Unesco Thesaurus

Unesco Thesaurus

A structured list of descriptors for indexing
and retrieving literature in the fields of
education, science, social science, culture
and communication

Compiled by Jean Aitchison

Published in 1977 by the
United Nations Educational, Scientific
and Cultural Organization
7 Place de Fontenoy, 75700 Paris
Printed by Unwin Brothers Limited, Old Woking, Surrey

ISBN 92-3-101469-2

Printed in the United Kingdom

PREFACE

The *Unesco Thesaurus* is intended to be used as a tool for the indexing and retrieval of information processed through the Computerized Documentation System of Unesco as well as by any information/library service whose documentation coverage is closely related to Unesco's fields of activities.

Its terminology widely reflects the topical diversity of the documentation produced by Unesco in the fields of education, science and technology, social sciences, humanities and culture, communication, information, libraries and archives.

While providing an outline of major fields of knowledge, the *Unesco Thesaurus* has been devised so as to allow for in-depth expansion of any of the subject areas covered according to specific needs.

This thesaurus has been compiled by Mrs Jean Aitchison, an information systems consultant, who is well known for her work on *Thesaurus Construction* and as a compiler of various thesauri, notably the *Thesauro-facet* which was the first example of integrating a faceted classification with an alphabetical thesaurus.

The computer processing of the alphabetical thesaurus and of the hierarchical display was carried out by INSPEC (Institution of Electrical Engineers), London, using their thesaurus management software. The permuted index was generated by the Unesco Computerized Documentation System (CDS).

The translation and adaptation of the *Unesco Thesaurus* into French and Spanish is foreseen for 1979–80.

CONTENTS

INTRODUCTION

INTRODUCTION

1. Purpose

The thesaurus is designed to be the working tool of the Computerized Documentation System of Unesco. It will be used in indexing and retrieval of all documents and publications processed through the Computerized Documentation System, which include:

Unesco documents, current and retrospective
    Field mission reports
    Working series and Conference documents
    Main series documents
    General Conference documents
    Executive Board documents
Unesco publications
Unesco periodicals
Regional Office and affiliated Institute documents and publications
Unesco library acquisitions
On-going research and research reports received under the ISORID programme (International Information System on Research in Documentation)

The thesaurus terms feature in the publications issued by the Computerized Documentation System, namely

Unesco List of Documents and Publications (ULDP); issued quarterly, with annual cumulations;
Unesco Library Acquisitions (ULA); issued ten times a year;
Annual and multi-annual indexes to leading Unesco periodicals, e.g. *Cultures; Impact of Science on Society; International Social Science Journal; Museum; Nature and Resources; Prospects; Unesco Bulletin for Libraries;* and the *Unesco Courier*

Terms from the thesaurus are also used to retrieve information from the data base, either in retrospective searches (batch or on-line) or in SDI (Selective Dissemination of Information) searches.

The users of the Computerized Documentation System are institutions in Member States, including National Commissions; United Nations System and other intergovernmental organizations; international non-governmental organizations; experts and consultants; Unesco staff and visitors to the Organization.

2. History

The Computerized Documentation System of Unesco was developed during 1969–72 and became operational in 1973. Before indexing started, an unstructured list of descriptors was compiled of terms selected from the *Macrothesaurus* and from basic Unesco documents. In the course of indexing many terms were added and others deleted.

This list of terms formed the core of the draft edition of the *Unesco Thesaurus*, which was compiled between April 1973 and April 1974: separate thesaurus sections for the major Unesco subject fields were compiled in turn, starting with an Education Section, followed by Information and Communication, Social Sciences, Culture and Humanities, Science and Technology. Lastly a General Section was produced. The draft thesaurus of 5,000 terms, in these five separate sections, was then distributed to professional staff and specialists within Unesco for comment, while the Indexing and Retrieval Section of the Documentation Systems Division started to use it as a source of new index terms, on an experimental basis.

The present version of the thesaurus was produced between May and November 1976. The work involved more than the updating of the draft thesaurus with new terms generated during indexing. It was found necessary to make considerable extensions to certain subject areas, as the result of comments and recommendations received from Unesco programme divisions and experts. The main areas of expansion were in the fields of culture, international law, human rights, oceanography and related sciences. In addition, nearly all sections of the draft thesaurus were revised and updated to bring the work into line with the draft Broad System of Ordering of UNISIST. About 3,500 new terms were added bringing the total to approximately 8,500 terms.

The compilation of the alphabetical thesaurus and of the hierarchical display was computer-assisted using the INSPEC Thesaurus management software; the permuted index was generated by the Computerized Documentation System of Unesco.

3. Subject Coverage

The thesaurus covers major fields of knowledge in outline, at least to the depth of the sub-fields of UNISIST's draft 'Broad System of Ordering' (BSO). Within this framework, subjects of particular concern to Unesco are treated in detail. These subjects include education, communication, information and library science, culture, certain areas of social and political sciences and certain earth sciences, particularly oceanography and hydrology.

The thesaurus is issued in two volumes, containing a classified thesaurus, an alphabetical thesaurus, permuted index, and computer-generated hierarchical tree. The same descriptors appear in all four parts but with different arrangements. The subject coverage of the thesaurus is most easily seen in the classified part. The main subject categories are as follows:

A   General
B/H Science and Technology
J   Education
K/S Social Sciences
T/X Humanities and Culture
Y   Communication
Z   Information, Libraries and Archives

General (Section A)

This section gives schedules for languages, research, patenting, standardization and common terms. The Language schedule lists names of languages occurring in documents indexed at Unesco. The Research Section includes general research terms, applicable to most branches of research. Research terms of specific fields are classified with that field, for example, scientific research with the Science and Technology Section, economic research with the Economics Section, and so on. The brief list of common terms include such broad descriptors as Quality, Equipment and Time, which are too general to appear in any of the specialized subject sections. The names of countries[1] and geographical areas are given in the alphabetical thesaurus, but there is no geographical schedule in the classified thesaurus. There is a structured list in the computer-generated hierarchical tree, under the term 'Geographical areas and countries'.

Identifiers

Names of towns and cities, mountains, rivers and deserts are not included in the thesaurus. Neither are the names of persons, organizations and projects. These are recorded in an unpublished and frequently updated 'List of identifiers'. Names of oceans, seas, bays, gulfs and straits are, however, given in the thesaurus, because of the importance of these terms in the documentation of oceanography.

Science and Technology (Section B/H)

Unesco has a wide-ranging interest in science and technology, but requires depth retrieval in only a limited number of areas. Although it is possible to define the present areas requiring depth treatment, it is not so easy to predict what new subjects of special concern will emerge in the future. To meet this situation the thesaurus provides, in the classified part, an outline of science and technology which will allow for expansion in any subject area, as the need arises.

The structure of the schedules is compatible, although not identical, with the UNISIST draft Broad System of Ordering. Ideally, it should have matched the structure of BSO. This, however, was impossible, since the draft Unesco Thesaurus pre-dated the BSO, and to bring its revised version exactly into line with the 1976 draft of BSO, would have required more time than was available. Also, the BSO is still at the draft stage, and will, no doubt, be further amended before it is fully accepted.

Although the thesaurus does not attempt to treat any science and technology subject to the depth required in a research library or scientific information system, it does give medium depth treatment in certain areas of special interest to Unesco, namely, oceanography, hydrology, man and the biosphere, science policy and scientific and technical development are covered in the Science and Technology section.[2]

Education (Section J)

This section deals in depth with subjects within the field of education of special interest to Unesco. These are educational development, policy and planning, including problems of curricula and methods of education. Other areas of importance are adult education, literacy, primary, secondary and higher education, technical and special education, and the training of educational personnel.

Social Sciences (Section K/S)

This section is concerned with the social science subjects of politics, law, economics, behavioural science, administrative sciences, labour and employment, sociology, and the human environment (i.e. human settlement, housing, transport and environmental planning).

The depth of treatment varies, the greatest emphasis being given to Unesco subjects, such as human rights and international relations. As in the Science and Technology Section, the aim is to provide an adequate framework to facilitate the addition of new terms in the future.

The similarity of the Broad System of Ordering, and the Unesco Thesaurus is less obvious in this section, except in the area of economics which was redesigned on the lines of the BSO.

---

1. The descriptors employed in the thesaurus to represent the names of countries, dependencies or other areas of special geographical interest, do not imply the expression of any opinion whatsoever concerning the legal status of any country or territory, or of its authorities, or concerning the delimitations of its frontiers. Those descriptors are intended for use in indexing and retrieval of information.

2. A more comprehensive treatment of this subject is found in the *SPINES Thesaurus* (Unesco, 1976) which also covers engineering and medicine in greater detail than found in this thesaurus.

Culture and Humanities (Section T/X)

This section comprises philosophy, religion, history and associated studies, culture, including arts and leisure. History and religion are not dealt with in depth; although the outline is there for further expansion if needed. On the other hand, the section on cultural policy, administration and development is exhaustively covered.

Communication (Section Y)

This section is concerned with communication policy, planning and skills. The choice of terms reflects Unesco's interest in the development of the communication media, and the training of communication personnel. Communication technology is placed here rather than in the Science and Technology Section.

Information, Libraries and Archives (Section Z)

The information and library field is dealt with in depth in this section. An exhaustive treatment was necessary, because the thesaurus is used in the indexing and retrieval of information concerning on-going research and research reports under the ISORID programme (International Information System on Research in Documentation).

4. Source of Terms

Many thesauri and classification systems were consulted during compilation. A debt is acknowledged to those, listed in this section, which served as a source of terms and as a guide to the arrangement of the classified schedules.

General

The structure and layout of the Language Section was based on the 1976 draft Broad System of Ordering, Auxiliary Schedule 3 of the new Bliss Classification, and the English full edition of UDC 8. The SPINES Thesaurus and Auxiliary Schedule 2 of the Bliss Classification were used for the structural relationships between geographical terms.

Sources
Broad System of Ordering for UNISIST (BSO). 2nd (revised draft). The Hague, FID, 1976.
Bliss Bibliographic Classification, edited by J. Mills, 2nd edition. London, Butterworth, 1976.
    Auxiliary schedule 2. Place
    Auxiliary schedule 3. Language
Universal Decimal Classification. English full edition. UDC 8: Language. Linguistics. Literature. London, British Standards Institution, 1971.
SPINES Thesaurus: a controlled and structured vocabulary of science and technology for policy making, management and development. Paris, Unesco, 1976.

Science and Technology

The UNISIST Broad System of Ordering served as a check for subject coverage and layout in this section. The influence of the BSO is most clearly noticeable in the Physics Section where the schedule was redesigned to conform to BSO layout. The detailed facet structure

of the Chemistry Section was derived from the draft Chemistry Section (Class C) of the revised Bliss Classification. The INSPEC Thesaurus was used for terminology in physics, electronics, computers and instruments; the TEST Thesaurus and English full edition of UDC 54 were used for chemical terminology, and TEST, Thesaurofacet and the Construction Industry Thesaurus for engineering and technology. The MeSH Thesaurus was drawn upon for medical terms, and the Broad System of Ordering for the facet structure of the life sciences.

The Thesaurus of Water Resources, WATDOC's Thesaurus/Classification Concordance, the FAO's draft Thesaurus of Aquatic Sciences, the International Glossary of Hydrology and the United Nations List of Oceanographic Terms, were the main source of terms for oceanography and hydrology. The International Hydrographic Organization's Lists of Oceans and Seas was used for the names of oceans and seas given in the Oceanography Section.

TEST and Geothesaurus were drawn upon for terms in the Geology Section. The SPINES Thesaurus was published too late to be used as a major source of terms and term relationships in this section; although some terms on science policy and technology transfer were added after brief pre-publication access to the SPINES graphic displays.

Sources
Bliss Bibliographic Classification, edited by J. Mills. 2nd edition. London, Butterworth. In course of publication.
Draft schedules: AM   Mathematics
                   AY   Probability and statistics
                   C   Chemistry
                   D-DF Astronomy
                   E   Biology
                   F   Botany ⎫
                   G   Zoology ⎬ Preliminary analysis only
Broad System of Ordering for UNISIST. Provisional and revised drafts. The Hague, FID, 1975/76.
Construction Industry Thesaurus; compiled by M. Roberts and others. London, Department of the Environment, 1973.
Daniels, Ruth. *Classification of health services;* compiled for the Wessex Hospital Board. 1972. (Draft)
Draft Thesaurus of the Aquatic Sciences and Fisheries Abstracts (ASFA). Rome, FAO, 1973.
Geothesaurus. London, Geotitles Weekly. 1973.
INSPEC Thesaurus: a thesaurus of terms for physics, electrotechnology, computers and control: compiled by B. J. Field. 2nd edition. London, Institution of Electrical Engineers, 1975.
International Glossary of Hydrology. Paris, Unesco; Geneva, World Meteorological Organization, 1974.
Medical Subject Headings. Bethesda, National Library of Medicine.
North Atlantic Bibliography and Citation Index: Subject Index—Physical Oceanography; compiled by L. Otto. Rome, FAO, 1968.
Oceanography: a list of terms relating to oceanography and marine resources. New York, United Nations, Office of Conference Services, 1971. (Terminology bulletin No. 265.)
SPINES Thesaurus: a controlled and structured vocabulary of science and technology for policy making, management and development. Paris, Unesco, 1976.
Thesaurofacet: a thesaurus and faceted classification for engineering and related subjects; compiled by Jean Aitchison, Alan Gomersall and Ralph Ireland. Whetstone, English Electric Company, 1969.
Thesaurus of Engineering and Scientific Terms (TEST): a list of scientific and engineering terms and their relationships for use in vocabulary for indexing and retrieving technical information. New York, Engineers Joint Council, 1967.
Thesaurus of Water Resources Terms: a collection of water re-

*sources and related terms for use in indexing technical informa-
tion.* Washington, D.C., Department of the Interior, 1971.
Universal Decimal Classification. English full edition. 54.
  Chemistry. London, British Standards Institution, 1972.
WATDOC. UDC Water Thesaurus/Concordance. (Draft)

Education

Terms in this section were derived from the Unesco
IBE Thesaurus, the ERIC Thesaurus, the EUDISED
Thesaurus and the London Education Classification.
The facet structure follows that of the London
Education Classification. The term definitions included
in this section are almost all taken from the IBE
Thesaurus.

Sources

*Unesco : IBE Education Thesaurus: a faceted list of terms for
  indexing and retrieving documents and data in the field of
  education.* 2nd edition. Geneva, Unesco-IBE, 1975.
*EUDISED Multilingual Thesaurus for Information Processing in
  the field of Education;* prepared by Jean Viet for the Council
  of Europe. Paris, Mouton, 1974.
*London Education Classification: a thesaurus classification of
  British educational terms;* compiled by D. J. and Joy Foskett.
  2nd edition. London University Institute of Education
  Library, 1974. (Education Libraries Bulletin, supplement 6)
ERIC Thesaurus. Thesaurus of ERIC descriptors. New York,
  CCM Information Corporation, 1972.

Social Sciences

In this section the draft Glossary of Human Rights
published by the International Institute of Human
Rights, was a source of terms on international law,
and administration of justice as well as human rights.
Elizabeth Moys's Classification for Law Books was
also a source of law terms. Macrothesaurus was used
for the economic terms.

The structure of the Economics Section follows
the Broad System of Ordering. The new Bliss Classification was invaluable for the structuring of the Political
and Law Sections, and for detailed terminology and
structure in the Psychology Section. Viet's Thesaurus
for Information Processing in Sociology was drawn
upon for both sociological and political terms. The
London Classification of Business Studies was used
for terminology and schedule layout for the subjects
of management and labour relations. Extensions to the
Library of Congress schedules on Planning and
Housing compiled by the library of the Department of
the Environment (U.K.), provided a detailed source
of terms in environmental planning.

Sources

Bliss Bibliographic Classification, edited by J. Mills. 2nd edition.
  London. Butterworth. In course of publication
  Published schedules: I   Psychology
                         Q   Social welfare
  Draft schedules: R   Politics
                         S   Law
Broad System of Ordering for UNISIST. Provisional and revised
  draft. The Hague, FID, 1975/76.
International Institute of Human Rights. *Draft glossary of terms
  on human rights.* 1975.
London Classification of Business Studies; compiled by K.D.C.
  Vernon and V. Long. London Graduate Business School,
  1970. (With additions and amendments up to 1976)
*Macrothesaurus: a basic list of economic and social development
  terms;* compiled by J. Viet. Paris, OECD, 1972.
Moys, E. *A Classification scheme for law books.* London,
  Butterworth, 1970.
Thesaurus for Information Processing in Sociology; compiled by

Jean Viet under the auspices of the International Committee
  for Social Science Information and Documentation. Paris,
  Mouton, 1971.
United Kingdom. Department of the Environment Library.
  Extensions to the NAC Environmental Planning and Housing
  schedules of the Library of Congress Classification System.
  (Unpublished.)

Culture

Jean Viet's provisional Unesco List of Cultural
Development Descriptors and the Cultural Development Thesaurus prepared for the Council of Europe,
formed the basis of the section on cultural development and administration. The definitions in this
section are Jean Viet's. For the sections on arts,
languages, literature, religion and philosophy the new
Bliss schedules were indispensable, both as a source
of terms and as a guide for the arrangement of the
schedules. These Bliss schedules have far greater depth
than is at present required in the Unesco Thesaurus,
but could be used for future extension.

Sources

Bliss Bibliographic Classification; edited by J. Mills. 2nd edition.
  London, Butterworth. In course of publication.
  Published schedules: P   Religion
  Draft schedules: AA/AK   Philosophy
                         L   History
                         V/VU   Fine Arts
                         VV/VX   Music
                         W/X   Linguistics, language and
                                  literature
Viet, J. *Cultural Development: Unesco list of descriptors* (draft).
  Paris, Maison des Sciences de l'Homme, 1974.
Viet, J. *Cultural Development Thesaurus.* Strasbourg, Council of
  Europe, 1976.

Communication

Jean Viet's List of Mass Communication Descriptors
which includes terms taken from Unesco documents
and publications, was used as a source in this field.
The INSPEC Thesaurus was checked to verify and
supplement terminology in the Communication
Technology Section.

Sources

*INSPEC Thesaurus: a thesaurus of terms for physics, electro-
  technology, computers and control;* compiled by B. J. Field.
  2nd edition. London, Institution of Electrical Engineers, 1975.
Viet, J. *Mass communication: list of descriptors.* Paris, Maison
  des Sciences de l'Homme, 1975.

Information, Libraries and Archives

The second edition of Terminology of Documentation, by Gernot Wersig and Ulrich Neveling, was used
as a source of terms and definitions included in this
section. The definitions of archive terms were taken
from the glossary by F. B. Evans and others, published
in the *American Archivist.* The two publications by
Jack Mills and associates, listed below, influenced the
schedule structure, particularly for types of libraries
and information materials.

Sources

Evans, F. B. and others. A basic glossary for archivists, manuscript curators and records managers. *The American Archivist,*
  37 (1974) 3, p. 415–433.
International Federation for Documentation. *Subject descriptors
  to be used in ISORID.* 1972.

Library Association (U.K.). *Classification of library sciences; a scheme compiled by J. Mills and other members of the Classification Research Group and adopted for use in Library and Information Science Abstracts (LISA).* London, Library Association. (Unpublished.)

Daniels, R. and J. Mills. *Classification of library and information science.* London, Library Association, 1975.

Wersig, G. and U. Neveling. *Terminology of documentation: a selection of 1200 basic terms published in English, French, German, Russian and Spanish.* Paris, Unesco, 1976.

5. Notes on the Structure of the Thesaurus

The thesaurus has a four-part structure, giving a multi-aspect approach to term interrelationships. The first part of the thesaurus provides a classified arrangement of the descriptors. The second part arranges the same descriptors in alphabetical order, with the conventional thesaural relationship of synonym, narrower, broader and related terms. The third part supplements the alphabetical thesaurus with a permuted index. The fourth part contains computer-generated hierarchies of the generic relationships (BT/NT) in the alphabetical thesaurus.

Each part of the thesaurus gives a different view of the terms and their interrelationships, and although there is some overlapping of information, the four sections tend to be complementary rather than repetitive. This style of thesaurus is essentially a species of Thesaurofacet, supplemented by machine-generated hierarchies in the INSPEC style. It differs from the original Thesaurofacet in that it repeats in the alphabetical thesaurus relationships displayed in the schedules, as well as giving relationships not shown in the classification. For Unesco's purposes, it was thought more useful to produce a comprehensive alphabetical thesaurus.

The Classified Thesaurus

The classification gives an overview of the subject matter, with the aim of making possible the speedy scanning of entire subject fields and sub-fields, for the selection of relevant terms. To achieve this the classification schedules are designed to give a fairly comprehensive picture of the terms in each subject area. This is done by showing non-hierarchical as well as purely generic relations; also synonyms and asterisked cross-references to terms whose main location is in other subject fields. The information, however, is not entirely complete, and the user also needs to consult the alphabetical thesaurus for definition of individual terms and additional cross-references, which would have over-complicated the schedules if included in the display. The schedules may also be supplemented by hierarchies, machine-derived from the BT/NT relationships in the alphabetical thesaurus. These are helpful for checking hierarchies which cut across several classes. The classification also gives a useful indication of where new terms should be inserted in the system and what their thesaural relationships should be.

Facet analysis

The main subject divisions in the classified thesaurus are Science and Technology, Education, Social Sciences, Culture and Humanities, Communication, Information, Libraries and Archives. These broad subject sections are divided into disciplines, for example, Physical sciences, Life sciences, Earth sciences in the Science and Technology Section; Political science and Sociology in the Social Sciences Section. Within each discipline there are further divisions of the main classes, following the traditional groupings, where these exist: for example, Music, Graphic arts, Performing arts in the schedule for Arts. Where no obvious traditional divisions exist, facet techniques are used to establish the main classes. This is the case in Education where the subject is divided into facets representing persons (Teachers, Students); organizations (Schools, Universities), processes (Teaching, Educational planning, Educational management).

Within each main class or facet, the aim is to display the subject in the most meaningful way. In some sciences, commonly accepted sub-classes are the best method of arranging the terms. An example of this type of arrangement is found in Chemistry where Physical chemistry is divided into Reaction chemistry, Thermochemistry, Electrochemistry and so on. Where no traditional sub-classes may be discerned, facet techniques are again used to find helpful groupings of terms, for example, in the field of Music, which is divided into eight facets, including theory and study, techniques, performance, musical character, music for particular media, and instruments. The characteristics of division are shown in brackets in the schedule in italics, preceding the facet array. This enables the user to understand quickly the arrangement of the subject. For example:

	(By musical character)
W75	Musical character
W75.05	Mechanical music
W75.10	Electronic music
W75.13	Abstract music
	....
	....
	....
	(By music for particular media)
W76	Vocal music
	UF Choral music
	Operatic music
	....
	....
W77	Instrumental music
	....
	....
	(By instruments)
W78	Musical instruments
W78.10	Keyboard instruments
W78.20	String instruments
	....
	....

These signposts are particularly useful when no appropriate generic headings are available, for example, in the Mass Media schedules under the Press.

Y70.05/25	Press
	(By organizations)
Y70.08	Press councils

Y70.10	(*By form of publication*)
	Newspaper press
	*Newspapers Z15.30.40
Y70.10.20	News items
	*Press releases Y60.35.10
Y70.10.25	News agencies
Y70.10.30	News flow
Y70.10.30B	News transmission
	UF News dispatches
Y70.10.40	Press conferences
Y70.15	Periodical press
	*Periodicals Z15.30.50
	(*By coverage*)
Y70.18.10	Local press
Y70.18.20	National press
Y70.18.70	Underground press

Synonyms

Synonyms are shown in the schedules immediately below the preferred term, preceded by the symbol UF (Use for). It was decided to include these in the classified display, to increase the user's understanding of the terms. This is especially useful where a subject field has not been elaborated in detail, and where more specific terms lead into the broader term. This tells the user the scope of the broad 'containing' term. For example:

X80/89	Sport
	UF Games
X83	Ball games
	UF Football
	Cricket
	Golf
	Tennis
X84.10	Aquatic sports
	UF Diving
	Water-skiing
	Sailing
X84.10.10	Swimming

Listing all synonyms in the display enables the user to recognise a concept by the name most familiar to him. For example:

Hovercraft
UF Air cushion vehicles
Ground effect vehicles

Hierarchical relationships

The schedules display a variety of term interrelationships. The most common relationship is the hierarchical or generic relationship. For example:

R79/84	People-in-need
R84	Socially disadvantaged
R84.45	War disadvantaged
R84.45.10	War wounded
R84.45.20	War prisoners
R84.45.40	Refugees

The above example has four levels of hierarchy, but it is possible to show more. By using cross-references (indicated by asterisks) it is possible to extend the hierarchies to include narrower concepts occurring in other schedules, for example:

R80/83	Handicapped
R83	Mentally disadvantaged
R83.30	Mentally handicapped
	*Backward students J90.20.03B

	*Educationally subnormal J90.20.03C
	*Ineducable J90.20.03A
R83.30.50	Mongols

In the classified display it is not usual to show broader terms located in other schedules using the asterisk device. This information is given in the alphabetical thesaurus—but only at one hierarchical level. For full hierarchies the machine-generated hierarchies should be scanned.

Non-hierarchical (associative) relationships

The schedules also show non-hierarchical relations, for example:

Whole/part relationship

C87/99	Solar system
C88	Sun
C90	Planets
J25.03.04	School buildings
J25.03.04A	Classrooms

Process/agent relationship

W67	Microphotography
	(*By equipment*)
W67.30	Microform equipment
E32	Air pollution
	(*By pollutants*)
E32.70	Smoke
E32.72	Fumes

Thing/characteristic relationship

R23/29	Family
R27	Family role
R28	Family environment

Cross-references to non-hierarchically related terms in other schedules, or located elsewhere in the same schedule, are shown, as for hierarchical relationships, preceded by an asterisk. Not every associated relationship is given in the schedules, but a large number are. Cross-references are included where they will increase the usefulness of the display. Examples of non-hierarchical cross-references occurring in the schedules are given below:

R25.60	One-parent families
	*Unmarried mothers R26.20.20
S56	Air transport
	*Air safety E73.90.10
	*Air traffic S68.10
	*Aircraft S67
P58	Personality
	UF Disposition
	Temperament
	*Personality development P64
	*Personality change P64.20

Another reason for including cross-references, whether hierarchical or associative, is to facilitate retrieval of closely-related concepts, when using the notation for a computer search. Terms are not only coded with their own class number, but also with the number of the terms where they are located as cross-references. For example, 'Personality change' is coded P64.20 and *P58. If a search is made on 'Personality' P58 'OR' *P58, the terms 'Personality development' and 'Personality change' will also be retrieved.

Notation

The notation was designed with computer searching in mind. The Education and Information Sections were compiled earliest and these were given a hierarchical notation. The resulting class numbers were long and lacking mnemonics. It was unfortunate that these schedules were also the most specific and likely in any case to have a longer notation. In other schedules the hierarchical notation was replaced by a semi-hierarchical notation, giving a shorter number, but at the same time allowing computer (broader to narrower) searching of the schedules. An example of full hierarchical notation in the Education Section is shown below:

J20	Educational planning and administration
J20.05	Economics of education
J20.05.05	Educational finance
J20.05.05B	Educational budgets
J20.05.05BC	Educational budgetary control

In contrast the semi-hierarchical notation appears as follows:

H70/99	Computer science
H80/83	Computer hardware
H82	Computer storage devices
H82.10	Digital storage

The oblique device used for the broad class numbers is also clumsy, but it allows for shorter notation in the detailed arrays of the schedule.

Although it was not intended that the notation should be used for manual filing systems or for shelving, the complexity of the notation is not so excessive as to prohibit such an application.

Non-descriptors

Some broader headings are used in the classification, for the sake of improving the display. These are not to be used as descriptors, and are marked (†) in the schedules, with a scope note to this effect in the alphabetical section.

The Alphabetical Thesaurus

The alphabetical section of the thesaurus lists in alphabetical order the terms displayed in the classification. The information under each term is in the format recommended in the UNISIST 'Guidelines for the establishment and development of monolingual thesauri' (ISO 2788). The information includes scope notes (SN), synonyms (UF), narrower terms (NT), broader terms (BT) and related terms (RT). In addition to this basic information the entry also gives the top term (TT) of the hierarchy in which the descriptor appears in the computer-generated hierarchies. The class number or numbers of the term in the classified thesaurus appears to the right of the main terms. The main class number is given first, followed by one or more asterisked class numbers, which indicate additional locations of the term. The alphabetical thesaurus also includes lead-in and 'use' entries from non-descriptors to the preferred index terms.

The alphabetical thesaurus was derived from the classified thesaurus. It repeats all the relationships shown in the classified display to one hierarchical level. In addition it supplements the classified thesaurus by listing relationships, particularly associative (RT), which are not displayed in the schedules. Scope notes and definitions are given in the alphabetical thesaurus, rarely in the classified thesaurus.

Thesaural relationships in the alphabetical section

ISO 2788 rules that the BT/NT relationship should in general be used only for generic relationships (except in the case of geographical and anatomical systems). However, the BT/NT relationship may be taken to include the part/whole relationship, if the code BTP/NTP is used to distinguish the part-whole from the true generic relationship, coded BTG/NTG. In the Unesco Thesaurus, it is accepted that only the generic usage of the BT/NT relationship is valid. Having accepted this rule, it is nevertheless sometimes difficult to decide what is a generic relationship, particularly in the Social sciences. For example, is Social progress a type of Social change and therefore NT to it; or is it an associated phenomenon, and therefore RT? On many occasions during compilation, there were incidences where a term was inadvertently coded both RT and NT to the same concept. A common error was to forget that phenomena listed under a subject discipline such as chemistry or sociology were not narrower terms, but related terms. For example, Sensory process psychology is NT to Psychology, as being a type of Psychological study; but Higher mental processes is RT, being phenomena studied. The temptation was to make all major subdivisions of a discipline in the classification NT to that discipline, particularly as this would have increased the number of machine-generated hierarchies available. It was indeed also a temptation to make all terms indented under a given term in the classified thesaurus, NT to that term, because that would have simplified the construction of the alphabetical thesaurus. However, to have done so would have contravened the standard rules for determining thesaural relationships, since many terms indented under a heading in the classification obviously are associatively, rather than generically related to that heading.

Term wordform control

Number. The EJC (Engineers Joint Council) rules are followed on singulars and plurals.

Direct form. The direct form is used for descriptors with more than one word. The second or other words in the compound term are picked up by the Permuted Index.

Oblique. Occasionally it has been necessary to include compound terms containing an oblique. This arose where there was no single term available to express the concept. For example, for library science and information science there is no general descriptor covering both disciplines; consequently it has been necessary to coin the term Information/Library to precede administration, personnel and other aspects common to both sciences.

Pre-coordinated terms. The thesaurus contains some pre-coordinated terms, that is, compound terms made up of two or more words. The majority of these terms are combinations of two words, for example Scientific institutions or Cultural financing. There are a few longer terms such as Democratization of education, Right to freedom from inhuman treatment; but these are not frequent. Compound terms are needed in the Computerized Documentation System because of the variety of indexes produced. These list information under single descriptors, and not under terms in combination, so that it is important that each descriptor be meaningful and fairly specific.

Homographs. A homograph is a word with the same spelling as another, but having a different meaning. In the Unesco Thesaurus a homograph is differentiated by a note in parenthesis. For example:

Springs
Springs (components)

Alphabetization. The word-by-word arrangement is used in alphabetization, for example:

Social values
Social welfare
Social work
Socialism
Socialization

Hyphenated words take precedence over non-hyphenated

Pre-coordinate indexing
Precision

and oblique terms follow the term alone

Information transfer
Information users
Information/library aims

The Permuted Index

The Permuted Index supplements the alphabetical thesaurus in that it gives access to the descriptors via the second, third or more constituent terms in compound class numbers. In the main alphabetical thesaurus the term appears only under the first word of the compound term. In the Permuted Index the term appears under every constituent word, including the first word, for example, in the case of Primary school teacher:

Primary school curriculum
Primary school teachers
. . . .

. . . .
Primary school curriculum
Primary school teachers
Parochial schools
. . . .

. . . .
Pre-primary school teachers
Primary school teachers

Without the Permuted Index, terms might be overlooked in the alphabetical thesaurus, particularly when the first word of the descriptor is less significant than the other constituent words.

Hierarchical Display

The hierarchical chains are derived by the computer from the broader/narrower (BT/NT) term relationships in the alphabetical thesaurus. All the hierarchical chains are arranged in alphabetical order of the top term of their hierarchy. These top terms (TT) are given in the alphabetical thesaurus so that the latter can be used in conjunction with the hierarchical display. A term can appear in more than one hierarchical chain and also more than once in any particular hierarchy.

The hierarchies can be used to advantage to search quickly for hierarchies cutting across more than one schedule in the classified thesaurus, especially where asterisked cross-references have not been made. The hierarchies would have been more numerous if the number of generic relationships had not been limited by the nature of the subject matter, and by the strict thesaurus rules on allowable BT/NT relationships.

6. How to use the Thesaurus

Use all parts of the thesaurus to obtain a complete picture of term interrelationships. Each part of the thesaurus has a particular function.

1. *Use the Classified Thesaurus*
(a) To obtain an over-view of a broad subject area or sub-field.
(b) To ascertain quickly the depth of coverage given to the subject sought.
(c) To make a quick overall check of the subject field for synonyms, broader, narrower, and related terms of the terms sought.
(d) To carry out broad computer searches of the 'explosion' type, using the shorthand of the class code to bring out a detailed hierarchy, without having to list the name of each constituent term.

2. *Use the Alphabetical Thesaurus*
(a) To check for definitions and scope notes.
(b) To check for synonyms, broader and narrower and related terms at one level of hierarchy. Relationships, additional to those in the classified thesaurus, are included.
(c) To locate the term in the classified thesaurus by checking the class number or numbers given against the term (additional class numbers are preceded by asterisks, e.g., F98.05 *V15.50).
(d) To locate the term in the computer-generated hierarchy by checking for the top term (TT) of the hierarchy.
(e) To produce cross-references for printed indexes using the thesaurus descriptors as headings. The 'see' references may be derived from the synonyms and 'see also' references from the broader, narrower and related term data.

3. *Use the Permuted Index*

To trace compound terms by the second (or third) constituent word, which is hidden in the 'direct form'

entry in the alphabetical thesaurus.
For example:

Alphabetical Thesaurus	*Role* of education
	Discharge of rivers
Permuted Index brings out also	Role of *education*
	Discharge of *rivers*

4. *Use the Hierarchical Display*

To check quickly for hierarchies, particularly those which cut across several schedules in the classification. Hierarchies are generated only from (BT/NT) broader/narrower terms. Look in the alphabetical thesaurus for the top term (TT) of the hierarchy in which that term appears. Turn to the hierarchical display and find the top term of the hierarchy in the alphabetical sequence of hierarchical chains.

7. Key to Abbreviations and Symbols

Classified Thesaurus
SN	Scope note
UF	Use for
*	Cross-references to terms in other schedules
(†)	Non-descriptor

Alphabetical Thesaurus
SN	Scope note
UF	Use for
NT	Narrower term
BT	Broader term
RT	Related term
TT	Top term in the Hierarchical Display
*	Class numbers of cross-references

8. Updating

It must be accepted that the thesaurus will have to be frequently updated as terminology in Unesco documents and publications reflects new interests and subject emphasis.

The faceted framework of the classification schedule should assist in placing in the system new terms or groups of terms. Mechanization of the thesaurus file will reduce the clerical, as opposed to the intellectual effort of updating.

New terms may be taken into the system by raising to full index term status, terms which were previously lead-in or entry terms. For example:

M93.60   Trade Union rights
        UF Right to strike

The term 'Right to strike' could be made a full descriptor, with its own notation, M93.60.20. An entry would also have to be made in the alphabetical thesaurus, giving broader, narrower and related-term details.

An example of a more complex extension is given below, showing how the section on Memory in the Psychology Section could be expanded. The original schedule gives only two terms under Memory:

P53	Memory
	*Memory disorders F79.40
P53.10	Memorization

An enlarged schedule could include a dozen terms or more, for example:

P53	Memory
	*Memory disorders F79.40
	(*By type*)
P53.05	Visual memory
P53.08	Long term memory
P53.10	Short term memory
	(*By characteristics*)
P53.40	Memory retention
	UF Recall (memory)
	Recognition (memory)
	Reconstruction (memory)
P53.45	Spontaneous memory recovery
P53.50	Forgetting
	(*By activity*)
P53.70	Memorization
	UF Memory training
P53.70.10	Repetitive memory training
P53.70.30	Mnemonic systems

Entries would then be made for these new terms in the alphabetical thesaurus giving the relationship derived from the scdedules, and any additional relationships.

It is also possible to expand complete subject areas within the thesaurus. In this edition, there are few or no subdivisions under certain subject fields, for example, veterinary medicine, space vehicles, polymer chemistry, molecular physics in the Science and Technology Section, or under the history or art of particular countries (e.g. Arab art, Latin American history) in the Culture and Humanities Section. These fields could be expanded by drawing upon the relevant glossaries, classification systems, thesauri and the know-how of subject experts, if the present outline coverage proved limited.

9. Acknowledgements

I should like to thank the many subject specialists on the Unesco staff whose advice and help were indispensable.

I should also like to thank the staff of INSPEC, especially Mr John Carmichael, Head of Systems Development Department, for their work on mechanizing the thesaurus. I am particularly grateful to my husband, Tom Aitchison, for taking a substantial share in the burden of checking and editing the output.

My thanks are also due to Mrs Catherine Downs, for her skill in laying out and typing the facet schedules.

Jean Aitchison

CLASSIFIED THESAURUS

Summary

A   GENERAL SECTION

Summary

Languages
Linguistics X02/54

A02	International languages
A02.10	International auxiliary lingua
A02.20	Esperanto
A03	Indo-European languages
	UF European languages
A03.10	Indic languages
	Dravidian languages A07.10/30
	(ancient)
A03.10.10	Sanskrit
	(modern)
A03.10.25	Panjabi
A03.10.30	Sindhi
	UF Punjabi
A03.10.30/49	Hindustani
A03.10.35	Hindi
A03.10.40	Urdu
A03.10.45	Gujurati
A03.10.50	Bengali
A03.10.55	Oriya
A03.10.60	Assamese
A03.10.65/70	Dardic languages
A03.10.68	Kashmiri
A03.10.70	Romany language
A03.10.80	Nepali
A03.10.85	Marathi
A03.10.90	Sinhala
	UF Sinhalese
A03.15	Iranic languages
A03.15.10	Persian
A03.15.20	Kurdish
A03.15.30	Pushto
A03.15.50	Armenian
A03.18	Greek (classical)
A03.20	Greek (modern)
A03.25	Macedonian
A03.28	Albanian
A03.30/39	Celtic languages
A03.32	Gaelic
A03.32.40	Irish Gaelic
A03.35	Welsh
A03.38	Breton
A03.40	Italic languages
A03.40.10	Latin
A03.45/59	Romance languages
A03.46	Romanian
A03.48	Catalan
A03.50	Italian
A03.52	Spanish
A03.56	Portuguese
A03.58	French
A03.60/80	Germanic languages
A03.62	German
A03.64	Dutch
A03.66	Flemish
A03.67	Afrikaans
A03.69	Faeroese
A03.70	Icelandic

A01/11

		Languages (cont.)
A03		Indo-European languages (cont.)
A03.60/80		Germanic languages (cont.)
A03.72		Norwegian
A03.74		Swedish
A03.76		Danish
A03.80		English
A03.82		Baltic languages
A03.82.10		Lithuanian
A03.82.20		Latvian
A03.85		Slavic languages
A03.85.10		Russian
A03.85.15		Ukrainian
A03.85.20		Byelorussian
A03.85.30		Kazakh
A03.85.35		Bulgarian
A03.85.40		Serbo-Croatian
		UF Croatian
A03.85.50		Slovene
A03.85.60		Polish
A03.85.70		Slovak
A03.85.80		Czech
A04/07		Oriental languages
		UF Asian languages
A05		*Hamito-Semitic and Caucasian Languages* (†)
A05.10/40		Hamito-Semitic languages
A05.15		Semitic languages
A05.15.10		Hebrew
A05.15.20		Arabic
A05.15.60		Amharic
A05.20/40		Hamitic languages
		UF Egyptial languages
A05.25		Libyan-Berber languages
A05.35		Cushitic languages
A05.35.10		Somali
A05.50		Caucasian languages
A05.50.10		Darghi
A05.50.30		Georgian
A05.80		Basque language
A06		Eurasian and North Asian languages
A06.10/30		Uralic languages
A06.12		Samoyedic languages
A06.15		Hungarian
A06.20		Estonian
A06.25		Finnish
A06.30		Lappic
A06.35/45		Altaic languages
A06.36		Turkish
A06.38		Azerbaijani
A06.40		Mongolian languages
A06.45		Tungus
A06.50		Palaeosiberian languages
A06.60		Eskimo languages
A06.70		Korean
A06.80		Japanese
A07		South and South-East Asian languages
A07.10/30		Dravidian languages
A07.15		Tamil
A07.18		Telegu

A01/11   **Languages** (cont.)

A04/07	Oriental languages (cont.)
A07	South and South-East Asian languages (cont.)
A07.10/30	Dravidian languages (cont.)
A07.25	Malayalam
A07.30	Kannada
A07.40	Andaman languages
A07.45	Mon-Khmer languages
A07.45.10	Cambodian
	UF Khmer language
A07.50	Annam-Muong
A07.55	Munda languages
A07.60/90	Sino-Tibetan languages
	UF Indo-Chinese languages
A07.65	Tibeto-Burmese
A07.65.10	Tibetan
A07.65.30	Burmese
A07.75	Thai languages
A07.75.10	Siamese
A07.75.20	Laotian
A07.75.30	Annamese
A07.75.40	Vietnamese
A07.85	Chinese
A08	Austronesian and Oceanic languages
A08.10/40	Malayo-Polynesian languages
A08.15	Indonesian
	UF Bahasian
A08.18	Pilipino
A08.20	Tagalog
A08.25	Formosan
A08.30	Malagasy
A08.32	UF Malgasi
A08.35	Malay language
A08.40	Javanese
A08.50	Polynesian
A08.50.10	Hawaiian
A08.50.30	Samoan
A08.50.40	Tahitian
A08.55	Melanesian
A08.60	Micronesian
A08.65	Maori
A08.70	Australian aboriginal languages
A08.75	Tasmanian languages
A08.80	Papuan languages
A09	African languages
	Hamito-Semitic languages A05.10/40
A09.10	Khoin languages
	UF Bushman languages
	Hottentot languages
A09.20	Bantu languages
A09.20.30	Swahili
	UF Kiswahili
A09.50	Sudanic languages
A09.60	Bantuide languages
A09.60.10	Yoruba
A09.80	Igbo
A10	Amerindian languages
A10.10	North American Indian languages

A01/11   **Languages** (cont.)

A10/10	Amerindian languages (cont.)
A10.30	Central American Indian languages
	UF Mexican Indian languages
A10.50	South American Indian languages
A10.50.10.	Kechua

(By number of languages used)

A11.10	Monolingual
A11.20	Bilingual
	Bilingualism X23
A11.40	Multilingual
	Multilingualism X23.10
A11.50	Pluralingual

A20/59   **General Terms** (†)

This schedule includes terms which are too general to be placed in any of the subject sections of the Theraurus.
Where possible use a more specific descriptor.

A36.10	Concepts
A36.20	Images
A36.30	Theory
A36.40	Hypothesis
A36.50	Practice
A36.70	Aims
	UF Objectives
A36.75	Goals
A36.85	Ratio
A37	Time
A37.10	Age
A37.30	Frequency
A37.30.10	Daily
A37.30.15	Weekly
A37.30.20	Monthly
A37.30.25	Quarterly
A37.30.40	Yearly
A37.80	Future
A38	Species
A39	Properties
	UF Characteristics
A39.40	Shape
A40	Quality
A40.10	Reliability
A40.25	Validity
A40.30	Failure
A40.32	Faults
A40.35	Damage
A40.38	Deterioration
A41	Quantity
A41.20	Shortages
	UF Scarcity
A41.40	Size
A42.10	Programmes
A42.10.30	Accelerated programmes
A42.10.40	Country programming

A20/59		**General Terms** (cont.)
	A42.30	Missions
	A42.30.10	Expert missions
	A43.80	Competitions
	A43.85	Prizes
	A44	Equipment
		UF Appliances
	A44.30	Sites
	A45.10	Analysis
	A45.15	Evaluation
		UF Assessment
	A45.70	Verification
	A46.10	Methods
	A46.50	Techniques
	A48.10	Specialization
	A48.40	Interdisciplinary
	A50	Development
	A50.20	Exploitation
	A50.40	Progress
	A50.42	Modernization
	A50.45	Reform
	A50.50	Innovations
	A50.70	Mechanization
	A52.10	Admission
	A54.10	Conservation
	A54.15	Preservation
	A54.30	Storage
	A54.45	Resources
	A54.50	Needs
	A58.10	Conflict
	A58.50	Participation

A60/64		**Standardization**
		Inspection H28.30
		Quality A40
		Quality control H28.20
		Testing H28
	A63	Standards
		Building standards G59.35
		Information/library standards Z30.05.50
		Educational standards J20.03.14A
	A63.10	International standards
	A63.20	Physical standards
	A63.30	Specifications
	A63.40	Codes of rules
	A63.80	Professional standards

A65/69		**Patenting**
		(By end products)
	A67.10	Patents
	A67.70	Trade marks
		(By services)
	A68.20	Patent offices

A70/99		**Research**

Archive research Z86.20
Communication research Y06
Cultural research T14/19
Information/library research Z26
Educational research J05
Psychological research P12/15
Research libraries Z62.48
Scientific research B25/29
Social science research K10
Testing H28

(By objectives)

A71.10	Discoveries
	Scientific discoveries B16.10

A71.20	Inventions
	Patents A67.10

(By research type)
A73.10	Interdisciplinary research
	UF Multidisciplinary research

A73.30	Fundamental research

A73.40	Applied research
	Research and development B28
A73.40.20	Problem focused research
A75	Research policy

(By management)
A76	Research management
	UF Research administration
A76.10	Research planning
A76.15	Research programmes
A76.20	Research coordination
A76.20.10	Research registers
A76.40	Research priorities
A76.45	Research trends
A76.60	Economics of research
A76.60.10	Research finance
A76.60.10G	Research grants

(By institutions and bodies)
A77	Research centres
	UF Research institutions
	Research units
	Scientific institutions B24.30.10
A77.10	Research foundations
A77.20	Research councils

(By personnel)
A78	Research workers
A78.40	Research training

(By sociology)
A79	Sociology of research

(By projects)
A81	Research projects
A81.10	Experimental projects
	Experimental development B28.10
A81.40	Pilot projects

(By research activities)
A83/91	Research work
A84.40	Exploration
	Ocean exploration D86.20
	Resource exploration E93
	Scientific expeditions B26
	Space exploration G63.55
A84.50	Observation

A70/99		**Research** (cont.)
	A83/91	Research work (cont.)
	A85	Field work
	A85.10	Surveys
		Economic surveys N04.60
		Soil surveys D43
	A85.10.10	Sample surveys
	A85.10.30	Survey data
	A85.10.40	Survey analysis
	A85.20	Questionnaires
	A85.30	Interviews
		Interviewing for job Q72.30.10
	A86	Case studies
	A88	Experimentation
		Experimental biology F05.10
		Experimental botany F36.10
		Experimental chemistry C33/39
		Experimental physics C03
		Experimental psychology P14
		Measurement and instruments H10/24
		Testing H28
	A88.10	Experiments
		Educational experiments J05.20
	A88.40	Experimental methods
		(By methods)
	A89/91	Methodology
	90	Research methods
		Cross-cultural analysis T15.70
		Data analysis H67
		Evaluation A45.15
		Experimental methods A88.40
		Systems analysis H37
	A90.05	Research strategy
	A90.10	Causal analysis
	A90.12	Comparative analysis
	A90.20	Cross-national analysis
	A90.30	Typological analysis
	A91	Research techniques
	A91.50	Models
		UF Modelling
		Cultural models T15.30
		Economic models N04.55
		Educational models J05.30
		Mathematical models B91
	A91.50.20	Simulation models
		UF Simulation
		Simulation techniques
		(By facilities)
	A93	Research facilities
		Laboratories B37.10
		Research ships D86.30
	A93.30	Observatories
		UF Research stations
		Astronomical observatories C78
		Meteorological observatories D64.50
		Oceanographic stations D86.10
		Seismological observatories D11.70
		(By results)
	A94	Research results
		Scientific research results B29
		Discoveries A71.10
		Innovations A50.50
		Inventions A71.20

B/H SCIENCE AND TECHNOLOGY
Summary

B01/39	**Science of Science and Technology**
B02	**Science**
B04	**Science philosophy**
B05	**Sociology of science**
B08	**History of science**
B15/19	**Science policy**
B20/24	**Science planning and administration**
B25/29	**Scientific research**
B30	**Technology transfer**
B34	**Scientific personnel**
B36/39	**Scientific facilities**

B01/39   **Science of Science and Technology**
                              Scientific information Z08.10

    B02   **Science**
                              SN Science in general

                              UF Natural sciences
                              Science education J60.40
                              Science museums T96.30

    B03.10   Scientific activities

    B04   **Science Philosophy**
                              UF Philosophy of technology

    B04.30   Ethics of science
                              Bioethics F06
                              Medical ethics F98.05

    B05   **Sociology of Science**

                              UF Science and society
                              Science popularization Z08.10.10
                              Scientific communities B34.10
                              Scientific cultures T53.72

    B08   **History of Science**

                              UF Science history
                                 Technology history

B15/19   **Science Policy**

                              UF Technology policy

    B16   Scientific development
                              UF Technological development
                              Scientific research B25/29

    B16.03   Technological change
                                   UF Technological development
                                      Technological evaluation
                                      Technological revolution

    B16.05   Scientific progress
                                   UF Technological progress

    B16.10   Scientific discoveries
                                   UF Technological discoveries

    B16.15   Scientific innovations
                                   UF Technological innovations

    B16.30   Scientific initiation
                                   UF Technological initiation

    B16.35   Scientific potential
                                   UF Technological potential

    B16.35.30   Technological gap

    B17   Science forecasting
                                   UF Technological forecasting

    B18   Scientific cooperation
                                   UF Technological cooperation

B20/24   **Science Planning and Administration**

    B21   Science planning
                                   UF Technology planning

    B21.10   Scientific programmes
                                   UF Technological programmes

    B21.20   Science statistics
                                   UF Technology statistics

    B22/23   Economics of science
                                   UF Economics of technology

    B23   Science finance
                                   UF Technology finance

    B23.10   Science budgets

B20/24		**Science Planning and Administration** (cont.)
	B22/23	Economics of science (cont.)
	B23	Science finance (cont.)
	B23.30	Scientific expenditure
	B23.50	Science financing
		UF Technology financing
	B24	Science administration
		UF Technology administration
	B24.30	Scientific organizations
		UF Technological organizations
	B24.30.10	Scientific institutions
		UF Technological institutions

B25/29   **Scientific Research**
Agricultural research G06
Biological research F05
Chemical research C32
Ecological research E11
Geographical research D35.10
Hydrological research D67
Medical research F51
Oceanographic research D86
Scientific facilities B36/39

For research on specific disciplines combine 'Scientific research' with descriptor for discipline, except where the term is enumerated, e.g. Medical research.

For research methods, personnel, etc., combine with terms in schedule for Research at A70/99. For facilities see B36/39 Scientific facilities.

(By expeditions)
B26   Scientific expeditions

(By research and development)
B28   Research and development
               UF Industrial research

(By operations)
B28.10   Experimental development
               UF Development research
                  Experimental projects A81.10
                  Experimentation A88
                  Pilot projects A81.40
                  Process development N38.70.10
                  Product development N38.70.30

(By results)
B29   Scientific research results
               SN Includes applications
                  Patenting A65/69
                  Scientific discoveries B16.10
                  Scientific innovations B16.15
                  Technology transfer B30

B30   **Technology Transfer**

               UF Transfer of technology
                  Transfer of techniques
               Foreign industries N40.15
               Indigenous industries N40.10
               Industrial development N37
               Scientific research results B29

(By type and method of transfer)
B30.10   Horizontal technology transfer
               UF Adaptation of technology

B30.20   Vertical technology transfer

B30.30   Diffusion of technology

B30.40   Implantation of technology
               UF Fixation of technology
                  Penetration of technology

B30		**Technology Transfer** (cont.)
	B30.60	International technology transfer *International instruments M75* *International assistance L84* *Donor countries L84.60* *Recipient countries L84.65* *Technical assistance L84.50.60*
	B30.80	Technical transfer services *Scientific information systems Z68.50* *Patent offices A68.20*

B34		**Scientific Personnel**
		UF Technical personnel Technological personnel *Medical personnel F98.20*
	B34.10	Scientific communities
	B34.25	Higher technical personnel
	B34.30	Scientists
	B34.35	Technologists
	B34.38	Engineers
	B34.40	Environmentalists
	B34.42	Geophysicists
	B34.43	Geologists
	B34.44	Geographers
	B34.48	Hydrologists
	B34.50	Oceanologists
	B34.55	Oceanographers
	B34.80	Technicians
	B35	Scientific personnel training *Technical education J60.45* *Technical training J60.34.30* *Science education J60.40*

B36/39		**Scientific Facilities**
	B37.05	Scientific buildings
	B37.10	Laboratories *Chemical laboratories C34* *Educational laboratories J25.03.02D* *Medical laboratories F51.40*
	B38	Scientific equipment *Measurement and instruments H10/24* *Medical equipment F94* *Oceanographic equipment D98*
	B38.10	Laboratory equipment UF Laboratory apparatus Laboratory instruments *Chemical laboratory equipment C34.30*

B40/99   Mathematical Sciences

B40/69   Mathematics

B70/99   Statistics

Mathematical Sciences

Mathematics

*Geomathematics D05
*Mathematics education J60.38
*Mathematical physics C02.60
*Statistical mathematics B75/99

B41	Mathematical logic
	UF Formal logic
B41.40	Algorithms
B42	Number theory
B42.10	Arithmetic
B42.10.60	Digital arithmetic
B43	Algebra
B43.20	Boolean algebra
B43.30	Group theory
B43.40	Linear algebra
B43.40.10	Determinants
B43.40.20	Matrix algebra
B43.40.30	Eigenvalues
B43.40.50	Tensors
B43.40.60	Vectors
B43.65	Polynomials
B46	Geometry
B46.10	Analytical geometry
B46.10.10	Trigonometry
B46.10.30	Differential geometry
B47	Combinatorial mathematics
	UF Combinatorial analysis
B48	Set theory
B50	Topology
	UF Homology
B50.10	Graph theory
B51	Convergence (mathematics)
B56	Equations
B56.10	Differential equations
B56.10.20	Partial differential equations
B56.20	Non-linear equations
B56.30	Integral equations
B58	Functions (mathematics)
	*Transforms B62
B60/68	Mathematical analysis
	*Eigenvalues B43.40.30
B61	Calculus
B61.10	Integral calculus
B61.20	Differential calculus
B61.30	Variational calculus
	UF Calculus of variations
B62	Transforms
B62.10	Fourier transforms
B63	Functional analysis
B63.10	Harmonic analysis
B64	Fourier analysis
B65	Series (mathematics)
	*Convergence (mathematics) B51
B67	Numerical analysis
	*Monte Carlo methods B97
B67.10	Approximation theory
B67.10.10	Least squares approximation
B67.30	Interpolation

B40/69		**Mathematics** (cont.)
	B60/68	Mathematical analysis (cont.)
	B67	Numerical analysis (cont.)
	B67.35	Iterative methods
	B67.40	Error analysis
	B67.50	Numerical methods
	B67.70	Graphical methods
		UF Nomograms

B70/99		**Statistics**

Communication statistics Y20.20.50
Cultural statistics T15.20
Information/library statistics Z30.05.55
Educational statistics J20.03.20
Museum statistics T91.10.20
Science statistics B21.20
Statistics education J60.38.40

	B72/73	Descriptive statistics
		Statistical data Z15.15.50S
	B72.30	Statistics presentation
	B75/99	Statistical mathematics
		UF Mathematical statistics
		Statistical physics C05
	B76/79	Statistical methods
	B77	Non-parametric statistics
	B78	Decision theory
		UF Statistical decision
	B79	Statistical inference
	B79.10	Estimation
		Expectation B82
	B79.30	Statistical tests
	B80/89	Probability theory
		UF Statistical probability
	B82	Expectation
	B82.10	Probable error
	B82.40	Standard error
	B82.60	Risk
	B83	Statistical distributions
		UF Probability distribution
		(By distribution parameters)
	B83.30	Averages
	B83.35	Central tendency
	B83.50	Statistical dispersion
	B83.50.10	Standard deviation
	B83.60	Variability
	B84	Random processes
		UF Random data
		Stochastic processes
	B84.20	Markov processes
	B84.50	Queueing theory
	B84.70	Random walk
	B86	Game theory
	B87	Renewal theory
	B90/99	Statistical design
		UF Design of experiments
		Experimental design
	B91	Mathematical models
		UF Models
		Modelling
		Statistical models
	B93	Statistical analysis

B70/99		**Statistics** (cont.)
	B75/99	Statistical mathematics (cont.)
	B90/99	Statistical design (cont.)
	B93	Statistical analysis (cont.)
	B93.10	Multivariate analysis
		UF Multidimensional analysis
	B93.10.10	Discriminant analysis
	B93.10.30	Factor analysis
	B93.20	Variance analysis
	B93.30	Correlation
	B93.30.10	Regression analysis
	B93.40	Optimization
	B93.40.10	Minimization
	B94	Time series
		Harmonic analysis B63.10
	B94.10	Forecasting
	B96	Sampling theory
	B97	Monte Carlo methods

C00/69   Physical Sciences

C01/27	Physics
C02	Theoretical physics
C03	Experimental physics
C04/12	Physics of energy phenomena
C13.01/49	Particle physics
13.50	Nuclear physics
C13.70/99	Atomic, molecular and ion physics
C14	Vacuum physics
C15/27	Bulk matter physics
C16/20	Physical properties
C21	Radiation effects
C22	Dispersion and surface physics
C23	Plasma physics
C24	Fluid physics
C25/27	Condensed matter physics
C25.20/80	Physics of liquids
C26/27	Physics of solids
C28	Crystallography
C30/69	Chemistry
C33/39	Experimental chemistry
C36/39	Chemical analysis
C40/54	Physical chemistry
C55/69	Chemistry of elements and compounds
C62/63	Inorganic chemistry
C64/66	Organic chemistry
C68	Polymer chemistry

Physical Sciences

Physics

Astrophysics C76
Atmospheric physics D48/63
Biophysics F26
Geophysics D03/14
  Physical chemistry C40/54
  Physics education J60.40.15

C02	**Theoretical Physics**
C02.10	Relativity
C02.30	Gravitation
	UF Gravity
C02.60	Mathematical physics

C03	**Experimental Physics**
	SN For measurements and instruments see H10/24
C03.30	High temperature techniques
C03.40	Cryogenics
	UF Low temperature physics
C03.50	High pressure techniques

C04/12	**Physics of Energy Phenomena**
	SN Any state of matter
C05	Statistical physics
C05.20	Statistical mechanics
C06	Thermodynamics
	Atmospheric thermodynamics D51.10
	Thermochemistry C47.10
C06.05	Heat
	Heat transfer C07.20
C06.20	Thermodynamic properties
	UF Enthalpy
	Entropy
	Free energy
C06.30	Temperature
	Atmospheric temperature D51.10.10
	Body temperature F24
	Temperature control H51.10
	Temperature measurement and instruments H20.20
	Soil temperature D40.15
	Water temperature D83.50
C06.30.05	High temperatures
	High temperature techniques C03.30
C06.30.10	Low temperatures
	Cryogenics C03.40
C06.30.30	Temperature distribution
	UF Temperature gradients
C06.40/90	Phase transformations
	UF Thermodynamic changes of state
	(By liquid-vapour transformations)
C06.45	Vaporization
C06.45.10	Boiling
C06.45.20	Evaporation
C06.50	Condensation
	Atmospheric condensation D60/63
C06.50.10	Humidity
	Atmospheric humidity D62
C06.50.20	Moisture
	Soil moisture D74.20.10
C06.50.30	Water vapour
C06.55	Liquefaction of gases

C01/27		**Physics** (cont.)
C04/12		**Physics of Energy Phenomena** (cont.)
	C06	Thermodynamics (cont.)
	C06.40/90	Phase transformations (cont.)
		(By solid-liquid transformations)
	C06.60	Freezing
	C06.65	Melting
		UF Fusion
	C06.70	Solidification
		Crystallization C28.40.10
		(By solid-vapour transformation)
	C06.80	Sublimation
		(By solid-solid transformations)
	C06.85	Solid-state phase transformation
		(By properties)
	C06.85.10	Phase equilibrium
		UF Phase diagrams
		Phase rule
	C07	Transport processes (physics)
		Electrical conductivity C19.05
	C07.05	Diffusion
	C07.10	Energy transfer
	C07.10.10	Energy dissipation
		UF Energy losses
	C07.12	Energy conversion
	C07.15	Mass transfer
	C07.20	Heat transfer
	C07.20.10	Heating
	C07.20.20	Cooling
	C07.20.30	Convection
	C07.20.40	Heat conduction
	C07.20.50	Radiative transfer
	C07.20.70	Thermal diffusion
		Thermal diffusivity C18.25
	C08	Mechanics
		SN Non-linear, wave, particle and bulk matter together
		Mechanical variables control H49
		Mechanics of solids C27.01/65
	C08.10/40	Classical mechanics
	C08.15	Statics
	C08.15.10	Density
	C08.15.20	Mass
	C08.15.30	Weight (mass)
	C08.20	Kinematics
	C08.20.10	Velocity
		UF Speed
	C08.20.30	Acceleration
	C08.20.40	Ballistics
	C08.30	Dynamics
		Fluid dynamics C24.20/70
		Geodynamics D23/25
		Friction C27.60.10
		Gravitation C02.30
		Vibrations C17.10
	C08.30.10	Force
	C08.30.15	Pressure
		Fluid pressure C24.10
	C08.30.20	Momentum
	C08.30.30	Rotation
	C08.30.40	Stability
	C08.50	Continuum mechanics
	C08.70	Quantum theory
		UF Quantum mechanics
		Quantum field theory C13.05

C01/27		**Physics** (cont.)
C04/12		**Physics of Energy Phenomena** (cont.)
	C08	Mechanics (cont.)
	C08.70	Quantum theory (cont.)
	C08.70.30	Wave mechanics
	C09.01/60	Electricity

          Atmospheric electricity D57.10
          Electrochemistry C47.30
          Electrical properties of substances C19
          Electrical variables control H48
          Electromagnetism C09.80

	C09.10	Electrodynamics
	C09.20	Electrostatics
	C09.20.10	Static electricity
	C09.22	Electric fields
	C09.25	Electric charge
	C09.30	Electric potential

          UF Voltage

	C09.35	Electric currents
	C09.35.10	Electric discharges

          UF Gas discharges
          Lightning D57.10.20

	C09.40	Electrical faults
	C09.70/90	Magnetism

          Magnetic measurements and instruments H22
          Magnetic properties of substances C19.40
          Magnetic variables control H48.30
          Geomagnetism D10

	C09.80	Electromagnetism

          UF Electromagnetic fields

	C10	Radiation physics

          SN Wave and particle together
          Radiation technology G64.80
          Radiation chemistry C47.50
          Radiation measurement and instruments H25
          Radiation effects C21

	C10.05/90	Radiation

          Atmospheric radiation D56
          Cosmic radiation C76.20
          Electromagnetic waves C11.50
          Light C12.10
          Radiative transfer C07.20.50

	C10.10.40	Infrared radiation
	C10.10.50	Ultraviolet radiation
	C10.50	Radioactivity

          UF Ionizing radiation

	C11	Wave physics

          Fluid waves C24.30.90

          (By phenomena and properties)

	C11.10	Wave propagation
	C11.15	Absorption (wave)
	C11.18	Interference

          Radio wave interference Y80.10.70

	C11.20	Diffraction
	C11.22	Refraction
	C11.25	Reflection
	C11.30	Polarization
	C11.33	Scattering
	C11.35	Wave frequency
	C11.38	Wavelength

          (By type of wave)
          Fluid waves C24.30.90

	C11.50	Electromagnetic waves

C01/27		**Physics** (cont.)
C04/12		**Physics of Energy Phenomena** (cont.)
	C11	Wave physics (cont.)
	C11.50	Electromagnetic waves (cont.)
		Light C12.10
	C11.50.30	X-rays
		X-ray analysis H26
	C11.50.40	Gamma rays
	C11.50.60	Radio waves
	C11.50.60M	Microwaves
	C12	Optics
		Atmospheric optics D57.20
		Optical measurements and instruments H23
		Optical properties of substances C20
		Optical variables control H50
		Particle optics C13.10
		Wave physics C11
	C12.10	Light
	C12.20	Image formation
	C12.70	Quantum optics
		UF Quantum electronics
		Masers G29.45
		Lasers G29.50
C13.01/49		**Particle Physics**
		UF Elementary particle physics
		Particle measurements and instruments H24
	C13.05	Quantum field theory
		UF Field physics
	C13.10	Particle optics
		UF Electron optics
		Ion optics
	C13.10.10	Particle beams
		UF Electron beams
		Ion beams
	C13.20	Elementary particles
		UF Alpha particles
		Beta particles
		Baryons
		Bosons
		Fermions
		Hadrons
		Leptons
		Mesons
		Strange particles
		Electrons C13.25.10
		Neutrons C13.30.10
	C13.20.25	Protons
	C13.20.30	Photons
	C13.25	Electron physics
		Electron diffraction H24.20
		Electron microscopes H24.30
	C13.25.10	Electrons
	C13.30	Neutron physics
	C13.30.10	Neutrons
	C13.40	High energy physics
		Particle accelerations H24.10
C13.50		**Nuclear Physics**
		Nuclear engineering G64
		Radioactivity C10.50
	C13.50.10	Nuclear structure and properties
		SN Includes binding energy and masses, shape, charge, radius, spin, parity, moments, spacing and nuclear force

C01/27		**Physics** (cont.)
C13.50		**Nuclear physics** (cont.)
	C13.50.20/40	Nuclear reactions
		UF Nuclear scattering
	C13.50.30	Nuclear fission
	C13.50.40	Nuclear fusion
		UF Thermonuclear reactions
	C13.50.70	Nuclear reactor theory
		Neutron physics C13.30
C13.70/99		**Atomic, Molecular and Ion Physics**
	C13.70	Atomic physics
	C13.70.10	Atoms
	C13.70.20	Atomic mass
	C13.70.40	Atomic structure
		Crystal atomic structure C28.30.10
	C13.75	Molecular physics
		SN Includes molecular beams, spectra, collision processes, dissociations, moments, spin, etc.
		Molecular structure C48.10/90
	C13.90	Ion physics
	C13.90.10	Ions
	C13.90.30	Ionization
		Atmospheric ionization D57.40
	C14	**Vacuum Physics**
		Vacuum measurement H16
	C15/27	**Bulk Matter Physics**
	C16/20	**Physical Properties**
		SN General physical properties of substances
		Chemical properties C41
		Thermodynamic properties C06.20
	C17	Mechanical properties of substances
		Mechanics of solids C27.01/65
	C17.10	Vibrations
		Vibration measurement H15.50
	C17.30	Acoustics
		UF Acoustic waves
		Sound
		Atmospheric acoustics D57.50
		Electroacoustics C19.25
		Noise S07.10
	C17.30.05	Sound wave propagation
		UF Acoustic wave propagation
	C17.30.10	Acoustic properties
		Sea water acoustic properties D90.50.60
	C17.30.10B	Sound velocity
		UF Acoustic velocity
	C17.30.40	Underwater sound
		UF Hydroacoustics
		Underwater communication G52.10
	C17.30.70	Ultrasonics
		UF Ultrasound
	C18	Thermal properties of substances
		UF Boiling points
		Calorific value
		Critical point
		Emissivity
		Solidification points
		Vapour points
		Volatility
		Thermal measurements and instruments H20
		Thermal variables control H51

C01/27		**Physics** (cont.)
C15/27		**Bulk Matter Physics** (cont.)
C16/20		**Physical Properties** (cont.)
	C18	Thermal properties of substances (cont.)

                 Thermodynamic properties C06.20
                 Temperature C06.30

	C18.05	Specific heat
	C18.10	Latent heat
	C18.20	Thermal conductivity
	C18.25	Thermal diffusivity
	C18.30	Thermal resistance
	C19	Electrical properties of substances

         UF Electrical impedance
             Electrical inductance
             Electrical reactance
             Electrical resistance
       Electrical measurements and instruments H21
       Electrical variable control H48

	C19.05	Electrical conductivity
	C19.05.20	Superconductivity
	C19.10	Dielectric properties

             UF Capacitance
                 Dielectrics
                 Electric strength
                 Permittivity

	C19.15	Electromechanical effects
	C19.15.10	Piezoelectricity
	C19.20	Photoelectricity
	C19.25	Electroacoustics
	C19.30	Thermoelectricity
	C19.40	Magnetic properties of substances

         Magnetic measurements and instruments H22
         Magnetic variables control H48.30

	C20	Optical properties of substances

         Optics C12
         Optical measurements and instruments H23
         Optical variables control H50
         Sea water optical properties D90.50.50

	C20.10	Light absorption
	C20.40	Luminescence
	C20.50	Transparency
	C20.55	Opacity
	C20.70	Colour
	C20.75	Visibility
	C21	**Radiation Effects**

         UF Radiation damage
       Radiobiology F27

	C22	**Dispersion and Surface Physics**
	C22.10	Dispersion physics

         Dispersions C53.20/90

	C22.10.30	Colloid physics

           Colloids C53.40

	C22.30/80	Surface physics

         SN Includes surface discharges, surface energy, etc.
       Surface chemistry C51

	C22.35	Surface tension
	C22.40	Capillarity
	C22.50	Surface films
	C22.50.10	Thin films

C01/27		**Physics** (cont.)
C15/27		**Bulk Matter Physics** (cont.)

C23   **Plasma Physics**

         UF Plasma

C24   **Fluid Physics**

         SN Liquids and gases together
         Fluid measurement and instruments H17

C24.05/70   Fluid mechanics
         Hydromechanics C25.30/50

C24.10   Fluid pressure
         Atmospheric pressure D52
         Water pressure D83.80
         Pressure measurement and instruments H17.40
         Pressure control H49.55

C24.15   Fluid mechanical properties
         Capillarity C22.40
         Viscosity C25.10.10

C24.15.10   Compressibility

C24.15.20   Fluid density

C24.20/70   Fluid dynamics
         Hydrodynamics C25.45

C24.30   Flow
         UF Gas flow
             Fluid flow
             Liquid flow
             Water flow
         Flow control H49.50
         Flowmeters H17.10

C24.30.05   Laminar flow

C24.30.10   Turbulent flow

C24.30.12   Vortices

C24.30.15   Boundary layer flow

C24.30.18   Capillary flow

C24.30.20   Channel flow
         UF Open channel flow

C24.30.20S   Streamflow

C24.30.25   Flow in pipes
         (By elements and phenomena)

C24.30.30   Boundary layers

C24.30.38   Wakes

C24.30.40   Jets

C24.30.43   Sprays

C24.30.45   Drops

C24.30.50   Turbulence

C24.30.55   Cavitation

C24.30.65   Bubbles

C24.30.70   Surges

C24.30.80   Water hammer

C24.30.90   Fluid waves
         Water waves C25.45.20

C24.40   Aerodynamics

C24.60   Magnetohydrodynamics
         UF MHD
         Plasma physics C23
         Magnetohydrodynamic conversion G25.30

C24.80   Gas physics
         UF Structure of gases
         Electric discharges C09.35.10

C25/27   **Condensed Matter Physics**

         SN Liquids and solids together

C25.10   Rheology

C25.10.10   Viscosity

C01/27		**Physics** (cont.)
C15/27		**Bulk Matter Physics** (cont.)
C25/27		**Condensed Matter Physics** (cont.)
	C25.20/80	Physics of liquids
	C25.30/50	Hydromechanics
		Hydraulic engineering G40/54
		Underwater sound C17.30.40
	C25.40	Hydrostatics
	C25.40.10	Buoyancy
	C25.40.20	Flotation
	C25.45	Hydrodynamics
		Dynamic oceanography D92
		Flow C25.30
		Magnetohydrodynamics C24.60
		Water discharge D82.80
	C25.45.10	Water currents
		Ocean currents D92.20
	C25.45.20	Water waves
		Ocean waves D92.50
	C25.60	Liquid structure
	C25.70	Liquid crystals
	C26/27	Physics of solids
	C27.01/65	Mechanics of solids
		UF Mechanical behaviour of solids
		Mechanical properties of solids
	C27.10	Stress (mechanical)
	C27.15	Mechanical strength
	C27.20	Hardness
	C27.25	Elasticity
	C27.28	Plasticity
	C27.30	Deformation
		UF Strain
	C27.30.10	Elastic deformation
	C27.30.40	Plastic deformation
	C27.30.40C	Creep
	C27.40	Fracture
		UF Cracking
	C27.45	Fatigue
	C27.60	Tribology
	C27.60.10	Friction
	C27.60.20	Wear
	C27.60.30	Lubrication
		Lubricants G35.15.10
		Lubrication systems G35.15
	C27.70/99	Solid state physics
		Crystallography C28
		Dielectric properties C19.10
		Electromechanical effects C19.15
		Magnetic properties of substances C19.40
		Superconductivity C19.05.20
	C27.80	Semiconductor physics
		Semiconductors G29.30
C28		**Crystallography**
	C28.05	Crystals
		Liquid crystals C25.70
	C28.10	Crystalline state
	C28.10.70	Amorphous state
	C28.30	Crystal structure
		UF Crystal orientation
		Crystal morphology
		Crystal symmetry

C28		**Crystallography** (cont.)
	C28.30	Crystal structure (cont.)
	C28.30.10	Crystal atomic structure
		UF Crystal lattic structure
	C28.30.30	Crystal defects
		UF Crystal dislocations
		Crystal impurities
		Lattic defects
		Twinning (crystal)
	C28.30.40	Crystal microstructure
		UF Grain boundaries
		Grain structure
		Crystal inclusion
		Microstructure
	C28.30.40B	Solid solutions
	C28.35	Crystal chemistry
	C28.40	Crystal growth
	C28.40.10	Crystallization
	C28.40.40	Nucleation
	C28.80	Crystal examination
		Electron microscopes H24.30
		Neutron diffraction H24.25
	C28.80.10	X-ray crystallography

C30/69		**Chemistry**
		Agricultural chemistry G09.30
		Biochemistry F25
		Chemistry education J60.40.20
		Chemical oceanography D94
		Geochemistry D13
		Chemical technology G77/93
		Materials science G70/93
		Petrochemistry G92.30.10
		Phytochemistry F38.40
		Soil chemistry D41
		Water chemistry D84.35
		Zoochemistry F42.50

	C32	**Chemical Research**
		Chemical laboratories C34
		Experimental chemistry C33.39

	C33/39	**Experimental Chemistry**
		UF Chemical experiments
		Practical chemistry
		(By laboratories and equipment)
	C34	Chemical laboratories
	C34.30	Chemical laboratory equipment
		SN Includes flasks, beakers, test tubes,
		balances, furnaces
		Autoclaves G79.30
	C34.30.50	Reagents
		(By operations)
	C35.10	Microchemistry
		UF Microtechniques (chemistry)
		Microscopes H23.50.10
	C35.50	Preparative chemistry
		SN Includes chemical separation, solvent extraction,
		decomposition, synthesis, etc.

	C36/39	**Chemical Analysis**
		UF Analytical chemistry

C30/69		**Chemistry** (cont.)
C33/39		**Experimental Chemistry** (cont.)
C36/39		**Chemical Analysis** (cont.)

	(By method)
C37.05	Instrumental analysis
C37.10	Trace analysis
C37.12	Semimicroanalysis
C37.15	Microanalysis
C37.20	Systematic chemical analysis
	SN Includes dry tests, wet tests, spot tests
C37.20.10	Sampling (chemical analysis)
C37.25	Qualitative analysis
C37.28	Quantitative analysis
C37.30	Gravimetric analysis
C37.35	Volumetric analysis
	UF Titration
C37.40	Electroanalysis
	UF Electroanalytical chemistry
C37.40.10	Polarographic analysis
C37.40.30	Potentiometric analysis
C37.45	Thermal chemical analysis
	UF Thermogravimetric analysis
C37.50	Optical chemical analysis
	Optical measurements and instruments H23
C37.50.20	Colorimetric analysis
C37.50.40	Spectrochemical analysis
C37.55	X-ray chemical analysis
C37.60	Radiochemical analysis
C37.70	Chromatographic analysis
	UF Chromatography
	Gas chromatography
	Liquid chromatography
	(By properties analysed)
C38.05/40	Chemical variables measurement
C38.10	pH measurement
C38.20	Moisture measurement
	(By substances analysed)
	Water analysis D84.40
C39.20	Gas analysis
C39.50	Biochemical analysis
C40/54	**Physical Chemistry**
	(By properties)
C41	Chemical properties
	Chemical variables measurement C38.05/40
	Permeability C51.10
	Photosensitivity C47.80
	Porosity C51.20
	Salinity D90.50.35
	Solubility C52.30
C41.05	Acidity
C41.10	Alkalinity
V41.15	pH
	UF Hydrogen ion concentration
C42/46	Reaction chemistry
C43	Chemical thermodynamics
C44/46	Chemical mechanics
C45.10	Chemical statics
C45.10.10	Chemical equilibrium
	Phase equilibrium C06.85.10
C45.30/90	Chemical kinetics

C30/69		**Chemistry** (cont.)
C40/54		**Physical Chemistry** (cont.)
	C42/46	Reaction Chemistry (cont.)
	C44/46	Chemical Mechanics (cont.)
	C45.30/90	Chemical Kinetics (cont.)

                               *Sorption C51.50
                               *Transport processes (physics) C07

	C45.35	Chemical diffusion
	C45.35.10	Dialysis
	C45.35.20	Osmosis
	C45.50	Catalysis
		UF Catalysts

(By type of reaction)

	C46	Chemical reactions

                 *Electromechanical reactions C47.30.50/90
                 *Photochemical reactions C47.60.30

(By reaction mechanism)

	C46.05	Chemical effects
	C46.10	Synthesis (chemical)
		UF Formation (chemical)
	C46.20	Decomposition reactions
		UF Thermal decomposition
	C46.20.10	Degradation
	C46.20.20.	Fermentation
	C46.20.40	Dissociation reactions

                         *Radiolysis C47.40.20

	C46.20.40H	Hydrolysis
	C46.25	Separation (chemical)
		UF Concentration (chemical)
	C46.30	Addition reactions
	C46.30.20	Polymerization
	C46.35	Elimination reactions
	C46.40	Combination reactions
		UF Fusion reactions
	C46.45	Replacement reactions
		UF Substitution reactions
	C46.50	Exchange reactions
	C46.50.20	Ion exchange
	C46.60	Redox reactions
		UF De-oxidation
		Reduction
		Hydrogenation
	C46.60.20	Oxidation
		UF De-hydrogenation

                         *Combustion C47.10.10

	C46.65	Rearrangement reactions
	C46.65.10	Isomerization
	C46.65.30	Ring closure reactions

(By special reactions)

	C46.80/99	Corrosion
		SN Includes atmospheric, gas, biological, stress, cavitation, and erosion corrosion
	C46.85	Electrochemical corrosion
	C46.85.10	Water corrosion
		UF Sea water corrosion
	C47.10	Thermochemistry

                 *Chemical thermodynamics C43
                 *Heat transfer C07.20
                 *Latent heat C18.10

	C47.10.10	Combustion
		UF Flames
		Flammability
		Ignition
		Combustion products

C30/69		**Chemistry** (cont.)
C40/54		**Physical Chemistry** (cont.)
	C47.10	Thermochemistry (cont.)
	C47.10.10	Combustion (cont.)

Ashes E32.76
Smoke E32.70
Explosions E73.20
Fire E73.10
Thermal engineering G32

	C47.30	Electrochemistry
		Electrodes G27.50
	C47.30.10	Electrolytes
		UF Electrolytic solutions
	C47.30.20	Electrolytic cells
		Batteries G25.10
	C47.30.50/90	Electrochemical reactions
		SN Includes polarization, electroosmosis, electrosynthetics, etc.
		Electrochemical corrosion C46.85
	C47.30.55	Electrolysis
	C47.35	Magnetochemistry
	C47.40	Radiochemistry
	C47.40.20	Radiolysis
	C47.50	Radiation chemistry
		SN Chemical processes produced by high energy radiation
	C47.60	Photochemistry
	C47.60.30	Photochemical reactions
	C47.60.30B	Photosynthesis
	C47.80	Photosensitivity
	C48	Chemical structure
		UF Structural chemistry
		Atomic structure C13.70.40
		Crystallography C28
	C48.10/90	Molecular structure
		Molecular biology F11
		Molecular physics C13.75
	C48.20	Molecules
	C48.20.10	Macromolecules
		Polymers C68.20
	C48.30	Chemical bonds
		UF Valency
	C48.50	Stereochemistry
		UF Allotropy
		Isomerism
		Polymorphism
	C49	States of matter
		Dispersions C53.20/90
		Mixtures C53.10
		Solutions C52.10
		Phase transformations C06.40/90
	C49.10	Fluids
		Fluid physics C24
	C49.10.10	Gases
	C49.10.20	Vapours
	C49.10.30	Liquids
		Liquid crystals C25.70
		Physics of liquids C25.20/80
	C49.30	Semi-solids
	C49.30.20	Gels

C30/69		**Chemistry** (cont.)
C40/54		**Physical Chemistry** (cont.)
	C49	States of matter (cont.)
	C49.50	Solids

                        Amorphous state C28.10.70
                        Crystalline state C28.10
                        Mechanics of solids C27.01/65
                        Solid state physics C27.70/99

	C50/53	Mixed-phase chemistry
	C51	Surface chemistry

                        Surface physics C22.30/80

	C51.05	Surfaces
	C51.10	Permeability
	C51.20	Porosity
	C51.25	Diffusivity
	C51.30	Adhesion
	C51.50	Sorption
		UF Desorption
	C51.50.10	Adsorption
	C51.50.30	Absorption (chemical)
	C52	Solution chemistry
	C52.10	Solutions
		(By property)
	C52.30	Solubility
		(By components)
	C52.50	Solutes
	C52.50.10	Dissolved gases
	C52.60	Solvents
	C53	Colloid chemistry

                        Colloid physics C22.10.30

	C53.10	Mixtures
	C53.20/90	Dispersions
	C53.30	Suspensions
	C53.40	Colloids
		Gels C49.30.20
	C53.40.10	Foams
	C53.40.20	Aerosols
	C53.40.40	Emulsions
	C53.40.50	Sols

	C55/69	**Chemistry of Elements and Compounds**
	C56/59	Chemical elements
		Metals G73
	C57	Isotopes
		Radioisotopes G64.80.10
	C58	Non-metals
		SN Non-metallic elements
	C58.10	Hydrogen
	C58.20/29	Halogens
	C58.21	Chloride
	C58.22	Bromide
	C58.23	Iodine
	C58.24	Fluorine
	C58.30	Nitrogen
	C58.32	Phosphorus
	C58.34	Arsenic
	C58.36	Oxygen
	C58.36.10	Ozone
	C58.40	Sulphur
	C58.42	Selenium

C30/69		**Chemistry** (cont.)
C55/69		**Chemistry of Elements and Compounds** (cont.)
	C56/59	Chemical elements (cont.)
	C58	Non-metals (cont.)
	C58.45	Tellurium
	C58.48	Carbon
	C58.50	Silicon
	C58.55	Germanium
	C58.60	Helium
	C58.62	Neon
	C58.65	Argon
	C58.70	Krypton
	C58.72	Xenon
	C58.75	Radon
	C59	Metalloids

*Antimony G73.50.10
*Arsenic C58.34
*Boron G73.30.15
*Germanium C58.55
*Polonium G73.60.60
*Silicon C58.50
*Tellurium C58.45

C60   Chemical radicals
UF Free radicals
*Ions C13.90.10

C61   Compounds
UF Salts (compounds)
C61.10   Acids
C61.20   Bases (chemical)
C61.30   Complex compounds
*Organic complex compounds C66.80
C61.30.10   Coordination compounds

C62/63   **Inorganic Chemistry**

C63   Inorganic compounds
UF Inorganic acids
Inorganic bases
Inorganic salts
Intermetallics
*Air D50.10
*Minerals D21.40/90
*Water D81/83

(By specific inorganic compounds)
C63.20   Silicates
C63.40   Carbon dioxide
C63.50   Salt
UF Common salt
Sodium chloride

For others divide as UDC 54 Chemistry, Second English full edition

C64/66   **Organic Chemistry**

C65/66   Organic compounds
UF Organic acids
Organic bases
Organic salts
Esters
*Biochemicals F25.18/50
C66.05   Organic matter
C66.10   Organometallic compounds
*Coordination compounds C61.30.10

(By general types of organic compounds)
C66.25   Ethers
C66.28   Carbonyl compounds

C30/69		**Chemistry** (cont.)
C55/69		**Chemistry of Elements and Compounds** (cont.)
C64/66		**Organic Chemistry** (cont.)
	C65/66	Organic compounds (cont.)
	C66.28	Carbonyl compounds (cont.)

UF Aldehydes
    Ketones

	C66.30	Hydrocarbons
	C66.40/55	Aliphatic compounds
	C66.45	Alkanes

    UF Alkyl compounds

	C66.50	Alkenes

    UF Olefines
        Alkylene compounds

	C66.55	Alkynes

    UF Acetylene compounds

	C66.60	Carbohydrates
	C66.65	Alicyclic compounds

    UF Terpenes

	C66.70	Aromatic compounds

    UF Isocyclic compounds

	C66.75	Heterocyclic compounds
	C66.75.30	Alkaloids
	C66.80	Organic complex compounds

For detailed classification of organic compounds divide as UDC 54
Chemistry, Second English full edition

	C68	**Polymer Chemistry**

UF Macromolecular chemistry
*Polymer and plastic technology G86
*Macromolecules C48.20.10
*Polymerization C46.30.20

	C68.20	Polymers

UF Homopolymers
    Organic polymers
    Resins (polymers)
    *Natural resins G86.08
    *Plastics G86.10
    *Rubber G86.40.10

	C68.20.70	Inorganic polymers

C70/99 Space Sciences

C72/99 Astronomy

C80 Astronomical bodies and systems

C70/99	**Space Sciences**
	Space communication Y80.30.45
	Aerospace medicine F95.65
	Exobiology E15.20
	Space technology G63.50/99
C71	**Space**
C72/99	**Astronomy**
	(By theories, properties and processes)
C73	Cosmology
	SN Nature and origin of the universe
	UF Cosmogony
C74	Spherical astronomy
	UF Positional astronomy
C75	Celestial mechanics
C76	Astrophysics
C76.20	Cosmic radiation
	UF Cosmic rays
	Solar radiation C88.05
	(By observation and measurement)
C77/79	Practical astronomy
C78	Astronomical observatories
	UF Astronomical observations
	Space stations G63.70
C78.10	Planetaria
C79	Astronomical measurements and instruments
C79.10	Astronomical telescopes
C79.30	Radioastronomy
	UF Radiotelescopes
	(By bodies and systems)
C80	Astronomical bodies and systems
	UF Celestial bodies
C81	Universe
	UF Cosmos
C82	Interstellar space
C83	Cosmic matter
	UF Interstellar matter
C83.10	Nebulae
C84	Stars
C84.10	Novae
C84.20	Quasars
C84.30	Pulsars
C84.40	Black holes
C85/86	Galaxies
	UF Stellar systems
C86	Milky way
C87/99	Solar system
C88	Sun
C88.05	Solar radiation
C88.10	Solar disturbances
	UF Solar activity
	Sun spots
C88.20	Solar corona
C88.30	Solar eclipses
C90	Planets
	Earth (planet) D04
C92	Satellites
	Artificial satellites G63.60.30
C92.10	Moon
C95	Interplanetary matter
C95.20	Asteroids
C95.30	Meteors
C95.40	Meteorites
C95.50	Comets

D   Earth Sciences

D03/14	**Geophysics**
D15/18	**Geology**
D29	**Palaeontology**
D30/34	**Geomorphology**
D35	**Geography**
D38/44	**Soil science**
D45/64	**Meteorology**
D65/84	**Hydrology**
D85/99	**Oceanography**

D   Earth Sciences

D03/14

Geophysics
Marine geophysics D88

D04	Earth (planet)
D05	Geomathematics
D07	Terrestrial rotation
	UF Earths rotation
D07.30	Seasons
D07.40	Diurnal variations
D08	Terrestrial age
	UF Earths age
D08.30	Geochronology
D09	Isostasy
D10	Geomagnetism
	UF Terrestrial magnetism
D10.15	Geoelectricity
D11	Seismology
	Earthquake engineering G58.50.10
D11.05	Earthquakes
	Submarine earthquakes D88.50
	(By frequency and distribution)
D11.10	Seismic areas
D11.20	Seismicity
	(By instruments and observations)
D11.50	Seismometers
	UF Seismographs
	Seismoscopes
D11.70	Seismological observatories
	UF Seismological centres
D12	Terrestrial heat
	UF Crustal temperature
	Geothermics
	Geotemperature
D13	Geochemistry
D13.40	Biogeochemistry
D14	Geophysical measurements and instruments
	UF Geodetics
	Earth measurement
	Geophysical prospecting D26.30
	Seismometers D11.50
D14.10	Geodesy
D14.30	Gravimeters

D15/28

Geology
Geology education J60.40.40
Hydrogeology D74.05
Marine geology D89

D15.30	Geological data
D16/17	Stratigraphy
	UF Historical geology
D16.30	Palaeogeology
D17	Geological ages
	Geochronology D08.30
D17.10	Precambrian period
D17.15	Palaeozoic period
D17.20	Mesozoic period
D17.25	Cenozoic period
D17.30	Tertiary period
D17.40	Quarternary period
	UF Ice age
	Stone age U16

D15/28		**Geology** (cont.)
	D18/26	Physical geology
	D19/20	Petrology
		UF Lithology
		Petrography
		Geochemistry D13
		(By rock types)
	D20	Rocks
		UF Stones (rocks)
		Building stones G60.65
		Quarrying G61.30
		Soils D39
		(By properties and phenomena)
	D20.10	Rock properties
	D20.15	Rock mechanics
		(By type)
	D20.20	Boulders
	D20.25	Igneous rocks
	D20.15.10	Plutonic rocks
		UF Intrusive rocks
	D20.25.10G	Granite
	D20.25.40	Volcanic rocks
		UF Andesite
		Basalt
		Extrusive rocks
		Phonolite
		Pyroclastic rocks
		Rhyolites
	D20.30	Metamorphic rocks
		UF Schists
	D20.30.10	Gneiss
	D20.30.30	Marbles
	D20.30.50	Slates
	D20.35/99	Sedimentary rocks
		Sedimentology D25.10.05
	D20.40/70	Clastic deposits
		UF Conglomerate rocks
	D20.45/55	Arenaceous rocks
	D20.48	Sandstones
	D20.50	Sands
	D20.55	Gravels
	D20.60	Argillaceous rocks
		UF Siltstones
	D20.60.10	Clays
	D20.60.40	Marls
	D20.60.60	Shales
		UF Oil shales
		Mudstones
	D20.70	Rudaceous rocks
	D20.80/99	Non-clastic rocks
		UF Aluminous sediments
		Chert
		Endogenic rocks
		Evaporitic rocks
		Flysch sediments
		Molasse sediments
		Non-clastic sediments
		Phosphatic sediments
		Siliceous sediments
	D20.85	Carbonate rocks
		UF Carbonate sediments
	D20.85.10	Limestone
	D20.85.30	Chalk
	D20.90	Carbonaceous rocks

D15/28		**Geology** (cont.)
	D18/26	Physical geology (cont.)
	D19/20	Petrology (cont.)
	D20	Rocks (cont.)
	D20.35/99	Sedimentary rocks (cont.)
	D20.80/99	Non-clastic rocks (cont.)
	D20.90	Carbonaceous rocks (cont.)

                           UF Lignite
                            Coal G83.10

	D20.90.10	Asphalts
	D20.90.40	Bituminous sands
	D21	Mineralogy
	D21.10/40	Mineral deposits

                           UF Ore deposits
                           Mineral maps H34.10.30
                           Mineral resources E82
                           Bituminous sands D20.90.40
                           Shales D20.60.60

	D21.20	Metallic deposits

                           UF Metalliferous mineral deposits

	D21.25	Non-metalliferous mineral deposits
	D21.25.10	Salt deposits

                           UF Rock salt deposits

	D21.30	Fossil fuel deposits
	D21.30.10	Gas fields
	D21.30.30	Oil fields
	D21.35	Submarine mineral deposits
	D21.40/90	Minerals
	D21.45	Metalliferous minerals

                           SN Includes aluminium ores, copper ores, lead ores,
                               tin ores, titanium ores, zinc ores, etc.
                           UF Ores (metal sources)

	D21.45.10	Iron ores

                               UF Pyrite

	D21.50/90	Non-metalliferous minerals

                           UF Ores (non-metallic)
                              Silicate minerals

	D21.55	Asbestos
	D21.60	Feldspar
	D21.65	Clay minerals

                               UF Kaolin

	D21.70	Silica minerals
	D21.70.10	Quartz
	D21.75	Carbonate minerals
	D21.75.10	Dolomite
	D21.80	Sulphate minerals
	D21.80.10	Anhydrite
	D21.80.20	Gypsum
	D21.85	Mica
	D21.90	Gems

                           UF Gemmology

	D21.90.10	Diamonds
	D22	Earths structure
	D22.10	Earths core

                           UF Barysphere

	D22.30	Earths crust

                           UF Lithosphere

	D23/25	Geodynamics

                           UF Geological processes

	D24	Endogenous processes

                           UF Internal geodynamics
                           Seismology D11

D15/28		**Geology** (cont.)
	D18/26	Physical geology (cont.)
	D23/25	Geodynamics (cont.)
	D24	Endogenous processes (cont.)
	D24.10	Thermal springs
		UF Geysers
	D24.20	Volcanology
	D24.20.10	Volcanoes
		Submarine volcanoes D89.20.50
	D24.20.30	Volcanic eruptions
	D24.20.40	Volcanic products
	D24.20.50	Volcano surveillance
	D24.40	Tectonics
		UF Geological deformation
		Geological faults
		Oryogenesis
		Schistosity
		Tectonic maps H34.10.10
	D24.40.10	Continental drift
	D24.40.50	Landslides
	D24.40.50A	Avalanches
	D24.40.55	Land subsidence
	D25	Exogenous processes
	D25.10	Sedimentation
	D25.10.05	Sedimentology
	D25.10.10	Sediment
	D25.10.20	Moraines
		UF Eskers
	D25.10.40	Sediment transport
	D25.30	Erosion
		Soil erosion D42.10
	D25.30.10	Coastal erosion
	D25.40	Glaciology
		Ice D63.50
		Moraines D25.10.20
		Sea ice D90.80
		Floating ice D90.80.10
	D25.40.05	Glaciation
	D25.40.10	Ice caps
	D25.40.20	Glaciers
	D25.40.30	Land ice
	D25.40.35	Permafrost
		UF Frozen ground
	D26	Experimental geology
	D26.30	Geophysical prospecting
		UF Electrical prospecting
		Gravimetric prospecting
		Seismic prospecting
	D27	Economic geology
		Fuels G82
		Mineral deposits D21.10/40
		Mineral resources E82
		Resource exploration E93
	D28	Engineering geology
	D28.10	Mining geology
	D28.30	Petroleum geology
		Petroleum production G84.20

D29		**Palaeontology**
		UF Palaeobiology
		Palaeozoology

Palaeontology (cont.)

D29.10	Fossils
D29.20	Invertebrate palaeontology
D29.25	Vertebrate palaeontology
D29.30	Micropalaeontology
D29.50	Palaeobotany
	UF Palynology
D29.60	Palaeobiochemistry
D29.65	Palaeoecology
D29.80	Palaeoclimatology
D29.85	Palaeohydrology

D30/34   **Geomorphology**
                                             (By land form)

D31/34	Topography
	Glaciology D25.40
	Submarine topography D89.15/60
D33	Land forms
	UF Land features
	Wetlands D80
D33.05	Continents
D33.10	Islands
D33.10.10	Archipelangos
D33.10.30	Atolls
D33.12	Reefs
	UF Barrier reefs
D33.12.10	Coral reefs
D33.15	Peninsulas
D33.20	Mountains
	UF Highlands
	Volcanoes D24.20.10
D33.22	Hills
D33.23	Cliffs
D33.25	Plateaus
D33.30	Valleys
D33.30.10	Canyons
D33.30.30	Gullies
D33.35	Basins
	Drainage basins D73.20
	River basins D76.10
D33.38	Plains
D33.38.10	Coastal plains
D33.40	Coasts
	UF Coastal topography
	Bays D99.80
	Gulfs D99.40
	Coastal plains D33.38.10
	Coastal waters D90.15
	Coastal erosion D25.30.10
	Mangrove areas D96.10.90
D33.40.10	Coastal zones
D33.40.20	Shores
D33.40.25	Beaches
D33.40.25B	Beach sand
D33.40.25D	Dunes
D33.40.30	Intertidal areas
	UF Foreshores
	Tidal zones
D33.40.40	Fjords
D33.40.50	Estuaries

D30/34		**Geomorphology** (cont.)
	D31/34	Topography (cont.)
	D33	Land forms (cont.)
	D33.40	Coasts (cont.)
	D33.40.60	Deltas
	D33.50	Karst
	D33.55	Caves

UF Speleology

(By vegetation)

	D33.60	Deserts

*Desert soils D39.30
*Arid zones D46.40.40

	D33.60.10	Desert science
	D33.60.50	Oasis
	D33.62	Jungle
	D33.62.20	Taiga
	D33.63	Grasslands
	D33.63.10	Pampas
	D33.63.20	Savannah
	D33.63.30	Steppe
	D33.68	Tundra
	D34	Water features

*Bays D99.80
*Canals S60.70
*Estuaries D33.40.50
*Gulfs D99.40
*Lagoons D77.70
*Lakes D77
*Oceans D99.10
*Rivers D76
*Seas D99.20
*Straits D99.60
*Wetlands D78

D35		**Geography**

*Cartography H34
*Geographers B34.44
*Geography education J60.40.50
*Topography D31/34

	D35.10	Geographical research
	D35.10.10	Geographical exploration

UF Geographical expeditions

	D35.10.30	Geographical data
	D35.15/49	Regional geography

SN For geographical areas and countries see entries in the alphabetical thesaurus and computer-generated hierarchies
Climatic zones D46.46

	D35.17	Global geography
	D35.19	Continental geography

*Continents D33.05

	D35.21	National geography
	D35.23	Local geography
	D35.50	Physical geography

*Phytogeography F38.80
*Zoogeography F42.80

	D35.60/80	Human geography

*Cultural geography T19

	D35.65	Anthropogeography
	D35.70	Economic geography
	D35.80	Political geography
	D35.90	Historical geography
	D35.90.10	Palaeogeography

D38/44		**Soil Science**
		UF Pedology
		Soil conservation E94.20
		Soil resources E84
	D39	Soils
		(By type)
	D39.10	Clay soils
	D39.15	Sandy soils
	D39.18	Loams
	D39.20	Peat soils
	D39.25	Loess
	D39.28	Laterites
	D39.30	Desert soils
	D39.35	Volcanic soils
	D39.40	Salt affected soils
	D39.42	Saturated soils
	D39.42.10	Waterlogging
	D39.45	Unsaturated soils
		(By properties)
	D40.05	Soil properties
		Capilliarity C22.40
		Permeability C51.10
		Porosity C51.20
	D40.10/90	Soil physics
	D40.15	Soil temperature
	D40.20	Soil mechanics
		Earthquake engineering G58.50
	D40.20.30	Soil compaction
	D40.40	Soil profiles
	D41	Soil chemistry
		Soil moisture D74.20.10
	D41.05	Soil constituents
	D41.20	Soil fertility
	D41.40	Soil genesis
		UF Soil formation
		(By problems)
		Soil resources E84
		Soil conservation E94.20
	D42.10	Soil erosion
	D42.30	Soil deterioration
		Soil pollution E38.10
		(By activity)
	D43	Soil surveys
		Soil maps H34.10.45
D45/64		**Meteorology**
		UF Atmospheric sciences
	D46	Climatology
		Palaeoclimatology D29.80
		Climatic maps H34.10.55
	D46.10	Climate
	D46.10.10	Climatic data
	D46.20	Bioclimatology
	D46.25	Agroclimatology
	D46.30	Microclimatoology
	D46.40	Climatic zones
	D46.40.10	Cold zones
	D46.40.20	Temperate zones
	D46.40.30	Tropical zones
	D46.40.35	Equatorial zones

D45/64		**Meteorology** (cont.)
	D46	Climatology (cont.)
	D46.40	Climatic zones (cont.)
	D46.40.40	Arid zones
	D46.40.50	Humid zones
	D46.60	Weather
	D46.60.20	Weather forecasting
		UF Weather reports
	D46.60.20S	Synoptic modelling
	D46.60.50	Weather modification
		UF Artificial precipitation
		Cloud seeding
		Rain making
	D48/63	Atmospheric physics
		UF Aeronomy
	D50	Atmosphere
		UF Terrestrial atmosphere
		Air pollution E32
	D50.10	Air
	D50.20/35	Lower atmosphere
	D50.25	Troposphere
	D50.30	Ozonosphere
	D50.35	Stratosphere
	D50.40/80	Upper atmosphere
		(By temperature distribution)
	D50.53	Mesosphere
		(By physiochemical processes)
	D50.65	Ionosphere
	D50.66	Magnetosphere
	D50.68	Radiation belts
		UF Van Allen belts
		(By dynamic/kinetic processes)
	D50.72	Exosphere
	D51	Atmospheric dynamics
	D51.10	Atmospheric thermodynamics
	D51.10.10	Atmospheric temperature
	D52	Atmospheric pressure
	D53	Atmospheric formations
	D53.10	Air masses
	D53.30	Frontal systems
		UF Cold fronts
	D54	Atmospheric circulation
	D54.10	Winds
	D55	Atmospheric disturbances
	D55.10	Anticyclones
	D55.30	Low pressure systems
	D55.30.10	Cyclones
		Typhoons D55.30.30B
	D55.30.30	Storms
		UF Gales
		Thunderstorms
	D55.30.30B	Typhoons
		UF Hurricanes
		Tropical cyclones
	D55.30.30D	Tornadoes
		UF Whirlwinds
	D56	Atmospheric radiation
		Solar radiation C88.05
	D56.10	Sunlight
	D56.20	Daylight
	D56.40	Sky
	D56.70	Auroras

D45/64		**Meteorology** (cont.)
	D48/63	Atmospheric physics (cont.)
	D57.10	Atmospheric electricity *Static electricity C09.20.10
	D57.10.20	Lightning
	D57.20	Atmospheric optics
	D57.40	Atmospheric ionization *Auroras D56.70 *Ionosphere D50.65
	D57.50	Atmospheric acoustics
	D58/63	Hydrometeorology
	D59	Hydrological cycle
	D59.30	Evapotranspiration
	D60/63	Atmospheric condensation
	D61.10	Clouds
	D61.20	Dew
	D61.25	Fog
	D61.30	Mist UF Haze
	D62	Atmospheric humidity UF Atmospheric water content
	D63	Precipitation UF Atmospheric precipitation *Drought D70.30.10
	D63.10	Rain UF Rainfall
	D63.30	Snow UF Hail Sleet
	D63.50	Ice *Glaciology D25.40
	D63.50.10	Frost
	D64	Meteorological measurements and instruments
		(By data)
	D64.05	Meteorological data
		(By phenomena measured)
	D64.10	Atmospheric pressure measurement
	D64.10.10	Barometers
	D64.20	Precipitation measurement
	D64.20.10	Rain gauges
	D64.30	Atmospheric humidity measurement
	D64.30.10	Hygrometers
	D64.40	Wind measurement
		(By observation and methods)
	D64.50	Meteorological observatories
	D64.60	Meteorological satellites UF Sounding rockets
	D64.70	Radar meteorology
D65/84		**Hydrology** UF Land hydrology *Fluid mechanics C24.05/70 *Hydraulic engineering G40/54 *Hydrodynamics C25.45 *Hydrologists B34.48 *Hydrology education J60.40.65 *Hydrometeorology D58/63 *Oceanography D85/99 *Palaeohydrology D29.85
	D66.05	Hydrosphere
	D66.40	Hydrography

D65/84		**Hydrology** (cont.)
	D66.40	Hydrography (cont.)
		Hydrographic surveying D97.05/40
		(By research)
	D67	Hydrological research
	D67.10	Hydrological data
		(By hydrological services)
	D68	Hydrological networks
		(By water resources)
	D70	Water resources
	D70.05	Regime of waters
	D70.10	Water requirements
	D70.12	Water consumption
	D70.15	Water yield
	D70.20	Water balance
	D70.30	Water shortages
	D70.30.10	Drought
		(By management)
	D70.50	Water resources management
		Quality of water D83.20
		Water supply G41
	D70.50.10	Hydrological forecasting
	D70.50.20	Water utilization
	D70.50.30	Water conservation
	D70.50.50	Water resources development
		(By disasters)
	D71	Floods
		Flood control G46
	D71.50	Water damage
		(By water collection and sources)
	D72/79	Water sources
		Glaciers D25.40.20
		Precipitation D63
		Snow melt D82.40
	D73	Drainage
	D73.10	Run-off
	D73.20	Drainage basins
		UF Hydrological basins
	D73.30	Watersheds
	D74	Groundwater
		UF Underground water
	D74.05	Hydrogeology
		UF Geohydrology
		Hydrogeological maps H34.10.50
	D74.10	Hydrogeochemistry
	D74.20	Soil water
	D74.20.10	Soil moisture
	D74.20.30	Capillary water
	D74.30	Wells
		UF Artesian wells
		Water wells
	D74.40	Springs
		Thermal springs D24.
	D74.60	Aquifers
	D74.70	Underground streams
	D75/80	Surface water
		Oceans D99.10
		Dams G41.10.10
		Reservoirs G41.10.20
		Seas D99.20
	D76	Rivers

D65/84		**Hydrology** (cont.)
	D72/79	Water sources (cont.)
	D75/80	Surface water (cont.)
	D76	Rivers (cont.)

> *River and lake engineering G50*
> *Canals S60.70*
> *Deltas D33.40.60*
> *Estuaries D33.40.50*

	D76.10	River basins
	D76.40	Discharge of rivers
	D76.70	Streams

> *Underground streams D74.70*

	D77	Lakes

> *River and lake engineering G50*

	D77.50	Ponds
	D77.70	Lagoons
	D78	Wetlands
	D78.10	Marshes
	D78.20	Swamps
	D78.40	Bogs
	D78.50	Fens
	D79	Running water

> *Rivers D76*
> *Springs D74.40*
> *Streams D76.70*
> *Underground streams D74.70*

	D79.10	Channels
	D79.40	Waterfalls
	D80	Standing water

> *Lakes D77*
> *Ponds D77.50*
> *Reservoirs G41.10.20*
> *Wetlands D78*

(By water types and properties)

	D81/83	Water

> *Aquatic environment E04.60*
> *Hydrodynamics C25.45*
> *Hydrobiology E15.30*

(By type of water)

	D82.10	Freshwater

> *Limnology E15.30.10*

	D82.20	Saline water

> UF Salt water
> *Sea water D90.50*

	D82.20.10	Brackish water
	D82.35	Stagnant water
	D82.40	Snow melt

(By phenomena)
Flow C24.30

	D82.60	Capillary conductivity

> *Capillary flow C24.30.18*

	D82.62	Capillary fringe

> *Capillary water D74.20.30*

	D82.65	Percolation
	D82.68	Infiltration
	D82.70	Water loss
	D82.70.10	Seepage
	D82.80	Water discharge

(By properties)

	D83	Water properties

> *Acidity C41.05*
> *Alkalinity C41.10*
> *Diffusivity C51.25*

D65/84		**Hydrology** (cont.)
	D81/83	Water (cont.)
	D83	Water properties (cont.)

                         pH C41.15
                         Salinity D90.50.35
                         Sea water properties D90.50.29/90
                         Surface tension C22.35
                         Taste F15.90.40
                         Viscosity C25.10.10

	D83.20	Quality of water
		UF Potable water
		Water pollution E35
		Water treatment E66
	D83.30	Water hardness
	D83.50	Water temperature
		Sea water temperature D90.50.25
	D83.70	Water level
		Sea level D90.35
	D83.80	Water pressure
		Sea water pressure D90.50.40
		(By measurements and instruments)
	D84	Hydrological measurement and instruments
		Fluid measurement and instruments H17
		Hydrographic surveying D97.05/40
		Precipitation measurement D64.20
		Oceanographic instruments D98.50
		Oceanographic measurements D97
	D84.10	Hydrographs
	D84.35	Water chemistry
	D84.40	Water analysis
		Sea water analysis D97.75
	D84.40.10	Water sampling
		For methods of analysis, see Chemical Analysis C36/39

D85/99		**Oceanography**
		UF Marine science
		Oceanology
		Hydrology D65/84
		Oceanography education J60.40.70
		Marine resources E86
		Oceanologists B34.50
		Oceanographers B34.55
		Underwater technology G52
	D86	Oceanographic research
		Oceanographic equipment D98
		Oceanographic measurements D97
	D86.10	Ocean stations
	D86.20	Ocean exploration
		UF Oceanic expeditions
	D86.30	Research ships
		UF Oceanographic research ships
	D86.40	Oceanographic laboratories
	D86.60	Oceanographic data
	D87/92	Physical oceanography
	D88	Marine geophysics
		UF Submarine geophysics
		SN See also terms at Geophysics D03/14
	D88.50	Submarine earthquakes
	D89	Marine geology
		SN See also terms at Geology D15/28
		Coasts D33.40
	D89.10	Submarine geology
		Submarine mineral deposits D21.35

D85/99		**Oceanography** (cont.)
	D87/92	Physical oceanography (cont.)
	D89	Marine geology (cont.)
	D89.10	Submarine geology (cont.)
	D89.10.20	Ocean floor UF Ocean bottom Sea bed
	D89.15/60	Submarine topography UF Bottom topography *Ocean floor D89.10.20*
	D89.20.10	Continental shelf
	D89.20.20	Continental slope
	D89.20.30	Submarine plains UF Abyssal plains
	D89.20.40	Submarine ridges UF Submarine hills Submarine mountains
	D89.20.50	Submarine volcanoes
	D89.20.55	Submarine valleys UF Submarine basins
	D89.20.60	Submarine canyons
	D90	Ocean structure
	D90.10	Water masses
	D90.15	Coastal waters
	D90.20	Deep sea
	D90.30	Ocean stratification UF Ocean thermal stratification *Sea water temperature D90.50.25*
	D90.30.10	Oceanic troposphere SN Warm water sphere
	D90.30.20	Oceanic stratosphere SN Cold water sphere
	D90.30.40	Thermoclines
	D90.35	Sea level *Sea level measurement D97.65*
	D90.50	Sea water UF Marine water Ocean water *Sea water measurements D97.70/90* *Sea water composition D97.75.05* *Water corrosion C46.85.10*
	D90.50.20/90	Sea water properties
	D90.50.25	Sea water temperature
	D90.50.30	Sea water density
	D90.50.35	Salinity
	D90.50.40	Sea water pressure
	D90.50.50	Sea water optical properties
	D90.50.60	Sea water acoustic properties *Sound velocity C17.30.10B*
	D90.80	Sea ice
	D90.80.10	Floating ice UF Ice packs
	D90.80.20	Icebergs
	D92	Dynamic oceanography UF Ocean dynamics *Flow C24.30* *Hydrodynamics C25.45*
	D92.05	Ocean circulation
	D92.10	Ocean variability
	D92.20	Ocean currents *Ocean current measurement D97.55*
	D92.20.30	Tidal currents

D85/99		**Oceanography** (cont.)
	D87/92	Physical oceanography (cont.)
	D92	Dynamic oceanography (cont.)
	D92.20	Ocean currents (cont.)
	D92.20.30	Tidal currents (cont.)
		UF Tidal flow
	D92.20.40	Wind driven currents
	D92.30	Tides
		Tidal currents D92.20.30
		Tide measurement D97.60
		(By type)
	D92.30.20	Wind tides
		(By properties and phenomenon)
	D92.30.30	Tidal energy
		Tidal power stations G24.50.10
	D92.30.35	Tidal cycle
	D92.30.38	Tidal constant
	D92.30.40	Tidal friction
	D92.30.45	Tidal curve
	D92.30.47	Tidal lamination
		UF Tidal stratification
	D92.30.50	Tidal range
	D92.30.52	Tidal rise
		(By effects)
	D92.30.60	Tidal effects
		(By tidal area)
	D92.30.70	Tidal waters
		UF Tide waters
		Intertidal areas D33.40.30
		(By prediction)
	D92.30.80	Tidal prediction
		UF Tide tables
	D92.50	Ocean waves
		Ocean wave measurement D97.50
		(By type)
	D92.50.10	Tsunami
		UF Seismic sea waves
		Tidal waves
	D92.50.20	Internal waves
	D92.50.30	Surf
		UF Breakers
		(By properties)
	D92.50.35	Ocean wave height
	D92.50.38	Ocean wave frequency
	D92.50.40	Ocean wave length
	D92.50.42	Ocean wave velocity
	D92.50.45	Ocean wave energy
		(By part)
	D92.50.50	Ocean wave base
	D92.50.55	Ocean wave crest
	D92.50.60	Ocean wave front
	D92.50.65	Ocean wave profile
		(By process)
	D92.50.70	Ocean wave motion
	D92.50.72	Ocean wave action
	D92.50.74	Ocean wave growth
	D92.50.76	Ocean wave decay
	D92.70	Aquatic drift
		UF Flotsam
		Jetsam
	D94	Chemical oceanography
		UF Marine chemistry

D85/99		**Oceanography** (cont.)
	D94	Chemical oceanography (cont.)

                                        Desalination E66.50
                                        Sea water analysis D97.75

	D95	Marine environment
		UF Ocean environment
		Marine ecosystems D96.20
		Marine pollution E35.50
	D96	Marine biology
		Marine acquaculture G18.60.30
	D96.10	Marine ecological zones
		UF Life zones
	D96.10.10	Littoral zone
	D96.10.20	Bathyal zone
	D96.10.25	Abyssal zone
	D96.10.30	Hadal regions
	D96.10.40	Pelagic zone
	D96.10.40B	Neritic province
	D96.10.40H	Oceanic province
	D96.10.50	Benthic zone
	D96.10.60	Aphotic region
	D96.10.65	Disphotic region
	D96.10.70	Euphotic region
	D96.10.80	Brackish water environment
	D96.10.85	Intertidal environment
	D96.10.90	Mangrove areas
	D96.20	Marine ecosystems
	D96.30/90	Marine life
	D96.35	Plankton
		Phytoplankton D96.40.40
		Plankton recorders D98.30.10
		Zooplankton D96.60.10
	D96.40	Marine plants
	D96.40.10/30	Marine algae
		UF Gymnodinium
		Kelps
	D96.40.25	Seaweeds
	D96.40.40	Phytoplankton
	D96.40.50	Marine microorganisms
		UF Marine bacteria
	D96.60	Marine animals
		Fisheries G18
		Marine fish G18.20.30
		Shellfish G18.20.50
	D96.60.10	Zooplankton
	D97	Oceanographic measurements
		Oceanographic instruments D98.50
	D97.05/40	Hydrographic surveying
		Sonar G36.50.10
	D97.10	Bathymetry
		UF Bathymetric surveying
		Bathyspheres G52.50.10
	D97.10.10	Bathymeters
		UF Bathometers
	D97.10.20	Bathythermographs
	D97.10.30	Bathymetric charts
	D97.30/40	Sounding
		UF Depth sounding
	D97.32	Depth recorders
	D97.35	Fathometers

D85/99   **Oceanography** (cont.)

D97	Oceanographic measurements (cont.)	
D97.05/40	Hydrographic surveying (cont.)	
D97.30/40	Sounding (cont.)	
D97.40	Echo sounding	
D97.40.10	Echo sounders	
D97.50	Ocean wave measurement	
D97.50.10	Wave recorders	
D97.55	Ocean current measurement	
D97.55.10	Current meters	
D97.55.20	Drift bottles	
D97.60	Tide measurement	
D97.60.10	Tide gauges	
D97.65	Sea level measurement	
D97.70/90	Sea water measurements	
D97.75	Sea water analysis	
D97.75.05	Sea water composition	
D97.80	Sea water temperature measurement	

                                     UF Ocean temperature measurement
                                         Sea temperature measurement
                              Bathythermographs D97.10.20
                              Temperature probes H20.20.20

D97.80.30	Thermistor chains	
D97.82	Sea water pressure measurement	
D97.84	Salinity measurement	
D97.84.10	Salinity recorders	

                                  UF Salinometers

D97.85	Sea water density measurement	
D97.87	Sea water optical measurements	

                              Light detectors H23.70
                              Turbidimetry H23.38

D97.88	Sea water acoustic measurements	

                              Sound velocity meters H19.20

D98	Oceanographic equipment	

                              Bathyspheres G52.50.10
                              Capstans G37.70.20
                              Diving equipment G52.50.30
                              Floats G53.70
                              Grabs G37.70.50
                              Hydrophones G29.70.40
                              Winches G37.70.10
                              Wire ropes G35.42.10

D98.10	Oceanographic buoys	
D98.30	Oceanographic samplers	
D98.30.10	Plankton recorders	
D98.40	Underwater cameras	

                              Underwater photography W53.30

D98.50	Oceanographic instruments	

                              Bathythermographs D97.10.20
                              Bathymeters D97.10.10
                              Current meters D97.55.10
                              Depth recorders D97.32
                              Drift bottles D97.55.20
                              Echo sounders D97.40.10
                              Fathometers D97.35
                              Flowmeters H17.10
                              Oceanographic measurements D97
                              Plankton recorders D98.30.10
                              Salinity recorders D97.84.10
                              Sonar G36.50.10
                              Thermistor chains D97.80.30
                              Telemetry Y80.30.35
                              Tide gauges D97.60.10
                              Wave recorders D97.50.10

D85/99		**Oceanography**(cont.)
D99		**Oceans and Seas by Name**
	D99.10	Oceans
	D99.10.10	Arctic Ocean
	D99.10.20	Atlantic Ocean
	D99.10.20A	North Atlantic Ocean
	D99.10.20B	South Atlantic Ocean
	D99.10.30	Indian Ocean
	D99.10.50	Pacific Ocean
	D99.10.50A	North Pacific Ocean
	D99.10.50B	South Pacific Ocean
	D99.10.80	Antartic Ocean
	D99.20	Seas
	D99.20.08	Baltic Sea
	D99.20.09	North Sea
	D99.20.10	Greenland Sea
	D99.20.11	Norwegian Sea
	D99.20.12	Barents Sea
	D99.20.13	White Sea
	D99.20.14	Kara Sea
	D99.20.15	Laptev Sea
		UF Nordenskjold Sea
	D99.20.16	East Siberia Sea
	D99.20.17	Chukchi Sea
	D99.20.18	Beaufort Sea
	D99.20.19	Labrador Sea
	D99.20.20	Lincoln Sea
	D99.20.21	West Coast of Scotland Inland Sea
	D99.20.22	Irish Sea
		UF St. Georges Channel
	D99.20.23	Caribbean Sea
	D99.20.26/33	Mediterranean Sea
	D99.20.27	Alboran Sea
	D99.20.28	Balearic Sea
		UF Iberian Sea
	D99.20.29	Ligurian Sea
	D99.20.30	Tyrrhenian Sea
	D99.20.31	Ionian Sea
	D99.20.32	Adriatic Sea
	D99.20.33	Aegean Sea
	D99.20.34	Dead Sea
	D99.20.35	Sea of Marmara
	D99.20.36	Black Sea
	D99.20.36A	Sea of Azov
	D99.20.37	Caspian Sea
	D99.20.38	Red Sea
	D99.20.39	Arabian Sea
	D99.20.40	Laccadive Sea
	D99.20.41	Andaman Sea
		UF Burma Sea
	D99.20.42/60	East India Archipelago Seas
		UF Indonesian Seas
	D99.20.43	Salu Sea
	D99.20.44	Celebes Sea
	D99.20.45	Molucca Sea
	D99.20.46	Halmahra Sea
	D99.20.47	Ceram Sea
	D99.20.48	Banda Sea
	D99.20.49	Arafura Sea
	D99.20.50	Timor Sea

D85/99		**Oceanography** (cont.)
D99		**Oceans and Seas by Name** (cont.)
	D99.20	Seas (cont.)
	D99.20.42/60	East India Archipelago Seas (cont.)
	D99.20.51	Flores Sea
	D99.20.52	Bali Sea
	D99.20.53	Java Sea
	D99.20.54	Savu Sea
	D99.20.61	South China Sea
		UF Nan Hai
	D99.20.62	East China Sea
		UF Tung Hai
	D99.20.63	Yellow Sea
		UF Hwang Hai
	D99.20.64	Sea of Japan
	D99.20.65	Seto Naikai Inland Sea
	D99.20.66	Sea of Okhotsk
	D99.20.67	Bering Sea
	D99.20.68	Philippine Sea
	D99.20.69	Tasman Sea
	D99.20.70	Coral Sea
	D99.20.71	Solomon Sea
	D99.20.72	Bismarck Sea
	D99.40	Gulfs
	D99.40.05	Gulf of Bothnia
	D99.40.10	Gulf of Finland
	D99.40.15	Gulf of Riga
	D99.40.20	Gulf of St. Lawrence
	D99.40.25	Gulf of Mexico
	D99.40.30	Gulf of Guinea
	D99.40.35	Gulf of Suez
	D99.40.40	Gulf of Aqaba
	D99.40.45	Gulf of Aden
	D99.40.50	Gulf of Oman
	D99.40.55	Gulf of Iran
		UF Persian Gulf
	D99.40.60	Gulf of Thailand
	D99.40.65	Gulf of Tomini
	D99.40.70	Gulf of Boni
	D99.40.75	Gulf of Alaska
	D99.40.80	Gulf of California
	D99.60	Straits
	D99.60.05	Kattegat
	D99.60.10	Skagerrak
	D99.60.15	Northwest Passage
	D99.60.20	Davis Strait
	D99.60.25	Hudson Strait
	D99.60.30	Bristol Channel
	D99.60.35	English Channel
	D99.60.40	Strait of Gibraltar
	D99.60.45	Rio de la Plata
	D99.60.50	Mozambique Channel
	D99.60.55	Malacca Strait
	D99.60.58	Singapore Strait
	D99.60.60	Alaska Coastal Waters
		UF British Columbia Coastal Waters
	D99.60.65	Makassar Strait
	D99.60.70	Bass Strait
	D99.80	Bays

D85/99		**Oceanography** (cont.)
D99		**Oceans and Seas by Name** (cont.)
	D99.80	Bays (cont.)
	D99.80.10	Baffin Bay
	D99.80.20	Hudson Bay
	D99.80.30	Bay of Biscay
	D99.80.40	Bay of Fundy
	D99.80.50	Bay of Bengal
	D99.80.60	Great Australian Bight

E   Environmental Sciences

E10/29	Ecology
E30/49	Environmental pollution
E31/49	Pollution
E50/59	Environmental management
E60/79	Environmental engineering
E61/64	Sanitary engineering
E65	Air pollution treatment
E66	Water treatment
E67	Noise control
E68	Public health
E70/79	Safety
E80/99	Natural resources

E

Environmental Sciences
Earth sciences D
Environmental education J60.50

E03/05	Environment
	Human environment S
	Social environment S51
E05	Natural environment
	Atmosphere D50
	Biosphere E12
	Ecosystems E16
E05.20	Terrestrial environment
	Terrestrial ecosystems E16.30
E05.40	Aquatic environment
	Aquatic ecosystems E16.50
	Marine environment D95

E10/29

Ecology
UF Environmental biology
Bioclimatology D46.20
Ecomuseums T96.30.30
Palaeoecology D29.65

E11	Ecological research
E11.10	Ecological analysis
E12	Biosphere
E12.10	Biomes
	UF Ecological regions
E12.20	Habitats
E12.30	Phytotrons
	UF Biotrons

(By biology of specific environment)

E15.10	Aerobiology
E15.20	Exobiology
	UF Astrobiology
	Space biology
E15.30	Hydrobiology
	Aquatic animals F43.10
	Aquatic plants F37.10.80
	Aquaculture G18.60
	Marine biology D96
E15.30.10	Limnology
	UF Freshwater biology

(By biological communities)

E16	Ecosystems
	UF Biological communities
E16.10	Aerial ecosystems
	Aerobiology E15.10
E16.30	Terrestrial ecosystems
E16.50	Aquatic ecosystems
	Marine ecosystems D96.20
	Hydrobiology E15.30

(By relationships)

E17	Ecological relationships
E17.10	Autecology
	SN Organism and its environment
E17.30	Synecology
	SN Population and its environment
E17.40	Food chains
E18	Symbiosis

(By plant and animal ecology)

E19	Plant ecology
	Aquatic plants F37.10.80
	Phytogeography F38.80
E19.10	Plant life
E19.40	Plant adaptation

E10/29		**Ecology** (cont.)
	E20	Animal ecology
		Aquatic animals F43.10
		Zoogeography F42.80
	E20.10	Wild animals
	E20.10.10	Game animals
	E20.30	Animal behaviour
		UF Ethology
	E20.30.10	Animal migration
		UF Bird migration
	E20.30.20	Hibernation
	E20.40	Animal life
	E21	Human ecology
		Human biology F52
		(By balance and changes)
	E23	Ecological balance
		UF Biological equilibrium
		Ecosystem stability
		Natural equilibrium
	E24	Environmental changes
	E24.05	Ecological crisis
		UF Ecological balance distruption
	E24.10	Human activities effects
		Environmental deterioration E30/49
	E24.10.10	Biological control
		(By response to environment)
	E24.40	Adaptation (biological)
		Plant adaptation E19.40

E30/49		**Environmental Deterioration**
		Amenities destruction S07
		Environmental changes E24

E31/49		**Pollution**
		Pollution control E56
		Visual pollution S07.50
		(By location)
	E32	Air pollution
		(By pollutants)
		Combine with terms for gases, vapours and chemicals
		Automobile emission E42
		Radioactive fallout E40.10
		(By particulate pollutants)
	E32.70	Smoke
		UF Soot
	E32.72	Fumes
		UF Odours
	E32.75	Dust
	E32.76	Ashes
		UF Cinders
	E32.78	Smog
	E35	Water pollution
		(By biological causes)
		Combine with appropriate terms
		Aquatic microorganisms F37.10.80B
		Bacteria F29.10.10
		Viruses F29.10.20
		(By chemical pollutants)
		Combine with term for particular chemical
		Fertilizers G14.50.10
		Pesticides G14.30.10
		Detergents G93.10.20
	E35.10	Oil pollution

E30/49		**Environmental Deterioration** (cont.)
E31/49		**Pollution** (cont.)
	E35	Water pollution (cont.)
	E35.15	Eutrophication
		(By physical pollutant)
		Wastes E63.10
		Sewage E64.10
		(By sea water and river)
	E35.50	Marine pollution
	E35.70	River pollution
	E38	Land pollution
	E38.10	Soil pollution
		(By pollutant source)
	E40	Radioactive pollution
	E40.10	Radioactive fallout
	E41	Industrial pollution
		Waste water E64.15
	E42	Automobile emission
		(By pollutants)
	E44	Pollutants
		UF Contaminants
		Impurities (pollutants)
		Dangerous materials E73.40
		Radioactive wastes E63.10.20
		See alphabetical thesaurus for complete list
E50/59		**Environmental Management**
		UF Environmental control
		Environmental protection
		Environmental planning S70/99
	E51/53	Environmental conservation
		Resource conservation E94
		Amenities conservation S79
	E52	Conservation techniques
	E53	Conservation of nature
		Countryside conservation S91.30
	E53.30	Wildlife protection
	E53.30.10	Wildlife
		Wild animals E20.10
		Wild plants F37.10.70
	E53.50	Nature reserves
		Zoological gardens S92.40.20
	E54	Environmental legislation
		Water law M62.40
		Environmental planning legislation S75
	E54.10	Air pollution legislation
		UF Clean air acts
	E56	Pollution control
		Environmental engineering E60/79
		Pollution E31/49
	E56.10	Environmental monitoring
		UF Pollution monitoring
E60/79		**Environmental Engineering**
	E61/64	Sanitary engineering
	E62	Disposal of the dead
	E62.10	Cemeteries
	E62.30	Crematoria
		UF Cremation
	E63	Waste disposal and handling
		UF Waste handling

E60/79		**Environmental Engineering** (cont.)
	E61/64	Sanitary engineering (cont.)
	E63	Waste disposal and handling
	E63.10	Wastes

E63.10 Wastes
*Waste water E64.15
*Sewage E64.10

E63.10.10 Refuse
UF Trash

E63.10.20 Radioactive wastes

E63.30 Waste collection

E63.50 Waste treatment
UF Waste reclamation
*Waste heat recovery G32.30

E64 Sewage disposal and handling
UF Sewage engineering

E64.10 Sewage
E64.15 Waste water
E64.20 Sewers
E64.30 Sewage treatment

E65 Air pollution treatment
*Air conditioning G32.70
*Filtration G78.70.10

E65.40 Emission control
*Automobile emission E42

E66 Water treatment
UF Chlorination
Fluorination
*Decontamination G78.60.40
*Filtration G78.70.10

E66.40 Water demineralization
E66.50 Desalination

E67 Noise control
*Noise S07.10
*Sound insulation G36.20

E68 Public health
*Health F54
*Health services R97
*Immunization F92.10.05
*Pest control G14.30
*Preventive medicine F92
*Sanitary engineering E61/64

E68.30 Drug control
E68.50 Food control

E70/79 **Safety**
UF Safety engineering
*Public health E68
*Safety education J60.54

*(By hazards)
E71/74 Hazards accidents and disasters (†)
E72 Disasters
E72.10 Natural disasters
*Disaster relief work R98
*Floods D71
*Earthquakes D11.05
*Landslides D24.40.50
*Typhoons D55.30.30B
*Volcanic eruptions D24.20.30

E72.10.50 Famine
E72.10.60 Epidemics
*Epidemiology F92.10

E72.50 Man-made disasters
*Nuclear explosions E73.60.10

E60/79		**Environmental Engineering** (cont.)
E70/79		**Safety** (cont.)
	E71/74	Hazards accidents and disasters (cont.)
	E73	Accidents
	E73.10	Fire
		Fire protection E76.10
	E73.10.40	Forest fires
	E73.20	Explosions
	E73.30	Electrical safety
		UF Electrical accidents
	E73.40	Dangerous materials
		Radioactive wastes E63.10.20
	E73.40.10	Poisons
		Toxicology F69.70
	E73.60	Radiation hazards
		Radioactive pollution E40
	E73.60.10	Nuclear explosions
		(By location)
	E73.70	Occupational safety
		UF Industrial safety
		Occupational diseases F73.60
	E73.70.10	Mining safety
	E73.80	Domestic safety
		UF Domestic accidents
		Home accidents
	E73.90	Transport safety
		UF Traffic accidents
	E73.90.10	Air safety
		UF Air accidents
	E73.90.20	Road safety
		UF Road accidents
	E73.90.30	Rail safety
		UF Rail accidents
	E73.90.50	Marine safety
		UF Marine accidents
		(By safety measures)
	E76	Safety measures
		UF Accident prevention
	E76.10	Fire protection
	E76.20	Radiation protection
	E76.30	First aid
	E76.40	Rescue
		UF Escape
		(By devices)
	E78	Safety devices
	E78.10	Protective clothing
	E78.30	Restraint systems
		UF Safety belts
	E78.50	Warning devices
		UF Alarm systems
		Theft protection L59.20
E80/99		**Natural Resources**
		Human resources R10.20
		Water resources D70
		(By type of resources)
	E81	Energy resources
		UF Power resources
		Power industry N48
		(By type of energy)
	E81.05/50	Energy
		Solar radiation C88.05

E80/99		**Natural Resources** (cont.)
	E81	Energy resources (cont.)
	E81.05/50	Energy (cont.)
	E81.10	Electrical energy
	E81.15	Nuclear energy
	E81.20	Water power
	E81.25	Steam power
	E81.40	Geothermal energy
	E81.45	Wind power
		(By fuels)
	E81.60	Fuel resources
		Fuels G82
	E81.60.10	Coal resources
	E81.60.30	Oil resources
	E81.60.50	Gas resources
		UF Natural gas resources
		(By consumption and shortage)
	F81.85	Energy balance
	E81.90	Energy consumption
	E81.95	Energy shortages
		UF Energy depletion
		Energy crisis
		Energy conservation E94.10
	E82	Mineral resources
		Minerals D21.40/90
	E83	Land resources
		Land use S81
	E84	Soil resources
	E85	Plant resources
	E85.10	Forest resources
	E86	Marine resources
		Fishery resources G18.10/30
	E88	Animal resources
		UF Living resources
		Animal husbandry G15
		Wildlife E20.10
	E89	Food Resources
	E89.30	Food shortages
		Famine E72.10.50
		(By exploration and development)
	E92	Resource development
	E93	Resource exploration
		(By conservation)
	E94	Resource conservation
		Conservation of nature E53
		Environmental control E50/59
		Resource management N12.20
		Water conservation D70.50.30
	E94.10	Energy conservation
	E94.20	Soil conservation

F   Life Sciences

F03	**Natural history**
F04/49	**Biology**
F35/39	**Botany**
F40/47	**Zoology**
F48	**Anthropology**
F50/99	**Medical sciences**
F51	**Medical research**
F52	**Human biology**
F54	**Health**
F55/73	**Pathology**
F74/87	**Psychiatry**
F88/90	**Clinical medicine**
F91	**Surgery**
F92	**Preventive medicine**
F93	**Medical technology**
F94	**Medical equipment**
F95	**Medical specialities**
F96	**Systems of medicine**
F98	**Medical profession**

F   # Life Sciences

F03   **Natural History**

UF Nature study
Natural history museums T96.30.10

F04/49   **Biology**

Agricultural biology G09.10
Ecology E10/29
Biology education J60.40.75
Human biology F52

F04   Biological effects

(By research)
F05   Biological research
F05.10   Experimental biology

(By ethics)
F06   Bioethics

(By measurement)
F07   Biometrics
F07.30   Biomass

(By biological sciences and phenomena)
F08   Life
F08.10   Living substances

F09   Evolution
F09.20   Biogenesis

F10   Genetics
Animal genetics F42.55
Human genetics F52.30
Plant genetics F38.50

F10.10   Heredity
F10.10.30   Eugenics
F10.30   Cytogenetics
Chromosomes F12.30
F10.30.10   Genes
F10.50   Mutation
UF Biological change
Genetic variation

F10.70   Natural selection

F11   Molecular biology

F12   Cell biology
UF Cytology
Cytochemistry

F12.10   Cells
F12.30   Chromosomes

F13   Histology
Plant histology F38.20
Zoohistology F42.25
F14/16   Anatomy
Animal anatomy F42.20
Human anatomy F52.40
Medical sciences F50/99
Plant ecology F38.10

F15   *Anatomical systems (†)*
F15.10   Cardiovascular systems
UF Circulatory systems
F15.10.10   Heart
F15.10.30   Blood vessels
UF Arteries
Capillaries
Veins
F15.20   Respiratory systems
F15.30   Digestive systems
F15.40   Haemic and lymphatic systems

F04/49		**Biology** (cont.)
	F14/16	Anatomy (cont.)
	F15	Anatomical systems (cont.)
	F15.50	Endocrine systems
	F15.50.10	Endocrinology
	F15.60	Urogenital systems
	F15.70	Locomotory systems
		UF Muskuloskeletal systems
	F15.80/90	Nervous systems
		Motor development F22.70
	F15.82	Neurobiology
	F15.83	Neurology
	F15.84	Brain
		Brain research F51.70
		Brain surgery F86
	F15.86	Psychophysiology
	F15.90	Sensory systems
		UF Sense organs
		Sensory systems psychology
	F15.90.10	Sight
		UF Eyes
	F15.90.20	Hearing
		UF Ears
	F15.90.30	Smell (sense)
	F15.90.40	Taste
	F15.90.50	Touch
		UF Tactile sense
		Pain F71.20
	F16	Regional anatomy
	F16.10	Head
	F16.30	Torso
	F16.40	Limbs
	F18/24	Physiology
		SN Study of the normal functions of the body
		Human physiology F52.60
		Medical sciences F50/99
		Physiological effects F52.60.10
		Plant physiology F38.30
		Zoophysiology F42.30
	F18.50	Biorhythms
	F18.50.10	Photoperiodism
	F19	Sex
	F19.10	Male
	F19.30	Female
	F20	Life cycle
	F20.10	Birth
		Reproduction (biological) F21
	F20.20	Puberty
		Adolescence R18.10
	F20.20.10	Menstruation
	F20.40	Maturity
	F20.60	Ageing
		Old age R20
	F20.60.10	Menopause
	F20.60.70	Gerontology
	F20.80	Death
	F20.80.10	Euthanasia
		UF Mercy killing
	F21	Reproduction (biological)
		Birth F20.10
	F21.10	Fertility
	F21.30	Pregnancy

F04/49		**Biology** (cont.)
	F18/24	Physiology (cont.)
	F22	Physiological development
		UF Development biology
		Physical development
		Developmental psychology P60/69
		Life cycle F20
	F22.05	Embryology
	F22.05.10	Embryos
	F22.10	Growth
	F22.70	Motor development
	F22.70.30	Handiness
	F24	Body temperature
		UF Hypothermia
	F25	Biochemistry
		Biochemical analysis C39.50
		Human biochemistry F52.25
		Molecular biology F11
		Palaeobiochemistry D29.60
		Phytochemistry F38.40
		Zoochemistry F42.50
	F25.10	Metabolism
	F25.15	Biosynthesis
		(By substances)
	F25.18/50	Biochemicals
	F25.20	Enzymes
	F25.30	Vitamins
	F25.40	Hormones
	F25.45	Proteins
	F25.47	Lipids
	F25.55	Trace elements
	F26	Biophysics
		UF Biomechanics
		Human biophysics F52.20
		Bioengineering F93.30/60
		Bionics H38.40
	F27	Radiobiology
	F28/29	Microbiology
	F29	Bacteriology
	F29.10	Microorganisms
	F29.10.10	Bacteria
	F29.10.20	Viruses
	F29.10.20A	Virology
		UF Viral genetics
	F30	Parasitology
	F30.10	Parasites
	F31	Immunology
		Immunization F92.10.50
	F31.10	Antigens
	F31.20	Antibodies
	F34	Taxonomy
		Botanical taxonomy F39
		Animal taxonomy F45/47
F35/39		**Botany**
		UF Plant biology
		Botanical gardens S92.40.10
		Plant ecology E19
	F36	Botanical research
	F36.10	Experimental botany
	F37	Vegetation

F04/49		**Biology** (cont.)
F35/39		**Botany** (cont.)
	F37	Vegetation (cont.)
	F37.10	Plants
		Crops G14.60/99
	F37.10.10	Trees
		Forestry G16
		(By part)
	F37.10.40	Leaves
		(By habitat)
	F37.10.70	Wild plants
	F37.10.80	Aquatic plants
		Marine plants D96.40
		Phytoplankton D96.40.40
	F37.10.80A	Aquatic algae
	F37.10.80B	Aquatic microorganisms
	F38.10	Plant anatomy
	F38.15	Plant morphology
	F38.20	Plant histology
	F38.30	Plant physiology
	F38.30.20	Plant transpiration
		UF Stomata (plant)
	F38.30.50	Plant development
		UF Plant embryology
	F38.30.50G	Plant growth
	F38.40	Phytochemistry
		UF Plant biochemistry
		Plant chemistry
	F38.45	Plant metabolism
	F38.50	Plant genetics
		UF Plant breeding
		Plant mutation
		Plant reproduction
	F38.60	Phytopathology
		UF Plant disease
	F38.80	Phytogeography
		UF Distribution of plants
		Plant geography
	F38.80.10	Flora
	F39	Botanical taxonomy
		UF Systematic botany
	F39.10	Thallophyta
	F39.10.10	Algae
		UF Algology
		Aquatic algae F37.10.80A
	F39.10.30	Fungi
		UF Mycology
	F39.10.50	Lichens
	F39.20	Byrophyta
		UF Bryology
		Liverworts
		Mosses
	F39.30	Pteridophyta
		UF Ferns
		Pteridology
	F39.40/80	Spermatophyta
		UF Seed plants
		Trees F37.10.10
	F39.50	Gymnospermae
		UF Conifers
	F39.70	Angiospermae

F04/49		**Biology** (cont.)
F35/39		**Botany** (cont.)
	F39	Botanical taxonomy (cont.)
	F39.40/80	Spermatophyta (cont.)
	F39.70	Angiospermae (cont.)
		UF Flowering plants
	F39.70.10	Flowers

F40/47		**Zoology**
		UF Animal biology
		Animal ecology E20
		Zoological gardens S92.40.20
	F41	Experimental zoology
	F42.10	Animal anatomy
	F42.20	Animal morphology
	F42.25	Zoohistology
	F42.30	Zoophysiology
		UF Animal physiology
	F42.30.10	Animal metabolism
	F42.30.30	Animal development
		UF Animal embryology
	F42.30.30G	Animal growth
	F42.50	Zoochemistry
		UF Animal biochemistry
	F42.55	Animal genetics
	F42.60	Animal breeding
		UF Animal reproduction
	F42.70	Zoopathology
		UF Animal disease
		Animal pathology
		Veterinary medicine F95.70
	F42.80	Zoogeography
	F42.80.10	Fauna
	F43	Animals
		Birds F47.25
		Amphibia F47.15
		Insects F46.35.40
		Mammals F47.50
		Reptiles F47.20
		Wild animals E20.10
		(By habitat)
	F43.10	Aquatic animals
		Fish G18.20
		Marine animals D96.60
	F43.30	Domestic animals
		Animal husbandry G15
		(By purpose)
		Game animals E20.10.10
	F43.60	Laboratory animals
	F43.60.10	Vivisection
	F45/47	Animal taxonomy
		UF Zoological taxonomy
		Systematic zoology
	F46	Invertebrata
	F46.10	Protozoa
	F46.15	Parazoa
	F46.18/40	Metazoa
	F46.20	Coelenterata
	F46.25	Echinodermata
	F46.30	Mollusca

F04/49		**Biology** (cont.)
F40/47		**Zoology** (cont.)
	F45/47	Animal taxonomy (cont.)
	F46	Invertebrata (cont.)
	F46.18/40	Metazoa (contd.)
	F46.35	Anthropoda
		UF Articulata
	F46.35.10	Crustacea
	F46.35.20	Myriapoda
	F46.35.40	Insects
	F46.35.40E	Entomology
	F47	Vertebrata
		Fish G18.20
	F47.15	Amphibia
	F47.20	Reptiles
	F47.25	Birds
	F47.25.10	Ornithology
	F47.50	Mammals
	F47.50.10	Primates
	F47.50.10H	Human species
		Man R13
		For other mammals—alphabetically by name, e.g.
	F47.50.20CAM	Camels

F48   **Anthropology**

UF Physical anthropology
Human biology F52
Cultural and social anthropology T08/13

F48.10   Prehistoric man

F50/99   **Medical Sciences**

UF Biomedical sciences
Medical education J60.42
Medical information systems Z68.50.50
Medical libraries Z62.68.20M

F51   **Medical Research**

(By laboratories)

F51.40   Medical laboratories
Laboratory animals F43.60

(By subject of research)

F51.70   Brain research

For other subjects combine with appropriate terms e.g.

Cancer research (Medical research & Cancer)

F52   **Human Biology**

Anthropology F48
Human ecology E21

Combine with terms at F04/49 Biology, except where precoordinated below

F52.20   Human biophysics
F52.25   Human biochemistry
F52.30   Human genetics
F52.40   Human anatomy
Combine with terms at F14/16 Anatomy
F52.60   Human physiology
Combine with terms at F18/24 Physiology
F52.60.10   Physiological effects
SN Effects of electricity, ionizing radiation, chemicals, heat, pressure, vibrations, weightlessness on the human body

F50/99		**Medical Sciences** (cont.)
F52		**Human Biology** (cont.)
	F52.60	Human physiology (cont.)
	F52.60.10	Physiological effects (cont.)

UF Fatigue (physiology)
Human body environmental effects
Stress physiology
Aerospace medicine F95.65
Radiation effects C21
Sports medicine F95.60

F54   **Health**
Addiction R73.50/90
Health education J60.52
Public Health E68
Health services R97
Right to health M93.10.10

	F54.10	Nutrition

Dietetics F90.20
Nutrition education J60.52.30
Hunger R71.30
Food G94.10
Malnutrition F61.30
Nutrition and metabolic diseases F61

	F54.10.05	Nutrients
	F54.10.40	Calories
	F54.30	Hygiene

UF Cleanliness
Personal hygiene

	F54.40	Exercise

Sport X80/89

	F54.60	Rest

Sleep P44.10

	F54.80	Mental health

UF Mental hygiene
Mental diseases F77/83

F55/73   **Pathology**

UF Human pathology
Phytopathology F38.60
Zoopathology F42.70

	F56/73	Diseases

UF Illness
Sickness
Mental diseases F77/83

	F57	Infectious diseases

Epidemics E72.10.60

	F57.40	Bacterial diseases

Bacteria F29.10.10

(By individual infectious diseases)

	F57.50	Smallpox
	F57.52	Measles
	F57.55	Influenza
	F57.58	Typhoid
	F57.60	Diphtheria
	F57.62	Cholera
	F57.65	Dysentry
	F57.68	Malaria
	F57.70	Rabies
	F57.72	Poliomyelitis
	F57.75	Tuberculosis
	F57.78	Tetanus

F50/99		**Medical Sciences** (cont.)
F55/73		**Pathology** (cont.)
F56/73		Diseases (cont.)
F57		Infectious diseases (cont.)
F57.80		Venereal disease
F57.85		Leprosy
F58		Cardiovascular diseases
F58.10		Heart diseases
F59		Respiratory diseases
F59.10		Asthma
F59.20		Bronchitis
F59.40		Pneumonia
F60		Digestive system diseases
F60.10		Dental diseases
		Dentistry F95.30
F60.40		Liver diseases
F61		Nutrition and metabollic diseases
F61.10		Obesity
F61.30		Malnutrition
		Famine E72.10.50
		Hunger R71.30
F62		Haemic and lymphatic systems diseases
F63		Endocrine diseases
F64		Skin diseases
F65		Urogenital diseases
		UF Urology
		Genito-urinal disease
		Enuresis F71.50.10
		Gynaecology F95.20
F66		Locomotory system diseases
		UF Musculoskeletal system diseases
F66.10		Arthritis
F67		Nervous system diseases
		Psychiatry F74/87
		Poliomyelitis F57.72
F67.10		Speech disorders
		UF Speech pathology
		Stammer
		Stutter
		Speech defective R82.30
		Psycholinguistics X30
		Speech therapy F90.30
F67.20		Spastic disorders
F67.25		Epilepsy
F67.30/50		Sensory system diseases
F67.35		Vision defects
		Ophthalmology F95.40
		Blind R82.10
F67.35.10		Blindness
F67.35.20		Partial sight
F67.35.30		Colour blindness
F67.40		Deafness
		UF Hearing defects
		Deaf R82.20
F67.45		Dyslexia
		Dyslexic R82.50
F68		Neoplasms
F68.10		Cancer
		UF Carcinogens
F69.10		Injuries
		SN Fractures, wounds, burns, etc.

F50/99		**Medical Sciences** (cont.)
F55/73		**Pathology** (cont.)
	F56/73	Diseases (cont.)
	F69.70	Toxicology
		UF Toxicity
		Poisons E73.40.10
	F70	Allergies
	F71	Symptoms of diseases
	F71.10	Sleep disorders
	F71.20	Pain
	F71.30	Shock
	F71.50	Incontinence
	F71.50.10	Enuresis
	F72	Handicaps
		Handicapped R79/83
	F72.10	Physical handicaps
		Blindness F67.35.10
		Deafness F67.40
		Physically handicapped R82
		Speech disorders F67.10
		(Diseases by climate and occupation)
	F73.10	Tropical diseases
		UF Tropical medicine
	F73.60	Occupational diseases
		UF Industrial diseases
		Industrial medicine
F74/87		**Psychiatry**
		UF Medical psychology
	F75/83	Psychopathology
	F76	Mental deficiency
		UF Mental handicap
		Mental retardation
		Backwardness P47.40
		Mentally handicapped R83.30
	F77/83	Mental diseases
		UF Mental disorders
		Mental illness
		Mental health F54.80
		Mentally ill R83.10
	F78.10	Psychosomatic disorders
		Psychophysiology F15.86
		Psychosomatics P20.10
	F79	Rational processes disorders
	F79.35	Brain deterioration
	F79.40	Memory disorders
	F80	Psychoses
	F80.10	Affective psychoses
	F80.10.15	Manic-depressive psychoses
	F80.10.25	Melancholia
	F80.30	Schizophrenia
	F80.40	Paranoia
	F80.50	Organic psychoses
		UF Senile psychoses
		Toxic psychoses
		Traumatic psychoses
	F81	Neuroses
		UF Psychoneuroses
	F81.10	Nervous breakdown
	F81.15	Mental strain
	F81.20	Amnesia
	F81.25	Obsessional neuroses

F50/99		**Medical Sciences** (cont.)
F74/87		**Psychiatry** (cont.)
	F75/83	Psychopathology (cont.)
	F77/83	Mental diseases (cont.)
	F81	Neuroses (cont.)
	F81.30	Phobias
	F81.35	Anxiety states
	F81.40	Hysteria
	F81.45	Emotional disturbances
	F82	Personality disorders
	F83	Behavioural disorders
		Social deviance R73
	F83.10	Apathy
	F83.20	Maladjustment
	F83.50	Suicide
	F83.60	Antisocial behaviour
		Delinquency R77.10
		(By treatment)
	F85	Clinical psychology
	F85.10	Psychoanalysis
		Psychological tests P15
		Psychometrics P13
	F85.30	Psychotherapy
	F85.30.10	Occupational therapy
	F85.30.20	Psychodrama
	F85.30.30	Sociodrama
	F85.30.40	Hypnotherapy
	F85.30.50	Shock treatment
	F85.30.60	Drug psychotherapy
	F86	Brain surgery
F88/90		**Clinical Medicine**
		Clinical psychology F85
		(By diagnosis)
	F89	Medical diagnosis
		UF Prognosis
		(By treatment)
	F90	Medical treatment
		UF Clinical treatment
		First aid E76.30
		Psychotherapy F85.30
	F90.05	Nursing
	F90.10/50	Therapy
		UF Therapeutics
	F90.15	Pharmacy
		Pharmaceutical technology G80.10
	F90.15.10	Drugs
		UF Medicines
		Drug addiction R73.60
		Drug psychotherapy F85.30.60
	F90.15.10A	Antibiotics
		UF Penicillin
	F90.15.40	Pharmacology
	F90.20	Dietetics
		UF Diet therapy
	F90.25	Physiotherapy
	F90.25.10	Electrotherapy
	F90.25.30	Radiotherapy
		UF Radiology
		Radiation therapy
	F90.30	Speech therapy

F50/99		**Medical Sciences** (cont.)
F88/90		**Clinical Medicine** (cont.)
	F90	Medical treatment (cont.)
	F90.10/50	Therapy (cont.)
	F90.50	Rehabilitation
		UF Aftercare (medical)

F91   **Surgery**
                                             Brain surgery F86
                                             Surgical instruments F94.20.30

	F91.50	Organ transplantation
	F91.60	Plastic surgery
	F91.80	Anaesthesiology
	F91.80.10	Anaesthetics

F92   **Preventive Medicine**
                                             Public health E68

	F92.10	Epidemiology
		UF Infectious diseases control
		Epidemics E72.10.60
	F92.10.05	Immunization
		Immunology F31
	F92.10.05B	Vaccination
	F92.10.10	Quarantine
	F92.20	Medical inspection
	F92.20.40	Dental inspection

F93   **Medical Technology**

                                             UF Medical ultrasonics
                                                 Nuclear medicine
                                                 Laser medicine
                                             Electrotherapy F90.25.10

	F93.30/90	Bioengineering
		UF Biomedical electronics
		Biomedical engineering
	F93.35	Prosthetics
	F93.35.10	Artificial organs
	F93.35.20	Artificial placentas
	F93.35.40	Artificial limbs
	F93.45	Sensory aids
	F93.45.10	Hearing aids
	F93.70	Life support systems
		UF Breathing apparatus
		Oxygen tents
		Incubators
		Respirators

F94   **Medical Equipment**
                                             Life support systems F93.70
                                             Medical technology F93

	F94.10	Therapeutic equipment
		UF Bandages
		Drugs F90.15.10
	F94.20	Medical instruments
	F94.20.30	Surgical instruments

F95   **Medical Specialities**

                                             (By age and sex)

	F95.15	Paediatrics
	F95.18	Geriatrics

F50/99		**Medical Sciences** (cont.)
F95		**Medical Specialities** (cont.)
	F95.20	Gynaecology
	F95.20.40	Obstetrics
	F95.20.60	Abortion
		(By parts of the body)
	F95.25	Orthopaedics
		Prosthetics F93.35
	F95.30	Dentistry
	F95.35	Chiropody
	F95.40	Ophthalmology
		(By special application)
	F95.50	Forensic medicine
	F95.60	Sports medicine
	F95.65	Aerospace medicine
		Exobiology E15.20
F95.70		**Veterinary Medicine**
		Zoopathology F42.70
F96		**Systems of Medicine**
		SN Includes Vedic medicine, Homeopathy, Herbal medicine
	F96.20	Acupuncture
	F96.30	Osteopathy
	96.40	Naturopathy
	F96.70	Folk medicine
F98		**Medical Profession**
		(By ethics)
	F98.05	Medical ethics
		(By personnel)
	F98.20	Medical personnel
		UF Surgeons
		Psychiatrists
	F98.20.10	Physicians
		UF Doctors
	F98.20.30	Nurses
	F98.20.50	Paramedical personnel
		UF Auxiliary medical personnel
		Dentists
		Dietitians
		Opticians
		Pharmacists
		Physiotherapists

G   Technology

G		**Technology**
		Industries N39/49
		Science and technology B
		Interdisciplinary science and technology H
		Technical education J60.45
		Technology transfer B30

G05/15		**Agriculture**
		UF Farming
		Agricultural economics N50/59
		Agricultural education J60.48
		Agricultural enterprises Q12.60
		Agricultural policy N52.10
		Agricultural production N54
		Agricultural products N54.40
		Agricultural workers Q88.50
		Agroclimatology D46.25
		Land reform N61.50
		Soil science D38/44
		(By research)
	G06	Agricultural research
	G06.50	Agricultural innovations
		(By buildings)
	G07	Agricultural buildings
		UF Farm buildings
		(By machinery)
	G08	Agricultural engineering
	G08.10	Agricultural machinery
		(By agricultural sciences)
	G09.10	Agricultural biology
	G09.10.10	Agricultural genetics
		Animal breeding F42.60
		Plant genetics F38.50
	G09.30	Agricultural chemistry
		(By land)
	G10	Agricultural land
		Land pollution E38
		Land resources E83
		Soils D39
	G10.10	Arable land
	G10.20	Grazing land
		UF Pasture

G12/15		**Farming Systems**
	G13	Mixed farming

G14		**Agronomy**
		(By type)
	G14.10	Arable farming
	G14.15	Horticulture
		UF Market gardening
		(By methods of cultivation)
	G14.20	Cultivation
	G14.20.10	Planting
	G14.20.20	Harvesting
	G14.20.30	Food production
		Food shortages E89.30
		Food resources E89
		(By culture in special environments)
	G14.20.50	Dry farming
	G14.20.60	Hydrophonics
		Aquaculture G18.60
		(By control and improvement)
	G14.30	Pest control

G05/15		**Agriculture** (cont.)
G12/15		**Farming Systems** (cont.)
G14		Agronomy (cont.)
	G14.30	Pest control (cont.)
	G14.30.10	Pesticides
	G14.30.20	Pests
	G14.30.20L	Locusts
	G14.30.20T	Termites
	G14.40	Weed control
	G14.40.10	Herbicides
	G14.50	Land amelioration
		Soil science D38/44
	G14.50.10	Fertilisers
		UF Manure
		(By crops)
	G14.60/99	Crops
		Agricultural products N54.40
		Plants F37.10
	G14.63	Grain crops
	G14.63.10	Cereals
	G14.64	Fruit
	G14.65	Vegetables
	G14.66	Grasses
	G14.68	Forage
	G14.70	Straw
	G14.72	Hay
	G14.74	Seeds
	G14.75	Nuts
	G14.76	Sugar cane
	G14.77	Sugar beet
	G14.85	Medicinal plant
	G14.95	Tobacco

G15   **Animal Husbandry**

UF Livestock management
Animal resources E88
Forage G14.68

	G15.10	Dairy farming
	G15.20	Stock farming
	G15.30	Apiculture
		UF Beekeeping
		(By animals)
	G15.50	Livestock
		(By products)
	G15.70	Animal products
		Agricultural products N54.10
		Dairy products G94.10.30

G16   **Forestry**

Forestry resources E85.10
Trees F37.10.30

	G16.10	Forests
	G16.10.10	Tropical forests
	G16.20	Forest management
		UF Afforestation
		Deforestation
	G16.25	Forest protection
		Forest fires E73.10.40

G16		**Forestry** (cont.)
	G16.30	Silviculture
		SN Covers planting, tending of stands, including tree surgery
	G16.40	Forest engineering
		SN Includes machines, equipment and operations
		(logging, felling, etc.)
		(By products)
	G16.50/60	Forest products
	G16.60	Wood
		Wood technology G96.20
	G16.60.10	Softwood
	G16.60.20	Hardwood
		(By industry)
	G16.80	Forest industry
G18		**Fisheries**
		Marine biology D96
		(By resources)
	G18.10/30	Fishery resources
	G18.20	Fish
	G18.20.10	Freshwater fish
	G18.20.30	Marine fish
	G18.20.50	Shellfish
		(By location)
	G18.22	Freshwater fishing
	G18.25	Sea fishing
		UF Marine fishing
	G18.25.10	Coastal fishing
	G18.25.30	Deep sea fishing
		(By equipment)
	G18.30	Fishing vessels
		UF Catchers
		Gill netters
		Long liners
	G18.30.40	Seiners
	G18.30.60	Trawlers
	G18.40	Fishing gear
		UF Fishing dredges
	G18.40.20	Gill nets
	G18.40.30	Seine nets
	G18.40.40	Trawl nets
		(By operations)
	G18.50	Fishing operations
		(By production)
	G18.60	Aquaculture
		UF Fish farming
	G18.60.10	Freshwater fish culture
	G18.60.30	Marine acquaculture
		(By industry)
	G18.80	Fishing industry
		Fishing rights M86.20.10
G20/69		**Engineering**
		Agricultural engineering G08
		Communication technology Y80
		Engineering education J60.45.60
		Engineering industry N44
		Engineers B34.38
		Environmental engineering E60/79
		Forest engineering G16.40

G20/69   **Engineering** (cont.)

    G21/29   **Electrical Engineering**
            UF Electrotechnology
            Electric heating G32.10.50
            Electric lighting G31.10
            Electrical energy E81.10
            Electrical installations G60.30.10
            Electrical industry N48.10

    G22/26   Electric power systems
    G23/25   Electric power generation
                  UF Electric power supply
    G24   Electric power stations
    G24.10   Nuclear power stations
                       Nuclear reactors G64.10
    G24.30   Thermal power stations
    G24.30.10   Steam power stations
    G24.30.10G   Geothermal power stations
    G24.30.20   Gas turbine power stations
    G24.30.30   Diesel power stations
    G24.40   Wind power stations
    G24.50   Hydroelectric power stations
                       Hydraulic engineering G40/54
    G24.50.10   Tidal power stations
    G25   Direct energy conversion
                  UF Direct power generation
    G25.10   Batteries
                     UF Electrochemical conversion
    G25.10.10   Fuel cells
    G25.20   Solar power generation
    G25.20.10   Solar cells
    G25.30   Magnetohydrodynamic conversion
    G25.40   Thermionic conversion
    G25.50   Thermoelectric conversion
    G26   Electric power transmission
    G26.05   Electric power distribution
    G26.10   Electric power transmission lines
    G26.10.10   Electric cables
    G26.40   Substations

    G27   Electrical equipment
               UF Electric power apparatus
               Circuits G29.10
    G27.10   Electric machines
    G27.10.10   Electric generators
    G27.10.30   Electric motors
    G27.12   Transformers
    G27.15   Converters
    G27.15.20   Inverters
    G27.18   Rectifiers
    G27.20   Electric control equipment
    G27.22   Electrical protection gear
    G27.22.10   Fuses
    G27.22.50   Earthing
    G27.25   Switchgear
    G27.25.10   Circuit breakers
    G27.26   Switches
    G27.26.30   Relays
    G27.28   Electric conductors
    G27.30   Resistors
    G27.31   Voltage dividers
    G27.32   Electric reactors

G20/69		**Engineering** (cont.)
G21/29		**Electrical Engineering** (cont.)
	G27	Electrical equipment (cont.)
	G27.35	Inductors
		UF Coils
	G27.36	Cores (electric)
	G27.38	Windings (electric)
	G27.40	Electric wiring
	G27.45	Electric connectors
		UF Plugs (electric)
		Sockets (electric)
	G27.48	Electric contacts
	G27.50	Electrodes
	G27.55	Dielectric devices
	G27.55.10	Electrical insulation
		UF Insulators
	G27.55.40	Capacitors
	G27.55.50	Piezoelectric devices
	G27.65	Electromechanical devices
	G27.70	Magnetic devices
	G27.70.40	Magnetostrictive devices
	G27.75	Electrochemical devices
		Batteries G25.10

G28/29		**Electronic Engineering**
		UF Electronics
		Bioengineering F93.30/90
		Communication engineering Y80
		Computers H71/76
		Control technology H40/54
	G29	Electronic equipment
	G29.10	Circuits
		UF Electronic circuits
		Computer circuits H81
	G29.10.05	Printed circuits
	G29.10.10	Amplifiers
	G29.10.20	Oscillators
	G29.10.40	Logic and switching circuits
	G29.10.60	Integrated circuits
	G29.20	Electron tubes
	G29.30	Semiconductors
	G29.30.10	Transistors
	G29.30.30	Thermistors
	G29.40	Superconductors
	G29.45	Masers
	G29.50	Lasers
	G29.60/69	Optoelectronic devices
	G29.65	Photoelectric devices
		UF Photoelectric cells
		Photocells
		Solar cells G25.20.10
	G29.70	Electroacoustic devices
		UF Acousto-electric devices
		Echosounders D97.40.10
		Hearing aids F93.45.10
		Piezoelectric devices G27.55.50
	G29.70.30	Microphones
	G29.70.40	Hydrophones
	G29.80	Thermoelectric devices
		Thermocouples H20.20.30
		Thermoelectric conversion G25.50

G20/69		**Engineering** (cont.)
G30/31		**Illuminating Engineering**
	G31	Lighting
	G31.10	Electric lighting
	G31.40	Street lighting

G32		**Thermal Engineering**
	G32.05	Heat engines
		Gas turbines G34.15.40
		Internal combustion engines G34.40
		Steam turbines G34.15.20
	G32.10	Heating systems
		UF Space heating
	G32.10.20	Central heating
	G32.10.30	District heating
		(By source of heat)
	G32.10.50	Electric heating
	G32.10.80	Solar heating
	G32.20	Heat storage
	G32.30	Waste heat recovery
	G32.40/50	Heating equipment
	G32.42	Heat exchangers
	G32.45	Boilers
	G32.50	Furnaces
	G32.60	Solar power engineering
		Solar heating G32.10.80
		Solar power generation G25.20
	G32.60.10	Solar stills
	G32.65	Refrigeration engineering
	G32.65.10	Refrigerators
	G32.65.40	Freezers
	G32.70	Air conditioning
		UF Ventilation
	G32.80	Heat pumps
	G32.90	Thermal insulation

G33/37		**Mechanical Engineering**
	G34	Machines
		Electric machines G27.10
	G34.10/50	Prime movers
	G34.15	Turbines
	G34.15.10	Water turbines
	G34.15.20	Steam turbines
	G34.15.40	Gas turbines
	G34.40	Internal combustion engines
	G34.40.10	Diesel engines
	G35	Mechanical components
	G35.10	Cooling systems
	G35.15	Lubrication systems
		Lubrication C27.60.30
	G35.15.10	Lubricants
	G35.20	Mechanical transmission systems
	G35.20.10	Gears
	G35.20.30	Clutches
	G35.20.50	Brakes
	G35.25	Shafts

G20/69		**Engineering** (cont.)
G33/37		**Mechanical Engineering** (cont.)
	G35	Mechanical components (cont.)
	G35.30	Reciprocating parts
		SN Includes pistons, connecting rods, big ends, tappets, push rods, etc.
		UF Pistons
	G35.32	Springs (components)
	G35.35	Seals
	G35.42	Ropes
	G35.42.10	Wire ropes
	G35.45	Joints
	G36	Acoustic engineering
		Acoustic measurements and instruments H19
	G36.20	Sound insulation
		Noise control E67
	G36.50	Acoustic equipment
		Electroacoustic devices G29.70
	G36.50.10	Sonar
	G37	Materials handling
		UF Mechanical handling
	G37.10	Lifting equipment
	G37.10.05	Hoists
	G37.10.10	Elevators
		UF Lifts
	G37.20	Excavating equipment
		UF Earth moving equipment
	G37.30	Conveyors
	G37.35	Escalators
		(By components and auxiliaries)
	G37.70.10	Winches
	G37.70.20	Capstans
	G37.70.50	Grabs
G38/54		**Fluid Power Engineering**
G39		**Steam Engineering**
		Steam power E81.25
		Steam power stations G24.30.10
		Steam turbines G34.15.20
G40/54		**Hydraulic Engineering**
		UF Water engineering
		Fluid mechanics C24.05/70
		Hydroelectric power stations G24.50
		Hydrology D65/84
	G41	Water supply
		Quality of water D83.20
		Water analysis D84.40
		Water pollution E35
		Water resources D70
		Water supply industry N48.40
		Water sources D72/79
		Water treatment E66
		(By storage)
	G41.10	Water storage
	G41.10.10	Dams
	G41.10.20	Reservoirs
	G41.10.30	Water towers
	G41.10.60	Water tanks
		(By distribution)
	G41.40	Water distribution
	G41.40.10	Water mains

G20/69		**Engineering** (cont.)
G38/54		**Fluid Power Engineering** (cont.)
G40/54		**Hydraulic Engineering** (cont.)
	G41	Water supply (cont.)
	G41.40	Water distribution (cont.)
	G41.40.30	Pumping stations
	G42	Irrigation
		UF Irrigation engineering
		(By systems)
	G42.10	Irrigation systems
		UF Gravity irrigation
		Subsurface irrigation
		Surface irrigation
		(By parts)
	G42.50	Irrigation canals
	G44	Drainage engineering
	G44.10	Land drainage
	G45	Land reclamation
		UF Reclamation engineering
	G46	Flood control
		Floods D71
	G48	Sediment control
		Sediments D25.10.10
	G48.30	Dredging
	G49	Harbour and coastal engineering
		Harbours S60.60
		Ports S60.50
		Docks S60.55
		Sediment control G48
	G49.30	Piers
		UF Jetties
	G49.35	Lighthouses
	G49.40	Coastal protection
		UF Breakwaters
		Coastal erosion control
	G50	River and lake engineering
		Lakes D77
		Flood control G46
		Rivers D76
		Sediment control G48
	G50.10	River control
	G50.40	Weirs
	G51	Waterway engineering
		UF Canal engineering
		Canals S60.70
	G51.20	Locks (waterways)
	G52	Underwater technology
		Oceanography D85/99
		Oceanographic equipment D98
		Oceanographic instruments D98.50
		Oceanographic measurements D97
		Underwater navigation H55.60
	G52.10	Underwater communication
		Hydrophones G29.70.40
	G52.30	Underwater excavation
		UF Deep sea mining
		Underwater mining
		Submarine mineral deposits D21.35
	G52.30.10	Underwater oil and gas extraction
		UF Offshore drilling
		Underwater drilling
	G52.40	Underwater construction
	G52.40.20	Submarine cable laying

G20/69		**Engineering** (cont.)
G38/54		**Fluid Power Engineering** (cont.)
G40/54		**Hydraulic Engineering** (cont.)
	G52	Underwater technology (cont.)
	G52.45	Underwater salvage
		UF Marine salvage
	G52.50	Diving
		UF Deep sea diving
		Bathymetry D97.10
	G52.50.10	Bathyspheres
		UF Bathyscopes
		Deep ocean vehicles
	G52.50.30	Diving equipment

(By hydraulic equipment)

	G53	Hydraulic equipment
		UF Pneumatic equipment
		Water turbines G34.15.10
		Oceanographic equipment D98
	G53.10	Hydraulic accumulators
	G53.15	Hydraulic motors
		UF Pneumatic motors
	G53.20	Valves
	G53.30	Fluid apertures
		SN Includes inlets, outlets, vents, diffusers, etc.
	G53.30.10	Nozzles
	G53.30.20	Orifices
	G53.30.40	Ducts
	G53.30.50	Pipes
		UF Pipelines
		Tubes
	G53.40	Pumps
	G53.45	Fans
	G53.50	Compressors
	G53.60	Inflatable devices
	G53.70	Floats
	G53.75	Buoys
		Oceanographic buoys D98.10

(By structure)

	G54	Hydraulic structures
		Dams G41.10.10
		Irrigation canals G42.50
		Locks (waterways) G51.20
		Reservoirs G41.10.20
		Water towers G41.10.30
	G54.10	Conduits
		UF Aquaducts
		Culverts
		Flumes
		Penstocks
		Canals S60.70
		Channels D79.10
		Pipes G53.30.50
	G54.20	Spillways
	G54.25	Sluices

G55		**Vacuum Engineering**
		Vacuum metallurgy G76.15
		Vacuum measurement H16
		Vacuum physics C14
G56/60		**Construction Engineering**
		Construction industry N47
	G57	Civil engineering
		Bridges S60.25

G20/69		**Engineering** (cont.)
G56/60		**Construction Engineering** (cont.)
	G57	Civil engineering (cont.)

        Hydraulic engineering G40/54
        Public works Q12.30.30
        Transport infrastructure S60
        Tunnels S60.30

	G57.10	Demolition
	G57.20	Excavation
		UF Earth works
	G57.40	Road engineering
		Roads S60.20
	G58	Structural engineering
	G58.10/36	Structures
	G58.15	Substructures
		UF Foundations
	G58.18	Superstructures

       (By structural elements of buildings)

	G58.20	Structural members
		SN Includes beams, girders, columns, panels, joists, struts, arches, etc.
	G58.30	Structural elements (buildings)
	G58.30.10	Roofs
	G58.30.20	Walls
	G58.30.25	Ceilings
	G58.30.30	Floors
	G58.30.40	Stairs
	G58.30.50	Chimneys
	G58.30.60	Windows
	G58.30.68	Doors
	G58.40	Structural analysis
		UF Structural design
		Deformation C27.30
		Stress (mechanical) C27.10
		Stress analysis H28.70
		Soil mechanics D40.20
	G58.50	Earthquake engineering
		Seismology D11
	G59	Building design
		Architecture W21/24
		Buildings W22
		Housing design S41
	G59.20	Open plan design

       (By standards)

	G59.35	Building standards

       (By costs)

	G59.40	Building costs
		UF Quantity surveying
	G60.01/20	Building operations
		SN Includes bricklaying, joinery, plastering, glazing, decorating, etc.
		Carpentry G96.20.30A
	G60.05	Building maintenance
	G60.10	Reconstruction
	G60.15	Prefabrication
	G60.30	Building services
		Air conditioning G32.70
		Heating systems G32.10
		Lighting G31
	G60.30.10	Electrical installations
	G60.30.50	Water services (buildings)
		UF Plumbing

G20/69		**Engineering** (cont.)
G56/60		**Construction Engineering** (cont.)

	G60.60/80	Building materials

                                                    Cement G91.10
                                                    Concrete G91.30

Cement G91.10
Concrete G91.30
Thermal insulation G32.90
Wood G16.60

	G60.65	Building stones
	G60.70	Bricks
	G60.75	Tiles
	G60.90	Construction equipment

Excavating equipment G37.20
Materials handling G37

G61		**Mining**

UF Mines
       Mining engineering
Extractive industries N41
Gas extraction technology G85.20.10
Mining geology D28.10
Mining safety E73.70.10
Petroleum production G84.20
Underwater excavation G52.30

(By product)

	G61.10	Coal mining
	G61.20	Metal mining

(By methods of mining)

	G61.25	Open cast mining
	G61.30	Quarrying
	G61.35	Underground mining

(By operation)

	G61.40	Mining operations

SN Includes blasting, drilling tunnelling, waste
      disposal
UF Shaft sinking

(By equipment)

	G61.50	Mining equipment

SN Includes hoists, winders, air conditioning equipment,
      pumps, conveyors, excavating equipment, etc.
UF Mine hoists
      Mine windows

	G61.70	Mining services

UF Mine drainage
      Mine lighting
      Mine transport
      Mine ventilation

G62		**Transport Engineering**

Road engineering G57.40
Transport S50/69
Vehicles S61/66

	G62.10	Road vehicle engineering

UF Automobile engineering
      Motor vehicle engineering
Motor industry N44.75
Road vehicles S64

	G62.40	Railway engineering

Locomotives S65.20
Railway networks S60.40

	G62.60	Marine engineering

UF Naval engineering
Ships S66

	G62.60.05	Marine engines

G20/69		**Engineering** (cont.)
G62		**Transport Engineering** (cont.)
	G62.60	Marine engineering (cont.)
	G62.60.10	Naval architecture UF Ship design
	G62.60.50	Shipbuilding *Shipbuilding industry N44.60*
	G62.80	Hovercraft UF Air cushion vehicles Ground effect machines Hovercraft engineering

G63   **Aerospace Engineering**

UF Aerospace technology
Aerodynamics C24.40
Aerospace medicine F95.65
Aerospace navigation H55.55
Air transport S56
Law of space M81

G63.10	Flight dynamics
G63.10.10	Astrodynamics
G63.20	Aircraft engineering *Aircraft S67*
G63.20.10	Aircraft engines

G63.50/99   **Space Technology**
Exobiology E15.20
Space sciences C70/99

G63.55	Space exploration UF Astronauts Space flight Space research
G63.60	Spacecraft *Missiles G66.70.80*
G63.60.10	Rockets
G63.60.30	Artificial satellites *Communication satellites Y80.80.50* *Meteorological satellites D64.60* *Satellite navigation H55.48*
G63.60.50	Space vehicles UF Spaceships
G63.70	Space stations UF Space observatories
G63.80	Ground support systems UF Space ground services

G64   **Nuclear Engineering**
Nuclear energy E81.15
Nuclear physics C13.50
Nuclear power stations G24.10
Nuclear weapons G66.70.30

G64.10	Nuclear reactors *Nuclear reactor theory C13.50.70* (By energy)
G64.10.10	Thermal reactors SN Includes heterogeneous and homogeneous thermal reactors, heavy and light water moderated, graphite moderated, etc.
G64.10.15	Fast reactors
G64.10.20	Fusion reactors UF Controlled thermonuclear reactions *Nuclear fusion C13.50.40*

G20/69		**Engineering** (cont.)
G64		**Nuclear Engineering** (cont.)
	G64.10	Nuclear reactors (cont.)

(By purpose)

	G64.10.30	Power reactors

         *Nuclear power stations G24.10

	G64.10.35	Nuclear propulsion

(By part)

	G64.10.45/70	Nuclear reactor components

         SN Includes cooling systems, moderators, control
            rods, fuel handling systems, etc.

	G64.10.50	Nuclear fuels

         *Nuclear fuel processing G64.80.20
         *Plutonium G73.30.68
         *Uranium G73.30.65

(By safety)

	G64.10.80	Nuclear reactor safety

         SN Includes shut down systems, leak detection, etc.
         UF Nuclear accidents
         *Nuclear explosions E73.60.10
         *Radiation hazards E73.60
         *Radiation protection E76.20

	G64.80	Radiation technology

         *Radiation chemistry C47.50
         *Radiation effects C21
         *Radiation hazards E73.60
         *Radiation measurement and instruments H25
         *Radiation protection E76.20
         *Radioactivity C10.50
         *Radioactive wastes E63.10.20

	G64.80.05/50	Isotope technology
	G64.80.10	Radioisotopes

            *Radiochemistry C47.40

	G64.80.10B	Radioactive tracers
	G64.80.20	Nuclear fuel processing

         UF Spent fuel processing

G66		**Military Engineering**

         UF Military technology
    *Armed forces L53
    *Military education J60.47

(By activities)

	G66.10	Military operations
	G66.20	Warfare

         *War L90

	G66.20.10	Air warfare
	G66.20.10B	Bombing
	G66.20.20	Naval warfare

         UF Submarine warfare

	G66.20.30	Land warfare

         SN Includes field engineering, fortifications,
            siege and defence works

	G66.20.30B	Urban warfare
	G66.20.4O	Unconventional warfare

         *Guerilla activities L73.60
         *Subversive activities L73.10
         *Terrorism L73.65

	G66.20.50	Nuclear warfare

         *Nuclear weapons G66.70.30

	G66.20.70	Chemical/biological warfare

         UF Biological warfare
            Poison gases

	G66.30	Military strategy

         UF Military tactics

	G66.30.10	War games

G20/69		**Engineering** (cont.)
G66		**Military Engineering** (cont.)
	G66.40	Military logistics
		(By equipment)
	G66.60/90	Military equipment
	G66.70	Weapons
		UF Armaments
	G66.70.10/29	Conventional weapons
		UF Artillery
		Small arms
	G66.70.20	Guns
	G66.70.25	Armoured vehicles
		UF Tanks (Weapons)
	G66.70.30	Nuclear weapons
		UF Atomic weapons
		Nuclear explosions E73.60.10
	G66.70.80	Missiles
		UF Ballistic missiles
		Guided missiles

G67   **Production Engineering**

UF Production processes
Production technology
Materials handling G37

(By process)

	G67.10	Metalworking

SN Includes cold and hot working, drawing, forging, forming,
sheet metalworking, extrusion, rolling, tubemaking, etc.
UF Extrusion
Forging
Rolling
Sheet metalworking
Art metalwork W34

	G67.20	Metal removal

SN Includes shaping, shearing, sawing, flame cutting,
finish, machining, (honing, reburring, etc.)
UF Deburring
Finish machining
Flame cutting
Honing
Sawing
Shaping

	G67.20.10	Machining
		UF Milling
	G67.20.30	Grinding
	G67.20.40	Boring
	G67.30	Joining
	G67.30.10	Welding
	G67.30.20	Brazing
	G67.50	Finishing (process)
		UF Polishing
	G67.50.40	Coating
		UF Electrodeposition
		Electroplating
		Coatings G71.70
	G67.60	Dispatching
		UF Goods dispatching
		Packaging G96.40
		(By equipment)
	G67.70	Machine tools
		(By place of work)
	G67.80	Workshops
		Educational works J25.03.02F

G20/69		**Engineering** (cont.)
G67		**Production Engineering** (cont.)
	G67.80	Workshops (cont.)

           Printing workshops W59
           Repair workshops T92.30.30

G68   **Precision Engineering**
Control technology H40/54
Machine tools G67.70
Measurement and instruments H10/24

G70/93   **Materials Science**
Chemistry C30/69
Materials testing H28.40/70
Mineralogy D21
Production engineering G67

G71   Materials
SN See Computer generated hierarchies for full list of materials
Animal oils G92.10.10
Bitumens G84.10.80
Cement G91.10
Ceramics G89.10
Glass G90.10
Concrete G91.30
Leather G96.10.10
Metals G73
Mineral oils G84.05/10
Natural resins G86.08
Paper G96.27.10
Plastics G86.10
Textiles G95.50
Vegetable oils G92.10.30
Wood G16.60

(By purpose)
Additives G93.40.10
Adhesives G93.20.10
Building materials G60.60/80
Cleaning agents G93.10
Dyes G87.40.10
Electrical insulation G27.55.10
Fuels G82
Lubricants G35.15.10
Pesticides G14.30.10
Thermal insulation G32.90

G71.70   Coatings
    Paints G87.10.10

(By form)
Fibres G95.30

G71.75   Chemicals
UF Industrial chemicals
Biochemicals F25.81/50
Inorganic compounds C63
Organic compounds C65/66
Petrochemicals G92.30.30

G71.80   Porous materials
G71.83   Powders
G71.85   Composite materials

(By characteristics)
Dangerous materials E73.40

G72/76   **Metallurgy**
Metal industry N44.10

(By metals)
G73   Metals
(By Group 1 elements)
G73.10.10   Potassium

G70/93		**Materials Science** (cont.)
G72/76		**Metallurgy** (cont.)
	G73	Metals (cont.)
	G73.10.20	Sodium
	G73.10.30	Lithium
	G73.10.40	Rubidium
	G73.10.50	Cesium
	G73.10.60	Francium
		(By Group 2 elements)
	G73.20.10	Calcium
	G73.20.15	Strontium
	G73.20.20	Barium
	G73.20.25	Radium
	G73.20.30	Beryllium
	G73.20.35	Magnesium
	G73.20.40	Zinc
	G73.20.45	Cadmium
	G73.20.50	Mercury
	G73.20.55	Copper
	G73.20.60	Silver
	G73.20.65	Gold
		(By Group 3 elements)
	G73.30.10	Aluminium
	G73.30.15	Boron
	G73.30.20	Scandium
	G73.30.25	Yttrium
	G73.30.30	Rare earths
	G73.30.40	Gallium
	G73.30.45	Indium
	G73.30.48	Thallium
	G73.30.60	Actinium
	G73.30.62	Thorium
	G73.30.65	Uranium
	G73.30.68	Plutonium
		(By Group 4 elements)
	G73.40.10	Tin
	G73.40.15	Lead
	G73.40.20	Titanium
	G73.40.30	Zirconium
	G73.40.40	Hafnium
		(By Group 5 elements)
	G73.50.10	Antimony
	G73.50.20	Bismuth
	G73.50.30	Vanadium
	G73.50.40	Niobium
	G73.50.50	Tantalum
		(By Group 6 elements)
	G73.60.10	Chromium
	G73.60.20	Molybdenum
	G73.60.30	Tungsten
	G73.60.60	Polonium
		(By Group 7 elements)
	G73.70.10	Manganese
	G73.70.20	Technetium
	G73.70.30	Rhenium
		(By Group 8 elements)
	G73.80.10	Iron
	G73.80.30	Cobalt
	G73.80.40	Nickel

G70/93		**Materials Science** (cont.)
G72/76		**Metallurgy** (cont.)
	G73	Metals (cont.)
	G73.80.70	Platinum
		(By value)
	G73.85	Precious metals
		Gold G73.20.65
		Platinum G73.80.70
		Silver G73.20.60
		(By ferrous and non-ferrous)
	G73.90	Ferrous metals
		Iron G73.80.10
		Steels G74.80
	G73.95	Non-ferrous metals
		Aluminium G73.30.10
		Copper G73.20.55
		Lead G73.40.15
		Magnesium G73.20.35
		Tin G73.40.10
		Zinc G73.20.40
	G74	Alloys
	G74.10	Copper alloys
	G74.10.10	Brass
	G74.10.40	Bronze
	G74.20	Aluminium alloys
	G74.50	Chromium alloys
	G74.60	Nickel alloys
	G74.70/80	Iron alloys
		UF Ferrous alloys
		Ferrous metals
	G74.80	Steels
	G74.80.10	Stainless steels
		For others use 'Alloys' in combination with the descriptor for the metal.
	G75	Physical metallurgy
		Corrosion C47.80/99
		Crystallography C28
		Physical chemistry C40/54
		Phase transformations C06.40/90
	G75.20	Metallography
		SN Includes macroscopic, surface, microscopic, radiographic and x-ray metallography
		Crystal examination C28.80
		(By metallurgical engineering)
	G76	Metallurgical engineering
		UF Metal technology
		Metal mining G61.20
		Production engineering G67
	G76.05	Extractive metallurgy
		UF Electrowinning
		Extraction metallurgy
		Metal extraction
		Metalliferous minerals D21.45
	G76.05.60	Pyrometallurgy
		UF Smelting
	G76.10/90	Production metallurgy
		UF Metal production
	G76.12	Metal refining
	G76.15	Vacuum metallurgy
	G76.20	Foundry practice
	G76.20.10	Casting
	G76.30	Metal treatment
	G76.30.20	Heat treatment
	G76.50	Powder metallurgy

G70/93		**Materials Science** (cont.)
G72/76		**Metallurgy** (cont.)
	G76	Metallurgical engineering (cont.)
	G76.10/90	Production metallurgy (cont.)
		(By particular metals)
	G76.70	Iron and steel making
		UF Steel making
G77/93		**Chemical Technology**
		Chemical industry N43
		Chemistry C30/69
	G78	Chemical engineering processes
		UF Chemical treatment
		Unit operations
		Water treatment E66
	G78.15	Fluid handling
	G78.20	Size reduction
	G78.22	Size enlargement
	G78.26	Liquefaction technology
	G78.30	Distillation
	G78.32	Process heating
	G78.33	Evaporation technology
	G78.33.10	Dehydration
	G78.35	Drying
	G78.40	Extraction technology
	G78.50	Mixing technology
	G78.60	Purification
	G78.60.40	Decontamination
	G78.70	Separation technology
		UF Centrifuging processes
		Crystallization technology
		Sedimentation process (chemical)
	G78.70.10	Filtration
		UF Filters
	G78.70.40	Leaching
	G78.80	Sorption technology
	G79	Chemical engineering equipment
	G79.10	Chemical reactors
	G79.20	Centrifuges
	G79.30	Autoclaves
	G79.40	Stills
		(By technology of particular chemical and specific-purpose products)
	G80.10	Pharmaceutical technology
		Drugs F90.15.10
	G80.40	Explosives technology
	G80.40.10	Explosives
	G81/85	Fuel technology
	G82	Fuels
	G83	Coal technology
	G83.10	Coal
	G83.20	Peat
	G84	Petroleum technology
		UF Petroleum fuel technology
		Oil industry N48.20
		Petrochemicals technology G92.30
	G84.08	Petroleum
		UF Crude oil
		(By products)
	G84.10	Petroleum products
		SN Includes light oils, gas oils, fuel oils, greases, etc.

G70/93	**Materials Science** (cont.)
G77/93	**Chemical Technology** (cont.)
G81/85	Fuel technology (cont.)
G84	Petroleum technology (cont.)
G84.10	Petroleum products (cont.)

Petrochemicals G92.30.30

G84.10.20	Gasoline UF Petrol
G84.10.80	Bitumens *Asphalts D20.90.10*
G84.20	Petroleum production UF Oil extraction industry Oil drilling Oil wells *Oil fields D21.30.30* *Submarine oil and gas extraction G52.30.10*
G85	Gas technology *Gas industry N48.30*
G85.10/50	Gas fuels
G85.20	Natural gas
G85.20.10	Natural gas production UF Gas extraction technology *Submarine oil and gas extraction G52.30.10*
G85.20.40	Manufactured gas
G85.60	Gas supply
G86	Polymer and plastics technology *Polymers C68.20*
G86.08	Natural resins *Rubber G86.40.10*
G86.10	Plastics
G86.10.10	Polyethylene
G86.10.12	Polypropylene
G86.10.15	Polystyrene
G86.10.25	Ester polymers UF Perspex
G86.10.35	Polyvinyl chloride UF PVC
G86.10.38	Polyvinyl fluoride UF PVF
G86.10.40	Teflon UF PTFE
G86.10.50	Polyesters
G86.10.55	Nylon
G86.10.65	Polyurethanes
G86.10.70	Epoxy resins
G86.10.75	Amino resins UF Urea formaldehyde
G86.10.85	Silicon resins
G86.40	Rubber technology
G86.40.10	Rubber UF Elastomers
G86.40.10B	Synthetic rubber
G87.10	Paint technology
G87.10.10	Paints
G87.40	Dyes technology
G87.40.10	Dyes
G87.40.30	Inks
G88.10	Lime and gypsum technology *Gypsum D21.80.20*
G88.10.20	Lime

G70/93		**Materials Science** (cont.)
G77/93		**Chemical Technology** (cont.)
	G89	Ceramics technology
		Ceramic art W36
	G89.10	Ceramics
	G89.10.40	Refractories
	G90	Glass technology
		Art glass W38
		Glassware W38.10
	G90.10	Glass
	G90.30	Glass blowing
	G91	Cement and concrete technology
	G91.10	Cement
	G91.30	Concrete
	G92.10	Vegetable and animal oils technology
	G92.10.10	Animal oils
	G92.10.30	Vegetable oils
	G92.30	Petrochemicals technology
	D92.30.10	Petrochemistry
	D92.30.30	Petrochemicals
	D93.05/20	Cleaning agents technology
	G93.10	Cleaning agents
	G93.10.10	Soap
	G93.10.20	Detergents
	G93.10.30	Polishes
	G93.20	Adhesives technology
	G93.20.10	Adhesives
		UF Glue
		Sealants
	G93.40	Processing agents technology
	G93.40.10	Additives
		UF Antifreezes
		Inhibitors
		Preservatives
		Thickeners
		Solvents C52.60
G94/97		**Other Technologies**
	G94	Food technology
		Crops G14.60/99
		Food industry N43.30
		Food production G14.20.30
	G94.10	Food
		Cereals G14.63.10
		Fish G18.20
	G94.10.05	Food preservation
	G94.10.05A	Frozen food
	G94.10.10	Beverages
		UF Coffee
		Tea
	G94.10.10A	Alcoholic drinks
		UF Beer
		Spirits
		Wines
	G94.10.20	Meat
	G94.10.30	Dairy products
		UF Butter
		Eggs
	G94.10.30C	Milk
	G94.10.70	Synthetic food

G70/93		**Materials Science** (cont.)
G94/97		**Other Technologies** (cont.)

G95		Textile technology
		Textile arts W41
		Textile industry N45
G95.10		Textile machinery
G95.20		Textile processes
		UF Spinning
		Textile finishing
		Weaving
G95.30		Fibres
		UF Animal fibres
		Cotton
		Natural fibres
		Wool
G95.30.30		Synthetic fibres
G95.50		Textiles
		UF Cloth
		Textile products
G96.10	Leather technology	
G96.10.10	Leather	
G96.15	Clothing manufacture	
	Clothing industry N45.20	
G96.15.10	Clothing	
G96.20	Wood technology	
	Wood G16.60	
G96.20.30	Woodworking	
G96.20.30A	Carpentry	
G96.25/29	Paper technology	
	UF Paper making	
	Pulp technology	
	Paper industry N46	
G96.27	Paper	
G96.27.10	Printing paper	
G96.27.10B	Newsprint	
G96.30	Furniture manufacture	
G96.30.10	Furniture	
G96.40	Packaging	
G96.40.30	Containers	
	SN Includes bins, barrels, crates, drums, flasks, etc.	
	UF Bottles	
	Boxes	
G96.60	Toy manufacture	
G96.60.10	Toys	
	Educational toys J55.05.07	
G97.10	Catering	
	UF Corporate catering	
	Cooking G98.10	
	Hotel and catering industry N49.10	
G97.10.10	Hotels	
	UF Hotel management	
G97.10.30	Canteens	
G97.10.40	Restaurants	
G97.30	Laundry technology	
G97.30.10	Laundries	

G98	**Domestic Science**
	SN Includes home catering, cleaning, laundry, dress making, etc.
	UF Home economics
	Household management
	Household science

G70/93	**Materials Science** (cont.)
G98	**Domestic Science** (cont.)

Catering G97.10
Domestic science education J60.90
Laundries G97.30.10

(By process)

G98.10	Cooking
	UF Cookery
G98.40	Domestic engineering
	UF Household engineering
G98.40.10	Domestic appliances
	UF Household appliances
	Kitchen appliances

H   Interdisciplinary Science and Technology

H Interdisciplinary Science and Technology

H05 **Design**
Artistic design W12

H05.10	Industrial design
H05.30	Technical drawing
	Technical drawings Z15.72.72
H05.60	Computer-assisted design

H10/24 **Measurement and Instruments**
Astronomical measurements and instruments C79
Chemical analysis C36/39
Computers H71/76
Geophysical measurements and instruments D14
Hydrological measurements and instruments D84
Meteorological measurements and instruments D64
Oceanographic measurements D97
Precision engineering G68
Surveying H30/34
Telemetry Y80.30.35
Testing H28

(By units and tolerances)

H11.10	Units of measurement
H11.10.10	Metric system
H11.40	Measurement tolerances
H11.50	Calibration

(By instruments generally)

H12	Instruments

UF Instrumentation
Measurement instruments
Scientific instruments
Medical instruments F94.20
Navigational instruments H56.70
Oceanographic instruments D98.50
Surveying instruments H33

H12.10	Gauges
H12.20	Sensors

UF Detectors
Monitors
Probes

H12.20.10	Monitoring
H12.30	Transducers
H12.40	Display devices

UF Consoles
Dials
Displays
Instrument panels
Screens (display)
Displays (computer) H83.70

H12.45	Recording instruments
H12.50	Indicating instruments

(By motive power)

H12.75	Electrical instruments

(By characteristics measured)

H13/15	Mechanical measurements and instruments
H14	Dimensional measurements and instruments

UF Height measurement
Length measurement
Surveying instruments H33

H14.10	Depth measurement
	Sounding D97.30/40
H14.20	Distance measurement
H14.40	Position measurement
H14.50	Volume measurement

H10/24		**Measurement and Instruments** (cont.)
	H13/15	Mechanical measurements and instruments (cont.)
		(By static, kinematic and dynamic property measurement)
	H15.10	Force measurement
	H15.10.10	Strain measurement
		UF Strain gauges
	H15.15	Weight measurement
	H15.20	Density measurement
		Fluid density measurement H17.50
	H15.30	Velocity measurement
	H15.40	Rotation measurement
	H15.50	Vibration measurement
	H16	Vacuum measurement
	H17	Fluid measurement and instruments
	H17.05/20	Flow measurement and instruments
	H17.10	Flowmeters
		UF Water meters
		Current meters D97.55.10
	H17.10.10	Anemometers
	H17.10.20	Pitot tubes
	H17.10.30	Venturimeters
	H17.30	Liquid level measurement
		Sea level measurement D97.65
	H17.40	Pressure measurement and instruments
		UF Pressure gauges
		Atmospheric pressure measurement D64.10
		Sea water pressure measurement D97.82
	H17.40.20	Manometers
	H17.40.30	Pressure transducers
	H17.50	Fluid density measurement
		Sea water density measurement D97.85
	H17.50.10	Hydrometry
		UF Hydrometers
	H18	Time measurement and instruments
		Radiocarbon dating U93.20
	H18.10	Clocks
	H19	Acoustic measurements and instruments
		Sea water acoustic measurements D97.88
	H19.10	Noise measurement
	H19.20	Sound velocity meters
	H19.70	Acoustic holography
	H20	Thermal measurements and instruments
		UF Calorimetry
		Heat measurement
		Radiometry
	H20.20	Temperature measurement and instruments
		Sea water temperature measurement D97.80
	H20.20.10	Thermometers
	H20.20.20	Temperature probes
	H20.20.30	Thermocouples
	H20.20.70	Pyrometers
	H21	Electrical measurements and instruments
		SN Includes measurement of charge, power, electrical waves, etc.
	H21.10	Electric current measurement
	H21.20	Voltage measurement
	H21.30	Electrical resistance measurement
	H22	Magnetic measurements and instruments
		UF Flux meters
	H23	Optical measurements and instruments
		Optical chemical analysis C37.50
		Sea water optical measurements D97.87

H10/24		**Measurement and Instruments** (cont.)
	H23	Optical measurements and instruments (cont.)
	H23.20	Photometry
	H23.20.10	Spectrophotometry
	H23.25	Calorimetry
	H23.30	Interferometry
		UF Interferometers
	H23.32	Diffractography
	H23.35	Refractometry
		UF Refractometers
	H23.38	Turbidimetry
		UF Transparency measurement
	H23.45	Telescopes
		Astronomical telescopes C79.10
	H23.50	Microscopy
	H23.50.10	Microscopes
		Electron microscopes H24.30
	H23.60	Spectroscopy
		UF Spectrography
		Spectrochemical analysis C37.50.40
	H23.60.10	Spectrometers
	H23.70	Light detectors
	H23.75	Holography
		Acoustic holography H19.70
	H23.80	Optical devices
	H23.80.10	Lenses
	H23.80.30	Mirrors
	H24	Particle measurements and instruments
		SN Includes particle diffraction, interferometry, spectroscopy, etc.
		UF Elementary particle measurements and instruments
		Nuclear instruments
	H24.10	Particle accelerators
		UF Cyclotrons
		Synchrotrons
	H24.20	Electron diffraction
	H24.25	Neutron diffraction
	H24.30	Electron microscopes
		UF Electron microscopy
	H24.40	Mass spectroscopy
		UF Mass spectrometry
	H25	Radiation measurement and instruments
	H25.20	Radiation detectors
	H26	X-ray analysis
		X-ray crystallography C28.80.10
	H26.20	X-ray spectroscopy
	H26.30	X-ray diffraction
	H27	Radiography
H28		**Testing**
		Chemical analysis C36/39
		Educational tests J45.16.05
		Experimentation A88
		Standardization A60
		Statistical tests B79.30
	H28.20	Quality control
	H28.30	Inspection
	H28.40/70	Materials testing
	H28.50	Destructive testing
		SN Includes creep, fatigue, fracture, hardness, wear, testing, etc.

H28		**Testing** (cont.)
	H28.40/70	Materials testing (cont.)
	H28.60	Non-destructive testing
		SN Includes fractography, diffractography, ultrasonic, magnetic, radiography and x-ray testing
		Metallography G75.20
	H28.70	Stress analysis
		UF Experimental stress analysis
		Stress (mechanical) C27.10
	H28.70.10	Photoelastic stress analysis
	H28.80	Tests

H29		**Maintenance**
		UF Maintenance engineering
		Repair
		Document maintenance Z42.35
		Building maintenance G60.05
	H29.10	Cleaning
		Finishing (process)
	H29.40	Restoration
		Restoration of paintings T83.10

H30/34		**Surveying**
		Hydrographic surveying D97.05/40
		(By methods)
	H31.10	Triangulation
	H31.20	Photogrammetry
	H31.30	Tacheometry
	H31.35	Aerial surveying
		(By instruments)
	H33	Surveying instruments
		UF Geodimeters
		Sextants
		Theodolites
		Gravimeters D14.30
		(By cartography)
	H34	Cartography
		UF Mapping
		Charts Z15.72.10
	H34.10	Maps
	H34.10.10	Tectonic maps
	H34.10.20	Quarternary maps
	H34.10.30	Mineral maps
	H34.10.40	Metallogenic maps
	H34.10.45	Soil maps
	H34.10.50	Hydrogeological maps
	H34.10.55	Climatic maps
	H34.10.60	Vegetation maps
		For other subjects, combine Maps with appropriate terms

H35/39		**Systemology**
		UF Systems engineering
		Operations research Q30.10
		(By systems performance)
	H36.10	Performance
		UF Efficiency
		Failure A40.30
	H36.10.50	Accuracy
	H36.10.60	Errors

H35/39   **Systemology** (cont.)

	(By analysis)
H37	Systems analysis
	UF Systems design
	Systems theory
	Models A91.50
	(By cybernetics)
H38	Cybernetics
H38.10	Artificial intelligence
H38.10.40	Automata theory
H38.20	Pattern recognition
H38.40	Bionics
	UF Biocybernetics
H38.40.10	Man-machine systems
H38.40.30	Ergonomics
	UF Human engineering
	Human biology F52

H40/54   **Control Technology**

                                           UF Automation

	(By theory)
H43	Control theory
	UF Control system analysis
	Control system synthesis
	Cybernetics H38
	(By type of system)
H44	Control systems
	SN Includes adaptive, closed-loop, discrete, distributed parameter, non-linear, optimal, sampled data, stochastic, time-varying and other types of control systems.
H44.10	Automatic control
	(By specific variables)
H45/52	Control of specific variables
	Noise control E67
H47	Humidity control
	UF Moisture control
H48	Electrical variables control
	UF Voltage control
H48.30	Magnetic variables control
H49	Mechanical variables control
H49.10	Speed control
H49.30	Positioning
H49.50	Flow control
H49.55	Pressure control
H50	Optical variables control
H51	Thermal variables control
H51.10	Temperature control
	UF Thermostats
	(By control applications)
H53.05	Remote control
H53.10	Process control
H53.40	Numerical control
	Machine tools G67.70
	(By equipment)
H54	Control equipment
	UF Actuators
	Controllers
	Governors
	Servomechanisms
	Servomotors
	Relays G27.26.30
	Switches G27.26
	Hydraulic equipment G53
	Electric control equipment G27.20

H55/59		**Navigation**
	H55.05	Position finding
		UF Direction finding
		(By method)
	H55.20	Magnetic navigation
	H55.25	Inertial navigation
	H55.35	Radio navigation
	H55.40	Radar navigation
	H55.45	Sonar navigation
	H55.48	Satellite navigation
		(By application)
	H55.50	Marine navigation
	H55.55	Aerospace navigation
	H55.60	Underwater navigation
		Sonar navigation H55.45
	H55.65	Tracking
		(By equipment)
	H56.70	Navigational instruments
	H56.70.10	Compasses
	H56.70.60	Gyroscopes
H60/69		**Data Processing**
		UF Automatic data processing
		Coding Y80.10.35C
		Computers H71/76
		Data retrieval Z54.40
		Data transmission Y80.30.20/30
	H61	Data
		Climatic data D46.10.10
		Geographical data D35.10.30
		Geological data D15.30
		Hydrological data D67.10
		Meteorological data D64.05
		Oceanographic data D86.60
		Statistical data Z15.15.50S
		Survey data A85.10.30
		(By media)
	H62/64	Data bearing media
		Catalogue cards Z52.80.15C
		Data preparation equipment H83.20
		Computer storage devices H82
		Microforms Z15.77
		Non-book materials Z15.60/99
		(By magnetic media)
	H63.10	Magnetic tapes
	H63.20	Magnetic cards
	H63.30	Magnetic discs
	H63.40	Magnetic cores
	H63.50	Magnetic films
		(By punched media)
	H64.10	Punched cards
	H64.20	Punched tapes
		(By operation)
	H65	Data collection
	H66	Data handling
		File management (index) Z48.54
		File organization (index) Z52.20
		File organization (computer) H88
	H66.10	Data preparation
	H67	Data analysis

H60/69		**Data Processing** (cont.)
	H67	Data analysis (cont.)
	H67.10	Data sampling
	H68	Data exchange

H70/99		**Computer Science**

Data processing H60/69
Computer science education J60.41

(By computer systems and types)

	H71/76	Computers
		UF Computer systems
	H72	Calculating machines
	H73	Digital computers
		UF Digital computing
		Digital systems
		Electronic digital computers

(By purpose and application)

	H73.05	General purpose computers
	H73.10	Special purpose computers
	H73.10.10	Digital differential analysers
	H73.15	Minicomputers
	H73.25	Satellite computers

(By operational conditions)

	H73.30	On-line systems

On-line information processing Z47.30
On-line information systems Z68.18

(By type of digital system)

	H73.35	Remote access
	H73.40	Fast-response computer systems
	H73.42	Sampled data systems
	H73.45	Multiaccess systems
	H73.50	Parallel processing systems
	H73.50.10	Multiprocessing systems
	H73.60	Real-time systems

On-line systems H73.30

	H73.70	Time-sharing systems
	H76	Analogue computers
		UF Network analysers
	H76.20	Differential analysers
	H76.40	Electrolytic tanks
	H77	Hybrid computers
		UF Analogue digital computers

(By networks)

	H78	Computer networks

(By hardware)

	H80/83	Computer hardware
	H81	Computer circuits

Logic design H90
Logic and switching circuits G29.10.40

	H82	Computer storage devices
	H82.10	Digital storage

Magnetic tapes H63.10
Magnetic discs H63.30
Magnetic films H63.50
Magnetic cores H63.40

	H82.30	Direct access
		UF Direct access storage
		Random access
	H83	Computer peripheral equipment
		UF Input-output media
	H83.10	Data communication equipment

Satellite computers H73.25

H70/99		**Computer Science** (cont.)
	H80/83	Computer hardware (cont.)
	H83	Computer peripheral equipment (cont.)
	H83.10	Data communication equipment (cont.)

                                Telemetry Y80.30.35

	H83.10.10	Computer terminals
	H83.10.20	Computer interfaces
	H83.20	Data preparation equipment
		Data bearing media H62/64
	H83.30	Keyboards
		UF Console typewriters
	H83.40	Computer graphic equipment
		UF Computer graphics
	H83.40.10	Light pens
	H83.40.30	Remote consoles
	H83.50	Character recognition equipment
		UF Optical character recognition equipment
	H83.60	Printers (computer)
		Computer output microform Z15.77.40
	H83.70	Displays (computer)
		UF Visual displays (computer)
	H83.80	Data converters
		UF Analogue-digital converters
		Digital-analogue converters
		(By programming)
	H84/87	Computer programming
		Algorithms B41.40
	H85	Program and systems documentation
		UF Decision tables
	H86	Computer languages
		UF Program languages
	H86.20	Machine oriented languages
	H86.30	Problem oriented languages
	H86.40	Procedure oriented languages
	H87	Computer software
		UF Computer programs
	H87.10	Complete computer programs
	H87.20	Subroutines
	H87.25	Macros
		UF Macrogenerating programs
	H87.30	Program processors
		UF Program assemblers
		Program compilers
		Program interpreters
	H87.40	Operating systems (computer)
	H87.40.10	Supervisory and executive programs
		UF Multiprocessing programs
	H87.45	Report generators
	H87.50	Time-sharing programs
	H87.55	Input-output programs
	H87.60	Utility programs
		UF Service programs
	H87.80	Program testing
		UF Program diagnostics
		Program debugging
		(By file organization)
	H88	File organization (computer)
		(By theory and design)
	H89	Computer metatheory
	H90	Logic design
	H90.10	Switching theory

H70/99		**Computer Science** (cont.)
		(By techniques)
	H93	Computer techniques
		Computer-assisted instruction J55.15.04
	H93.40	Teleprocessing
		(By applications)
	H95	Computer applications
		Computer linguistics X15
		Computer-assisted instruction J55.15.04
		Information processing automation Z47
		Library automation Z42.03
		Photocomposition W62.30
		(By administration and management)
	H97	Computer management
		(By centres)
	H97.10	Computation centres
		(By personnel)
	H97.50	Computer personnel
		UF Programmers
		Systems analysts

J	**EDUCATION**
	Summary
J03	**Educational history**
J05	**Educational research**
J05.40	**Comparative education**
J10	**Educational philosophy, policy and development**
J14	**Educational sociology**
J20	**Educational planning and administration**
J25	**Educational facilities**
J30	**Teaching profession**
J35	**Educational personnel**
J40	**Educational management**
J45	**Educational psychology**
J46	**Study**
J50	**Teaching**
J55	**Teaching materials and equipment**
J60	**Curriculum**
J60.10/99	**Curriculum subjects**
J60.11/32	**Curriculum subjects—basic**
J60.33/35	**Curriculum subjects—vocational and professional**
J60.36/99	**Curriculum subjects—traditional disciplines**
J70	**Educational systems and institutions**
J70.07	**Schools**
J70.08/10	**Higher education**
J70.11/13	**Out-of-school education**
J70.14	**Adult education**
J70.15/20	**Continuing, community and mass education**
J70.21/50	**Education of specific categories of students**
J90	**Students**

J   **Education**

Use for general works on education

J03   **Educational History**

J03.50   Educational biographies

J05   **Educational Research**
Curriculum research J60.02.04
Reading research J60.30.70

J05.15   Evaluation of education

J05.20   Educational experiments

J05.30   Educational models

For other terms combine with terms for research methods at A70 'Research' generally. For research on specific educational problems, combine 'Educational research' with appropriate terms throughout the Education section, except where the concept is already precoordinated, for example, 'Reading research' J60.30.70

J05.40   **Comparative Education**

J05.40.10   International education

J05.40.20   Intercultural education

(By method)
For other methods combine with terms for research techniques and with terms for individual countries and geographical areas

J10   **Educational Philosophy, Policy and Development** (†)

J10.05   Educational philosophy

J10.10   Educational theory
Educational models J05.30

J10.10.10   Principles of education

J10.20/59   Educational policy
Educational planning J20.03

J10.21   Educational strategies

J10.25   Educational aims
UF Educational objectives

J10.25.10   Educational goals

J10.30   Role of education

(By political policy)
J10.40   State and education

J10.40.10   State responsibility for education

(By religious policy)
J10.45   Church and education

(By rights and opportunities)
J10.50   Right to education
UF Universal education
Academic freedom J30.05.03

J10.50.10   Educational opportunities

J10.50.10A   Access to education

J10.50.10B   Equal education
UF Non-discriminatory education

J10.50.10E   Educational discrimination

J10.50.10L   Educational priority areas

J10.60   Educational development
UF Advancement of education

J10.60.05   Educational trends

J10.60.10   Educational reform
UF Educational regeneration
Educational renewal
Educational renovation

J10.60.20   Educational innovations

J10.60.30   Democratisation of education

J10.60.40   Diversification of education

J14	**Educational Sociology**

Educational psychosociology J45.40/69

(Note: Use the terms in Section R Sociology for social environment, family relationships and other social problems. This section contains terms for problems specifically of an educational sociological nature)

(By social environmental problems)

J14.10   Disadvantaged schools

(By welfare services)

J14.15   Educational welfare
            School meals J40.32.10

J14.15.15   School health services

(By student sociology)

J14.20   Student sociology
            UF Student customs
                Student life
            Student interests J46.07
            Student participation J45.48.40

J14.20.02   Student unrest

J14.20.06   Student movements

J14.20.10   Student organisations

J14.20.40   Student housing

(By industrial relationships)

J14.30   Industry and education
            SN Sociological relationships only

(By employment problems)

J14.40   Education and employment
            Transition from school to work J45.70.50
            Youth employment Q55.60
            Youth unemployment Q55.60.20

J14.40.10   Student employment

J20	**Educational Planning and Administration (†)**

J20.03   Educational planning
            Educational planners J35.02.10
            Educational policy J10.20/59

(By factors of concern to educational planners)

J20.03.02   Education and development

J20.03.03   Educational needs

J20.03.04   Educational demand

J20.03.06   Educational resources
            Educational facilities J25
            Educational financial resources J20.05.05F

J20.03.06B   Educational manpower
            Teacher supply J30.22

J20.03.10   Educational input

J20.03.11   Educational output

J20.03.14   Quality of education

J20.03.14A   Educational standards

J20.03.16   Educational levels

J20.03.20   Educational statistics

J20.03.22   Educational population

J20.03.22C   School-age population

J20.03.22D   Enrolment trends

J20.03.22E   Enrolment ratios

J20.03.22F   Enrolment projections

J20.03.22H   Attendance rate

J20.03.22J   Educational wastage

J20.03.22K   Drop-out rate

J20.03.22M   Student mobility

J20		**Educational Planning and Administration** (cont.)
	J20.03	Educational planning (cont.)
	J20.03.24	School mapping (cont.)
		UF School distribution
		School location
	J20.03.26	School size
		(By planning activities)
	J20.03.35	Educational forecasting
	J20.03.40	Educational programmes
	J20.03.45	Educational plans
	J20.03.50	Educational projects
		UF National educational projects
	J20.03.60	Educational assistance
		Educational advisers J35.02.20
		Educational financing J20.05.05K
	J20.03.62	Educational missions
	J20.05	Economics of education
		SN Techniques of economics applied to educational systems
		Use with terms in the general economics schedule
	J20.05.05	Educational finance
		Educational financial management J40.28
	J20.05.05B	Educational budgets
	J20.05.05BC	Educational budgetary control
	J20.05.05C	Educational costs
	J20.05.05F	Educational financial resources
		Educational income J40.28.02
	J20.05.05K	Educational financing
		UF Financial aid to education
		Educational assistance J20.03.60
		Educational grants J40.17
	J20.08	Educational administration
		(By organisations)
	J20.08.10/20	Educational administrative bodies
	J20.08.12	International educational bodies
		UF Intergovernmental educational bodies
		Non-governmental educational bodies
	J20.08.14	Regional educational bodies
	J20.08.16	National educational bodies
	J20.08.18	Government educational bodies
		UF Central government educational bodies
		Departments of education
		Ministries of education
		Regional government educational bodies
	J20.08.18L	Local government education authorities
	J20.08.20	Private educational organizations
		UF Voluntary educational organizations
	J20.08.20B	Educational foundations
		UF Educational charities
		Educational trusts
	J20.08.20E	Educational associations
		Teacher associations J30.30
		(By activities)
	J20.08.30	Educational legislation
		UF Educational acts
		Educational bills
		Educational laws
		Educational statutes
	J20.08.40	Educational supervision
	J20.08.40A	Accreditation
	J20.08.40C	School supervision
	J20.08.40E	Educational inspection
	J20.08.45	Educational coordination
	J20.08.50	Educational cooperation

J		**Education**

		Educational Planning and Administration (cont.)
	J20.08	Educational administration (cont.)
	J20.08.50	Educational cooperation (cont.)
	J20.08.50F	University cooperation

J25.   **Educational Facilities**

UF School facilities
Playgrounds X95.20
Playing fields X97.50

	J25.03	Educational buildings

UF Academic buildings
    College buildings

(By specific buildings, rooms and parts)
Academic libraries Z62.30.10

	J25.03.02B	Lecture theatres
	J25.03.02C	University campuses
	J25.03.02D	Educational laboratories

        UF College laboratories
          School laboratories J25.03.04D

	J25.03.02F	Educational workshops

        UF College workshops
          School workshops J25.03.04F

	J25.03.04	School buildings

        (By specific buildings)

	J25.03.04A	Classrooms
	J25.03.04D	School laboratories
	J25.03.04F	School workshops

For others combine 'School buildings' with terms from appropriate schedules

School gymnasia (School buildings & Gymnasia) School swimming pools (School buildings & Swimming pools)

(By educational buildings by architecture and design)
Combine with terms from Construction engineering section G56/60

	J25.08	Educational equipment

UF College equipment
    School equipment
Teaching materials and equipment J55

	J25.08.04	School furniture

                       The Teaching Profession

Teachers J35.03

(By professional status and ethics)

	J30.05	Teacher status

UF Teacher professional recognition

	J30.05.03	Academic freedom
	J30.05.05	Academic unity
	J30.06	Teacher professional ethics
	J30.06.20	Teacher responsibility
	J30.07	Teacher professional standards
	J30.10	Teacher role

UF Teacher influence

(By recruitment and conditions of service)

	J30.20	Teacher recruitment
	J30.22	Teacher supply
	J30.22.10	Teacher shortage
	J30.22.30	Teacher-student ratio
	J30.22.40	Class size
	J30.25	Teacher conditions of employment

UF Teachers working conditions

J30		**The Teaching Profession** (cont.)
	J30.25	Teacher conditions of employment (cont.)
	J30.25.10	Teacher salaries
		UF Teacher wages
	J30.25.20	Teacher leave
	J30.25.20A	Teacher sick leave
	J30.25.30	Teacher promotion
	J30.25.35	Teacher dismissal
	J30.25.40	Teacher retirement
	J30.25.45	Teaching load
	J30.25.60	Teacher strikes
	J30.25.80	Teaching abroad

For others combine 'Teacher conditions of employment' with terms from the Labour section Q50/59

(By organisations)

	J30.30	Teacher associations
		UF Teacher professional associations
	J30.30.10	Teacher trade unions
		UF Teacher labour unions

(By education and training)

	J30.35/80	Educational personnel training
	J30.40	Teacher training
		UF Teacher education
		Teacher educators J35.03.30
		Teacher training curriculum J60.07.60
		Teacher training schools J70.10.45

(By type of teacher)

	J30.40.05	Pre-primary teacher training
	J30.40.10	Primary teacher training
	J30.40.13	Secondary teacher training
	J30.40.15	Special teacher training
	J30.40.20	Vocational teacher training
	J30.40.22	Teacher educator training

(By courses)

	J30.40.25	Education courses
		UF Teacher training courses

(By training methods)

	J30.40.30	Pre-service teacher training
	J30.40.35	In-service teacher training
	J30.40.37	Practice teaching
	J30.40.39	Teacher supervision

(By qualification)

	J30.40.50	Teacher qualifications
	J30.40.50A	Teacher certification

J35		**Educational Personnel**

SN Use for academic and school personnel

(By executive officers)

	J35.02	Educational administrators

SN Academic and school administrators

UF Chancellors
Deans (academic)
Directors (academic)
Examiners
Head teachers
Heads of departments (academic)
Inspectors (education)
Principals (academic)
Rectors (academic)
Superintendents (academic)
Vice chancellors

J35		**Educational Personnel** (cont.)
	J35.02	Educational administrators (cont.)
	J35.02.10	Educational planners
	J35.02.20	Educational advisers

(By teaching personnel)

	J35.03	Teachers
		UF School teachers
		Teacher training J30.40
		Teaching profession J30

(By students taught)

	J35.03.10	Pre-primary school teachers
	J35.03.12	Primary school teachers
	J35.03.15	Secondary school teachers
	J35.03.20	Academic teaching personnel
		UF College teachers
		Faculty
		Lecturers
		Professors
		Readers
		Tutors
	J35.03.22	Vocational school teachers
		UF Technical teachers
	J35.03.25	Adult educators
	J35.03.30	Teacher educators

(By teachers function)

	J35.03.40	Training officers
		UF Trainers
	J35.03.42	Itinerant teachers
	J35.03.45	Visiting teachers
		UF Visiting professors
	J35.03.48	Part-time teachers

(By teacher characteristics)

	J35.03.50	Women teachers
	J35.03.50B	Married women teachers
	J35.03.55	Student teachers
	J35.03.58	Student assistants
		UF Teaching assistants

(By subject specialisation)

	J35.03.70	Literacy workers
	J35.03.72	Special education teachers
		For subjects taught combine 'Teachers' with subject taught, e.g. Mathematics teachers (Teachers & Mathematics education)

(By support personnel)

	J35.05	Educational support personnel
		SN Academic and school support personnel
	J35.05.02	Academic librarians
		SN College librarians
	J35.05.04	School librarians
	J35.05.06	Teachers librarians
	J35.05.20	Educational guidance personnel

(By ancillary personnel)

	J35.07	Paraprofessional educational personnel
		SN Academic auxiliary personnel
		School auxiliary personnel
	J35.07.02	Teacher aides
	J35.07.04	Educational technicians
		SN College technicians
		School technicians
	J35.07.06	Educational laboratory personnel
		SN Academic laboratory personnel
		School laboratory personnel

J35   **Educational Personnel** (cont.)

               (By youth leaders)

J35.09   Community leaders

J35.09.10   Youth leaders

J40   **Educational Management**

               SN Management of schools, colleges and other educational institutes

J40.02   Educational administrative structure

               SN Academic and school structure

               UF Academic boards

                   Academic departments

                   Boards of studies

                   Convocation

                   Courts (university)

                   Faculty boards

                   Graduate bodies

                   Senate (university)

J40.02.10   Governing boards

                   UF Boards of governors

J40.02.15   Examination boards

                   UF Examining bodies

J40.02.20   Self-governing educational bodies

J40.03   Educational admission

               UF Academic admission

                   School admission

J40.03.10   Admission criteria

J40.03.20   Student selection

J40.03.20C   Competitive selection

J40.03.30   Enrolment

                       UF Educational registration

                         School enrolment

                      Enrolment projections J20.03.22F

                      Enrolment ratios J20.03.22E

                      Enrolment trends J20.03.22D

J40.03.30D   Dual enrolment

J40.03.40   Readmission

J40.05   Educational grouping

               UF Academic grouping

                   School grouping

J40.05.01   School classes

                   UF Educational grades

                   Class size J30.22.40

J40.05.01C   Transition classes

                     UF Transfer classes

J40.05.05   Educational integration

                   UF Educational segregation

J40.05.07   Ability grouping

                   UF Educational sets

                     Streaming

               (By exchanges and transfers)

J40.07.02   Educational exchanges

                   UF Academic exchanges

                   School exchanges

J40.07.02A   Student exchanges

J40.07.02D   Exchange programmes

J40.07.04   Educational transfers

                   UF Academic transfers

                   School transfers

                   Transfer policy

J40.07.04K   Articulation

               (By attendance and absence)

J40.09   Educational attendance

                   SN School and college attendance

                   UF School attendance

J40   **Educational Management** (cont.)

J40.09		Educational attendance (cont.)
		(By period of attendance)
J40.09.10		Educational year
		UF Academic year
		School year
J40.09.13		Educational term
		UF Academic term
		School term
J40.09.15		Educational time-tables
		UF Academic time-tables
		School time-tables
J40.09.20		School time
		(By periods of absence)
J40.09.30		School holidays
		UF Academic vacations
J40.09.32		Educational leave
J40.09.35		Sabbatical leave
J40.11		Educational rules
		UF College rules
		School rules
		School discipline J45.50
J40.13		Educational ceremonies
		UF Academic ceremonies
		Educational celebrations
		Founders days
		School ceremonies
		Speech days
		Students rags
J40.15		School-leaving
		UF School-leavers
		School-leaving guidance J45.70.30
J40.15.04		School-leaving age
		(By stage of education)
J40.15.04C		Secondary school leaving
J40.17		Educational grants
		UF Educational awards
		Student grants
		Study grants
J40.17.02		Scholarships
J40.17.04		Research fellowships
J40.17.08		Fellowships
J40.17.14		Travel grants
J40.17.30		Student loans
J40.19		Educational courses
		(By administrative characteristics)
J40.19.02		Short courses
J40.19.04		Part-time courses
J40.19.06		Sandwich courses
J40.19.08		Accelerated courses
J40.19.10		Correspondence courses
J40.19.12		Elective courses
J40.19.13		Credit courses
		(By level and purpose)
J40.19.14		University courses
J40.19.16		Post-graduate courses
J40.19.20		Training courses
J40.19.20C		Industrial training courses
J40.19.24		Refresher courses
J40.19.28		Orientation courses
		(By technique)
J40.19.40		Programmed courses

J40		**Educational Management** (cont.)
	J40.21	Examinations
		Examination boards J40.02.15
		(By marks and standards)
	J40.21.02	Examination marks
	J40.21.04	Examination standards
		Equivalence between diplomas J40.23.10
		(By type of examination)
	J40.21.08	Oral examinations
		UF Viva voce
	J40.21.10	Practical examinations
	J40.21.12	Written examinations
	J40.21.12C	Theses
	J40.21.14	Internal examinations
	J40.21.15	External examinations
	J40.21.17	Entrance examinations
	J40.23	Qualifications
		Teacher qualifications J30.40.50
	J40.23.01	Educational background
		(By awards)
	J40.23.02	Educational certificates
		UF Leaving certificates
	J40.23.03	Degrees
		UF University degrees
	J40.23.03B	Bachelors degrees
	J40.23.03C	Masters degrees
	J40.23.03D	Doctoral degrees
	J40.23.06	Diplomas
		(By comparative standards)
	J40.23.10	Equivalence between diplomas
	J40.26	Educational records
		UF Academic records
		Correspondence files (academic)
		School records
		School reports
		Student records
	J40.28	Educational financial management
		UF College financial management
		School financial management
		Educational finance J20.05.05
	J40.28.02	Educational income
		UF College income
		School income
		Educational financial resources J20.05.05F
	J40.28.02F	Educational fees
		UF College fees
		School fees
	J40.28.04	Educational expenditure
		UF College expenditure
		School expenditure
	J40.28.04D	Educational wages
		Teacher salaries J30.25.10
		(By transport management)
	J40.30	Student transportation
		UF College transport
		School buses
		School transport
		(By domestic management)
	J40.32	Educational catering
		UF College catering
		School catering
	J40.32.10	School meals
		UF School meals programmes

J45	**Educational Psychology**

SN Use Section P Psychology for terms in the field of individual and social psychology. These include 'Higher mental processes' and 'Development psychology'. Use Section F74/87 'Psychiatry' for mental diseases and treatment. Psychological terms in this section are limited to those with a particularly educational connotation

J45.10/20	Learning
	Higher mental processes P46/59
J45.12	Learning processes
	Conceptualisation P49.30
	Memorisation P53.10
J45.12.05	Comprehension
J45.12.10	Attention
J45.12.20	Concentration
J45.12.30	Assimilation
J45.12.40	Retention
J45.12.50	Feedback (learning)
J45.12.60	Interest (learning)
	UF Curiosity
J45.12.60B	Boredom
J45.15	Learning methods
	Teaching methods J50.04/20
J45.15.05	Activity learning
J45.15.10	Verbal learning
J45.15.20	Visual learning
J45.15.25	Multisensory learning
J45.15.30	Symbolic learning
J45.15.40	Associative learning
J45.15.45	Sequential learning
J45.15.50	Rote learning
	(By persons taught)
J45.18	Adult training
	(By abilities)
J45.20.10	Learning readiness
J45.20.50	Learning disabilities
	Backwardness P47.40
J45.25	Academic achievement
	UF School achievement
J45.30/35	Educational measurement
	Examinations J40.21
J45.31	Educational assessment
	UF Educational rating
	Failure prediction (education)
	Success prediction (education)
	Talent recognition
J45.31.10	Intelligence quotient
J45.35	Educational testing
	(By individual tests)
	Reading tests J60.30.55
J45.35.10	Achievement tests
J45.35.20	Aptitude tests
J45.35.30	Intelligence tests
J45.40/69	Educational psychosociology
	(By environment)
J45.42	Educational environment
	(By behaviour and attitude)
J45.45	Teacher behaviour
J45.45.10	Teacher attitude
J45.45.20	Teacher authority
J45.45.40	Teacher participation

J45	**Educational Psychology** (cont.)
J45.40/69	Educational psychosociology (cont.)
J45.48	Student behaviour
	Truancy J45.58.40
J45.48.10	Student attitude
J45.48.30	Work attitude
J45.48.40	Student participation
	(By discipline)
J45.50	School discipline
	UF School authority
	Teacher authority J45.45.20
J45.50.20	School rewards
J45.50.30	School punishments
	UF Corporal punishment (school)
	Expulsion
	(By relationships)
J45.55	Teacher-student relationship
	(By testing)
J45.55.50	Interaction process analysis
J45.58	School-student relationship
J45.58.10	School adjustment
J45.58.20	School phobia
J45.58.40	Truancy
J45.58.50	Drop-out problem
	Educational wastage J20.03.22J
	School drop-outs J90.20.03P
J45.60	Parent-school relationship
	Parent attitude R28.20
	Parent-child relationship R28.40
	Parent participation R28.30
	Parent responsibility R28.25
	Parent role R27.30
J45.60.30	Parent-teacher relationship
J45.60.50	Parent-teacher organisations
J45.63	School-community relationship
J45.65	Teacher-administrator relationship
J45.68	Peer-group relationship
J45.70	Educational guidance
	UF Educational counselling
	Educational guidance personnel J35.05.20
J45.70.10	Vocational guidance
J45.70.30	School leaving guidance
J45.70.50	Transition from school to work
J46	**Study** (†)
	(By method of study)
J46.01	Study methods
J46.01.01	Individual study
	UF Private study
J46.01.02	Independent study
J46.01.04	Self-teaching methods
J46.01.05	Homework
	UF Home study
J46.01.07	Oral work
J46.01.09	Written work
J46.01.10	Library work (study method)
J46.01.12	Practical studies
J46.01.12B	Students projects
	(By time conditions)
J46.01.24	Study periods

J46		**Study** (cont.)
		(By subjects studied)
	J46.03	Creative writing
		Language education J60.37
		Mother tongue instruction J60.25/32
	J46.03.10	Oral composition
		(By interests)
	J46.07	Student interests
		Student sociology J14.20
	J46.07.03	Student leisure
	J46.07.06	After-school activities
		UF Extracurricular activities
	J46.07.06C	School clubs
		(By motivation)
	J46.09.02	Compulsory study
	J46.09.05	Voluntary study
		(By progress)
	J46.12	Student progress
J50		**Teaching**
	J50.01	Teaching skills
	J50.02	Teaching strategies
	J50.03	Teaching standards
	J50.04/20	Teaching methods
		Learning methods J45.15
	J50.05.10	Tutoring
		UF Coaching
	J50.05.15	Individualised instruction
	J50.05.20	Microteaching
	J50.05.30	Team teaching
		UF Group teaching
	J50.05.40	Remedial instruction
	J50.05.50	Sleep teaching
		(By type of media)
	J50.05.60	Multimedia instruction
		Multisensory learning J45.15.25
	J50.05.60A	Audiovisual instruction
		(By methods based on group learning and games theory)
	J50.06	Group work (teaching method)
	J50.06.10	Activity methods
	J50.06.20	Heuristic method (teaching)
	J50.06.25	Project method (teaching)
	J50.06.30	Play (teaching method)
	J50.06.35	Story telling
	J50.06.60	Academic games
	J50.06.65	Educational games
	J50.06.70	Dramatic presentation (teaching method)
	J50.06.75	Role playing
		(By methods identified by special names)
	J50.07	Teaching systems
		(List alphabetically by name, for example:)
	J50.07.01H	Headstart
	J50.07.01M	Monitorial system
	J50.07.01M2	Montessori system
		(By methods based on instruction by teacher)
	J50.09	Lessons
	J50.09.01	Classwork
		Rote learning J45.15.50
	J50.09.01D	Dictation
	J50.09.07	Diagrammatical teaching
	J50.09.09	Demonstrations (lessons)

J50		**Teaching** (cont.)
	J50.04/20	Teaching methods (cont.)
	J50.09	Lessons (cont.)
	J50.09.11	Experiments (lessons)
	J50.09.20	Direct method (teaching)
	J50.09.30	Tutorials
	J50.11	Lectures
		UF Expositions
	J50.11.01	Seminars
		(By methods based on group discussions)
	J50.12.06	Debates (teaching method)
	J50.12.08	Discussions (teaching method)
	J50.12.10	Questioning (teaching method)
	J50.12.14	Teach-ins (teaching method)
		(By methods based on visits and travel)
	J50.13	Educational visits
		UF School visits
		Student transportation J40.30
	J50.13.10	Educational walks
		UF School walks
	J50.13.20	Educational journeys
		UF School day trips
		School journeys
	J50.13.30	Study tours
		UF Educational travel abroad
	J50.13.30C	Educational cruises
		UF School cruises
		(By new methods)
	J50.18	Teaching method innovations
	J50.30/60	Training
		Training centres J70.14.12H
		Training courses J40.19.20
		Technical training J60.34.20
		Vocational training J60.34.20/40
		(By type of training)
	J50.40.01	Basic training
	J50.40.02	Further training
	J50.40.10	In-service training
		In-service teacher training J30.40.35
	J50.40.40	Retraining
		UF Vocational rehabilitation
		Refresher courses J40.19.24
	J50.40.60	Practical training
		UF Reality practice
		Practice teaching J30.40.37
	J50.40.70	Training abroad
		(By method)
	J50.45	Training methods
		(By organisations)
	J50.50	Training groups
		(By programmes)
	J50.55	International training programmes
J55		**Teaching Materials & Equipment**
	J55.03	Educational publications
	J55.03.01	Childrens books
	J55.03.04	Textbooks
	J55.03.04L	Textbook production
	J55.03.06	Reading materials
	J55.03.10	Teacher guides
	J55.03.20	College publications
	J55.03.24	School publications

J55		**Teaching Materials and Equipment** (cont.)
	J55.03	Educational publications (cont.)
	J55.03.30	Educational periodicals
	J55.04/15	Teaching aids

School museums T96.25

| | J55.05.01 | Educational exhibitions |

UF Educational displays

	J55.05.03	Educational collections
	J55.05.07	Educational toys
	J55.05.12	Educational laboratory equipment

SN Includes: Animals, Botanical gardens, Plants, Specimens, Realia

(By multi-media teaching aids)

| | J55.05.14 | Sensory aids (teaching) |
| | J55.05.14A | Audiovisual aids |

Audiovisual instruction J50.05.60A
Multimedia resource centres J55.20.20

| | J55.05.14AC | Chalkboards |
| | J55.05.14AD | Flannelgraphs |

For other aids use with terms from 'Audio-visual materials' at Z15.65/89

| | J55.05.14D | Tactile aids |
| | J55.05.14DB | Braille system |

(By mass media instructional aids)

	J55.07.02	Educational radio
	J55.07.03	Educational television
	J55.08	Educational films

UF Educational cinema

(By self-instruction aids)

	J55.15	Teaching machines
	J55.15.02	Automatic teaching
	J55.15.04	Computer-assisted instruction
	J55.15.06	Programmed instruction

UF Programmed materials
   Scrambled texts
   Tutor texts

(By subjects taught)

| | J55.15.10 | Language laboratories |

(By systems approach)

| | J55.17 | Educational technology |

(By resource centres)

| | J55.20 | Resource centres |

Teacher centres J70.10.45C

| | J55.20.20 | Multimedia resource centres |

UF Audio visual resource centres

J60		**Curriculum**
	J60.02	Curriculum development

UF Curriculum innovation
   Curriculum reform

	J60.02.04	Curriculum research
	J60.02.04D	Curriculum evaluation
	J60.02.04M	Curriculum study centres
	J60.02.06	Anticurriculum movement
	J60.02.06D	De-schooling
	J60.02.08	Curriculum planning

(By programmes and guides)

| | J60.03.12 | Instructional programmes |
| | J60.03.16 | Curriculum guides |

J60		**Curriculum** (cont.)
		(By type of curriculum)
	J60.05.20	Cross-disciplinary curriculum
		UF Interdisciplinary curriculum
		Multidisciplinary curriculum
	J60.05.20C	Integrated curriculum
		(By academic level)
	J60.07.10	Pre-primary curriculum
	J60.07.15	Primary school curriculum
	J60.07.18	Secondary school curriculum
	J60.07.20	Vocational school curriculum
	J60.07.30	University curriculum
	J60.07.60	Teacher training curriculum
J60.10/99		**Curriculum Subjects**
J60.11/32		**Curriculum Subjects — Basic (†)**
	J60.12	General education
	J60.15	Numeracy
	J60.17	Oracy
	J60.20	Literacy
		Reading instruction J60.30
		(By problems to be overcome)
	J60.20.10	Illiteracy
		Illiterates R84.80.10
		(By type)
	J60.20.15	Functional literacy
		(By person taught)
	J60.20.20	Adult literacy
		New literates J90.20.16
		(By instructors)
		Literacy workers J35.03.70
		(By methods)
	J60.20.30	Literacy methodology
	J60.20.30C	Literacy classes
		(By organisational activities)
	J60.20.50	Literacy campaigns
		UF Literacy projects
	J60.20.55	Literacy programmes
	J60.20.55D	Post-literacy programmes
	J60.20.70	Literacy promotion
	J60.25/32	Mother tongue instruction
		Creative writing J46.03
		Language education J60.37
	J60.26	Vocabulary instruction
		Vocabulary X46.10
	J60.27	Conversation instruction
		Conversation Y45.18
		Speech education J60.80.30
	J60.28	Listening instruction
		Listening Y45.40
		Story telling J50.06.35
	J60.28.10	Nursery rhymes
	J60.28.20	Fairy tales
	J60.30	Reading instruction
		Literacy J60.20
		Reading habit Y45.60.30
		Reading Y45.60
		Reading materials J55.03.06
		(By type of reading)
	J60.30.10	Oral reading
	J60.30.15	Silent reading

J60		**Curriculum** (cont.)
J60.10/99		**Curriculum Subjects** (cont.)
J60.11/32		**Curriculum Subjects — Basic** (cont.)
	J60.25/32	Mother tongue instruction (cont.)
	J60.30	Reading instruction (cont.)
	J60.30.18	Speed reading
		(By methods of instruction)
	J60.30.20	Initial teaching alphabet
	J60.30.25	Sight method
		(By level of ability)
	J60.30.32	Reading ability
	J60.30.35	Reading readiness
		(By problems)
	J60.30.45	Reading problems
		(By tests)
	J60.30.55	Reading tests
		(By programmes)
	J60.30.60	Reading programmes
		(By research)
	J60.30.70	Reading research
	J60.31	Spelling instruction *Spelling X40.40*
	J60.32	Handwriting instruction *Handwriting Y45.30.05*

J60.33/35   **Curriculum Subjects — Vocational and Professional** (†)

	J60.34	Vocational education *Vocational colleges J70.10.40/60*
	J60.34.10	Pre-vocational education
	J60.34.20/40	Vocational training *Vocational schools J70.07.09K*
	J60.34.20	Job training
	J60.34.30	Technical training
	J60.34.30A	Apprenticeship *Apprentice training schools J70.14.12HA*
	J60.34.30J	Industrial training *Industrial training courses J40.19.20C*
	J60.34.30L	Group training
	J60.34.50	Cooperative education UF Work experience programmes
	J60.35	Professional training UF Professional education *Archive science training Z90.70* *Communication personnel training Y30* *Cultural personnel training T49* *Information/library training Z38* *Social workers training R91.50* *Teacher training J30.40*

J60.36/99   **Curriculum Subjects — Traditional Disciplines** (†)

	J60.37	Language education UF Language learning Literature education *Language laboratories J55.15.10* *Mother tongue instruction J60.25/32*
	J60.37.10	Language teaching
	J60.38	Mathematics education
	J60.38.10	Modern mathematics
	J60.38.40	Statistics education
	J60.40	Science education
	J60.40.10	Basic science education
	J60.40.15	Physics education
	J60.40.20	Chemistry education

J60		**Curriculum** (cont.)
J60.10/99		**Curriculum subjects** (cont.)
J60.36/99		**Curriculum subjects—traditional disciplines** (cont.)
	J60.40	Science education (cont.)
	J60.40.40	Geology education
	J60.40.50	Geography education
	J60.40.65	Hydrology education
	J60.40.70	Oceanography education
	J60.40.75	Biology education
	J60.41	Computer science education
	J60.42	Medical education
	J60.42.10	Veterinary education
	J60.43	Psychology education
	J60.45	Technical education
		Technical training J60.34.20
		(By level)
	J60.45.10	General technical education
	J60.45.20	Pre-university science education
	J60.45.25	Higher technical education
		(By subject)
	J60.45.60	Engineering education
	J60.47	Military education
	J60.48	Agricultural education
	J60.48.10	Agricultural training
	J60.50	Environmental education
	J60.52	Health education
	J60.52.10	Alcohol education
	J60.52.20	Drug education
	J60.52.30	Nutrition education
	J60.52.40	Population education
	J60.52.50	Sex education
	J60.54	Safety education
	J60.56	Physical education
	J60.58	Humanities education
	J60.59	History education
	J60.60	Social science education
	J60.60.20	Social studies
	J60.62	Development education
	J60.63	Economics education
	J60.64	Commercial education
	J60.65	Distributive education
	J60.67	Management education
		UF Business education
	J60.70	Legal education
	J60.72	Civic education
		UF Citizenship education
	J60.72.10	Education for peace
	J60.73	Political science education
	J60.75	Religious education
	J60.77	Moral education
	J60.80	Cultural education
	J60.80.10	Music education
	J60.80.20	Movement studies
		UF Dancing studies
		Mime studies
		Poetry and movement studies

J60		**Curriculum** (cont.)
J60.10/99		**Curriculum Subjects** (cont.)
J60.36/99		**Curriculum Subjects — Traditional Disciplines** (cont.)
	J60.80	Cultural education (cont.)
	J60.80.30	Speech education
		UF Elocution education
	J60.80.40	Drama education
	J60.80.50	Art education
	J60.80.60	Architecture education
	J60.85	Handicrafts education
	J60.90	Domestic science education
		UF Home economics education
	J60.92	Catering education

For other subjects combine 'Curriculum' with terms in whole classification system.

J70   **Educational Systems and Institutions** (†)

	J70.01.02	Educational systems
		UF National educational systems
	J70.01.04	Educational institutions
		(By ownership)
	J70.02.02	Public education
		UF Public schools
		State education
		State schools
	J70.02.04	Private education
		UF Fee paying schools
		Independent schools
		Private schools
		(By financial and legal conditions)
	J70.03.04	Free education
	J70.03.08	Compulsory education
		(By location)
	J70.04.04	Boarding schools
		UF Residential education
		Residential schools
	J70.04.10	Home education
		Family education J70.17
		Pre-school education J70.07.03
	J70.04.20	Mobile educational services
		Mobile schools J70.07.09T
	J70.04.40	Urban education
	J70.04.45	Rural education

J70.07   **Schools**
Schoolchildren J90.04

		(By overall systems)
	J70.07.01	School systems
		(By level of education)
	J70.07.03	Pre-school education
		UF Early childhood education
	J70.07.04	Pre-primary education
		UF Pre-primary schools
	J70.07.04B	Nursery schools
		UF Kindergarten
	J70.07.04D	Day nurseries
		UF Creches
	J70.07.04K	Play groups
	J70.07.05	Primary education

J70		**Educational Systems and Institutions** (cont.)
J70.07		**Schools** (cont.)
	J70.07.05	Primary education (cont.)

        UF Elementary education
           First stage education
           Primary schools

J70.07.07   Secondary education
               UF Secondary stage education
                   Secondary schools

(By stages of secondary education)
J70.07.07B   Lower secondary education
J70.07.07C   Middle secondary education
J70.07.07D   Upper secondary education
J70.07.07G   Sixth forms
               UF Pre-university forms
                   Scholarship forms
                   Sixth form colleges
                   Top forms

(Schools by sex of student)
J70.07.08B   Boys schools

J70.07.08G   Girls schools

J70.07.08K   Coeducational schools

(Exceptional schools for normal children)
J70.07.09   Exceptional schools
         (By type of administration)
J70.07.09A   Experimental schools
J70.07.09E   One-teacher schools
J70.07.09G   Parochial schools
J70.07.09H   International schools
         (By curriculum)
J70.07.09K   Vocational schools
         (By religion)
J70.07.09L   Denominational schools
J70.07.09LC   Catholic schools
                   UF Convent schools

(By outdoor activities)
J70.07.09N   Holiday schools
               UF Camp schools
J70.07.09P   Open air schools
         (By mobility)
J70.07.09T   Mobile schools
               UF Itinerant schools
         Itinerant teachers J35.03.42
J70.07.09V   Ship schools
            Educational cruises J50.13.30C

(Special schools for exceptional children)
J70.07.11   Special schools
         Special education J70.26.10
J70.07.11A   Reformatory schools
               UF Correctional schools
                   Detention centres (schools)

(Schools peculiar to one or to several countries)
J70.07.15   National school types

List alphabetically, for example:
J70.07.15C   Community schools
               UF All age schools
                   Community colleges
J70.07.15CO   Comprehensive schools
               UF Multilateral schools
J70.07.15J   Junior colleges (USA)
J70.07.15L   Lycees
J70.07.15PO   Polytechnic schools (USSR)

J		**Education**

J70   **Educational Systems and Institutions** (cont.)

J70.07   Schools (cont.)

J70.07.15   National school types List alphabetically, for example: (cont.)

J70.07.15V   Volksschule

J70.08/10   **Higher Education**

UF Post-secondary education
Tertiary education
Third stage education
Students (college) J90.07

J70.10.09/10   Colleges
J70.10.10   Universities
J70.10.10A   University colleges
J70.10.10B   University institutes
J70.10.10H   Technological institutes
      UF Technological universities
J70.10.10J   Academies of science
J70.10.10L   Open universities
      UF Radio universities
      Universities-of-the-air
J70.10.10M   International universities
J70.10.10P   Polytechnics
J70.10.20   Technical colleges
      UF Technical schools
J70.10.30   Liberal arts colleges
J70.10.40/60   Vocational colleges
      Journalist schools Y30.40.10
      Information/Library schools Z38.20
      Vocational education J60.34
J70.10.45   Teacher training schools
J70.10.45C   Teachers centres
J70.10.50   Agricultural colleges

J70.11/13   **Out-of-School Education**

J70.12.30   Non-formal education
J70.13   Youth activities
J70.13.03   Youth movements
J70.13.05   Youth organisations
      UF Girl guides
      Scouts
      Students organisations J14.20.10
J70.13.05C   Youth clubs
J70.13.08   Youth participation

J70.14   **Adult Education**

UF Further education
Adult learning J45.18
(By persons taught)
Womens education J70.22
J70.14.02A   Workers education
J70.14.02P   Parent education
(By subjects studied)
Adult literacy J60.20.20
J70.14.04   Adult basic education
      UF Fundamental education
J70.14.04C   Polyvalent adult education
(By conditions of study)
J70.14.06   Leisure and education
(By teachers)
Adult educators J35.03.25

J70		**Educational Systems and Institutions** (cont.)
J70.14		**Adult Education** (cont.)
		(By organisation and programmes)
	J70.14.08	Adult education programmes
		(By institutions)
	J70.14.12	Adult education institutions
	J70.14.12B	Extension education
	J70.14.12BC	University extension
	J70.14.12BH	Agricultural extension
	J70.14.12E	Evening schools
		UF Evening colleges
		Evening courses
	J70.14.12H	Training centres
		Vocational schools J70.07.09K
	J70.14.12HA	Apprentice training schools
		UF Industrial schools
		Workshop schools
	J70.14.12L	Summer schools
J70.15/20		**Continuing Community and Mass Education**
	J70.16	Life-long education
		UF Continuous education
		Continuing education
		Permanent education
		Post-school education
	J70.16.10	Recurrent education
	J70.16.30	Informal education
	J70.16.50	Compensatory education
	J70.17	Family education
	J70.18	Community education
	J70.18.04	Community development
	J70.18.08	Community centres
	J70.19	Mass education
J70.21/50		**Education of Specific Categories of Students** (†)
	J70.22	Womens education
		UF Girls education
	J70.23	Mens education
		UF Boys education
	J70.24	Coeducation
	J70.26	Exceptional student education
		Exceptional students J90.20
		Special schools J70.07.11
	J70.26.10	Special education
		SN Education of physically and mentally handicapped
	J70.26.10B	Education of the blind
	J70.26.10D	Education of the deaf
		For others combine 'Special education' with terms at R79/84 and at J90.20
	J70.26.30	Migrant education
	J70.26.40	Refugee education
		For others, combine 'Exceptional child education' with terms in the R (Sociology) section
J90		**Students**
		Rights of students M95.60
		(By age groups)
	J90.03	Pre-school children
		SN Children under five years
	J90.04	Schoolchildren
	J90.07	Students (college)
		Student sociology J14.20

J90		**Students** (cont.)
	J90.07	Students (college) (cont.)
	J90.07.01	Undergraduates
		UF Freshmen
	J90.07.03	Graduates
		UF Postgraduates
	J90.07.09	Scholarship-holders
	J90.09	Out-of-school youth
	J90.09.01	Apprentices
	J90.12	Adult students
	J90.12.06	Trainees
		(By sex of students)
	J90.14.02	Women students
		UF Girl students
	J90.14.04	Men students
		UF Boy students
		(By exceptional students)
	J90.20	Exceptional students
		*Exceptional student education J70.26
	J90.20.01A	Geniuses
		UF Prodigies
	J90.20.01B	Gifted students
		UF Able students
		High achievers
	J90.20.01D	Overachievers
		(By low ability or achievement)
	J90.20.03A	Ineducable
	J90.20.03B	Backward students
		UF Retarded students
	J90.20.03C	Educationally subnormal
		UF ESN
	J90.20.03E	Low achievers
		UF Underachievers
	J90.20.03H	Slow learners
		UF Dull students
		Low ability students
	J90.20.03L	Late developers
	J90.20.03P	School drop-outs
		UF School failures
		(By place of origin)
	J90.20.07	Foreign students
		UF Alien students
		(By recently acquired literacy)
	J90.20.16	New literates

For other categories of students combine 'Students' with appropriate terms from the Social sciences section (in particular R79/84) for example:

         Students & Migrants

         Students & Physically handicapped

         Students & Blind

         Students & Maladjusted

         Students & Illiteracy

         Students & Refugees

K/S	**SOCIAL SCIENCES** Summary
K	**Social sciences (general)**
L	**Political science**
M	**Law**
N	**Economics. Finance**
P	**Behavioural sciences. Psychology**
Q05/44	**Administrative sciences**
Q45/99	**Labour and employment**
R	**Sociology**
S	**Human environment**

K   Social Sciences (General)

K10   Social science research

K20/25   Social science policy

K30/50   Social science planning and administration

K60   Social science personnel

K   **Social Sciences (General)**

SN For general studies of the subject.
   For specific social science subjects, see Section L/S of
   the classification, namely:
Administrative sciences Q05/44
Behavioural sciences P
Economics N
Employment and labour Q45/99
Human environment S
Political science L
Sociology R
See also
Social science education J60.60
Social science information Z08.30

K10   **Social Science Research**
Economics research N04
Market research N70.20
Population research R10.42
Psychological research P12/15

K10.20   Sociography

For specific techniques, etc. combine with terms in A70/99 Research

K20/25   **Social Science Policy**

K25   Social science development

K30/50   **Social Science Planning and Administration (†)**

K35   Social science planning
K45   Social science administration
K50   Social science organizations
K50.40   Social science institutions

K60   **Social Science Personnel**
Social workers R91

K60.10   Social scientists
K60.10.10   Sociologists
K60.30   Economists
K60.40   Psychologists

L   Political Science

L03   Political history

L05   Political development

L06/19   Political philosophy

L08/17   Political theory

L20/59   State

L22/31   Political systems

L32   Constitutional law

L34   Administrative law

L35/49   Government

L50/55   State security

L56/59   Law enforcement

L60/79   Internal politics

L80/99   International politics

L		**Political Science**
		Political science education J60.73
L03		**Political History**
L04		**Politics**
		Internal politics L60/79
		International politics L80/99
L05		**Political Development**
		Democratization R66.40
	L05.10	Political reform
L06/19		**Political Philosophy**
		Civil and political rights M92
L07		**Political Ethics**
		Political behaviour L76
L08/17		**Political Theory**
		UF Political thought
	L09/17	Political doctrines
		UF Political ideologies
		(By doctrines based on economic distribution)
	L10.10	Feudalism
	L10.20	Capitalism
		Capitalist systems N26.20
	L10.30	Collectivism
		Collectivist economy N26.70
	L10.30.10	Socialism
		Labour movement Q62
	L10.30.30	Communism
		UF Marxism-Leninism
		Bolshevism
	L10.70	Utopia
		(By doctrines relating to the power of the state versus individuals)
	L11.10	Totalitarianism
		UF Absolutism
		Authoritarianism
	L11.10.20	Fascism
	L11.10.20B	Nazism
		Racism R44.20
	L11.30	Liberalism
		Tolerance P73.45
	L11.40	Pluralism
	L11.50	Anarchism
		UF Nihilism
		Anarchy L26
		(By doctrines concerning the states relation with other states)
	L13.10	Neutralism
	L13.20	Isolationism
	L13.22	Separatism
	L13.25	Federalism
		Federation L28.20
	L13.28	Regionalism
	L13.30	Nationalism
		Cultural nationalism T58.35/50
		Tribalism R35.50
		Ethnocentrism T58.20
		National prestige R48.40
		Fascism L11.10.20
		Nazism L11.10.20B
	L13.35	Patriotism
	L13.40	Internationalism
	L13.45	Imperialism

L06/19		**Political Philosophy** (cont.)
L08/17		**Political Theory** (cont.)
	L09/17	Political doctrines (cont.)
	L13.50	Colonialism (cont.)
		Colonies L30.10
		Colonization L30.10.10
	L13.50.10	Neocolonialism
	L13.60	Militarism
		Anti-militarism L93.30
		(By doctrines relating to the receptivity to change)
	L16.10	Conservatism
	L16.30	Traditionalism
	L16.70	Radicalism

L20/59		**State**
		Church and state V63
		Nations R46/49
		State and education J10.40

L22/31		**Political Systems**
		UF Political regimes
		Political structures
		(By systems with single head of state)
	L23.05	Theocracy
	L23.10	Dictatorship
		UF Despotism
		Autocracy
		Fascism L11.10.20
		Nazism L11.10.20B
		Totalitarianism L11.10
		Tyranny L27
	L23.30	Monarchy
	L23.40	Empire
	L23.60	Republic
	L23.70	Presidential systems
		(By system having group rule)
	L24	Oligarchy
		Elite R57
		Aristocracy R56.30.10
	L24.30	Technocracy
		UF Meritocracy
		(By systems with rule by whole population)
	L25	Democracy
	L25.10	Representative democracy
	L25.10.10	Parliamentary systems
		UF Parliamentarianism
		Electoral systems L63
		(By systems with absence of rule)
	L26	Anarchy
		Anarchism L11.50
		(By systems with lack of freedom)
	L27	Tyranny
		Dictatorship L23.10
		Oppression L74
		Slavery R55.10
		Totalitarianism L11.10
		(By degree of centralization)
	L28.10	Unitary state
	L28.20	Federation
		UF Confederation
		Union (state)
		Federalism L13.25

L20/59		**State** (cont.)
L22/31		**Political Systems** (cont.)
	L28.20	Federation (cont.)
	L28.20.40	Member states
	L28.70	World government
		UF World state
		(By degree of control by government)
	L29	Self-government
		UF Atuonomous state
	L29.50	Newly-independent states
	L30	Non-self-governing territories
	L30.10	Colonies
		Colonialism L13.50
	L30.10.10	Colonization
	L30.10.50	Decolonization
	L30.40	Protectorates
	L30.60	Trust territories
L32		**Constitutional Law**
		Civil and political rights M92
	L32.10	Constitutions
	L32.10.10	Constitutional history
	L32.15	Rule of law
		UF Supremacy of the law
	L32.20/70	Political power
		UF Government power
		Political authority
		Economic power N23.50
		Sovereignty M85.10
	L32.25	Separation of powers
	L32.25.10	Independent judiciary
		(By type)
	L32.30	Legislative power
	L32.40	Judicial power
		UF Judicial review of constitution
	L32.50	Executive power
		(By specific powers)
	L32.60	Emergency powers
	L32.80	Citizenship
	L32.80.05	Nationality
		Right to nationality M92.40
	L32.80.10	Statelessness
	L32.80.20	Naturalization
		UF Denaturalization
L34		**Administrative Law**
	L34.10	Judicial control of administration
	L34.10.10	Administrative tribunals
		UF Courts of enquiry
	L34.10.30	Public enquiries
	L34.10.50	Ombudsman
L35/49		**Government**
	L36/41	Political institutions
	L37	Legislature
		UF Chamber of deputies
		Parliament
		Legislative power L32.30
		Parliamentary systems L25.10.10
		(By activities)
	L37.10	Legislative enactment

L20/59		**State** (cont.)
L35/49		**Government** (cont.)
	L36/41	Political institutions (cont.)
	L37	Legislature (cont.)
		(By type)
	L37.20	Single chamber legislature
		UF Unicameral legislature
	L37.25	Two chamber legislature
		UF Bicameral legislature
	L35.25.10	Lower house
		UF Congress
	L35.25.30	Upper house
		UF Senate
		(By members)
	L37.60	Members of parliament
		UF Congressmen
		Deputies
		Senators
	L38	Judiciary
		Independent judiciary L32.25.10
		Judicial control of administration L34.10
		Judicial power L32.40
	L39/41	Executive government
		Executive power L32.50
		Judicial control of administration L34.10
		(By part)
	L40.10	Head of state
		UF Sovereign
	L40.10.10	Presidency
	L40.30	Cabinet
	L40.40	Prime minister
	L40.50	Ministers
		UF Secretaries of State
		(By policy)
	L41	National policy
	L41.10	Government policy
	L42/49	Public administration
		Administrative law L34
		Administration of justice M33/39
		Economic administration N11.40
		Educational administration J20.08
		Government organizations Q13
		Law enforcement L56/59
		Social welfare administration R90
		(By action)
	L43.30	Government control
		UF Bureaucratic control
		State control
		State intervention
		Nationalization N26.30.10
		(By agencies)
	L44	Central government
		UF Federal government
		National government
		Central government organizations Q13.10
	L44.10	Civil service
		Bureaucracy Q11
		(By parts)
	L44.10.10	Government departments
		UF Ministries
		(By personnel)
	L44.10.70	Civil servants
		UF Public servants
	L46	Decentralized government

L20/59		**State** (cont.)
L35/49		**Government** (cont.)
	L42/49	Public administration (cont.)
	L46	Decentralized government (cont.)
	L46.10	Regional government

UF Colonial government
     Provincial government
     State government
     Regional government organizations Q13.30

	L46.30	Local government

UF Country government
     District government
     Local government organizations Q13.60

	L46.30.10	Municipal government

UF City government

	L48	Statutory bodies

Public enterprises Q12.30

L50/55   **State Security**
Defence L89

	L53	Armed forces

UF Defence forces
     Military forces
Military engineering G66
Peace-keeping forces L94.70.10
War L90

		(By personnel)
	L53.10	Military personnel

UF Soldiers

		(By law)
	L53.30	Military law

UF Martial law
Rights of soldiers M95.70

	L53.30.10	Conscription
	L53.30.30	Superior orders
	L53.30.40	Insubordination
	L53.30.50	Mutiny
		(By defence sector)
	L53.50	Armies
	L53.55	Navies
	L53.60	Air forces
	L53.80	Civil defence

L56/59   **Law enforcement**

UF Internal security
     Public order

	L57/59	Police

Crime R75/78

		(By powers)
	L58.05	Police powers
		(By abuse of powers)
	L58.10	Police brutality
		(By activities)
	L59	Police activities
	L59.10	Social protection
	L59.20	Theft protection
	L59.30	Search and seizure
	L59.30.10	Search warrants
	L59.35	Arrest
	L59.35.10	Warrant of arrest
	L59.40	Detention

UF Custody
     Preventive detention

L20/59		**State** (cont.)
L56/59		**Law Enforcement** (cont.)
	L57/59	Police (cont.)
	L59	Police activities (cont.)
	L59.40	Detention (cont.)

                                       Remand in custody M37.50.10
                                       Prisons R78.50

	L59.50/80	Criminal investigation
		(By persons)
	L59.55	Detectives
		(By process)
	L59.60	Evidence gathering
		Evidence M38
		Forensic medicine F95.50
	L59.60.10	Interception of communication
		UF Wire tapping
	L59.60.30	Interrogation

L60/79		**Internal Politics**
		UF Domestic affairs
		Internal affairs
		(By leadership and personnel)
	L61	Political leadership
		UF Political leaders
		Ruling class R57.10
	L61.10	Politicians
		Members of parliament L37.60
		(By parties)
	L62	Political parties
		UF Political factions
		Party system
	L62.05	One-party systems
	L62.10	Two-party systems
	L62.15	Multiparty systems
	L62.30	Political majorities
	L62.35	Political minorities
		Political opposition L68/73
		(By electoral system)
	L63	Electoral systems
		UF Voting system
	L63.05	Elections
		(By representation)
	L63.10	Political representation
		UF Suffrage
		Vote qualification
	L63.10.20	Equal representation
		UF Universal representation
		Right to vote and be elected M92.55
	L63.10.30	Womens suffrage
	L63.10.40	Proportional representation
	L63.10.60	Disenfranchisement
		(By ballot system)
	L63.60	Secret ballot
		(By popular vote)
	L63.80	Referendum
		UF Popular vote
		(By crisis)
	L64	Political crises
	L64.10	Political conflict
		(By action)
	L65/74	Political action
		Political development L05

L60/79		**Internal Politics** (cont.)
	L65/74	Political action (cont.)
	L66	Political support
	L68/73	Political opposition
		(By movements)
	L69	Political movements
		Labour movement Q62
	L69.10	Protest movements
	L69.30	Revolutionary movements
	L69.60	Liberation movements
	L69.60.10	Womens liberation movement
		UF Feminist movement
		Womens suffrage L63.10.30
		Womens rights M95.10
		Womens organizations Q14.70
		(By legitimate methods of opposition)
	L71	Legitimate opposition
		Pressure groups Y60.50.30
	L71.10	Petitioning
	L71.20	Non-violence
		UF Non-violent protest
		Passive resistance L74.80.20
	L71.30	Demonstrations
		(By non-legitimate methods of opposition)
	L73	Civil disturbances
		Civil war L90.15
	L73.10	Subversive activities
		UF Sedition
		Treason
		Conspiracy
	L73.10.10	Sabotage
	L73.20	Riots
	L73.30	Revolution
		UF Coup d'etat
		Insurrection
		Rebellion
	L73.35	Incitement to hate and violence
	L73.60	Guerilla activities
	L73.65	Terrorism
		Hi-jacking R76.35
		Hostage-holding R76.50
		Kidnapping R76.48
		(By action against the individual)
	L74	Oppression
		UF Deprivation of liberty
		Persecution
		Servitude
		Compulsory labour Q52.50.30
		Discrimination R54.10
		Inhuman treatment R78.15
		Police brutality L58.10
		Restriction on movement R78.20.60
		Slavery R55.10
	L74.20	Abuse of power
	L74.25	Intimidation
		(By resistance to oppress)
	L74.80	Resistance to oppression
		Right to resist oppression M92.35
	L74.80.20	Passive resistance
		(By political sociology)
	L75/77	Political sociology
		Political conflict L64.10
	L76	Political behaviour
	L76.10	Political attitude

L60/79		**Internal Politics** (cont.)
	L75/77	Political sociology (cont.)
	L76	Political behaviour (cont.)
	L76.20	Political participation
		UF Participation in politics
	L76.50	Political corruption
	L77	Political life

L80/99   **International Politics**
International law M70/89

(By organizations)
L81   International organizations
                  Member states L28.20.40
L81.10   Intergovernment organizations
L81.20   Non-governmental organizations
L81.70   Regional organizations
                  UF International regional organizations

(By cooperation)
L82/84   International cooperation
                  Cultural cooperation T26
                  Educational cooperation J20.08.50
                  Scientific cooperation B18
L83   Regional cooperation
                  UF Supranational regional cooperation
L84   International assistance
L84.40   Foreign aid
L84.50   Development aid
L84.50.20   Economic aid
L84.50.30   Financial aid
L84.50.60   Technical assistance
L84.50.80   Voluntary contribution

(By countries)
L84.60   Donor countries
                  UF Aid giving countries
L84.65   Recipient countries
                  UF Receiving countries

(By international relations)
L85/99   International relations
L86   Foreign relations
                  National prestige R48.40
L86.05   Foreign policy
L86.20   Diplomacy
                  UF Consular service
                       Diplomatic activity
                       Diplomatic service
                  Cultural diplomacy T26.20
L86.20.40   Diplomatic immunity
L86.30   Alliances
L86.40   Neutrality
                  Neutralism L13.10
L86.40.10   Neutral countries
L86.60   Non-aligned countries
L87   International equilibrium
                  UF Balance of power
L87.40   Collective security
L88   International conflict
L88.10   International tension
L88.15   Cold war
L88.40   Symmetrical conflict
L88.45   Asymmetrical conflict

L80/99		**International Politics** (cont.)
	L85/99	International relations (cont.)
	L88	International conflict (cont.)
		(By measures short of war)
	L88.50	Reprisals
	L88.55	Diplomatic relations suspension
	L88.60	Ultimatum
	L88.70	Economic sanctions
		Embargoes N75.60.40
	L89	Defence
		State security L50/55
	L89.10	Non-violent defence
	L89.30	Armament process
		Disarmament L96
	L89.30.10	Arms race
	L89.30.40	Arms sales
	L90	War
		UF Armed conflict
		Humanitarian law M98
		Military engineering G66
		War disadvantaged R84.45
		War propaganda Y60.55.20
		Peace-making L97
		Warfare G66.20
		(By studies)
	L90.05	Polemology
		UF War studies
		(By type)
	L90.10	World war
	L90.15	Civil war
		(By participants)
	L90.20	Aggressor nations
	L90.25	Belligerents
		(By action)
	L90.30	War aggression
	L90.30.10	Invasion
	L90.40	Self-defence (war)
		(By results)
	L90.60	War devastated countries
		War relief M98.70/80
	L91	Post-war measures
	L91.30	War reparations
	L93	Peace
		UF World peace
	L93.10	International understanding
	L93.15	International entente
	L93.20	Peaceful coexistence
	L93.30	Anti-militarism
	L93.50	Pacifism
	L93.50.10	Conscientious objection
	L94.50	Negative peace
		UF Passive world peace
	L94.60	Positive peace
		UF Active world peace
	L94.70	Controlled peace
	L94.70.10	Peace-keeping forces
		(By research)
	L95	Peace research
		UF Irenic studies
		Conflict research P83.70
		(By actions)
	L96	Disarmament
		Armament process L89.30

L80/99		**International Politics** (cont.)
	L85/99	International relations (cont.)
	L93	Peace (cont.)
	L96	Disarmament (cont.)
		Nuclear weapons G66.70.30
		Weapons G66.70
	L96.05	Arms control
		UF Gradual disarmament
	L96.10	Non-proliferation treaties
	L97	Peace-making
		UF Peace settlement
		Diplomacy L86.20
		Post-war measures L91
		Peace treaties M75.10.10
		Truces M98.10

M   Law

M04	**Legal history**
M06	**Sociology of law**
M08	**Law reform**
M10	**Legislation**
M15/29	**Legal theory**
M30/32	**Legal profession**
M33/39	**Administration of justice**
M40/49	**Legal systems**
M50/54	**Public law**
M52	**Criminal law**
M55/68	**Civil law**
M70/89	**International law**
M90/99	**Human rights**
M98	**Humanitarian law**

M   **Law**

UF Legal sciences
Law enforcement L56/59
Legal education J60.70

M04   **Legal History**

M06   **Sociology of Law**

M08   **Law Reform**

UF Legal reform

M10   **Legislation**

UF Laws
Archive legislation Z88.60.10
Communication legislation Y20.80
Cultural legislation T33
Economic legislation N11.40.40
Educational legislation J20.08.30
Environmental legislation E54
Information/library legislation Z30.65
Population legislation R10.80.50

M10.10   Statutes
UF Acts

M10.10.20   Bills

M10.20   Regulations
UF Prerogative instruments
Statutory instruments

M15/29   **Legal Theory**

UF Jurisprudence

M16   Analytical jurisprudence
M16.10   Concept of law
UF Nature of law
M16.40   Sources of law
M17   Justice
Social justice R05.10

M18   Rights and privileges
UF Immunities
Diplomatic immunity L86.20.40
Human rights M90/99
Rights of states M84/89

M20   Schools of legal theory
M20.10   Natural law
M26   Comparative law

M30/32   **Legal Profession**

Legal education J60.70

M31.20   Legal advice
Legal aid R95.10.40

M31.30   Advocacy
M32   Lawyers
UF Barristers
Solicitors
Notaries

M33/39   **Administration of Justice**

UF Legal administration
Right to justice M92.80/99

M34   Courts
UF Tribunals
Administrative tribunals L34.10.10
International courts M77.30

M33/39		**Administration of Justice** (cont.)
	M34	Courts (cont.)
	M34.10	Supreme court
	M34.20	Higher courts
	M34.30	Appeal courts
	M34.40	Lower courts
		UF Magistrates courts
	M34.50	Criminal courts
	M34.60	Juvenile courts
	M35	Law officers
	M35.10	Judges
	M35.20	Magistrates
	M35.30	Public prosecutors
	M35.60	Juries
		UF Jurists
		Trial by jury M37.20.30
	M36/39	Legal practice and procedure
		UF Due process of law
		Judicial proceedings
		Law suits
		Legal actions
		Litigation
	M37.10	Hearings
		Right to fair hearing M92.90
	M37.20	Trials
	M37.20.10	Trial in camera
	M37.20.30	Trial by jury
	M37.20.60	Political trials
		(By parties to action)
	M37.30	Defendants
		UF Accused
		Rights of accused M92.95
	M37.35	Plaintiffs
	M37.40	Counsel (legal)
		Right to counsel M92.95.10
		Right to legal aid M95.95.20
		(By court rules and procedures)
	M37.50	Court rules and procedures
	M37.50.10	Remand in custody
		UF Detention awaiting trial
	M37.50.20	Bail
	M37.50.40	Contempt of court
		(By pre-trial activity)
	M37.60	Summons
	M37.65	Brief preparation
		UF Defence preparation (legal)
		(By trial/hearing practice)
	M37.70	Pleadings
	M37.80	Mediation
	M37.80.10	Arbitration
	M37.80.20	Conciliation
		(By evidence)
	M38	Evidence
		UF Burden of proof
		Documentary evidence
		Privileged evidence
		Evidence gathering L59.60
		(By form of evidence)
	M38.30	Witnesses
		(By admissibility of evidence)
	M38.40	Admissibility of evidence
		UF Expert testimonies
		Direct evidence

M33/39		**Administration of Justice** (cont.)
	M36/39	Legal practice and procedure (cont.)
	M38	Evidence (cont.)
	M38.40	Admissibility of evidence (cont.)

Circumstantial evidence
Hearsay
Confession

		(By remedies)
	M39	Legal decisions
		UF Legal costs
		Legal damages
		Legal remedies
	M39.10	Judgments
		UF Sentencing
		Verdicts
		Punishment R78
	M39.10.10	Acquittal
	M39.10.20	Conviction (legal)
	M39.10.40	Decrees
	M39.30	Injunctions
	M39.70	Appeals (legal)
M40/49		**Legal Systems**
		UF Jurisdictions
		(By period)
	M41	Historical systems of law
	M41.10	Antiquarian law
		UF Roman law
	M41.30	Code Napoleon
	M41.40	Moslem law
		UF Islamic law
	M42	Primitive law
	M43	Modern law
		(By forms of law)
	M44	Customary law
		UF Common law
	M45	Codified law
		UF Statute law
	M46	Case law
	M46.20	Law reports
	M48	Ecclesiastical law
		UF Common law
		Church law
		Religious law
		(By nationality)
		For law and legal codes of individual countries combine 'legal systems' with name of country, e.g.
		French law (France & Legal systems)
M50/54		**Public Law**
		Administrative law L34
		Constitutional law L32
		Military law L53.30
	M52	Criminal law
		Crime R75/78
M55/68		**Civil Law**
		UF Private law
	M56	Contract law
	M56.10	Contracts

M55/68		**Civil Law** (cont.)
	M56	Contract law (cont.)
	M56.30	Agreements
	M56.40	Conventions
	M56.50	Charters
	M57	Torts
	M57.20	Liability (legal)
	M57.40	Libel
	M57.70	Trespass
	M58	Commercial law
	M58.30	Company law
	M60/64	Property law

UF Realty law
Right to property M93.45

	M61	Inheritance law
	M62	Real property law
	M62.40	Water law
	M64	Personal property law
	M64.10/50	Intellectual property

UF Industrial property
Patents A67.10
Trade marks A67.70
Right of intellectual property M94.30

	M64.20	Copyright
	M64.20.10	Copyright transfer
	M64.30	Literary property
	M64.35	Artistic property
	M64.50	Neighbouring rights
	M66	Family law

Adoption R96.10.30
Divorce R22.35.30
Marriage R22
Rights of the child M95.05
Womens rights M95.10

	M67	Labour law

UF Industrial law
Labour legislation

M70/89		**International Law**
	M72	Private international law
	M72.20	Conflict of laws
M74/89		**Public International Law**
	M75	International instruments

UF International agreements
International covenants
International conventions
International declarations
International statements
International recommendations
Alliances L86.30
Cultural agreements T26.10
Economic agreements N75.80

	M75.10	Treaties

Non-proliferation treaties L96.10

	M75.10.10	Peace treaties

(Instruments by characteristics and aspects)

	M75.30	Bilateral agreements
	M75.35	Reciprocal agreements
	M75.40	Most favoured nation

M70/89		**International Law** (cont.)
M74/89		**Public International Law** (cont.)
	M75	International instruments (cont.)
		(Instruments by processes)
	M75.60	Ratification
	M77	International disputes
	M77.20	International arbitration
	M77.30	International courts
		(By subject)
	M79	Law of the sea
		UF Freedom of the seas
		International maritime law
		International waters
		Piracy at sea
		Territorial waters M86.20
		Sea transport S58.10
	M80	Law of the air
		UF Freedom of the air
		International law of the air
		Air transport S56
		Territorial air space M86.30
	M81	Law of space
		UF International space law
		(By rights and responsibility of states)
	M84/89	Rights of states
		Collective human rights M96
	M85.10	Sovereignty
		UF Independence of state
	M85.20	Recognition rights
	M85.30	Equality of states
	M85.50	State responsibility
	M85.70	State succession
		UF Sovereignty
		Right of self-determination M96.20
	M86	Territorial rights
	M86.10	Boundaries
		UF Frontiers
	M86.20	Territorial waters
		UF Territorial seas
		Navigational waters
	M86.20.10	Fishing rights
	M86.30	Territorial air space
M90/99		**Human Rights**
	M92	Civil and political rights
		UF Civil liberties
		Civil rights
		Freedom
		Liberty
		Political freedom
		Political rights
		Academic freedom J30.05.03
	M92.05	Right to dignity
		UF Right to the inviolability of the human person
		Right to integrity of the human person
	M92.10	Right to freedom from inhuman treatment
		UF Prisoners minimum standard of treatment
		Right to freedom from cruelty
		Right to freedom from degrading punishment
		Right to freedom from torture
	M92.15	Right to freedom of thought
		UF Freedom of conscience
		Freedom of thought, conscience and religion
	M92.15.10	Religious freedom

M90/99		**Human Rights** (cont.)
	M92	Civil and political rights (cont.)

M92.20/29   Right to freedom of expression
       UF Freedom of expression
       Right to communicate M94.50
       Right to information M94.60

M92.22   Freedom of speech

M92.24   Freedom of the press

M92.28   Right of reply

M92.30   Right to life

M92.32   Right to die

M92.35   Right to resist oppression

M92.40   Right to nationality

M92.45   Right to free movement of persons

M92.48   Right to freedom of residence
       UF Right to chose residence

M92.50   Right to political asylum
       UF Political asylum

M92.55   Right to vote and be elected
       UF Right to be elected
          Suffrage rights
       Equal representation L63.10.20

M92.60   Right of association
       UF Right of peaceful association
       Trade union rights M93.60

M92.62   Right of assembly
       UF Right to peaceful assembly

M92.65   Right of petition

M92.68   Right to privacy

M92.68.10   Right to confidentiality

M92.75/79   Right to non-discrimination
       UF Equality rights
          Right to equality

M92.77   Equal opportunity

M92.78   Equal rights of men and women
       Women's rights M95.10

M92.80/99   Right to justice
       UF Right to equitable administration of justice

M92.82   Legal status
       UF Right to legal personality

M92.84   Equality before the law
       UF Equal protection of the law

M92.86   Right to habeas corpus

M92.88   Right to an effective remedy

M92.90   Right to a fair hearing
       UF Access to courts
          Access to tribunals
          Right to a fair trial
          Right to independence of judges
          Right to a speedy trial

M92.92   Right to presumption of innocence

M92.95   Rights of accused
       UF Rights of defendants
          Rights of suspects

M92.95.10   Right to counsel

M92.95.20   Right to legal aid

M93   Social and economic rights
       Right to economic development M96.30
       Right to natural resources control M96.40

M93.05   Right to environmental quality

M93.10   Right to social welfare

M93.10.10   Right to health

M90/99		**Human Rights** (cont.)
	M93	Social and economic rights (cont.)
	M93.10	Right to social welfare (cont.)
	M93.10.20	Right to social security
	M93.15	Right to marry
	M93.20	Family rights
		UF Right to found a family
		Rights of spouses
		Right to privacy M92.68
	M93.30	Right to adequate living standards
		UF Right to freedom from hunger
	M93.35	Right to work
		UF Right to earn
	M93.40	Right to rest and leisure
		UF Right to leisure
	M93.45	Right to property
	M93.60	Trade union rights
		UF Right to form unions
		Right to join unions
		Right to strike
		Right of association M92.60
	M94	Cultural rights
		UF Right to culture
		Right to education J10.50
		Right to rest and leisure M93.40
	M94.05	Access to culture
	M94.10	Right to cultural identity
	M94.20	Right to cultural participation
	M94.30	Right of intellectual property
	M94.30.10	Rights of authors
	M94.40	Right to artistic freedom
	M94.50	Right to communicate
		Right to freedom of expression M92.20/29
	M94.60	Right to information
		UF Freedom of information
		Free flow of information Z10.05
	M95	*Rights of special groups* (†)
	M95.05	Rights of the child
		UF Childrens rights
	M95.10	Womens rights
		UF Womens status
		Equal education J10.50.10B
		Equal pay Q58.40
		Equal opportunity M92.77
		Equal rights of men and women M92.78
		Womens liberation movement L69.60.10
		Womens suffrage L63.10.30
	M95.20	Rights of the elderly
	M95.25	Rights of the handicapped
	M95.30	Rights of the mentally ill
	M95.35	Rights of hospital patients
	M95.40	Rights of prisoners
		Rights of war prisoners M98.20
	M95.60	Rights of students
	M95.70	Rights of soldiers
		Rights of war wounded M98.15
		For others use 'Human rights' with descriptor for specific class of person
	M96	Collective human rights
		Right to environmental quality M93.05
		Rights of states M84/89
	M96.10	Right to live in peace
	M96.20	Right of self-determination
	M96.30	Right to economic development

M90/99		**Human Rights** (cont.)
	M96	Collective human rights (cont.)
	M96.40	Right to natural resources control UF Right of sovereignty over natural resources

	M97	Human rights violation
		    UF Abuse of human rights
		         Human rights suppression
		         Restriction to rights and liberties
		    Oppression L74
		    Discrimination R54.10

M98		**Humanitarian Law**
		    UF Human rights in time of conflict
		         Law of war
		    War L90
		    Warfare G66.20

	M98.05	Conduct of war rules UF Rules for conduct of war
	M98.10	Truces UF Armistices
	M98.15	Rights of war wounded *War wounded R84.45.10*
	M98.20	Rights of war prisoners *War prisoners R84.45.20*
	M98.25	Rights of civilians
	M98.25.10	Internment
	M98.30	Occupied territories
	M98.50	War crimes
	M98.50.10	Genocide
	M98.50.20	Concentration camps
	M98.50.70	War criminals
	M98.70/80	War relief
	M98.75	War relief organizations
	M98.75.10	Red Cross

N   Economics. Finance

N   **Economics**
Cultural economics T30
Economic geography D35.70
Economic geology D27
Economics education J60.63
Economics of communication Y20.40
Economics of education J20.05
Economics of research A76.60
Economics of science B22/23
Economists K60.30
Employment and labour Q45/99
Housing economics S35
Information/library economics Z30.30/40
Social and economic rights M93
Social welfare and economics R89
Transport economics S52

NØ2   **Economic History**

N03.10   *(Economics by level of operation)*
                                   Macroeconomics
N03.50
                                   Microeconomics
                                        SN Economics of the management of enterprises
                                   Business management Q21

N04   **Economics Research**
         N04.10/20   Econometrics
                                        UF Economic measurement
         N04.15   Socio-economic indicators
                                        UF Cost of living index
                                           Economic indicators
                                           Retail price index
                                           Cultural indicators T15.10

         N04.30/40   Economic analysis
         N04.32   Input-output analysis
         N04.35   Socio-economic analysis
         N04.35.10   Social cost
         N04.40   Cost/benefit analysis
                                           Cost effectiveness N97.40

         N04.45   Economic evaluation
         N04.50   Economic forecasting
         N04.55   Economic models
         N04.60   Economic surveys

                                   For other research methods see section A70/99

N06/10   **Economic Theory**
                                   (By doctrines)
         N07   Economic doctrines
                                        Capitalism L10.20
                                        Feudalism L10.10
                                        Collectivism L10.30

                                   (By specific subjects)
         N08.10   Economic equilibrium
                                        UF Economic stability
         N08.20   Economic fluctuations
                                        UF Business cycles
         N08.20.10   Economic depression
                                           UF Economic recession
         N09   Income distribution
                                        SN Sharing out of the national income among the owners
                                           of the factors of production
                                        UF Distribution theory
                                           Wealth distribution
         N09.10   Wealth

N06/10   **Economic Theory** (cont.)

        N09   Income distribution (cont.)

        N09.20   Income
                          Investment return N90.50.40
                          National income N23.38
                          Profits N98.25
                          Wages Q58

        N09.30   Incomes policy
                          Wages policy Q58.05

N11   **Economic Planning and Administration** (†)

        N11.10   Economic policy
                          Agricultural policy N52.10
                          Customs policy N75.60.10
                          Financial policy N77
                          Industrial policy N36
                          Incomes policy N09.30
                          Labour policy Q51
                          Price policy N69.10

        N11.20   Economic planning
                          Agricultural planning N52.20
                          Development planning N15.10
                          Industrial planning N36.30
                          Planned economy N26.30

        N11.20.10   Socio-economic factors
                          Socio-economic indicators N04.15

        N11.40   Economic administration
        N11.40.40   Economic legislation

N12   **Economic Resources**
                          Factors of production N38.25/38
                          Financial resources N78
                          Human resources R10.20
                          Natural resources E80/99

        N12.30   Resource management
                          Resource conservation E94
                          Resource development E92
                          Right to natural resources control M96.40

        N12.30.10   Resource allocation

N13/20   **Economic and Social Development**

                          UF Social development
                          Agricultural development N53
                          Communication development Y15.30
                          Cultural development T20/99
                          Development education J60.62
                          Educational development J10.60
                          Industrial development N37
                          Information/library development Z28.40
                          Political development L05
                          Resources development E92
                          Right to economic development M96.30
                          Rural development S96.30
                          Scientific development B16
                          Social change R65/69
                          Social science development K25
                          Urban development S86

        N14   National development

                       (By policy and planning)
        N15   Development policy
                          Communication policy Y15
                          Cultural policy T23/26
                          Development aid L84.50
                          Economic policy N11.10

N13/20		**Economic and Social Development** (cont.)
	N15	Development policy (cont.)

Educational policy J10.20/59
Environmental planning policy S71
Information/library policy Z28.20
Research policy A75
Social policy R05
Social science policy K20/25
Science policy B15/19

	N15.05	Development strategies
	N15.10	Development planning
		(See alphabetical section for narrower terms)
	N15.10.10	Development plans
	N15.40	Development programmes
	N15.45	Development projects

(By growth)

	N16	Economic growth
		UF Growth theory
	N16.20	Growth rate

(By stage of development)

	N17.40	Underdevelopment
	N18	Developing countries
		UF Third world
		Recipient countries L84.65
	N18.60	Least developed countries
	N19	Developed countries
		Donor countries L84.60
	N19.60	Recessing countries

N21/26		**Economic Systems**

  UF Economy
(By sectors)

	N22.10	Public sector
	N22.20	Private sector

(By national, regional and international economics)

	N23	National economy
		Public finance N79/83
	N23.30/40	National accounting
		UF Social accounting
	N23.35	Gross national product
	N23.38	National income
		Income distribution N09
	N23.50	Economic power
	N23.60	Economic structure
	N24	Regional economy
	N25	International economic systems
		UF Economic communities
		International economy
		International monetary systems N92
		International trade N75

(By form of organization)

	N26.10	Craft systems
		SN Primitive, feudal, mercantalist systems
		Feudalism L10.10

(By form of economic organization)

	N26.20	Capitalist systems
		Capitalism L10.20
	N26.20.10	Private ownership
		Private enterprises Q12.20
	N26.20.30	Free market economy

N21/26		**Economic Systems** (cont.)
	N26.30	Planned economy
		Economic planning N11.20
	N26.30.10	Nationalization
		UF Nationalized economy
	N26.30.20	Public ownership
		Public enterprises Q12.30
	N26.50	Mixed economy
		Mixed enterprises Q12.35
	N26.70	Collectivist economy
		UF Communist economy
		Socialist economy
		Collectivism L10.30
		Cooperatives Q12.70
N28/30		**Economic Conditions**
		UF Economic situation
		Poverty R71.10
	N29.10	Prosperity
		Wealth N09.10
	N29.20	Affluent societies
	N30	Living conditions
		Housing S30/49
		Working conditions Q76
	N30.10	Standard of living
		UF Living standards
		Right to adequate living standards M93.30
	N30.20	Cost of living
		Socio-economic indicators N04.15
		Inflation N69.60
		Prices N69
N32		**Economic Sociology**
		Living conditions N30
	N32.20	Economic life
N34		**Economic Psychology**
		UF Economic behaviour
N35/49		**Industrial Economics**
		Industrial enterprises Q12.65
		Technology G
	N35.50	Business economics
		(By policy)
	N36	Industrial policy
	N36.30	Industrial planning
	N36.30.70	Location of industry
		(By development)
	N37	Industrial development
		Industralization R66.20
		Technological change B16.03
		Technology transfer B30
		(By production)
	N38	Production
		(By characteristics)
	N38.10	Productivity
	N38.15	Economics of scale
		UF Economic size
		(By results)
	N38.20	Products

N35/49		**Industrial Economics** (cont.)
	N38	Production (cont.)
		(By factors)
	N38.25/38	Factors of production
		Capital N90.10
		Labour Q50
		Natural resources E80/99
	N38.30	Raw materials
	N38.35	Industrial plant
		UF Factories
		Workshops G67.80
		(By type of production)
	N38.40	Large scale production
	N38.45	Mass production
		(By management)
	N38.70	Production management
		Industrial design H05.10
		Production engineering G67
		Quality control H28.20
	N38.70.10	Process development
	N38.70.30	Product development
		(By individual industries)
N39/49		**Industries**
		Communication industry Y90
		Cultural industry T30.30
		Forest industry G16.80
		(By characteristics)
	N40.10	Indigenous industries
	N40.15	Foreign industries
	N40.30	Capital intensive industries
	N40.35	Labour intensive industries
		(By product)
	N41	Extractive industries
		UF Mining industries
	N42/49	Manufacturing industries
	N43	Chemical industry
	N43.30	Food industry
		Food production G14.20.30
		Food technology G94
	N44	Engineering industry
	N44.10	Metal industry
	N44.60	Shipbuilding industry
	N44.70	Aerospace industry
	N44.75	Motor industry
	N45	Textile industry
	N45.20	Clothing industry
	N46	Paper industry
	N47	Construction industry
	N48	Power industry
	N48.10	Electrical industry
	N48.20	Oil industry
	N48.30	Gas industry
	N48.40	Water supply industry
	N49	Service industries
	N49.05	Tourist industry
		Tourism X90/93
	N49.10	Hotel and catering industry
	N49.60	Show business
		Film industry W91

N50/59		**Agricultural Economics**
		Agricultural enterprises Q12.60
		Agricultural workers Q88.50
		Agriculture G05/15
		Land economics N60/64
	N51	Rural economics
	N51.40	Subsistence agriculture
		(By policy)
	N52.10	Agricultural policy
	N52.20	Agricultural planning
		(By development)
	N53	Agricultural development
		(By production)
	N54	Agricultural production
		Food production G14.20.30
	N54.40	Agricultural products
N60/64		**Land Economics**
		UF Land and property economics
		Agricultural economics N50/59
		Agricultural land G10
		Land use S81
		Real property law M62
	N61	Agrarian structure
		UF Agrarian systems
	N61.50	Land reform
		UF Agrarian reform
	N62.10	Land tenure
	N62.20	Tenancy
	N62.20.10	Landlords
	N63	Land and property finance
		UF Property development finance
		Mortgages N88.50
	N63.10	Rents
	N63.20	Land value
N65/75		**Trade**
		UF Commerce
		Commercial education J60.64
	N66	Supply and demand
	N66.10	Supply
	N66.40	Demand
	N67	Markets
		Financial markets N90.50.10
	N67.40/60	Market structure
	N67.50	Monopolies
		UF Cartels
	N67.50.10	Economic concentration
		Mergers N94.20.10
	N67.60	Economic competition
	N68	Consumption
		Consumer society R50.45
		Consumers N70.70
		Cultural consumption T69
		Energy consumption E81.90
	N68.20	Purchasing
		UF Buying
	N69	Prices
		Costs N97.25
	N69.10	Price policy

N65/75		**Trade** (cont.)
	N69	Prices (cont.)
	N69.20	Price control
	N69.30	Economic value
		UF Value theory
	N69.30.10	Appreciation
	N69.30.20	Depreciation
	N69.60	Inflation
	N69.60.10	Deflation
	N70	Marketing
		UF Sales promotion
		Selling
		Advertising Y60.6
	N70.10	Salesmanship
	N70.20	Market research
		UF Consumer behaviour research
	N70.70	Consumers
	N70.70.30	Consumer protection
	N70.70.60	Consumer education
	N73	Home trade
		UF Domestic trade
	N73.10	Retail trade
		UF Distributive trade (retail)
	N73.40	Wholesale trade
		UF Distributive trade (wholesale)
	N75	International trade
		UF Foreign trade
		International economic systems N25
		International monetary systems N92
	N75.15	International competition
	N75.20	Balance of trade
	N75.30	Exports/imports
	N75.35	Free trade
	N75.60	Protectionism
	N75.60.10	Customs policy
	N75.60.30/80	Tariff barriers
	N75.60.35	Tariffs
	N75.60.40	Embargoes
	N75.60.70	Customs duties
		(By cooperation)
	N75.80	Economic agreements
N76/99		**Finance**
		Communication finance Y20.40.20
		Cultural finance T30.40/50
		Information/library finance Z30.40
		Educational finance J20.05.05
		Housing finance S35.10
		Land and property finance N63
		Research finance A76.60.10
		Science finance B23
		Social welfare finance R89.40
		(By policy)
	N77	Financial policy
		(By resources)
	N78	Financial resources
		(By public finance)
	N79/83	Public finance
		National accounting N23.30.40
	N80.10	State budget
		UF National budget

N76/99		**Finance** (cont.)
	N79/83	Public finance (cont.)
	N80.10	State budget (cont.)
	N80.10.60	Public debt
	N81	Public expenditure
	N81.10	State aid

                                              UF Government assistance
                                              Financial aid L84.50.30
                                              Financial support N89

		(By locality)
	N82	Local finance
	N82.50	Regional finance
		(By policy)
	N83	Fiscal policy
	N83.10	Taxation

                                              UF Tax
                                              Customs duties N75.60.70

		(By direct taxation)
	N83.10.30	Income tax
		(By indirect taxation)
	N83.10.60	Consumption tax

                                              UF Value added tax

		(By monetary systems and currency)
	N84	Monetary systems

                                              UF Monetary economics
                                              International monetary systems N92

	N84.05	Monetary policy
	N84.10	Money
	N84.20	Liquidity
	N84.30	Coinage
	N85	Currency
	N85.50	Currency devaluation
	N86	Financial institutions

                                              UF Building societies
                                                Investment trust companies
                                              Insurance N91

	N86.10	Banks
		(By financing)
	N87/89	Financing

                                              Communication financing Y20.40.20F
                                              Cultural financing T30.60
                                              Educational financing J20.05.05K
                                              Financial aid L82.50.30
                                              Information/library financing Z30.40.20
                                              Science financing B23.50

		(By form of financing)
	N88.15	Credit
	N88.20	Debts

                                              UF Liabilities

	N88.30	Gratuities
	N88.35	Gifts
	N88.40	Loans
	N88.50	Mortgages
	N88.60	Subsidies
	N88.75	Subscriptions
	N89	Financial support

                                              UF Financial assistance
                                              Social security R95

	N89.10	Subventions
	N89.20	Grants

                                              UF Allowances

N76/99		**Finance** (cont.)
	N87/89	Financing (cont.)
	N89	Financial support (cont.)
	N89.20	Grants (cont.)

                                  Educational grants J40.17
                                  Research grants A76.60.10G

	N89.20.10	Personal grants

                                      Research fellowships J40.17.04
                                      Scholarships J40.17.02

		(By capital and investment)
	N90.10	Capital
	N90.10.10	Capital flow
	N90.10.60	Capital gains
	N90.40	Savings
	N90.50	Investment

                                    Investment appraisal N94.10.10
                                    Foreign investment N92.50

	N90.50.10	Financial markets

                                    UF Commodity markets
                                        Capital markets
                                        Money markets
                                        Stock exchanges

	N90.50.20	Bank rate
	N90.50.40	Investment return

                                    UF Dividends
                                      Rents N63.10

	N90.50.50	Discount
	N90.50.55	Interest
	N90.50.60	Shares

                                    UF Stocks and shares

		(By insurance)
	N91	Insurance

                                    UF Insurance companies
                                    Social security R95

	N91.10	Accident insurance
	N91.20	Fire insurance
	N91.30	Life insurance
		(By international finance)
	N92	International monetary systems

                                    UF International finance
                                        Clearing systems (monetary)

	N92.10	Foreign exchange
	N92.10.10	Exchange rates
	N92.30	Balance of payments
	N92.50	Foreign investment

                                      UF Foreign capital

		(By financial administration)
	N93/99	Financial administration

                                    SN Management of the finance of enterprises
                                    UF Business assets management
                                        Financial management

	N94.10	Capital raising

                                    Capital N90.10

	N94.10.10	Investment appraisal

                                    UF Capital budgeting
                                        Capital appraisal

	N94.20	Business formation

                                    Company law M58.30

	N94.20.10	Mergers

                                    UF Take-overs

	N94.20.30	Liquidations

                                    UF Business failures

N76/99		**Finance** (cont.)
	N93/99	Financial administration (cont.)
	N94.20	Business formation (cont.)
	N94.20.35	Bankruptcy
	N95/99	Accounting
		UF Book-keeping
		Management accounting
	N96	Budgets
	N96.i0	Budgetary control
		UF Budgeting
	N97	Cost accounting
		UF Cost analysis
		Costing
	N97.25	Costs
		Social cost N04.35.10
	N97.25.10	Fixed costs
		UF Overhead costs
	N97.25.20	Variable costs
		UF Running costs
	N97.30	Cost reduction
		UF Expenditure cuts
	N97.40	Cost effectiveness
		Cost/benefit analysis N04.40
		(By accounting for external appraisal)
	N98	Financial statements
		Debts N88.20
		Income N09.20
	N98.10	Expenditure
	N98.20	Assets
	N98.25	Profits
	N98.30	Cash flow
	N99	Auditing

P   Behavioural Sciences. Psychology

P01/99	**Psychology**
P04	**History of psychology**
P06	**Applied psychology**
P08	**Comparative psychology**
P10	**Psychological schools**
P12/15	**Psychological research**
P18	**Behaviour (psychological processes in general)**
P20	**Physiological psychology**
P25	**Sensory process psychology**
P30/33	**Executive functions (psychology)**
P34/37	**Affective psychology**
P39/44	**Depth psychology**
P40	**Subconscious**
P44	**Unconscious**
P46/55	**Higher mental processes**
P56/59	**Individual psychology**
P60/69	**Developmental psychology**
P70/90	**Social psychology**
P73	**Attitude**
P75/88	**Social behaviour**
P78/83	**Social interaction**
P79/82	**Interpersonal relations**
P83	**Intergroup relations**
P85	**Group behaviour**
P87	**Community behaviour**
P88	**Mass behaviour**
P89	**Sociometry**

P01/99		**Psychology** *Psychologists K60.40* *Psychology education J60.43*
P04		**History of Psychology**
P06		**Applied Psychology** *Communication psychology Y38* *Educational psychology J45* *Indoctrination Y60.55.40* *Psychiatry F74/87* *Psychoanalysis F85.10* *Psychohistory U08.20* *Psycholinguistics X30* *Psychology of art W11.02* *Psychology of religion V29* *Social psychology P70/90*
	P06.20	Psychotechnics UF Psychotechnology
P08		**Comparative Psychology**
P10		**Psychological Schools** UF Dynamic psychology Freudian psychology Gestalt psychology Hormic psychology Introspective psychology Jungian psychology Neo-Freudian psychology Objective psychology Teleological psychology *Philosophical schools V03*
P12/15		**Psychological Research** *Conflict research P83.70* *Sociometry P89*
	P13	Psychometrics *Psychoanalysis F85.10*
	P14	Experimental psychology
	P15	Psychological tests UF Psychological measurements *Educational testing J45.35*
P18		**Behaviour** SN Psychological processes in general UF Human behaviour *Animal behaviour E20.30* *Behavioural disorders F38* *Language behaviour X30.20* *Moral behaviour V15.35* *Political behaviour L76* *Religious behaviour V29.10* *Social behaviour P75/88* *Student behaviour J45.48* *Teacher behaviour J45.45* *(By factors and influences)*
	P18.10	Psychological effects UF Psychological factors
	P18.10.30	Stress (psychological) *Mental strain F81.15*
		(By attributes)
	P18.50	Norms
	P18.60	Traits UF Psychological characteristics

P20		**Physiological Psychology**

	P20.10	Psychosomatics
		    UF Mind-body relationships
		        Psychophysics
		    Psychophysiology F15.86
		    Psychosomatic disorders F78.10

P25		**Sensory Process Psychology** *Sensory systems F15.90*
	P25.20	Consciousness UF Awareness
	P25.15	Sensation
	P25.20	Stimulus

	P25.25	Response
		    UF Automatic response
		        Reflex response

	P25.30/70	Sensorimotor activities
		    UF Perceptual and motor activities
		
		    (By abilities)
		    Ability P47.10
		    Aptitude P47.20
		    Intelligence P47
		    Skill P47.20.10
		
		    (By performance)

	P25.40	Achievement
		        UF Attainment
		            Academic achievement J45.25

		(By process)
	P25.50	Perception UF Perceptual processes
	P25.70	Motor processes UF Motor skills
P30/33		**Executive Functions (Psychology)** UF Psychology of executive functions
	P31	Involuntary actions
	P31.10/30	Instincts *Hunger R71.30*

	P31.20	Sexual behaviour
		        UF Sexuality
		            Birth control R10.85.10
		            Marriage R22
		            Sex F19
		            Sex education J60.52.50
		            Sexual offences R76.55

	P31.40	Habits UF Mannerisms

	P31.70	Handedness
		        UF Laterality
		            Left handedness

	P32	Voluntary actions
	P32.01/60	Motivation
	P32.05	Incentives
	P32.05.05	Rewards
	P32.10	Ambition
	P32.20	Aspiration
	P32.50	Achievement motivation *Academic achievement J45.25*
	P32.70	Will UF Volition
	P32.70.10	Self-discipline UF Self-control
	P32.70.20	Choice

P34/37		**Affective Psychology**
	P35.10	Fixation
	P35.20	Inferiority complex
	P35.25	Superiority complex
	P36	Moods
	P37	Emotions

        Apathy F83.10
        Boredom J45.12.60B
        Hatred P82.10
        Love P80.50
        Emotional development P66
        Emotional disturbance F81.45
        Emotional maturity P65.40

	P37.02	Pessimism
	P37.04	Depression
	P37.06	Suffering
		UF Distress
	P37.10	Sorrow
		UF Grief
		Sadness
	P37.12	Anger
	P37.15	Anxiety
	P37.20	Fear
		UF Panic
		Terror
	P37.24	Embarrassment
		UF Humiliation
	P37.26	Dissatisfaction
		UF Disappointment
	P37.28	Jealousy
		UF Envy
	P37.30	Frustration
	P37.35	Optimism
	P37.40	Humour
	P37.42	Laughter
	P37.45	Happiness
		UF Joy
	P37.48	Pleasure
		UF Enjoyment
	P37.50	Euphoria
	P37.55	Satisfaction
P39/44		**Depth Psychology**
	P40	Subconscious
		UF Trances
		Parapsychology V86/87
	P40.10	Inhibitions
	P40.20	Hypnosis
	P44	Unconscious
	P44.10	Sleep
		UF Dreams
		Sleep disorders F71.10
P46/59		**Higher Mental Processes**
	P47	Intelligence
		Intelligence tests J45.35.30
		Intelligence quotient J45.31.10
	P47.10	Ability
	P47.20	Aptitude
	P47.20.10	Skill
	P47.30	Talent

P46/59		**Higher Mental Processes** (cont.)
	P47	Intelligence (cont.)
	P47.40	Backwardness
	P47.50	Educability
	P48/55	Cognition UF Cognitive process *Learning J45.10/20*
	P49.30	Conceptualization UF Concept formation
	P50/52	Ideation
	P51.10	Intuition
	P51.20	Inspiration
	P52	Imagination
	P52.10	Creativity UF Originality
	P52.20	Visualization
	P53	Memory *Memory disorders F79.40*
	P53.10	Memorization
	P54	Thinking UF Thought process
	P54.20	Creative thinking
	P54.30	Reasoning *Decision making Q27.20* *Problem solving Q27.30*
	P54.30.05	Rationalization
	P54.30.10	Abstract reasoning
	P54.30.20	Deduction
	P54.30.30	Decision
P56/59		**Individual Psychology** *Individualism V03.30* *Individual development P62*
	P57.05	Individual
	P57.10	Mind UF Mentality Psychic
	P57.20	Identity UF Personal identity Self-condept *Cultural identity T58.10*
	P57.25	Ego
	P57.30	Egocentrism
	P57.50	Self-esteem
	P58	Personality UF Disposition Temperament *Personality development P64* *Personality change P64.20*
	P58.10	Character
	P58.10.10	Characterology *Graphology Q72.30.05*
	P59	Individual difference UF Difference psychology
	P59.10	Individuality
P60/69		**Developmental Psychology** *Learning J45.10/20*
	P62	Individual development UF Self-concept development

P60/69		**Developmental Psychology** (cont.)
	P63	Mental development
		UF Intellectual development
		Language development X30.40
	P63.40	Thought process development
	P64	Personality development
	P64.20	Personality change
	P65	Emotional development
	P65.40	Emotional maturity
	P65.45	Emotional immaturity
	P66	Moral development
		UF Conscience development
		(By age groups)
	P67	Child psychology
		UF Child development
		Infant psychology
	P67.40	Genetic psychology
	P68	Adolescent psychology
	P69.10	Adult psychology
	P69.70	Geriatric psychology
P70/90		**Social Psychology**
		UF Psychosociology
		Communication psychology Y38
		Economic psychology N34
		Educational psychosociology J45.40/69
		Ethnopsychology T58
		Industrial psychology Q78.10
		Occupational psychology Q95.40
		Psycholinguistics X30
		(By general social psychological processes)
	P71	Social processes
		Social change R65/69
		Social problems R70/84
	P71.20	Social action
		(By attitude)
	P73	Attitude
		Parent attitude R28.20
		Political attitude L76.10
		Student attitude J45.48.10
		Teacher attitude J45.45.10
		Work attitude J45.48.30
	P73.10	Attitude change
		UF Attitude adjustment
	P73.20	Prejudice
	P73.35	Dogmatism
	P73.40	Intolerance
	P73.45	Tolerance
	P73.60	Opinion
		Belief V07.35
	P73.60.10	Opinion change
		(By behaviour)
	P75/88	Social behaviour
	P76.10	Social values
		UF Value systems
	P76.15	Social conformity
		Social alienation R73.10
	P76.20	Social influence
	P76.25	Social control
		UF Social power
		Social pressure
		Taboos T13.38

P70/90	**Social Psychology** (cont.)

P75/88	Social behaviour (cont.)
P76.30	Social integration UF Social assimilation *Cultural integration T72*
P76.36	Socialization
P76.36.10	Internalization
P76.40	Social adjustment *Maladjustment F83.20*
P76.50	Social participation
P76.55	Social passivity UF Social apathy
P76.60	Institutionalization
P78/83	Social interaction
P79/82	Interpersonal relations UF Human relations *Interpersonal communication Y50* *(By specific persons)* *Documentalist-user relationship Z72.84* *Information scientist-user relationship Z72.82* *Librarian-user relationship Z72.86* *Parent-child relationship R28.40* *Parent-school relationship J45.60* *Parent-teacher relationship J45.60.30* *School-student relationship J45.58* *Teacher-administrator relationship J45.65* *Teacher-student relationship J45.55*
P80.10	Personal contact
P80.10.20	Sociability
P80.30/90	Interpersonal attraction UF Affinity Empathy
P80.40	Friendship
P80.50	Love UF Affection
P81	Interpersonal influence
P81.10	Dependency relationship
P82	Interpersonal conflict *Social conflict R74.40*
P82.10	Hatred
P82.20	Hostility
P82.30	Aggressiveness
P83	Intergroup relations UF Intergroup conflict *Class conflict R56.70* *Cultural relations T59.65* *Interethnic relations R40* *International relations L85/89* *Labour relations Q60/69* *Race relations R44* *Social conflict R74.40*
P83.50	Conflict resolution *Conciliation M37.80.20* *Arbitration M37.80.10* *Peace-making L97*
P83.70	Conflict research *Peace research L95*
P85	Group behaviour UF Group conformity Group influence Group integration Group participation Group unity Group conflict *Group communication Y55*

P70/90		**Social Psychology** (cont.)
	P85/88	Social behaviour (cont.)
	P85	Group behaviour (cont.)
	P85.10	Group dynamics
	P87	Community behaviour
		UF Community integration
		Community action R93.20.10
	P87.05	Community identification
	P87.10	Community participation
	P88	Mass behaviour
		UF Collective behaviour
		Mass communication Y60
		(By measurement techniques)
	P89	Sociometry

Q05/44   Administrative Science

Q10/19   Organizations

Q20/30   Management

Q31/39   Administration

Q40   Office services

Q10/19   **Organizations**

UF Complex organizations
     Secondary organizations
Communication organizations Y20.60.20
Cultural organizations T34
Educational systems and institutions J70
Groups R30/45
Information/library organizations Z30.60
International organizations L81
Scientific organizations B24.30
Social science organizations K50
(See under 'Organizations' in alphabetical section and computer-generated hierarchies for complete list of types of organizations)

Q11	Bureaucracy	

UF Bureaucratic organization
Civil service L44.10
Statutory bodies L48

Q12   Enterprises
        UF Business organizations

Q12.10   Transnational enterprises
           UF International enterprises
              Multinational enterprises
              Transnational corporations

Q12.20   Private enterprises
Q12.20.20   Partnerships
Q12.20.30   Joint stock companies
Q12.30   Public enterprises
        UF Nationalized enterprises
            Public corporations

Q12.30.20   Public utilities
Q12.30.30   Public works
Q12.35   Mixed enterprises
Q12.60   Agricultural enterprises
Q12.65   Industrial enterprises
Q12.70   Cooperatives
Q12.70.10   Agricultural cooperatives

Q13   Government organizations
        Government cultural organizations T34.35
        Government educational bodies J20.08.18
        Government information/library organizations Z30.60.30

Q13.10   Central government organizations
           Public administration L42/49
Q13.30   Regional government organizations
Q13.60   Local government organizations

Q14   Private organizations
        Private enterprises Q12.20
        (For complete list of private organizations see alphabetical section)

Q14.10   Associations
        Clubs X79
        Cultural associations T34.40
        Educational associations J20.08.20E
        Employers associations Q63
        Trade Unions Q64

Q14.10.10   Professional associations
        Information/library professional associations Z36.60
        Teacher associations J30.30

Q14.10.30   Learned societies
Q15.20   Institutions
        (See alphabetical section and computer-generated hierarchies for narrower terms)

Q15.30   Voluntary organizations
        Voluntary welfare organizations R90.10.10

Q15.40   Trusts

Q10/19		**Organizations** (cont.)
	Q14	Private organizations (cont.)
	Q15.70	Womens organizations
		Womens liberation movement L69.60.10

Q20/30   **Management**

             UF Management science

(By application)
Cultural management T32
Educational management J40
Environmental management E50/59
Financial administration N93/99
Forest management G16.20
Information/library management Z30.70/99
Office management Q40.10
Personnel management Q70/79
 Records management Z92
Research management A76
Resource management N12.30

Q21	Business management	
		UF Management of enterprises
		Joint management Q68.30
		Marketing N70
Q21.20	Industrial management	
		Production management N38.70
Q21.20.20	Factory management	
		UF Works management

(By theory)

Q23	Management theory
	SN Includes classical theories of management, behavioural theories of management, management styles, management grid

(By personnel)

Q24	Managers
	UF Executive personnel
	Management personnel
	Management education J60.67
	Specialists Q85
Q24.10	Directors
	UF Board of directors
Q24.20	Top management
	UF Chairman, Chief executives
	Managing directors
Q24.30	Middle management
	UF Cadres
	Middle and lower management
Q24.40	Entrepreneurs

(By managerial attributes and qualities)

Q24.70	Managerial characteristics
	UF Managerial qualities
	Responsibility V15.30.35
Q24.70.10	Leadership
Q24.70.30	Authority
Q24.70.70	Prestige

(By management activities)

Q25/29	Management operations
Q26	Planning
	Development planning N15.10
Q26.10	Policy making
	UF Planning of objectives
	Policy formation
	Policy formulation
	Policy planning

Q20/30		**Management** (cont.)

Q25/29 Management operations (cont.)
Q26 Planning (cont.)
Q26.10 Policy making (cont.)
Q26.10.10 Policy
Development policy N15
National policy L41
Q26.15 PPBS
UF Planning programming and budgeting systems
Q26.20 Programme planning
Q26.25 Long range planning
Q26.30 Strategic planning
UF Strategy formulation
Q26.30.10 Strategies
Q26.40 Operational planning
UF Strategy implementation

(By day-to-day management activities)
Q27.05 Management control
Q27.10 Delegation of authority
Q27.20 Decision making
Cybernetics H38
Decision theory B78
Evaluation A45.15
Forecasting B94.10
Rationalization P54.30.05
Systems analysis H37
Value judgment V12.30
Q27.25 Problem setting
Q27.30 Problem solving
Q27.45 Coordination
Q27.50 Integration
Q27.55 Centralization
Q27.57 Decentralization
Q27.60 Cooperation
Q27.70 Goal setting
UF Management by objectives
Objective setting
Q27.80 Supervision
Discipline V15.30.60

Q29.10 Managerial services
SN Services, normally internal, providing advice on
management methods and how they may be improved

Q29.10.10 Management audit
SN The systematic appraisal of management methods by teams
from either within the organization or outside

Q29.20 Project management
SN An exercise involving a team in the completion of
a specific task within a given time

(By techniques)
Q30 Management techniques
Forecasting B94.10
Futurology R68
Research methods A90
Systems analysis H37
Q30.10 Operations research
Decision theory B78
Game theory B86
Mathematic models B91
Monte Carlo methods B97
Optimization B93.40
Quality control H28.20
Queueing theory B84.50

Q20/30		**Management** (cont.)
	Q30	Management techniques (cont.)
	Q30/10	Operations research (cont.)
	Q30.10.20	Mathematical programming
		UF Linear programming
		Non-linear programming
	Q30.10.40	Network analysis
		UF Critical path analysis
		PERT
	Q30.30	Organization and methods study
	Q30.35	Work study
		UF Method study
		Time study
		Work measurement

Q31/39   **Administration**

(By field of application)
Church administration V64
Educational administration J20.08
Communication administration Y20.60
Cultural administration T31/34
Financial administration N93/99
Information/library administration Z30.50/99
Public administration L42/49
Science administration B24
*(For complete list of types of administration see
computer-generated hierarchies)*

		(By structure)
	Q34	Administrative structure
	Q34.30	Committees
	Q34.30.30	Advisory committees
		(By reform)
	Q35	Administrative reform
		(By personnel)
	Q37	Administrators
		Cultural administrators T41.20
		Educational administrators J35.02
		Information/library administrators Z34.10
		Managers Q24

Q40   **Office Services**

UF Secretarial work
Typing
Office workers Q89.40
Reprography W65/69
Shorthand X41

	Q40.10	Office management
		Records management Z92
		(By equipment)
	Q40.30	Office equipment
		Computers H71/76

Q45/99   Labour and Employment

Labour and Employment

Labour Economics

      Q50   Labour
                                  Human resources R10.20
                                  Labour law M67

                              (By policy and planning)
      Q51   Labour policy
      Q51.10   Labour planning
      Q51.50   Human resources development

                              (By supply and distribution and systems)
      Q52   Labour market
      Q52.10/40   Labour supply
                                  Teacher supply J30.22
      Q52.15   Manpower
                                  UF Labour force
                                        Working population
      Q52.15.20   Manpower needs
      Q52.20   Labour shortages
      Q52.30   Labour distribution
      Q52.30.10   Labour mobility
      Q52.30.20   Labour migration
      Q52.30.50   Redevelopment
                                        UF Re-employment
      Q52.40   Labour turnover

      Q52.50   Labour systems
      Q52.50.30   Compulsory labour
                                UF Forced labour
                                  Prison labour

                              (By productivity)
      Q53   Labour productivity

                              (By employment)
      Q55   Employment
                              UF Jobs

                              (By policy)
      Q55.05   Employment policy
                                  Right to work M93.35

                              (By opportunities)
      Q55.08   Employment opportunities
                               (By type)
      Q55.10   Full-time employment
      Q55.15   Part-time employment
                              (By problems)
      Q55.20   Full employment
      Q55.25   Overemployment
      Q55.30   Underemployment
      Q55.40   Unemployment
                              (By persons employed)
      Q55.60   Youth employment
                                  Child workers Q88.05
                                  Education employment J14.40
                                  Education and employment
                                Student employment J14.40.10
                                Young workers Q88.08
      Q55.60.20   Youth unemployment
      Q55.62   Womens employment
                              UF Womens work
                                Working women Q88.90
                              (By services)
      Q55.80   Employment services
                              UF Employment bureaux
                                      Employment exchanges

                              (By remuneration)
      Q58   Wages
                              UF Remuneration

Q48/59

Labour Economics (cont.)

Q58   Wages (cont.)

                (By policy)
Q58.05   Wages policy

                (By type of remuneration)
Q58.10   Salaries
                    Teacher salaries J30.25.10
Q58.20   Fees
Q58.25   Fringe benefits
                    SN Includes financial and non-financial benefits
                    UF Employees benefits

                (By standards and equality)
Q58.30   Minimum wage
Q58.40   Equal pay

                (By evaluation)
Q58.60   Wage determination
Q58.60.10   Job evaluation

Q60/69   **Labour Relations**

                    UF Industrial relations
                        Labour/management relations
                    Industrial psychology Q78.10

                (By movement)
Q62   Labour movement

                (By organizations)
Q63   Employers organizations

Q64   Trade unions
                    UF Labour unions
                    Trade union rights M93.60

                (By activities)
Q64.40   Collective bargaining
Q64.40.10   Collective agreements

                (By conflict between workers and employers)
Q65/67   Labour conflict
Q66   Labour disputes

                    (By workers actions)
Q66.10   Work-to-rule
                        UF Go-slow
Q66.20   Strikes
Q66.30   Sit-ins
                        UF Work-ins

Q66.40   Picketing

                    (By employers actions)
Q66.50   Lockouts

                    (By dispute procedure)
Q66.70   Industrial conciliation
                        UF Labour disputes conciliation
                            Industrial mediation
Q66.70.10   Industrial arbitration
                            UF Labour disputes arbitration

                (By participation of workers in management)
Q68   Workers participation
                    UF Employee participation
                        Industrial democracy
                        Joint consultation
                        Self-government in industry
                        Workers management

                    (By agents)
Q68.10   Works councils

                    (By form of democracy)
Q68.30   Joint management
                        UF Co-partnership of workers

Q60/69		**Labour Relations** (cont.)
	Q68	Workers participation (cont.)
	Q68.50	Workers control
		UF Employee ownership
		Co-ownership of workers
		Workers cooperatives

Q70/79   **Personnel Management**

Labour relations Q60/69
Personnel Q81/89
Vocational training J60.34.20/40

(By records)
Q71.50   Personnel records

(By recruitment and selection)
Q72   Recruitment
       Teacher recruitment J30.20

Q72.05   Job description
       UF Job analysis
          Job specification
       Work study Q30.35

Q72.10   Job requirements
       Job evaluation Q58.60.10

Q72.10.20   Occupational qualifications
       UF Job qualifications

Q72.30   Personnel selection
       UF Selection boards
          Selection procedures (personnel)

Q72.30.05   Graphology
       UF Handwriting analysis

Q72.30.10   Interviewing for job

Q72.30.40   Group selection

Q72.40   Appointment to job
       UF Placement in job

Q72.40.30   Probation period
       UF Trial period of employment

(By action of employee)
Q72.70   Job hunting

(By conditions of employment and working environment)
Q74   Conditions of employment
       Career development Q92
       Occupational status Q94
       Teacher conditions of employment J30.25
       Wages Q58

Q74.10   Working time
       UF Hours of work
       Leisure time X73

Q74.10.10   Overtime

Q74.10.30   Rest periods
       UF Free-time at work
          Right to rest and leisure M93.40

Q74.20   Leave
       UF Holidays from work
          Time off work
       Holidays X93

Q74.20.10   Sick leave

Q74.20.30   Absenteeism
       UF Absence from work

Q74.40   Termination of service
       UF Resignation

Q74.40.10   Dismissal

Q74.40.20   Redundancy

Q74.40.30   Retirement

Q70/79   **Personnel Management** (cont.)

Q74   Conditions of employment (cont.)

Q74.70   Employment abroad
                        Teaching abroad J30.25.80

          (By working environment)
Q76   Working conditions
            SN Includes working environment, lighting, temperature, etc.
            Culture of work T53.75
            Occupational safety E73.70
            Right to environmental quality M93.05

          (By type of work)
Q76.20   Repetitive work
            UF Monotonous work

          (By inspection)
Q76.70   Labour inspection

          (By sociology and psychology)
Q78   Industrial sociology
            Culture of work T53.75

Q78.10   Industrial psychology
               Labour conflict Q65/67
               Work attitude J45.48.30

Q80/99   **Personnel and Occupations** (†)

Q81/89   Personnel
            Archive personnel Z90
            Communication personnel Y25
            Cultural personnel T40/49
            Educational personnel J35
            Information/library personnel Z34
            Occupations Q90/99
            Personnel management Q70/79
            Religious persons V75/82
            Scientific personnel B34

          (By employment status)
Q82   Employers
Q83   Employees
Q84   Self-employed

          (By job authority level)
            Apprentices J90.09.01
            Managers Q24
            Administrators Q37
Q85   Specialists
            UF Advisers
               Consultants
              Educational advisers J35.02.20

Q85.20   Planners
               Cultural planners T41.10
               Communication planners Y25.40
               Educational planners J35.02.10
               Environmental planners S73
Q86   Supervisors
Q87   Assistants

          (By socio-economic groups)
Q88   Workers
            Unemployed R84.15
            Working class R56.10
Q88.05   Child workers
             UF Child labour
Q88.08   Young workers
Q88.10   Manual workers
Q88.20   Semi-skilled workers
Q88.30   Skilled workers
Q88.30.10   Craftsmen
Q88.40   Factory workers

Q80/99		**Personnel and Occupations** (cont.)
	Q81/89	Personnel (cont.)
	Q88	Workers (cont.)
	Q88.50	Agricultural workers
	Q88.75	Itinerant workers
	Q88.80	Foreign workers
	Q88.90	Working women
		UF Women workers
	Q88.90.10	Married women workers
		*Working mothers R26.20.10
	Q89	White collar workers
		*Managers Q24
	Q89.10	Professional personnel
		SN See alphabetical thesaurus and computer-generated hierarchies for complete list
		*Deontology V15.50
		*Professional occupations Q96
	Q89.20	Middle grade personnel
	Q89.40	Office workers
		UF Clerical workers
	Q90/99	Occupations
		UF Careers
		*Personnel Q81/89
		*Occupational qualifications Q72.10.20
		*Occupational safety E73.70
		*Vocational education J60.34
		(By choice)
	Q91	Occupational choice
		*Vocational guidance J45.70.10
		(By development)
	Q92	Career development
		UF Occupational development
	Q92.10	Promotion (job)
	Q92.30	Transfer (job)
		(By status)
	Q94	Occupational status
	Q94.10	Professional status
		*Professional occupations Q96
		*Professional personnel Q89.10
		*Professional standards A63.80
	Q95	Occupational sociology
		*Industrial sociology Q78
	Q95.10	Occupational life
		*Working conditions Q76
	Q95.40	Occupational psychology
		*Industrial psychology Q78.10
		*Work attitude J45.48.30
	Q95.40.10	Job satisfaction
		(By specific occupations)
	Q96	Professional occupations
		*Archeologists U58
		*Archive profession Z90.60
		*Architects W24
		*Communication personnel Y25
		*Civil servants L44.10.70
		*Cultural personnel T40/49
		*Economists K60.30
		*Historians U13
		*Information/librarian profession Z36
		*Legal profession M30/32
		*Medical profession F98
		*Military personnel
		*Politicians L61.10
		*Psychologists K60.
		*Religious persons

R   Sociology

R03	**Social history**
R05	**Social policy**
R08/20	**Demography**
R10	**Population**
R11	**Population migration**
R12/20	**People**
R21/29	**Marriage and family**
R22	**Marriage**
R23/29	**Family**
R30/45	**Groups**
R33/45	**Ethnic and racial groups**
R46/49	**Nations**
R50/69	**Society**
R51	**Social environment**
R52/64	**Social struct**
R65/69	**Social change**
R70/84	**Social problems**
R75/78	**Crime**
R79/84	**People-in-need**
R85/99	**Social welfare**

R   **Sociology**
Cultural sociology T52
Economic and social development N13/20
Economic sociology N32
Educational sociology J14
Industrial sociology Q78
Occupational sociology Q95
Political sociology L75/77
Social psychology P70/90
Sociography K10.20
Sociolinguistics X20/29
Sociologists K60.10.10
Sociology of art W06
Sociology of communication Y35
Sociology of knowledge V07.15
Sociology of law M06
Sociology of leisure X72
Sociology of religion V18
Sociology of research A79
Sociology of science B05

R03   **Social History**

R05   **Social Policy**
Economic and social development N13/20
Housing policy S31
Population policy R10.80
Social change R65/69
Social reform R65.20
Welfare policy R87

(By philosophy)
R05.10   Social justice
R05.15   Social responsibility

(By planning and programmes)
R05.30   Social planning
R05.40   Social programmes

R08/20   **Demography**

R10   **Population**

Educational population J20.03.22
Indigenous populations R34.10
Rural population S28.10
Urban population S23.30

R10.10   World population
R10.20   Human resources
           Human resources development Q51.50

(By statistics)
R10.36   Census
           UF Population statistics

(By research and forecasting)
R10.42   Population research
           UF Motivational population research

R10.44   Population projection
           UF Population forecasting

(By problems and growth)
R10.52   Population problems
R10.52.10   Overpopulation

R10.54   Population dynamics
R10.54.10   Population increase
           UF Population growth
R10.54.20   Population decrease
R10.57   Population equilibrium
R10.58   Population optimum

R08/20		**Demography** (cont.)
R10		**Population** (cont.)
	R10.58	Population optimum (cont.)
		(By population distribution and events)
	R10.62	Population density
	R10.65	Population distribution
	R10.65.10	Age composition
	R10.65.20	Age distribution
	R10.65.30	Sex distribution
	R10.70/80	Population events
	R10.71	Nuptiality
	R10.73	Natality
	R10.73.10	Birth rate
	R10.75	Mortality
	R10.75.10	Death rate
	R10.77	Morbidity
		*Disease
		(By population policy and control)
	R10.80	Population policy
	R10.80.10	Population programmes
	R10.80.50	Population legislation
	R10.85	Family planning
		Population education J60.52.40
	R10.85.10	Birth control
	R10.85.10C	Contraception
	R10.85.40	Family size
R11		**Population Migration**
		UF Migration of peoples
		Migration of population
		Labour migration Q52.30.20
		(By policy)
	R11.10	Migration policy
		(By mobile persons)
	R11.20	Migrants
		Itinerant workers Q88.75
	R11.20.10	Nomads
		Refugees R84.45.40
	R11.20.20	Gipsies
		(By type of migration)
	R11.30	Emigration
	R11.30.10	Brain drain
	R11.35	Immigration
	R11.35.10	Immigrants
	R11.50	Internal migration
	R11.55	Rural migration
		UF Rural exodus
	R11.60	Seasonal migration
	R11.80	Nomadism
		Nomads R11.20.10
R12/20		**People**
		People-in-need R79/84
		Personnel Q81/89
	R13	Man
		UF Humans
		Human race
		Mankind
		Human species F47.50.10H

R08/20		**Demography** (cont.)
R12/20		People (cont.)
		(By sex)
	R14.10	Men
	R14.10.10	Boys
	R14.30	Women
		Womens education J70.22
		Womens employment Q55.62
		Womens liberation movement L69.60.10
		Womens organizations Q14.70
		Womens rights M95.10
		Working women Q88.90
	R14.30.10	Girls
		(By age)
	R15/22	Age groups
		Age composition R10.65.10
		Age distribution R10.65.20
	R16	Generations (age)
	R16.20	Age differences
	R16.30	Generation gap
		UF Conflict of generations
	R17	Childhood
	R17.10	Early childhood
		UF Infancy
		Infants
	R17.30	Children
		UF Juveniles
		Minors
		Adopted children R96.10.30A
		Child workers Q88.05
		Handicapped children R80.10
		Rights of the child M95.05
		Schoolchildren J90.04
		Socially disadvantaged children R84.60
	R18	Youth
		Rural youth S28.10.30
		Underprivileged youth R84.65
		Youth activities J70.13
		Youth employment Q55.60
		Youth unrest R74.10
		Urban youth S23.30.10
	R18.10	Adolescence
	R18.10.10	Adolescents
	R19	Adults
		Adult education J70.14
		Maturity F20.40
	R19.10	Young adults
	R20	Old age
		Ageing F20.60
	R20.10	Elderly
		UF Aged
		Old people
		Old persons
		Rights of the elderly M95.20
R21/29		**Marriage and Family**
R22		**Marriage**
		Sexual behaviour P31.20
		Right to marry M93.15
		(By type)
	R22.10	Polygamy
	R22.15	Mixed marriage
		(By legal aspects)
	R22.20	Marriage contract

R21/29		**Marriage and Family** (cont.)
R22		**Marriage** (cont.)
	R22.22	Consent to marriage
	R22.23	Minimum marriage age

	R22.35	Marriage dissolution
		    UF Desertion (marriage)
		          Separation (marriage)

	R22.35.30	Divorce
		(By marital status)
	R22.40	Marital status
	R22.40.10	Married men UF Husbands
	R22.40.20	Married women UF Wives
	R22.40.30	Widows
	R22.40.35	Widowers

	R22.40.60	Unmarried
		    UF Bachelors
		          Celibacy
		          Single persons
		    Unmarried mothers R26.20.20

R23/29		**Family** *Family education J70.17* *Family law M66* *Family rights M93.20* *Family planning R10.85*
	R24.05	Households
		(By type of family)

	R25.10	Nuclear family
		    UF Biological family
		          Elementary family

	R25.30	Joint family UF Extended family
	R25.40	Clans UF Sibs
		(By problem)

	R25.50	Broken families
		    Family disorganization R28.60
		    Marriage dissolution R22.35

	R25.60	One-parent families
		    UF Fatherless families
		          Motherless families
		          Single-parent families
		    Unmarried mothers R26.20.20

	R25.70	Problem families
		(By family relations)

	R26	Kinship
		    UF Family relatives
		          Relatives (family)

	R26.10/20	Parents
		    Children R17.30
		    Parent education J70.14.02P
		    Parent-school relationship J45.60
		    Parent-teacher relationship J45.60.30

	R26.15	Fathers
	R26.20	Mothers
	R26.20.10	Working mothers
	R26.20.20	Unmarried mothers
	R26.30	Grandparents
	R26.60	Siblings UF Brothers

R21/29		**Marriage and Family** (cont.)
R23/29		**Family** (cont.)
	R26	Kinship (cont.)
	R26.60	Siblings (cont.)
		Sisters
	R26.60.05	Birth order
	R26.60.40	Only children
		(By role in family)
	R27	Family role
	R27.10	Breadwinners
	R27.20	Housewives
	R27.30	Parent role
		(By environment, behaviour, relationships, problems)
	R28	Family environment
	R28.10	Family life
	R28.15	Family influence
		(By behaviour and relationships)
	R28.20	Parent attitude
	R28.25	Parent responsibility
	R28.30	Parent participation
	R28.40	Parent-child relationships
	R28.40.10	Parental deprivation
		(By problems)
		Domestic violence R76.45.10
	R28.60	Family disorganization

R30/45   **Groups**

UF Social groups
Communities S16
Group work (social work) R93.10
Group work (teaching) J50.06
Organizations Q10/19
Team teaching J50.05.30

(By behaviour)
Group behaviour P85
Group communication Y55
Intergroup relations P83

(By purpose)
Discussion groups Y55.05

	R31.10	Experimental groups
	R31.10.10	Control groups
	R31.40	Working groups

(By size)

	R32	Group size
	R32.10	Small groups
		UF Primary groups
	R32.30	Majority groups
	R32.40	Minority groups
		UF Minorities
		Cultural minorities T61.35
		Ethnic minorities R34.20
		Language minorities X22.30
		Racial minorities R37.10
		Religious minorities V63.30

R33/45   **Ethnic and Racial Groups** (†)

	R34	Ethnic groups
		UF Ethnicity
		Ethnography T10
		Ethnology T11
	R34.10	Indigenous population
	R34.10.10	Natives

R30/45		**Groups** (cont.)
R33/45		**Ethnic and Racial Groups** (cont.)
	R34	Ethnic groups (cont.)
	R34.20	Ethnic minorities
		Immigrants R11.35.10
	R34.20.10	Foreigners
	R35	Tribes
	R35.10	Tribal conflict
	R35.30	Tribalism
	R36/37	Race
	R37	Racial groups
	R37.10	Racial minorities
	R37.30	White people
	R37.40	Coloured people
	R37.40.20	Blacks
	R37.45	Mixed race
		UF Half caste
	R37.50	Asians
	R37.50.10	Indians
	R37.60	Semitic people
	R37.60.10	Arabs
	R37.60.20	Jews
	R37.65	South American Indians
	R37.70	North American Indians
	R37.90	Eskimos
	R37.92	Lapps
	R37.95	Aboriginal people
		(By relations)
	R40	Interethnic relations
	R40.20	Multiracial societies
	R44	Race relations
		SN Use in connection with racial discrimination, etc., otherwise use Interethnic relations
		UF Racial problems
	R44.20	Racism
	R44.25	Racialism
	R44.30	Racial prejudice
	R44.40	Racial discrimination
	R44.40.10	Antisemitism
	R44.40.20	Racial segregation
		UF Apartheid
		Ghettos
	R44.50	Racial conflict
		UF Racial tension
		Racial violence
		Tribal conflict R35.10
	R44.60	Racial integration
	R44.60.10	Desegregation
	R44.70	Racial tolerance
R46/49		**Nations**
		Cultural nationalism T58.35/50
		National development N14
		Nationalism L13.30
		Nationality L32.80.05
		State L20/59
	R47.10	Nation building
	R48.40	National prestige

R50/69		**Society**

(By type)
*Affluent societies N29.10
*Changing society R66
*Future society R68.20
*Multiracial societies R40.20
*Non-industrial societies T10.10

R50.20   Industrial societies
R50.25   Post-industrial societies

R50.30   Contemporary society

R50.40   Mass society
         *Mass culture T53.38

R50.45   Consumer societies

(By system)
R50.70   Social systems

R51   **Social Environment**
     *Human environment S

R51.05   Quality of life

R51.10   Social factors

R51.20   Social life
       *Family life R28.10
       *Community life S16.10
       *Cultural life T52.30/50

R52/64   **Social Structure**

R53/57   Social stratification
R54   Social differentiation
       *Cultural differentiation T61
R54.05   Class differentiation
R54.10   Discrimination
       *Cultural discrimination T61.20
       *Racial discrimination R44.40
       *Religious discrimination V63.20
       *Right to non-discrimination M92.75/79
R54.10.10   Sex discrimination
R54.10.20   Birth discrimination
R54.10.30   Nationality discrimination
R54.10.50   Language discrimination

R54.30   Social inequality
       UF Social equality
       *Cultural inequality T61.10
       *Social disadvantage R71

R54.80   Social pluralism
       UF Dual society
       *Cultural pluralism T53.50/60

R55   Caste
R55.10   Slavery
R56   Social class
       *Class differentiation R54.05
R56.10   Working class
       UF Lower class
         Proletariate
R56.20   Middle class
       UF Bourgoisie
R56.30   Upper class
R56.30.10   Aristocracy

(By characteristics)
R56.60   Class consciousness
R56.70   Class conflict

R50/69		**Society** (cont.)
R52/64		**Social Structure** (cont.)
	R53/57	Social stratification (cont.)
	R57	Elite
		Cultural elite T61.50
		Technocracy L24.30
	R57.10	Ruling class
		UF Establishment
		Aristocracy R56.30.10
	R57.10.20	Power elite
	R57.30	Intelligentsia
	R58	Social status
		Occupational status Q94
	R58.10	Social origin
	R58.20	Socio-economic status
	R59	Role
		UF Social role
		Family role R27
		Role playing J50.06.75
		Teachers role J30.10
	R59.05	Role analysis
	R59.30	Role duties
	R59.35	Role rights
	R59.50	Role conflict
	R59.60	Role change
	R59.80	Creative role
	R62	Social mobility
	R62.10	Social success
	R62.30	Social promotion
R65/69		**Social Change**
		SN Social development and evolution
		Cultural change T62
		Economic and social development N13/20
		Social planning R05.30
		Social policy R05
		(By agents of change, equilibrium and dynamics)
		Social conflict R74
		Political movements L69
		Social protest R74.20
	R65.05	Social equilibrium
	R65.10	Social dynamics
		Cultural dynamics T62.10
		(By result of change)
	R65.15	Social progress
	R65.20	Social reform
	R65.30	Social disorganization
		(By form of change)
	R66	Changing society
		(By type of change)
		Decolonization L30.10.50
		Developing countries N18
		Recessing countries N19.60
		Urbanization S23.10
	R66.20	Industrialization
		UF Industrial revolution
		Technological change B16.03
	R66.40	Democratization
		Democratization of culture T71
		Democratization of education J10.60.30
		(By attitude to change)
	R67	Sociology of change
	R67.20	Innovation behaviour

R50/69		**Society** (cont.)
R65/69		**Social Change** (cont.)
	R67	Sociology of change (cont.)
	R67.40	Resistance to change
		(By future conditions)
	R68	Futurology
	R68.20	Future society

R70/84   **Social Problems**

SN Cause and effects of social needs
Disasters E72
Discrimination R54.10
Handicaps F72
Housing S30/49
Old age R20

	R71	Social disadvantage
		UF Deprivation
		Economic deprivation
		Social deprivation
		Social handicaps
		Underprivilege
		Cultural disadvantage T61.30
		Slums S33
		Unemployment Q55.40
	R71.10	Poverty
		Culture of poverty T53.70
	R71.30	Hunger
		Famine E72.10.50
		Malnutrition F61.30
	R71.40	Homelessness
	R72	Social isolation
	R73	Social deviance
		UF Social pathology
		Suicide F83.50
	R73.10	Social alienation
	R73.20	Opting out
		Drop-out problem J45.58.50
		Social drop-outs R74.50
	R73.40	Sexual deviance
		Sexual offences R76.55
	R73.50/90	Addiction
	R73.55	Gambling
	R73.60	Drug addiction
		UF Drug abuse
		Drug control E68.30
		Drug education J60.52.20
	R73.60.20	Narcotic drugs
	R73.70	Alcoholism
		UF Drunkenness
		Alcohol education J60.52.10
	R73.80	Smoking
	R74	Social unrest
		UF Social tensions
		Student unrest J14.20.02
	R74.10	Youth unrest
	R74.20	Social protest
	R74.40	Social conflict
		Civil disturbances L73
		Cultural conflict T58.70
		Racial conflict R44.50
	R74.50	Revolt

R70/84		**Social Problems** (cont.)
R75/78		**Crime**
		Administration of justice M33/39
		Criminal law M52
		Law enforcement L56/59
	R75.10	Criminology
	R76	Offences
		UF Crimes
		Addiction R73.50/90
		Civil disturbances L73
		Subversive activities L73.10
		Terrorism L73.65
		War crimes M98.50
		(By crimes against property)
	R76.10	Theft
		UF Burglary
		Larceny
		Robbery
	R76.15	Arson
	R76.20	Vandalism
		UF Malicious damage
	R76.25	Fraud
		UF Embezzlement
		Forgery
	R76.30	Blackmail
	R76.35	Hi-jacking
		(By crimes against the person)
	R76.40	Homicide
		UF Murder
	R76.40.10	Assassination
	R76.45	Violence
		UF Assault
		Mugging
		Cruelty V15.40.20
	R76.45.10	Domestic violence
		UF Violence in the home
		Battering
		Ill-treated children R84.60.10
	R76.48	Kidnapping
		UF Abduction
	R76.50	Hostage-holding
	R76.55	Sexual offences
		UF Prostitution
		White slave trade
		Rape
	R76.55.40	Pornography
		(By crimes against public order)
	R76.60	Disorderly conduct
		UF Hooliganism
	R76.68	Lynching
		(By crimes against the state)
	R76.70	Political offences
		Subversive activities L73.10
		Terrorism L73.65
	R76.70.10	Espionage
		(By offence against justice)
	R76.75	Perjury
	R76.78	Corruption
		UF Bribery
		Political corruption L76.50
		(By organization)
	R76.90	Transnational crime
	R76.90.40	Extradition

R70/84   **Social Problems** (cont.)

R75/78   **Crime** (cont.)

	(By offenders behaviour)
R77.10	Delinquency
R77.10.10	Juvenile delinquency
	UF Juvenile delinquents
	Juvenile offenders
	(By offenders)
R77.30	Criminals
	UF Delinquents
	Prisoners R78.50.30
	War criminals M98.50.70
R77.30.70	Gangs
	(By punishment)
R78	Punishment
	(By punishment involving violence to persons)
R78.08	Death penalty
	UF Capital punishment
R78.10	Corporal punishment
R78.12	Solitary confinement
R78.15	Inhuman treatment
	Right to freedom from inhuman treatment M92.10
R78.15.10	Torture
	(By non-custodial treatment)
R78.20	Non-custodial punishment
	UF Confiscation
	Disqualification
	Fines
	Intermediate treatment
	Suspended sentences
R78.20.10	Probation
R78.20.50	Social sanctions
	UF Blacklist
	Boycott
R78.20.60	Restriction on movement
	UF House arrest
	Right to free movement of persons M92.45
R78.20.60D	Deportation
	UF Expulsion
R78.20.60E	Exile
	(By imprisonment)
R78.50	Prisons
	UF Detention centres
	Imprisonment
	Concentration camps M98.50.20
	Detention L59.40
R78.50.10	Prison sentences
R78.50.20	Prison life
R78.50.25	Prison discharge
	UF Release from prison
R78.50.25A	Parole
R78.50.25D	Amnesty
	UF Pardon
	Reprieve
R78.50.30	Prisoners
	Rights of prisoners M95.40
	War prisoners R84.45.20

R79/84   **People-In-Need**

	UF Disadvantaged persons
	Elderly R20.10
R80/83	Handicapped
	SN Physically or mentally disadvantaged
	Rights of the handicapped M95.25

R70/84		**Social Problems** (cont.)
R79/84		**People-In-Need** (cont.)
	R80/83	Handicapped (cont.)
		(By children)
	R80.10	Handicapped children
		UF Disadvantaged children
		(By physically disadvantaged persons)
	R81/82	Physically disadvantaged
	R81.10	Sick persons
		UF Ill persons
		Mentally ill R83.10
		Patients R97.70
	R82	Physically handicapped
		UF Crippled
		Disabled
	R82.10	Blind
		UF Sight defective
		Visually defective
	R82.10.10	Partially sighted
	R82.20	Deaf
		UF Hearing defective
	R82.20.10	Deaf and dumb
	R82.30	Speech defective
		UF Dumb
	R82.40	Autistic
	R82.50	Dyslexic
	R82.60	Spastic
	R82.70	Multiply handicapped
		UF Deaf dumb and blind
		(By mentally disadvantaged)
	R83	Mentally disadvantaged (†)
	R83.10	Mentally ill
		Rights of the mentally ill M95.30
	R83.10.10	Maladjusted
	R83.30	Mentally handicapped
		UF Mentally deficient
		Mentally retarded
		Ineducable J90.20.03A
		Backward students J90.20.03B
		Educationally subnormal J90.20.03C
	R83.30.50	Mongols
	R84	Socially disadvantaged
		UF Deprived persons
		Socially deprived
		Socially handicapped
		Underprivileged
		One-parent families R25.60
		Prisoners R78.50.30
		Problem families R25.70
		Unmarried mothers R26.20.20
	R84.10	Poor
		UF Low income persons
		Paupers
		Beggars
	R84.15	Unemployed
	R84.30	Crime victims
		UF Victims of crime
		Ill-treated children R84.60.10
	R84.40	Illegitimate persons
	R84.45	War disadvantaged
		UF War handicapped
	R84.45.10	War wounded
		Rights of war wounded M98.15
	R84.45.20	War prisoners
		Rights of war prisoners M98.20

R70/84		**Social Problems** (cont.)
R79/84		People-In-Need (cont.)
	R84	Socially disadvantaged (cont.)
	R84.45	War disadvantaged (cont.)
	R84.45.40	Refugees
		UF Displaced persons
	R84.50	Social drop-outs
		UF Hippies
	R84.55	Vagrants
		UF Tramps
	R84.60	Socially disadvantaged children
	R84.60.10	Ill-treated children
		UF Battered children
		Child abuse
		Child battering
		Cruelty to children
		Neglected children
	R84.60.40	Deserted children
	R84.60.50	Orphans
	R84.65	Underprivileged youth
	R84.75	Culturally disadvantaged
	R84.80	Educationally disadvantaged
	R84.80.10	Illiterates

R85/99   **Social Welfare**

		(By philosophy, purposes and aims)
	R86	Social welfare philosophy
		Social justice R05.10
		Social responsibility R05.15
		Social values P76.10
		Right to social welfare M93.10
		(By policy)
	R87	Welfare policy
		Social policy R05
	R87.20	Social welfare aims
	R87.30	Social needs
		UF Social demands
		(By planning and administration)
	R88	Social welfare planning
	R89	Social welfare economics
	R89.40	Social welfare finance
	R90	Social welfare administration
		UF Social administration
		(By organizations)
	R90.10	Social welfare organizations
	R90.10.10	Voluntary welfare organizations
		UF International voluntary welfare organizations
		(By personnel)
	R91	Social workers
		(By training)
	R91.50	Social workers training
		(By social work)
	R93	Social work
	R93.05	Counselling
	R93.10	Group work (social work)
	R93.20	Community work
	R93.20.10	Community action
	R93.40	Residential social work
	R93.50	Day care
	R93.70	Voluntary social work
	R93.70.10	International voluntary services

R85/99	**Social Welfare** (cont.)
R93	Social work (cont.)
R93.70	Voluntary social work (cont.)
R93.70.10	International voluntary services (cont.)

(By social services)

R94/99	Social services

UF Welfare services
Educational welfare J14.15

R95	Social security

UF Child allowances
Family allowances
Health insurance
Industrial injuries benefits
National insurance
Social insurance
Supplementary benefits
Unemployment benefits
Right to social security M93.10.20

R95.10.10	Pensions
R95.10.40	Legal aid
R95.50	Relief in kind

SN Assistance in the form of food,
clothing, fuel, transport, etc.
Disaster relief work R98

R96	Personal social services

SN Care of particular groups of needy persons, for example,
handicapped, elderly, children, young people

R96.10	Child welfare

UF Child welfare services

R96.10.30	Adoption
R96.10.30A	Adopted children
R96.10.35	Foster care
R96.10.50	Residential child care

UF Orphanages

For other services use 'Social services' with term for needy person
from People-in-need R79/84

R97	Health services

UF Medical services
Social medicine
Family planning R10.85
Medical personnel F98.20
Medical sciences F50/99
Public health F68

R97.10	Hospitals
R97.40	Medical centres

UF Clinics
Health centres

R97.70	Patients

UF Hospital patients
Rights of hospital patients M95.35

R98	Disaster relief work

UF Emergency social services
Relief in kind R95.50

S   Human Environment

S05/10	Environmental quality
S12	Human needs
S15/49	Human settlement
S30/49	Housing
S50/69	Transport
S69	Travel
S70/99	Environmental planning
S84/89	Urban planning
S90/95	Open spaces
S96	Rural planning
S98	Regional planning

S   # Human Environment

UF Man made environment
Environmental sciences E
Social environment R51

SN Includes social aspects of the physical environment;
that is the quality and planning of human and community
environment—the built-environment, housing, transport,
infrastructure, etc.

S05/10   ## Environmental Quality
Cultural environment T52.10
Quality of life R51.05
Right to environmental quality M93.05

(By environmental assets)
S06.10   Amenities
Countryside S91
Cultural heritage T81.10
Cultural property T81.20
Landscape S91.40
Open spaces S90/95
S06.10.10   Natural heritage

(By deterioration)
S07   Amenities destruction
Amenities conservation S79
Industralization R66.20
Pollution E31/49
Traffic S68
S07.10   Noise
Noise control E67
S07.50   Visual pollution

S12   ## Human Needs
Food G94.10
Clothing G96.15.10
Domestic science G98
Housing S30/39
Leisure X70/99
Social needs R87.30
Travel S69

S15/49   ## Human Settlement

UF Community environment
S16   Communities
Community action R93.20.10
Community behaviour P87
Community centres J70.18.08
Community development J70.18.04
Community education J70.18
Community work R93.20
Religious communities V65
School-community relationships J45.63
Scientific communities B34.10
S16.10   Community life
S16.20   Local communities
Neighbourhoods S85.50

S18/24   Urban areas
UF Urban communities
Urban education J70.04.40
Urban planning S84/89
S20.05/40   Towns
UF Cities
Expanded towns S87.70
New towns S86.25
S20.08   Small towns
S20.10   Conurbations
S20.15   Metropolitan areas

S15/49		**Human Settlement** (cont.)
	S18/24	Urban areas (cont.)
	S20.05/40	Towns (cont.)
	S20.20	Ancient cities
		UF Historic cities
	S20.30	Industrial towns
	S20.40	Overspill towns
		UF Dormitory towns
		(By environment)
	S22	Urban environment
	S22.10	Built environment
		(By social considerations)
	S23	Urban sociology
		UF Urban life
		Urban society
	S23.10	Urbanization
	S23.30	Urban population
	S23.30.10	Urban youth
	S25/29	Rural areas
		UF Agricultural areas
		Rural communities
		Rural economics N51
		Rural education J70.04.45
		Rural planning S96
		Countryside S91
	S26	Villages
		(By environment)
	S27	Rural environment
		(By social aspects)
	S28	Rural sociology
		UF Rural life
		Rural society
	S28.10	Rural population
		Rural migration R11.55
	S28.10.10	Farmers
	S28.10.30	Rural youth
S30/49		**Housing**
		UF Dwellings
		(By policy)
	S31	Housing policy
		(By needs and problems)
	S32	Housing needs
		UF Housing demands
	S32.10	Housing shortages
		Homelessness R71.40
	S32.10.10	Squatting
	S33	Slums
		UF Sub-standard housing
		Slum clearance S86.20
		(By economics and finance)
	S35	Housing economics
	S35.10	Housing finance
		Mortgages N88.50
		(By agency providing housing)
	S37.10	Public housing
	S37.20	Private housing
		(By ownership and tenancy)
	S39.10	Home ownership
	S39.50	Rented housing
		Rents N63.10
		Tenancy N62.20

S15/49		**Human Settlement** (cont.)
S30/49		**Housing** (cont.)
	S39.50	Rented housing (cont.)

(By design and construction)

	S41	Housing design
		Building design G59
	S42	Housing construction
	S42.40	Housing improvement
		UF Housing reclamation

(By type of dwelling)

	S45.10	Houses
	S45.20	Apartments
		UF Flats
	S45.20.10	High rise flats
	S45.50	Mobi_ homes
		ᒪF Caravans

(By purpose)

	S47.30	Second homes

(By user)
Student housing J14.20.40

For others combine 'Housing' with descriptor for user, e.g. Housing for the elderly (Housing & Elderly)

S50/69		**Transport**

SN Transportation
Communication Y

(By policy and planning)

	S51	Transport policy
		Transport planning

(By economics)

	S52	Transport economics

(By scope and purpose)

	S54.10	International transport
	S54.20	Private transport
	S54.30	Public transport
		UF Passenger transport
		Road passenger transport
	S54.40	Freight transport
		UF Goods transport
	S54.50	Urban transport
	S54.60	Rural transport

(By mode of transportation)

	S56	Air transport
		UF Aviation
		Air safety E73.90.10
		Air traffic S68.10
		Aircraft S67
		Airports S60.10
		Law of the air M80
	S56.20	Civil aviation
	S57	Land transport
	S57.10	Road transport
		Road engineering G57.40
		Road safety E73.90.20
		Road traffic S68.20
		Road vehicles S64
		Roads S60.20
	S57.30	Railway transport
		Railway engineering G62.40
		Railway networks S60.40
		Trains S65

S50/69		**Transport** (cont.)
	S57	Land transport (cont.)
	S57.30	Railway transport (cont.)
	S57.30.10	Monorails
	S57.30.40	Underground railways
	S58	Water transport
	S58.10	Sea transport
		UF Shipping industry
		Harbours S60.60
		Law of the sea M79
		Ships S66
		Ports S60.50
	S58.20	Inland water transport
		Canals S60.70
		Waterway engineering G51
		(By transport infrastructure)
	S60	Transport infractructure
		Civil engineering G57
	S60.10	Airports
		UF Air terminals
	S60.20	Roads
		UF Motorways
	S60.25	Bridges
	S60.30	Tunnels
	S60.40	Railway networks
	S60.40.10	Railway tracks
	S60.40.40	Railway stations
	S60.50	Ports
	S60.55	Docks
	S60.60	Harbours
	S60.70	Canals
		(By vehicles)
	S61/66	Vehicles
		Transport engineering G62
	S63/65	Land vehicles
		UF Terrain vehicles
	S64	Road vehicles
		Road vehicle engineering G62.10
	S64.20	Motor vehicles
		UF Automobiles
		Motorcycles
		Tractors
	S64.20.40	Trucks
		UF Commercial vehicles
		Juggernauts
	S64.40	Bicycles
	S65	Trains
		UF Rolling stock
	S65.20	Locomotives
	S66	Ships
		Hovercraft G62.80
		Marine engineering G62.60
		Naval architecture G62.60.10
		Research ships D86.30
	S66.50	Submarines
	S67	Aircraft
		Aircraft engineering G63.20
		Spacecraft G63.60
	S67.30	Helicopters
		(By traffic)
	S68	Traffic
		Transport safety E73.90

S50/69		**Transport** (cont.)
	S68	Traffic (cont.)
		(By mode of transport)
	S68.10	Air traffic
	S68.20	Road traffic
	S68.30	Rail traffic
	S68.40	Marine traffic
		(By location)
	S68.70	Urban traffic
S69		**Travel**
		Tourism X90/93
	S69.10	Commuting
		UF Journey to work
	S69.20	Travel abroad
		UF International travel
		Study tours J50.13.30
	S69.40	International movement of persons
		Right to free movement of persons M92.45
S70/99		**Environmental Planning**
		UF Physical planning
		(By policy)
	S71	Environmental planning policy
		Housing policy S31
		(By public relations)
	S72.10	Public participation in planning
		(By personnel)
	S73	Environmental planners
		UF Planners (environment)
		(By administration)
	S74	Environmental planning administration
		(By legislation)
	S75	Environmental planning legislation
		UF Compulsory purchase
		(By control)
	S76	Environmental planning control
		SN Includes aesthetic control, advertising control, development control, planning permission processes
		(By environmental planning processes)
	S78/83	Environmental planning processes
		UF Environmental plan preparation
		Planning surveys
	S79	Amenities conservation
		Countryside conservation S91.30
		Preservation of monuments T84
		Noise control E67
	S80	Environmental design
		SN Includes site layout, buildings/street relationships, aesthetic design
		Architecture W21/24
	S80.10	Visual planning
		SN Views, skyline, colour, etc.
		Visual pollution S07.50
	S80.10.30	Perception of the environment
	S80.15/30	Urban design
		UF Civic design
	S80.20	Street furniture design
		SN Includes street lighting, bus stops, telephone kiosks, etc.
		Street lighting G31.40
	S80.50	Landscape design
		UF Landscape architecture
		Landscape S91.40

S70/99		**Environmental Planning** (cont.)
	S78/83	Environmental planning processes (cont.)
	S81	Land use
		UF Land use planning
	S82	Transport planning
		Traffic S68
		(By areas planned)
S84/89		**Urban Planning**
		UF Town planning
		Urban areas S18/24
		Urban design S80.15/30
		Urban spaces S93
		Urban traffic S68.70
		Urban transport S54.50
		(By district planned)
	S85.10	Urban centres
		UF Central areas
	S85.20	Industrial areas
	S85.30	Shopping areas
	S85.40	Residential areas
	S85.45	Suburbs
	S85.50	Neighbourhoods
		(By problem areas)
	S85.70	Development areas (urban planning)
		UF Action areas in urban planning
		Clearance areas
		Comprehensive development areas
	S85.70.10	Depressed areas
		UF Declining areas
		Twilight areas
		(By activities)
	S86	Urban development
	S86.20	Slum clearance
	S86.25	New towns
	S86.30	Town reconstruction
	S87	Urban expansion
		(By uncontrolled expansion)
	S87.10	Urban sprawl
		(By controlled expansion)
	S87.70	Expanded towns
	S88	Urban renewal
		UF Urban rehabilitation
		Town reconstruction S86.30
	S89	Urban decentralization
		UF Office dispersal
S90/95		**Open Spaces**
		UF Amenity open spaces
		Recreational open spaces
		Playgrounds X95.20
		Playing fields X97.50
	S91	Countryside
	S91.10	Access to countryside
		Outdoor pursuits X87
	S91.30	Countryside conservation
	S91.40	Landscape
		Landscape design S80.50
	S91.40.10	Landscape protection
	S92	Parks
	S92.10	National parks

S70/99		**Environmental Planning** (cont.)
S90/95		**Open Spaces** (cont.)
	S92	Parks (cont.)
	S92.30	Water recreational areas SN Includes rivers, canals, lakes, seafronts UF Bathing beaches Marinas Water parks
	S92.40	Public gardens
	S92.40.10	Botanical gardens
	S92.40.20	Zoological gardens
	S93	Urban spaces SN Includes town squares, market places UF Urban parks
	S94	Green belts
S96		**Rural Planning** *Rural areas S25/29* *Rural transport S54.60*
	S96.30	Rural development
S98		**Regional Planning**

T/X   **CULTURE AND HUMANITIES**
Summary

T   **Culture (general)**

U   **History and associated studies**

V   **Philosophy, Ethics and Religion**

W   **Arts**

X01/69   **Philology (Language and Literature)**

X70/99   **Leisure**

T   Culture

T04	**Cultural history**
T06	**Cultural philosophy**
T07	**Cultural creation**
T08/13	**Cultural and social anthropology**
T14/19	**Cultural research**
T16/19	**Cultural studies**
T20/99	**Cultural development**
T23/26	**Cultural policy**
T27/34	**Cultural planning and administration**
T35/39	**Cultural resources**
T40/49	**Cultural personnel**
T50/64	**Cultural conditions**
T65/69	**Cultural users**
T70/99	**Cultural action**
T78	**Cultural activities**
T80/84	**Preservation of cultural property**
T85/99	**Presentation of cultural property**
T87/99	**Museums**

T		**Culture**
		Cultural education J60.80
	T02	Civilisation
T04		**Cultural History**
		Art history W05
T06		**Cultural Philosophy**
		Cultural rights M94
		Cultural policy T23/26
		Concept of culture T17.20
	T06.10	Culturology
	T06.20	Culturalism
	T06.50	Cultural values
T07		**Cultural Creation**
		Artistic creation W11
		Cultural innovations T68.50
		Cultural discoveries T62.60
T08/13		**Cultural and Social Anthropology**
		UF Cultural anthropology
		Social anthropology
		Ethnic groups R34
		Ethnolinguistics X25
		Ethnopsychology T58
	T10	Ethnography
		Ethnographic museums T96.55
		Nomadism R11.80
		Tribes R35
	T10.10	Non-industrialized societies
	T10.30	Non-industrialized peoples
		Native art W15.13
	T11	Ethnology
	T12	Folk cultures
		Folk art W15.10
		Folk dance W85.10
		Folk literature X63.50
		Folk music W75.40
	T12.10	Folklore
		UF Folk wisdom
		Magic V95
		Mythology V41
	T13	Customs and traditions
		UF Traditions
		Festivals X78.20
		Traditional cultures T53.05
		Written tradition X61.10
	T13.10	Oral culture
	T13.15	Ceremonies
		Religious ceremonies V55
	T13.20	Rites
		UF Sacrificial rites
	T13.20.10	Initiation rites
	T13.22	Rituals
	T13.25	Commemorations
	T13.30	Feasts
		Religious festivals V53
	T13.35	Mores
		Social conformity P76.15
	T13.38	Taboos
	T13.50	Manners
	T13.50.10	Etiquette
	T13.55	Food customs

T08/13		**Cultural and Social Anthropology** (cont.)
	T13	Customs and traditions (cont.)
	T13.60	Fashion
		UF Costumes
		Dress
		Fashion design W43
T14/19		**Cultural Research**
		Linguistic research X10/19
		Literacy research X59.10
		(By tools and techniques)
	T15.10	Cultural indicators
	T15.20	Cultural statistics
		Book output Y90.24.10
		Film production statistics W91.10
		Information/library statistics Z30.05.55
		Museum statistics T91.10.20
	T15.20.10	Time budgets
	T15.20.30	Household cultural budgets
		UF Household cultural expenditure
	T15.30	Cultural models
	T15.70	Cross-cultural analysis
		For other techniques see A70/99 Research
T16/19		**Cultural Studies**
	T17	Theoretical cultural studies
	T17.20	Concept of culture
		UF Image of culture
	T17.70	Basic personality
		(By time)
		Ancient civilizations U23
	T18.50	Contemporary culture
		Contemporary art W17.70
		Contemporary literature X69.10.10
		Contemporary music W75.80.10
		(By place)
	T19	Cultural geography
	T19.05	Cultural atlases
	T19.10	European cultures
		European art W18.70
		European history U32
		Indo-European languages A03
	T19.10.20	Baltic culture
	T19.10.30	Slav culture
	T19.10.40	Central European cultures
	T19.10.60	Iberian cultures
	T19.20/30	Asian cultures
		UF Oriental cultures
		Asian art W18.20
		Asian history U35
		Oriental languages A04/07
	T19.25	Central Asian cultures
		UF Mongolian culture
		Malay culture
		Tamil culture
		Buddhism V46.35
	T19.25.30	Kushan
	T19.40	Arab culture
		Arab art W18.30
		Arab history U36
		Arabic A05.15.20
		Islamic art W15.30.30

T16/19		**Cultural Studies** (cont.)
	T19.50	African cultures
		*African art W18.50
		*African history U37
		*African languages A09
	T19.60	North American cultures
		*North American history U40
	T19.60.40	North American Indian culture
		*North American Indian languages A10.10
	T19.70	Latin American cultures
		*Latin American art W18.70
		*Latin American history U41
		*South American Indian languages A10.50
	T19.70.40	Incas
	T19.70.50	Aztecs
	T19.85	Oceanic cultures
		*Austronesian and oceanic languages A08
		*Oceanic art W18.90
	T19.90	Arctic cultures

T20/99   **Cultural Development**

T23/26   **Cultural Policy**
*Language policy X21
*Museum policy T90.10

	T24	Cultural aims
		*Cultural rights M94
	T24.10	Cultural democracy
	T24.40	Cultural objectives
	T26	Cultural cooperation
	T26.10	Cultural agreements
	T26.20	Cultural diplomacy
	T26.30	Cultural exchange
		*Programme exchange Y70.48.10

T27/34   **Cultural Planning and Administration** (†)

	T28	Cultural planning
		*Cultural policy T23/26
		(By factors)
		*Cultural needs T66
		(By tools)
		*Cultural models T15.30
		*Cultural indicators T15.10
		*Cultural statistics T15.20
		(By plans and programmes)
	T28.40	Cultural plans
	T28.50	Cultural programmes
	T30	Cultural economics
		UF Economics of culture
		*Cultural resources T35/39
	T30.10	Cultural costs
	T30.30	Cultural industry
		*Cultural goods T39.10
		*Film industry W91
		*Show business N49.60
	T30.35	Cultural supply
	T30.40/50	Cultural finance
	T30.45	Cultural accounting
	T30.45.10	Cultural budgets
		*Household cultural budgets T15.20.30
	T30.45.30	Cultural expenditure

T20/99		**Cultural Development** (cont.)
T27/34		**Cultural Planning and Administration** (cont.)
	T30	Cultural economics (cont.)
	T30.40/50	Cultural finance (cont.)
	T30.60	Cultural financing
		UF Cultural subsidies
	T30.60.10	Patronage of the arts
		(By administration)
	T31/34	Cultural administration
	T32	Cultural management
		(By legislation)
	T33	Cultural legislation
		(By organizations)
	T34	Cultural organizations
		UF Cultural institutions
		Cultural development centres T38.05
	T34.10	International cultural organizations
		UF Intergovernment cultural organizations
		Non-governmental cultural organizations (international)
	T34.25	Regional cultural organizations
	T34.30	National cultural organizations
	T34.35	Government cultural organizations
	T34.35.10	Central government cultural organizations
	T34.35.30	Regional government cultural organizations
	T34.35.50	Local government cultural organizations
	T34.40	Private cultural organizations
		UF Non-government cultural organizations
		Socio-cultural clubs X79.30
	T34.40.10	Cultural associations

T35/39		**Cultural Resources**
		Cultural heritage T81.10
		Cultural personnel T40/49
		Cultural property T81.20
	T36	Cultural productions
		Broadcasting programmes Y70.48
		Films W90
		Musical performances W74
		Theatrical performances W82.60
	T37/39	Cultural facilities
		Library buildings Z32.10
		Museum buildings T92.10
		Recreational buildings X95.40
	T38	Cultural centres
	T38.05	Cultural development centres
	T38.10	Arts centres
	T38.30	Socio-cultural centres
		Community centres J70.18.08
	T39	Cultural equipment
	T39.10	Cultural goods
		Books Z36.15
		Cultural industry T30.30
		Leisure equipment X98
		Radio receivers Y80.70.30C
		Record players Y80.60.40H
		Recordings Z15.80/89
		Television receivers Y80.70.30D

T40/49		**Cultural Personnel**
		Architects W24
		Authors Y25.10
		Communication personnel Y25
		Information/library personnel Z34

T20/99	**Cultural Development** (cont.)
T40/49	**Cultural Personnel** (cont.)
	Museum personnel T93
	(By persons with expert knowledge and appreciation)
T41.05	Connoisseurs
	(By cultural development personnel)
T41.10	Cultural planners
T41.20	Cultural administrators
T41.30	Cultural agents
	UF Animateurs
	Cultural animateurs
	Cultural workers
T41.70	Architect restorers
	UF Monument conservationists
	(By professional artists, directors, producers)
T42/47	Artists
	UF Professional artists
	Craftsmen Q88.30.10
T43	Visual artists
T43.10	Young artists
T43.20	Painters
T43.30	Sculptors
T43.40	Graphic designers
T43.50	Photographers
T44	Musicians
T44.10	Composers
T44.20	Conductors
T44.30	Instrumentalists
T44.50	Singers
	UF Opera singers
T44.70	Pop musicians
	UF Pop singers
T45	Theatre directors
T45.10	Theatre producers
T45.60	Theatre agents
T46	Film-makers
T46.10	Film directors
	Television and radio directors Y25.60.40
T46.20	Film producers
	Television and radio producers Y25.60.30
T47	Performers
	Sportsmen X89
T47.10	Actors
T47.10.10	Child actors
T47.10.30	Dancers
	UF Professional dancers
T47.10.30C	Choreographers
T47.10.40	Film actors
	UF Film stars
	(By amateurs)
T48	Amateurs
	UF Amateur artists
	Amateur sportsmen X98.50
T48.05	Amateurism
T48.10	Amateur musicians
T48.20	Amateur actors
	(By training)
T49	Cultural personnel training
T49.20	Cultural agents training
T49.40	Film-making training

T20/99		**Cultural Development** (cont.)
T40/49		**Cultural Personnel** (cont.)
	T49	Cultural personnel training (cont.)
	T49.40	Film-making training (cont.)

For others combine descriptor for particular artists with term 'Cultural personnel training'

T50/64		**Cultural Conditions**
	T51	Cultural situation
	T51.10	Cultural aspect
	T51.20	Cultural content
	T51.35	Cultural factors
	T52	Cultural sociology
	T52.10	Cultural environment
	T52.10.10	Cultural level
	T52.30/50	Cultural life

Cultural behaviour T67/69
Quality of life R51.05

	T52.35	Everyday life
	T52.45	Life styles
	T53	Cultural systems

UF Cultural types

	T53.05	Traditional cultures

Folk cultures T12

	T53.08	Established cultures
	T53.10	Dominant cultures
	T53.13	Minority cultures
	T53.15	Elite cultures

UF High cultures

	T53.25	New cultures
	T53.30	Subcultures
	T53.35	Counter-cultures

UF Anti-cultures

	T53.38	Mass culture
	T53.40	Living cultures
	T53.42	Spontaneous cultures
	T53.45	Disappearing cultures
	T53.50/60	Cultural pluralism

UF Diversity of cultures

	T53.52	Biculturalism
	T53.55	Multiculturalism

(By culture of a particular class or condition)

	T53.65	Working class cultures
	T53.70	Culture of poverty

(By predominant activity)

	T53.72	Scientific cultures
	T53.75	Culture of work
	T53.78	Artistic cultures
	T53.80	Literary cultures

(By culture of a particular nation)

	T53.85	National cultures

(By culture of a world-wide nature)

	T53.90	Universal culture
	T58	Ethnopsychology
	T58.10	Cultural identity

UF Cultural identification
Ethnic identity
Basic personality T17.70
Right to cultural identity M94.10

	T58.20	Ethnocentricism

UF Race attitude

T20/99		**Cultural Development** (cont.)
T50/64		**Cultural Conditions** (cont.)
	T58	Ethnopsychology (cont.)
	T58.20	Ethnocentricism (cont.)
		Racism R44.20
	T58.35/50	Cultural nationalism
	T58.38	National identity
	T58.40	National consciousness
	T58.42	National character
	T58.44	National stereotype
	T59	Cultural interaction
		UF Cultural contact
	T59.10	Acculturation
	T59.65	Cultural relations
	T59.70	Cultural conflict
	T60	`ultural isolation
		Cultural integration T72
		Cultural minorities T61.35
		Cultural participation T68
	T61	Cultural differentiation
	T61.10	Cultural inequality
		UF Cultural equality
		Cultural rights
	T61.20	Cultural discrimination
	T61.30	Cultural disadvantage
	T61.35	Cultural minorities
		Dominant cultures T53.10
	T61.50	Cultural elite
		Elite culture T53.15
	T62	Cultural change
		Acculturation T59.10
		Changing society R66
		Disappearing cultures T53.45
		New cultures T53.25
	T62.10	Cultural dynamics
	T62.20	Cultural equilibrium
	T62.30	Cultural revolution
	T62.40	Cultural reproduction
	T62.50	Cultural innovations
	T62.60	Cultural discoveries
	T63	Civilization crises
	T63.10	Cultural crises
T65/69		**Cultural Users**
		UF Cultural consumers
		Culturally disadvantaged R84.75
		Audiences Y95.30
		Library users Z72.30.10
		Museum users T98
		(By needs)
	T66	Cultural needs
		Cultural rights M94
	T66.10	Cultural demand
		Cultural supply T30.35
	T66.20	Cultural benefits
		(By behaviour)
	T67/69	Cultural behaviour
		UF Cultural behaviour patterns
		Cultural interaction T59
		Leisure time activities X75/93
		Time budgets T15.20.10

T20/99		**Cultural Development** (cont.)
T65/69		**Cultural Users** (cont.)
	T67/69	Cultural behaviour (cont.)
	T68	Cultural participation
		Cultural isolation T60
		Right to cultural participation M94.20
	T68.30	Cultural attendance
		Cinema attendance W88.60
		Museum attendance T97.10.10
		Theatre attendance W82.25.40
	T69	Cultural consumption
		UF Cultural goods consumption
		Cultural services consumption
		Household cultural budgets T15.20.30

T70/99		**Cultural Action**
		Environmental planning S70/99
		Information/library development Z28.40
	T71	Democratization of culture
		Cultural democracy T24.10
	T72	Cultural integration
		Cultural isolation T60
		Cultural identity T58.10
	T72.20	Enculturation
	T72.40	Cultural assimilation
	T73	Dissemination of culture
		UF Cultural communication
		Cultural diffusion
		Cultural transmission
		Cultural education J60.80
		Cultural tourism X92.10
		Presentation of cultural property T85/89
	T74	Animation culturelle
		SN Cultural activities encouragement
		Cultural agents T41.30
	T75	Socio-cultural action
		Socio-cultural activities T78.10

T78		**Cultural Activities**
		UF Cultural fields
		Cultural sectors
		SN Descriptors for individual activities are found in succeeding sections. In particular see:
	V16/82	Religion
	V50/59	Religious practice
	W	Arts
	W19/69	Visual arts
	W80/99	Performing arts (including theatre, cinema, dance, etc.)
	X55/69	Literature
	X70/99	Leisure
	Y	Communication
	Y70	Mass media (including radio and television)
	Z	Information libraries and archives
	Z15.65/89	Audiovisual materials
	Z62	Libraries
	Z75	Library extension work
	T78.10	Socio-cultural activities
		Socio-cultural centres T38.10
		Socio-cultural clubs X79.30

T80/84		**Preservation of Cultural Property**
		SN The preservation and restoration of cultural heritage
		Amenities conservation S79

T20/99		**Cultural Development** (cont.)
T80/84		**Preservation of Cultural Property** (cont.)
	T81.10	Cultural heritage
	T81.20	Cultural property
	T81.20.30	Movable cultural property

(By specific properties)

	T83	Preservation of works of art
		UF Conservation of works of art
		Restoration of works of art
		Works of art W08
	T83.10	Restoration of paintings
	T84	Preservation of monuments
		UF Ancient cities preservation
		Buildings preservation
		Conservation of monuments
		Historic cities preservation
		Historic monuments preservation
		Historic sites preservation
		Restoration of monuments
		Historic monuments W22.70.10

(By theft protection and insurance)
Combine 'Cultural property' with descriptors 'Theft protection' and 'Insurance'

T85/89		**Presentation of Cultural Property**
T86		**Cultural Exhibitions**
	T86.10	Art collections
	T86.30	Art galleries
		UF Picture galleries
	T86.70	Cultural demonstrations
T87/99		**Museums**
	T88	Museology
	T88.10	Museography
		Museographers T93.40
	T90	*Museum policy and development* (†)
	T90.10	Museum policy
	T90.10.40	Museum cooperation
	T90.30	Museum development
	T91	*Museum planning and administration* (†)
	T91.10	Museum planning
		(By planners tools)
	T91.10.20	Museum statistics
		(By programmes)
	T91.10.40	Museum programmes
	T91.30	Museum economics
	T91.30.10/30	Museum finance
	T91.30.15	Museum charges
	T91.30.20	Museum financing
	T91.40	Museum administration
	T91.40.10	Museum re-organization
	T91.40.40	Museum legislation
	T92	Museum facilities
	T92.10	Museum buildings
	T92.10.10	Museum architecture
	T92.30	Museum laboratories
	T92.30.30	Repair workshops
	T92.40	Museum equipment
		UF Showcases
	T93	Museum personnel

T20/99		**Cultural Development** (cont.)
T85/89		**Presentation of Cultural Property** (cont.)
T87/99		**Museums** (cont.)
	T93	Museum personnel (cont.)
	T93.10	Museum curators
	T93.40	Museographers
	T93.60	Museum training
	T94	Museum techniques
		UF Museum technical operations
	T95	Museum collections
	T95.10	Museum objects
		(Museums by type)
	T96.10	National museums
	T96.20	Regional museums
	T96.25	School museums
		(By subject)
	T96.30	Science museums
	T96.30.10	Natural history museums
	T96.30.30	Ecomuseums
	T96.35	Art museums
	T96.45	Historical museums
	T96.50	Archaeological museums
	T96.55	Ethnographic museums
	T96.70	Specialized museums
		UF Special subject museums
		(By mobility)
	T96.80	Museobuses
		(By special characteristics)
	T96.90	Musee imaginaire
		(By activities)
	T97	Museum activities
	T97.05	Museum educational programmes
	T97.10	Museum visits
		*Museum charges
	T97.10.10	Museum attendance
		(By users)
	T98	Museum users

U   History and Associated Studies

U01/49   History

U50/59   Archaeology

U60/65   Genealogy Heraldry

U70/72   Numismatics. Sigillography

U75/80   Epigraphy. Palaeography

U90/95   Chronology

History and Associated Studies

History

*History education J60.59
*Historical museums T96.45

U03	Philosophy of history
U05/14	Historiography
	SN The study of history and the agents of that study
U06	Historical writing
U06.50	Historical editing
	(History by method)
U08	Historical method
U08.10	Objective history
	UF Scientific history
U08.20	Psychohistory
U08.30	Quantitative history
U08.40	Oral history
U08.45	Documentary history
U10	Historical research
U11	Historical analysis
U13	Historians
	(History by period)
U15/19	Prehistory
	*Geological ages D17
	*Prehistoric man F48.10
U16	Stone age
U16.10	Palaeolithic period
	UF Old stone age
U16.30	Mesolithic period
U16.40	Neolithic period
	UF New stone age
U17	Iron age
U18	Bronze age
U20/24	Ancient history
U21	Antiquity
U21.10	Antiquities
U23	Ancient civilizations
	*Ancient art W17.30
	*Ancient religions V40/43
	*Ancient theatre W82.10
	*Antiquarian law M41.10
U23.10	Egyptology
U23.30	Assyriology
U25	Medieval history
U25.05	Middle ages
U30	Modern history
	(History by place)
U32	European history
U33	Byzantine history
U34	Russian history
U35	Asian history
U36	Arab history
U37	African history
U39/41	American history
U40	North American history
U41	Latin American history
U42	Australasian history
	For others combine 'History' with descriptor for name of place
U44	*(History by subject)*
	*Art history W05
	*Communication history Y04

U01/49		**History** (cont.)
	U44	*(History by subject)* (cont.)

Constitutional history L32.10.10
Cultural history T04
Economic history N02
Educational history J03
History of archives Z86.10
History of psychology P04
History of science B08
Information/library history Z24
Legal history M04
Literary history X56
Political history L03
Religious history V17
Social history R02.50

For others combine 'History' with terms for specific subjects

U50/59		**Archaeology**

Archaelogical museums T96.50

(By operations)

	U51	Archaeological field work
	U51.10	Archaeological surveying
	U51.30	Archaeological excavations
		UF Archaeological digging
	U52/53	Archaeological interpretation
	U52.10	Archaeometry
		SN Statistical, physical and chemical methods of archaeological interpretation
		Photogrammetry H31.20
	U52.10.40	Archaeological dating
		Radiocarbon dating U93.20
	U52.50	Archaeological sociology
		SN Social anthropological interpretation of archaeological remains

(By sites and remains)

	U55	Archaeological sites
	U56	Archaeological structures
		SN Includes cairns, barrows, cumuli, caves, walls, circles, fortifications, earthwork, buildings (temples, dwellings)
		Preservation of monuments T84
		Historic monuments W22.70.10

(By objects)

	U57	Archaeological objects
		UF Artifacts

(By personnel)

	U58	Archaeologists

U60/65		**Genealogy. Heraldry** (†)
	U62	Genealogy
		SN The investigation of pedigrees as a branch of knowledge
	U65	Heraldry
	U65.10	Flags

U70/72		**Numismatics. Sigillography** (†)
	U71	Numismatics
		UF Numismatology
		SN Study of coins, tokens and medals
	U72	Sigillography
		SN The study of seals

U75/80		**Epigraphy. Palaeography (†)**
	U76	Epigraphy
		SN The study of ancient inscriptions
		Tablets (documents) Z15.62.30
		Ancient scripts X39
	U78	Palaeography
		SN The study of ancient and medieval scripts
		Manuscripts Z15.42.10
		Archives Z85/99
		Graphonomy X37/42
U90/95		**Chronology**
		SN The science of computing time or periods of time and of assigning events to their true dates
		UF Historical chronology
		Geochronology D08.30
		Time A37
		Time measurement and instruments H18
	U93	Dating
	U93.20	Radiocarbon dating

V   Philosophy, Ethics and Religion

Philosophy, Ethics and Religion

Philosophy
Cultural philosophy T06
Educational philosophy J10.05
Information/library philosophy Z28.10
Ethics V15
Literary philosophy X57.10
Philosophy of history U03
Political philosophy L06/19
Science philosophy B04
Social welfare philosophy R86

(By viewpoints, doctrines and schools)

V02	Ideologies
	UF Doctrines

V03	Philosophical schools

    SN Includes pragmatism, utilitarianism, naturalism, evolutionism, realism, platonism, optimism, pessimism, stoicism, fatalism, nihilism scepticism, manism, dualism, electricism, phenomenology, etc.
    Determinism V06.60.05
    Humanism V33.50
    Pluralism L11.40
    Psychological schools P10
    Traditionalism L16.30

V03.10	Rationalism
V03.15	Empiricism
V03.15.10	Behaviourism
V03.15.20	Positivism
V03.20	Materialism
V03.25	Idealism
V03.30	Individualism
V03.60	Existentialism
V03.65	Structuralism
V03.70	Functionalism

(By branches, fields, topics and problems in philosophy)

06	Metaphysics

    SN Includes philosophy of nature, philosophy of life, infinity, etc.
    Cosmology C73
    Time A37

V06.10	Ontology
	SN Includes reality, absolute, existence
V06.60	Causality
	Causal analysis A90.10
V06.60.05	Determinism
V06.60.10	Cause and effect
V06.70	Teleology

V07	Epistemology

    Cognition P48/55
    Methodology A89/91

V07.10/20	Knowledge
	Dissemination of knowledge Z10.10.10
V07.15	Sociology of knowledge
V07.20	Structure of knowledge
	UF Classification of knowledge
	Classification systems Z50.05
	Taxonomy F34
V07.20.10	Typology
	Typological analysis A90.30
V07.30	Experience
V07.35	Belief
V07.40	Uncertainty

V08	Logic
	Mathematical logic B41

V01/14		**Philosophy** (cont.)
	V09	Truth
		UF Falsity
	V10	Philosophy of mind
		Psychology P01/99
		Mind P57.10
	V10.10	Human nature
	V11	Philosophy of action
		Behaviour P18
		Responsibility V15.30.35
	V11.10	Free-will
	V12	Axiology
		UF Theory of value
	V12.10	Value
		Cultural values T06.50
		Economic value N69.30
		Moral values V15.10
		Social values P76.10
	V12.30	Value judgment
V15		**Ethics**
		SN The science of morals
		UF Moral theology
		Moral philosophy
		Morality
		Ethics of science B04.30
		Communication ethics Y15.10
		Moral development P66
		Moral education J60.77
		Philosophy V01/14
		Political ethics L07
		Theology V20/29
	V15.10	Moral values
	V15.20	Moral order
		UF Moral standards
		Moral codes
	V15.25	Moral problems
	V15.25.20	Moral crises
	V15.30	Moral concepts
		UF Good
		Evil
		Guilt
		Ideals
		Right and wrong
		Sin
	V15.30.25	Obligation
		UF Moral obligation
	V15.30.30	Duties
	V15.30.35	Responsibility
		UF Moral responsibility
	V15.30.40	Accountability
	V15.30.50	Conscience
	V15.30.60	Discipline
	V15.35	Moral behaviour
		UF Moral actions
		Moral conduct
	V15.35.10	Misconduct
	V15.40	Virtue and vice
		UF Clemency
		Compassion
		Courage
		Honour
		Loyalty

V15		**Ethics** (cont.)
	V15.40	Virtue and vice (cont.)
		Mercy
		Obedience
		*Love P80.50
		*Hatred P82.10
		*Jealousy P37.28
		*Tolerance P73.45
		*Truth V09
	V15.40.20	Cruelty
	V15.50	Deontology
		UF Professional ethics
		*Communication ethics Y15.10
		*Medical ethics F98.05
		*Press ethics Y70.25
		*Teacher professional ethics J30.06
V16/82		**Religion**
		*Ecclesiastical law M48
		*Religious art W15.30
		*Religious education J60.75
		*Religious music W75.70
V17		**Religious History**
V18		**Sociology of Religion**
		*Psychology of religion V29
		*Religious conflict V29.20
		*Religious discrimination V63.20
		*Religious minorities V63.30
V20/29		**Theology**
		*Ethics V15
		*Philosophy V01/14
	V21	Scriptures
		UF Holy writings
		Bible
		Koran
	V22/25	Religious doctrines
		(By subject of doctrines)
	V23	God
	V24	Immortality
		UF After life
	V26	Religious belief
		UF Religious faith
	V26.30	Superstition
	V27/29	Religious experience
	V29	Psychology of religion
	V29.10	Religious behaviour
		UF Puritanism
		Religious fanaticism
	V29.20	Religious conflict
V30/49		**Religious Systems**
	V31	Deism
		UF Monotheism
	V32	Messianism
	V32.20	Millenarianism
	V33.10	Atheism
	V33.20	Agnosticism
	V33.50	Humanism
	V36	Primitive religions
	V36.10	Animism

V16/82		**Religion** (cont.)
V30/49		**Religious Systems** (cont.)
	V36	Primitive religions (cont.)
	V36.20	Totenism
	V36.30	Fetishism
	V38	Prehistoric religion
	V40/43	Ancient religions
	V41	Mythology
		UF Myths
	V42	Egyptian religion
	V43	Ancient Asiatic religions
	V43.10	Zoroastrianism
	V43.20	Taoism
	V43.30	Confucianism
	V43.40	Shinto
	V43.50	Shamanism
	V46	Modern religions
	V46.10	Brahmanism
	V46.20	Hinduism
	V46.25	Sectarianism
	V46.30	Jainism
	V46.33	Sikhism
	V46.35	Buddhism
	V46.37	Theravada
		UF Hinayana
	V46.38	Mahayana
		UF Jodo
		Lamaism
		Tantrism
		Zen
	V46.40	Islam
		UF Mohammedism
		Moslemism
	V46.50	Judaism
	V46.60	Christianity
	V46.60.20	Catholicism
		UF Roman Catholicism
	V46.60.30	Protestantism
V50/59		**Religious Practice**
	V52	Cults
	V53	Religious festivals
		UF Religious feasts
		(By formal devotions)
	V54.10	Preaching
	V54.20	Prayer
	V55	Religious ceremonies
		UF Funerals
		Religious rites
		Weddings
		(By personal devotion)
	V58.10	Asceticism
	V58.12	Fasting
	V58.20	Pilgrimages
V60/74		**Religious Institutions**
	V62/64	Church
		Church and education J10.45
		(By relations with state)
	V63	Church and state

V16/82	**Religion** (cont.)
V60/74	**Religious Institutions** (cont.)
V62/64	Church (cont.)
V63	Church and state (cont.)
	UF Religious authority
	Ecclesiastical law M48
	Religious freedom M92.15.10
V63.20	Religious discrimination
V63.30	Religious minorities
	(By administration)
V64	Church administration
	UF Church organization
V64.10	Pastoral work
V64.15	Missionary work
V64.50	Religious reform
	(By groups)
V65	Religious communities
	UF Religious groups
	Congregations
V65.30	Religious orders
	UF Monasteries
V65.30.20	Convents
	(By movements and sects)
V66.10	Religious movements
	UF Religious missions
V66.10.10	Ecumenical movement
V66.30	Sects
	(By facilities)
V68	Religious buildings
	UF Cathedrals
	Chapels
	Church buildings
V68.30	Mosques
V68.40	Temples
V68.80	Shrines
V75/82	**Religious Persons**
V76	Religious leaders
	UF Messiahs
V77	Prophets
V78	Priests (cultic)
	UF Exorcists
	High priests
	Magicians
V79	Saints
	UF Martyrs
V80	Ministers of religion
	UF Clergymen
	Priests (clergy)
	Rabbies
	(By persons in religious orders)
V81.10	Monks
V81.20	Nuns
V82.10	Believers
V82.20	Pagans
	UF Heathens
	(By particular religion)
	Jews R37.60.20
V82.30	Buddhists
V82.40	Hindus
V82.50	Moslems

V16/82		**Religion** (cont.)
V75/82		**Religious Persons** (cont.)
	V82.70	Christians
		UF Catholics
		Protestants

V83/99   **Esoteric Practices**

	V84	Mysticism

V85/92   **Occult**

UF Psychical research
Supernatural

	V86/87	Parapsychology
		UF Metaphysics
		Paranormal psychology
		Psychotronics
	V87	Extra-sensory perception
		UF Clairvoyance
		Precognition
	V87.10	Telepathy
		UF Object reading
	V87.40	Psychokinesis
		UF Mind over matter
	V88	Alchemy
	V89	Fortune telling
		UF Augury
	V90	Astrology
		UF Horoscopy
	V91	Physiognomy
		UF Phrenology
	V91.10	Palmistry
		UF Chiromancy
		Chirognomy
	V94	Spiritualism
	V95	Magic
		SN Ritual arts believed and designed to influence events
	V95.10	Witchcraft
		UF Sorcery
		Witchdoctors V78.30
	V95.20	Demonology
	V95.50	Voodoo

V97   **Sciosophic Movements**

UF Scientology

V98   **Secret Societies**

UF Rosicrucians

	V98.10	Freemasonry

W   Arts

W01/18   Art theory, techniques and styles

W19/69   Visual arts

W20/39   Fine arts

W21/24   Architecture

W25/29   Graphic arts

W30/39   Plastic arts

W40/49   Handicrafts

W50/69   Reproductive arts

W51/54   Photography

W55/64   Printing

W65/69   Reprography

W70/79   Music

W80/99   Performing arts

W82   Theatre

W83   Other theatrical arts

W84   Opera

W85   Dance

W86/99   Cinema

W	**Arts**
W01/18	**Art Theory, Techniques and Styles (†)**

UF Artistic culture
Art books Z15.36.30
Art libraries Z62.68.40
Cultural education J60.80

	(By history)
W05	Art history
	UF History of art
	(By sociology)
W06	Sociology of art
	(By products)
W08	Works of art
	UF Art objects
	Masterpieces
	Cultural property T81.20
W08.10	Antiques
W08.30	Representative works of art
W08.50	Art imitations
	UF Art forgeries
	(By philosophy and criticism)
W10	Aesthetics
	UF Philosophy of art
W10.20	Art criticism
	UF Art appreciation
	(By qualities)
W11	Artistic creation
W11.02	Psychology of art
W12	Artistic design
	UF Artistic composition
	Industrial design H05.10
W13	Expression
	UF Artistic expression
	Expressivity
W13.20	Improvisation
W13.30	Oral expression
W13.35	Physical expression
W13.50	Catharsis
	(By style)
W15	Art styles
	SN Use for individual European art styles, for example: Renaissance, Gothic, Baroque, Romanticism, Impressionism, Cubism, Surrealism, etc.
W15.02	Byzantine art
W15.05	Classical art
W15.10	Folk art
W15.13	Native art
	UF Primitive art
W15.15	Pop art
	UF Psychodelic art
	Graffiti
	Kitsch
W15.30	Religious art
W15.30.10	Iconography
W15.30.30	Islamic art
	(By period)
W17.20	Prehistoric art
	Rock painting W26.45
W17.30	Ancient art
W17.40	Medieval art

W01/18		**Art Theory, Techniques and Styles** (cont.)
	W17.50/80	Modern art SN Twentieth century art
	W17.70	Contemporary art *Pop art W15.15*
	W17.70.30	Avant-garde art
	W17.70.70	Experimental art
		(By place)
	W18.10	European art
	W18.10.30	Slav art
	W18.20	Asian art
	W18.20.10	Chinese art
	W18.30	Arab art *Islamic art W15.30.30*
	W18.50	African art
	W18.70	Latin American art
	W18.90	Oceanic art

For other countries combine the descriptor 'Arts' with geographical place name.

W19/69   **Visual Arts**

W20/39   **Fine Arts**

UF Decorative arts

W21/24   **Architecture**
Architecture education J60.80.60
Construction engineering G56/60
Environmental planning S70/99
Building design G59

	W22	Buildings *Apartments S45.20* *Educational buildings J25.03* *Houses S45.10* *Library buildings Z32.10* *Museum buildings T92.10* *Recreational buildings X95.40* *Religious buildings V68*
	W22.50	Palaces
	W22.70	Monuments
	W22.70.10	Historic monuments UF Historic sites *Ancient cities S20.20* *Preservation of monuments T84*
	W23	Interior architecture
		(By personnel)
	W24	Architects *Architect restorers T41.70* *Environmental planners S73*
	W24.10	Landscape architects

W25/29   **Graphic Arts**

UF Pictorial arts
Photography W51/54
Printing W55/64
Art education J60.80.50

	W26	Painting UF Paintings *(By medium)*
	W26.10	Oil painting *(By properties)*
	W26.30	Miniature painting

W19/69		**Visual Arts** (cont.)
W20/39		**Fine Arts** (cont.)
W25/29		**Graphic Arts** (cont.)
	W26	Painting (cont.)
		(By surface painted on)
	W26.40	Murals
	W26.45	Rock painting
	W27	Drawing
		UF Sketching
		Technical drawing
		(By product)
	W27.70	Cartoons
	W28	Commercial art
		Posters Z15.72.47
	W29	Calligraphy
		SN Handwriting as an art
W30/39		**Plastic Arts**
		Numismatics U71
		Sigillography U72
	W31	Sculpture
	W32	Engraving
		UF Glyptography
	W33	Jewelry
	W34	Art metalwork
	W35	Woodcarving
	W36	Ceramic art
		UF Stoneware
		Porcelain
	W36.10	Pottery
		UF Earthenware
	W37	Mosaics
		UF Inlay
	W38	Art glass
	W38.10	Glassware
		Glass technology G90
	W38.40	Stained glass
W40/49		**Handicrafts**
		UF Arts and crafts
		Basketry crafts
		Crafts
		Flower arrangement
		Minor arts
		Handicrafts education J60.85
	W41	Textile arts
		Textile technology G95
	W41.10	Tapestry
	W41.40	Carpets
	W43	Fashion design
		UF Dress design
		Haute couture
		Clothing manufacture G96.15
		Fashion T13.60
	W44	Needlework
		UF Embroidery
W50/69		**Reproductive Arts**
W51/54		**Photography**
		Amateur photography X77.60
		Microphotography W67

W19/69		**Visual Arts** (cont.)
W50/69		**Reproductive Arts** (cont.)
W51/54		**Photography** (cont.)
		Photographs Z15.72.49
		(By type)
	W52	Cinematography
	W53.10	Aerial photography
	W53.30	Underwater photography
		(By equipment)
	W54	Photographic equipment
	W54.10	Cameras
		Television cameras Y80.70.40
		Underwater cameras D98.40
	W54.10.20	Film cameras
	W54.20	Projectors
	W54.20.40	Slide projectors
W55/64		**Printing**
		UF Typography
		Book production Y90.22.10
		Publishing Y90.20/29
		(By process)
	W57	Printing processes
	W57.10	Relief printing
		UF Letterpress
	W57.20	Intaglio printing
		UF Photogravure
		Collotype
	W57.30	Stencil printing
		UF Screen printing
		Silk screen printing
	W57.40	Lithography
		UF Photolithography
	W57.70	Illustration printing
		UF Engraving (printing)
		Etching (printing)
		Half tones
		(By facilities and equipment)
	W58	Printing equipment
		UF Printing machines
		Printing paper G96.27.10
	W59	Printing workshops
		(By operations)
	W60/64	Printing operations
	W62	Composition
		UF Typesetting
	W62.20	Machine typesetting
	W62.30	Photocomposition
		UF Computer typesetting
	W63	Press work
	W64	Binding
W65/69		**Reprography**
		UF Document reproduction
	W66	Photocopying
		Photocopies Z15.72.60
	W66.20	Xerography
	W66.40	Diazo processes
	W67	Microphotography
		UF Microcopying
		Microforms Z15.77

W19/69		**Visual Arts** (cont.)
W65/69		**Reprography** (cont.)
	W67	Microphotography (cont.)
		(By equipment)
	W67.30	Microform equipment
		UF Microfilm readers
		(By application)
	W67.70	Micropublishing
	W68	Duplicating
		SN Includes carbon copy stencil and spirit duplicating
W70/79		**Music**
		Music education J60.80.10
		Musicians T44
		(By scores)
	W71	Music scores
		(By theory and study)
	W72	Musicology
	W72.10	Musical theory
	W72.30	Musical elements
		SN Includes musical time, pitch, tonality and musical harmony
	W72.30.10	Rhythm
	W72.50	Musical forms
		SN Includes fugues, concertos, marches, rondos, sonatas, symphonies, etc.
		(By techniques)
	W73	Musical composition
		(By performance)
	W74	Musical performances
		UF Conducting
	W74.05	Recitals
	W74.10	Musical concerts
	W74.50	Musical festivals
	W74.80	Amateur musical performances
		(By musical character)
	W75	Musical character
	W75.05	Mechanical music
	W75.10	Electronic music
	W75.13	Abstract music
	W75.15	Concrete music
	W75.20	Classical music
	W75.30	Traditional music
	W75.33	National music
	W75.35	Popular music
	W75.40	Folk music
	W75.50	Pop music
	W75.55	Jazz
	W75.60	Dance music
	W75.62	Ballet music
	W75.64	Film music
	W75.70	Religious music
	W75.80	Modern music
	W75.80.10	Contemporary music
		(By music for a particular media)
	W76	Vocal music
		UF Choral music
		Operatic music
	W76.10	Singing
	W76.30	Songs
	W76.30.10	Folk songs

W70/79		**Music** (cont.)
	W76	Vocal music (cont.)
	W76.50	Choirs
	W76.50.50	Amateur choirs
	W77	Instrumental music
		UF Chamber music
		Orchestral music
		(By instruments)
	W78	Musical instruments
	W78.10	Keyboard instruments
	W78.20	String instruments
	W78.30	Wind instruments
	W78.40	Brass instruments
	W78.50	Percussion instruments
		(By orchestras)
	W79	Orchestras
		UF Bands
	W79.50	Amateur orchestras
	W79.50.10	Youth orchestras
W80/99		**Performing Arts**
		UF Dramatic arts
		Audiences Y95.10
		Broadcasting Y70.30/90
		Drama education J60.80.40
		Performers T47
		Show business N49.60
		(By acting)
	W81	Acting
	W81.30	Gesture
	W81.40	Miming
		(By individual performing arts)
		Broadcasting Y70.30/90
W82		**Theatre**
		Drama X67
	W82.03	Theatrical life
		(By type)
	W82.10	Ancient theatre
	W82.11	Traditional theatre
	W82.12	National theatre
	W82.13	Commercial theatre
	W82.14	Popular theatre
	W82.15	Repertory theatre
	W82.16	Travelling theatre
		UF Strolling players
	W82.17	Open air theatre
	W82.18	Amateur theatre
	W82.18.10	School plays
	W82.20	Total theatre
		(By management)
	W82.25	Theatre management
	W82.25.05	Theatrical companies
	W82.25.05F	Folklore troupes
	W82.25.10	Theatre buildings
		Opera houses X95.40.30
	W82.25.10C	Theatre capacity
	W82.25.40	Theatre attendance
		(By theatrical production)
	W82.50	Theatrical production
		Theatrical directors T45

W80/99		**Performing Arts** (cont.)
W82		**Theatre** (cont.)
	W82.25	Theatre management (cont.)

Actors T47.10
Drama X67

	W82.50.10	Auditioning
	W82.50.20	Rehearsal
	W82.50.40	Stage management

SN Includes theatrical costumes, theatrical make-up and stage effects

	W82.50.40B	Scenery (stage)

UF Stage sets

	W82.60	Theatrical performances

UF Show (theatrical)

	W82.60.10	Dramatization
W83		**Other Theatrical Arts**
	W83.05	Concerts
	W83.10	Music-Hall
	W83.15	Variety shows
	W83.20	Circuses
	W83.25	Pantomime
	W83.30	Puppets

UF Marionettes

	W83.35	Mime

Miming W81.40

	W83.60	Play reading
	W83.70	Sound and music

UF Son et lumiere

W84		**Opera**

Opera houses X95.40.30

	W84.70	Musical comedy
W85		**Dance**

UF Dancing
Theatrical dance
Dancers T47.10.30

	W85.10	Folk dance
	W85.20	National dance
	W85.30	Modern dance

UF Ballroom dancing

	W85.60	Ballet

Ballet music W75.62

	W85.60.10	Classical ballet
	W85.60.20	Modern ballet
	W85.60.70	Choreography

Choreographers T47.10.30C

W86/99		**Cinema**

Educational films J55.08

(By publicity and management)

	W87	Film festivals
	W88	Cinema management
	W88.50	Cinema buildings
	W88.50.10	Cinema capacity
	W88.60	Cinema attendance

(By production)

	W89	Film-making

UF Filming
Shooting (films)
Cinematography W52
Film actors T47.10.40

W80/99		**Performing Arts** (cont.)
W86/99		**Cinema** (cont.)
	W89	Film-making (cont.)
		Film-makers T46
		Film-making training T49.40
		Film music W75.64
		Film scripts X68.20
		Photography W51/54
		Television production Y70.70.30
		(By facilities)
	W89.20	Film sets
		(By films)
	W90	Films
		Film clubs X79.30.20
		Film libraries Z62.63
		Educational films J55.08
		Film strips Z15.75.10
		Television films Y70.70.80
		(By form)
	W90.05	Full-length films
	W90.08	Short films
		(By subject content)
	W90.10	Thriller films
		UF Espionage films
	W90.15	Science fiction films
	W90.18	War films
	W90.20	Comedy films
	W90.25	Musical comedy films
		UF Musicals
	W90.30	Romance films
		UF Love story films
	W90.35	Historical films
	W90.40	Documentary films
	W90.45	News films
		UF Newsreels
	W90.50	Political films
	W90.60	Arts films
	W90.65	Ethnographic films
		(By user)
	W90.70	Children's films
		(By industry)
	W91	Film industry
	W91.10	Film production statistics
	W91.20	Film distribution

X01/69   Philology (Language and Literature)

X02/54	Linguistics
X05	Linguists
X07	Linguistic theory
X10/19	Linguistic research
X20/29	Sociolinguistics
X30	Psycholingistics
X35/46	Descriptive linguistics
X36	Phonetics
X37/42	Graphonomy
X43	Grammar
X44/46	Semantics
X47/50	Comparative and diachronic linguistics
X53/54	Translation
X55/69	Literature

X01/69   Philology (Language and Literature)

X02/54   **Linguistics**

             UF Language (linguistics)
       Communication Y
       Computer languages H86
       Index languages Z50
       Language education J60.37
       Languages A01/15

X05   **Linguists**
       Interpreters X54.40.10
       Translators Z34.60.20

X07   **Linguistic Theory**

X10/19   **Linguistic Research**

X11	Language collection	
X11.40	Language recording	
X12/15	Linguistic analysis	
	Speech analysis X36.50	
X12.20	Contextual analysis	
X12.50	Semantic analysis	
	UF Significance analysis	
X12.70	Syntactic analysis	
X14	Statistical linguistics	
	Statistical linguistics (indexing) Z48.52	
X15	Computer linguistics	
	Automatic indexing Z48.50/52	
	Automatic translation X54.10	

X20/29   **Sociolinguistics**

       SN Social and cultural functions of language
       UF Language and class
            Language and politics

X21	Language policy	
X21.20	Language of instruction	
X21.30	Linguistic unification	
X22.10	Language barriers	
X22.30	Language minorities	
	Language discrimination R54.10.40	
X23	Bilingualism	
X23.10	Multilingualism	
X25	Ethnolinguistics	

X30   **Psycholinguistics**

       UF Neurolinguistics
       Speech disorders F67.10
       Speech habits X36.10.10

X30.20	Language behaviour	
X30.40	Language development	

X35/46   **Descriptive Linguistics**

X36	Phonetics	
	SN Science of human speech sound	
	Phonetic writing X40	
	Speech Y45.10/20	
X36.10	Speech production	
	UF Articulation (speech)	
	Diction	
	Speech disorders F67.10	
X36.10.10	Speech habits	
X36.40	Phonology	
X36.50	Speech analysis	

X02/54		**Linguistics** (cont.)
X35/46		**Descriptive Linguistics** (cont.)
	X37/42	Graphonomy
		SN Linguistic aspects of writing
		UF Graphemics
		Handwriting Y45.30.05
		(By operation)
	X37.10	Transliteration
	X37.30	Transcription
	X37.40	Deciphering
		(By systems)
	X38/42	Writing systems
	X39	Ancient scripts
		Epigraphy U76
		Palaeography U78
	X39.10	Pictographic script
	X39.20	Ideographic scripts
		UF Ideograms
	X39.30	Hieroglyphics
	X39.40	Cuneiform writing
	X40	Phonetic writing
		UF Syllabic writing
		Alphabetic writing
		Punctuation marks
		Accents (writing)
		(By elements)
	X40.10	Alphabet
	X40.20	Letters (alphabet)
		UF Upper case letters
		Lower case letters
		(By spelling)
	X40.40	Spelling
		UF Orthography
	X41	Shorthand
		UF Stenography
	X42	Cryptography
	X43	Grammar
	X43.10	Morphology (linguistics)
		SN Studies of the smallest meaningful units of language and their formation into words
		UF Inflection
		Morpheme
		Nouns
		Phrases
		Prefix
		Suffix
		Syllables
		Verbs
		Words (morphology)
	X43.70	Syntax
		SN Study of rules of the relation of words to one another
		UF Clauses
		Sentences
		Syntactic relations Z50.70/79
		Syntactic analysis X12.70
	X44/46	Semantics
		Semantic relations Z50.52/69
		Semantic analysis X12.50
	X45	Semiology
		UF Semiotics
	X45.10	Symbolic language
		Codes Y80.10.35
	X45.10.20	Signs
	X45.10.30	Symbols

X02/54		**Linguistics** (cont.)
X35/46		**Descriptive Linguistics** (cont.)
	X44/46	Semantics (cont.)
	X46	Lexicography
		Dictionaries Z15.15.10
	X46.10	Vocabularies
		Index language vocabularies Z50.30/59
	X46.20	Terminology
		UF Nomenclature
	X46.20.60	Educational terminology
	X46.20.70	Communication terminology
	X46.20.80	Scientific terminology

X47/50		**Comparative and Diachronic Linguistics**
		SN Study of language change and variation
	X48	Etymology
		UF Language origins
	X49	Language change
	X50	Language varieties
		Computer languages H86
		Index languages Z50
		Symbolic languages X45.10
	X50.10	Spoken languages
	X50.30	Written languages
	X50.35	Formal language
	X50.40	Colloquial language
		UF Slang
		Jargon
	X50.50	Unwritten languages
	X50.55	Dead languages
	X50.60	Modern languages
	X50.65	Vernacular languages
	X50.65.10	Mother tongue
		Mother tongue instruction J60.25/32
	X50.70	Foreign languages
	X50.70.10	Second language
		Bilingualism X23
	X50.80	Dialects
		UF Dialectology
	X50.90	Language mixtures
		For individual languages see list at A01/11

X53/54		**Translation**
		Translations Z15.37.30
		(By personnel)
		Translators Z34.60.20
	X54.10	Automatic translation
	X54.10	Interpreting
	X54.40.10	Interpreters

X55/69		**Literature**
		UF Literary culture
		(By history)
	X56	Literary history
		(By philosophy and sociology)
	X57.10	Literary philosophy
	X57.50	Literary life
		(By theory, analysis, criticism and awards)
	X59.10	Literary research
	X59.20	Literary analysis
		UF Literary interpretation

X59.30	Literary criticism
X59.30.10	Book reviews
X59.50	Literary prizes

(By techniques)

X60	Literary composition
	UF Authorship
	Creative writing J46.03
	Editing Y90.22.40
	Translation X53/54
X60.10	Literary style
X60.20	Literary devices
	UF Alliteration
	Dialogue
	Literary characters
	Literary plot
	Metaphors

(By works of literature)

X61	Literary works
X61.10	Written tradition
	SN From the invention of printing
	UF Written expression
X61.30	Representative literary works
	UF Classical literary works
X62/68	Literary forms and genres
	UF Allegory
	Fantasy (literary)
	Humour (literary)
	Satire
	Correspondence Z15.42.30
	Biographies Z15.15.91
	Comics Z15.30.50K
	Speeches Y45.16.18
X63.10	Fiction
	Novels X60.40
X63.20	Popular literature
X63.20.05	Best sellers
X63.20.10	Romance stories
X63.20.20	Thrillers
X63.20.30	Science fiction
X63.50	Folk literature
	Fairy tales J60.28.20
X63.50.10	Legends
X63.50.20	Proverbs
X65	Poetry
	UF Verse
	Nursery rhymes J60.28.10
X65.40	Spoken poetry
X66	Prose
X66.10	Essays
X66.40	Novels
	Popular literature X63.20
X67	Drama
	UF Farce
	Plays
	Dramatization W82.60.10
	Mime W83.35
	Performing arts W80/99
	Radio drama Y70.50.55
	Television drama Y70.70.55
	Theatre W82
X67.10	Comedy
X67.20	Tragedy

X02/54		**Linguistics** (cont.)
X55/69		**Literature** (cont.)
	X62/68	Literary forms and genres (cont.)
	X68	Scripts
		UF Adaptations (scripts)
	X68.20	Film scripts
		(By period)
	X69.10	Modern literature
	X69.10.10	Contemporary literature
		(By language)
	X69.20	Foreign literature

For literature of particular languages combine with term for language, e.g.

French literature (Literature & French)

X70/99   Leisure

X75/93	**Leisure time activities**
X80/89	**Sport**
X90/93	**Tourism**
X94/99	**Recreational facilities**

X70/99   **Leisure**

UF Recreation
Right to rest and leisure M93.40
Students leisure J46.07.03

(By sociology)
X72   Sociology of leisure
UF Leisure utilization
Retirement Q74.40.30
X72.10   Leisure civilization
X72.40   Commercialized leisure

(By leisure time)
X73   Leisure time
Holidays X93
Leave Q74.20
Rest periods Q74.10.30

X75/93   **Leisure Time Activities**
Cultural activities T78
Time budgets T15.20.10

X76   Play
UF Playing activities
Play (teaching method) J50.06.30
Play groups J70.07.04K
Toys G96.60.10

X77   Hobbies
X77.10   Gardening
X77.40   Stamp collecting
UF Philately
X77.60   Amateur photography

X78   Entertainment
UF Amusement
Gambling R73.55
Performing arts W80/99
X78.10/30 Cultural events
X78.20   Festivals
Film festivals W87
Musical festivals W74.50
Religious festivals V53
X78.20.10   Pop festivals
X78.40   Fun fairs

X79   Clubs
School clubs J46.07.06C
Youth clubs J70.13.05C
X79.10   Old people's clubs
X79.30   Socio-cultural clubs
X79.30.10   Book clubs
X79.30.20   Film clubs
X79.30.30   Teleclubs
X79.30.40   Video clubs
X79.70   Sports clubs

X80/89   Sport
UF Games
Physical education J60.56
Sports clubs X79.70
Sports medicine F95.60
X81   Olympic games
X82.10   Acrobatics
X82.20   Gymnastics
X82.30   Athletics
X83   Ball games
UF Football
Cricket
Golf
Tennis

X75/93		**Leisure Time Activities** (cont.)
	X80/89	Sport (cont.)
	X84.10	Aquatic sports
		UF Diving
		Water-skiing
		Sailing
	X84.10.10	Swimming
	X84.30	Aerial sports
		UF Gliding
		Parachuting
		Sky diving
	X85	Combative sports
		UF Angling
		Wrestling
		Judo
		Boxing
		Fencing
	X85.10	Hunting
		SN Big game hunting
		UF Shooting (sport)
	X86.10	Equestrian sports
		UF Horse-riding
		Horse-racing
		Show-jumping
	X86.20	Winter sports
		UF Ice sports
		Skating
		Skiing
	X86.30	Mechanical sports
		UF Cycle racing
		Motoring (sport)
		Motor racing
		Roller skating
		Speedway racing
	X86.40	Animal sports
		UF Bull-fighting
		Greyhound racing
		Pigeon racing
	X87	Outdoor pursuits
		UF Caving
		Mountaineering
		Pot-holing
	X87.10	Camping
	X87.30	Hiking
		UF Rambling
		Walking
	X88	Indoor games
		UF Billiards
		Children's games
		Darts
		Toys G96.60.10
	X88.20	Card games
		(By personnel)
	X89	Sportsmen
		UF Professional sportsmen
	X89.10	Sports trainers
	X89.50	Amateur sportsmen
		(By status)
	X89.70	Amateur status
	X90/93	Tourism
		Tourist industry N49.05
		Travel S69
	X91	Tourist facilities
		UF Tourist equipment
		Tourist guides
		Tourist information

X75/93		**Leisure Time Activities** (cont.)
	X90/93	Tourism (cont.)
	X91	Tourist facilities (cont.)
	X91.10	Tourist accommodation
		Camping sites X96.10
		Hotels G97.10.10
		Hotel and catering industry N49.10
		(By type)
	X92.10	Cultural tourism
	X92.20	Weekend tourism
		Second homes S47.30
	X93	Holidays
		Holiday centres X96.20
		Holiday schools J70.07.09N
	X93.20	Holidays abroad
		UF Stay abroad
X94/99		**Recreational Facilities**
		Open spaces S90/95
		Tourist facilities X91
	X95.20	Playgrounds
	X95.40	Recreational buildings
		Cinema buildings W85.50
		Theatre buildings W82.25.10
	X95.40.30	Opera houses
	X95.40.40	Concert halls
	X96	Recreational centres
		UF Play centres
		Open air centres
		Cultural centres T38
		Sports centres X97.10
	X96.10	Camping sites
	X96.20	Holiday centres
	X96.20.10	Holiday camps
	X96.50	Youth hostels
	X97	Sports facilities
		Sports equipment X98.10
	X97.10	Sports centres
	X97.20	Gymnasia
	X97.30	Swimming pools
	X97.50	Playing fields
	X98	Leisure equipment
	X98.10	Sports equipment
		UF Physical education equipment

Y	**COMMUNICATION**
	Summary

Y04	**Communication history**
Y06	**Communication research**
Y15	**Communication policy**
Y20	**Communication planning and administration**
Y25	**Communication personnel**
Y30	**Communication personnel training**
Y35	**Sociology of communication**
Y38	**Communication psychology**
Y40/64	**Communication process**
Y45	**Communication skills**
Y50	**Interpersonal communication**
Y55	**Group communication**
Y60	**Mass communication**
Y65/79	**Communication media**
Y70	**Mass media**
Y80	**Communication technology**
Y90	**Communication industry**
Y90.10/40	**Book industry**
Y95	**Communication users**

Y		**Communication**
		Linguistics X02
		Transport S50/69
		Travel S69
Y04		**Communication History**
Y06		**Communication Research**
	Y06.10	Communication research programmes
Y15		**Communication Policy**
		(By rights and ethics
		Right to communicate M94.50
		Right to freedom of expression M92.20/29
	Y15.10	Communication ethics
		Right to privacy M92.68
		Right to confidentiality M92.68.10
		Interception of communication L59.60.10
		Press ethics Y70.25
		(By strategy)
	Y15.20	Communication strategies
		(By development)
	Y15.30	Communication development
	Y15.30.10	Book development
	Y15.30.10C	International book year
Y20		**Communication Planning and Administration (†)**
	Y20.20	Communication planning
		Communication planners Y25.40
		Communication policy Y15
	Y20.20.20	Communication programmes
	Y20.20.50	Communication statistics
	Y20.40	Economics of communication
	Y20.40.20	Communication finance
	Y20.40.20F	Communication financing
	Y20.60	Communication administration
	Y20.60.20	Communication organizations
		Broadcasting organizations Y70.32
		(By control and legislation)
	Y20.70	Communication control
	Y20.70.10	Censorship
	Y20.80	Communication legislation
		Copyright M64.20
	Y20.80.30	Broadcasting legislation
Y25		**Communication Personnel**
		Cultural personnel T40/49
		Linguists X05
	Y25.05	Writers
	Y25.10	Authors
	Y25.10.05	Scriptwriters
	Y25.13	Editors
	Y25.15	Journalists
		UF Reporters
	Y25.20	Publishers
	Y25.25	Printers
	Y25.28	Booksellers
	Y25.40	Communication planners
	Y25.60	Television and radio personnel
	Y25.60.10	Television and radio technical personnel
	Y25.60.20	Broadcasters

Y		**Communication**

Y25		**Communication Personnel** (cont.)
	Y25.60	Television and radio personnel (cont.)
	Y25.60.30	Television and radio producers
	Y25.60.40	Television and radio directors
Y30		**Communication Personnel Training**
	Y30.10	Communication planners training
	Y30.30	Television and radio personnel training
	Y30.40	Journalist training
	Y30.40.10	Journalist schools
	Y30.60	Book production training
	Y30.70	Publishers training
Y35		**Sociology of Communication**
	Y35.30	Communication impact
	Y35.40	Mass media exposure
Y38		**Communication Psychology**
		Communication process Y40/64
		Group communication Y55
		Interpersonal communication Y50
		Mass communication Y60
Y40/64		**Communication Process**
		Communication psychology Y38
		Information transfer Z10
	Y42	Communication (thought transfer)
	Y44	Communication channels of flow
	Y44.10	One-way communication
	Y44.30	Two-way communication
	Y44.30.20	Feedback (communication)
Y45		**Communication Skills**
		Acting W81
	Y45.10/20	Speech
		UF Speaking
		Verbal communication
		Phonetics X36
		Singing W76.10
		Speech disorders F67.10
		Speech education J60.80.30
		(By application)
	Y45.16	Public speaking
		Oral reading J60.30.10
	Y45.16.10	Speech-making
	Y45.16.18	Speeches
	Y45.18	Conversation
		Conversation (instruction) J60.27
	Y45.30	Writing
		Creative writing J46.03
		Graphonomy X37
		Literary composition X60
	Y45.30.05	Handwriting
	Y45.30.10	Letter writing
	Y45.30.20	Report writing
	Y45.30.30	Technical writing
	Y45.40	Listening
		Audiences Y95.30
		Listening groups Y95.30.25
		Listening instruction J60.28

Y40/64		**Communication Process** (cont.)
Y45		**Communication Skills** (cont.)
	Y45.45	Non-verbal communication
	Y45.50	Watching
	Y45.50.20	Televiewing
		UF Viewing
		Televiewers Y95.30.20
	Y45.60	Reading
		Literacy J60.20
		Reading instruction J60.30
		Readiing promotion Z75.20
		Library users Z72.30.10
	Y45.60.30	Reading habit
Y50		**Interpersonal Communication**
		UF Direct communication
		Human communication
		Individual communication
		Correspondence Z15.42.30
		Interpersonal relations P79/82
		Letter writing Y45.30.10
		Personal contact P80.10
		Speech Y45.10/20
		Teaching J50
		Telegraphy Y80.30.25
		Two-way communication Y44.30
	Y50.30	Telephone
		Telephone engineering Y80.30.10
	Y50.30.20	Radiotelephone
	Y50.30.40	Videotelephone
	Y50.50	Postal services
	Y50.50.40	Postage stamps
Y55		**Group Communication**
		Group behaviour P85
		Intergroup relations P83
		(By means)
		Group work (teaching method) J50.06
	Y55.05	Discussion groups
		Discussions (teaching method) J50.12.08
	Y55.10/30	Meetings
		Working groups R31.40
	Y55.12	Committee meetings
	Y55.20	Conferences
	Y55.20.10	International conferences
	Y55.20.70	Teleconferencing
	Y55.22	Symposia
	Y55.28	Public meetings
Y60		**Mass Communication**
		Communication impact Y35.30
		Mass behaviour P88
		Mass education J70.19
		Mass media Y70
		Public opinion Y95.15
		(By campaign and programmes)
	Y60.05.10	Mass communication campaigns
	Y60.05.20	Mass communication programmes
		(By activities)
	Y60.20	Publicity
		UF Public information
	Y60.20.40	Public image
	Y60.30/40	Public relations

Y40/64		**Communication Process** (cont.)
Y60		**Mass Communication** (cont.)
	Y60.30/40	Public relations (cont.)
	Y60.35	Public liaison
		(By means)
	Y60.35.10	Press releases
		(By promotion of UNESCO activities)
	Y60.35.60	UNESCO Public liaison
	Y60.35.60A	UNESCO publications
	Y60.35.60B	UNESCO clubs
	Y60.35.60C	UNESCO coupons
	Y60.35.60E	UNESCO voluntary assistance
	Y60.35.60G	Philatelic service
	Y60.35.60M	Anniversary celebrations
	Y60.35.60P	UNESCO awards and honours
	Y60.45	Popularization
	Y60.50	Persuasion
	Y60.50.30	Pressure groups
	Y60.55	Propaganda
		UF Psychological warfare
	Y60.55.20	War propaganda
	Y60.55.40	Indoctrination
	Y60.60	Advertising
		Marketing N70
	Y60.60.20	Advertising agencies
	Y60.60.30	Press advertising
	Y60.60.40	Radio advertising
	Y60.60.50	Television advertising
Y65/79		**Communication Media**
		Codes Y80.10.35
		Information materials Z15
		Linguistics X02/54
		Signs X45.10.20
		Speech Y45.10/20
		Symbols X45.10.30
	Y66	Multimedia
		Multimedia instruction J50.05.60
		Multimedia resource centres J55.20.20
	Y68.20	Exhibitions
		Cultural exhibitions T86
		Educational exhibitions J55.05.01
		Library exhibitions Z74.10.10
	Y68.20.10	Travelling exhibitions
Y70		**Mass Media**
		Mass communication Y60
		Mass media exposure Y35.40
		(By type of media)
		Cinema W86/99
	Y70.05/25	Press
		Book industry Y90.10
		Freedom of the press M92.24
		Press advertising Y60.60.30
		(By organisations)
	Y70.08	Press councils
		(By form of publication)
	Y70.10	Newspaper press
		Newspapers Z15.30.40
	Y70.10.20	News items
		Press releases Y60.35.10
	Y70.10.25	News agencies

Y65/79		**Communication Media** (cont.)
Y70		**Mass Media** (cont.)
Y70.05/25		Press (cont.)
Y70.10		Newspaper press (cont.)
Y70.10.30		News flow
Y70.10.30B		News transmission
		UF News dispatches
Y70.10.40		Press conferences
Y70.15		Periodical press
		Periodicals Z15.30.50
		(By coverage)
Y70.18.10		Local press
Y70.18.20		National press
Y70.18.70		Underground press
		(By profession)
Y70.20		Journalism
		Journalists Y25.15
		(By standards of behaviour)
Y70.25		Press ethics
		Right to privacy M92.68
Y70.30/90		Broadcasting
		Broadcasting legislation Y20.80.30
		Educational radio J55.07.02
		Educational television J55.07.03
		(By administrative bodies)
Y70.32		Broadcasting organizations
		UF Broadcasting corporation
		(By ownership)
Y70.34		Commercial broadcasting
		(By coverage)
Y70.36		National broadcasting
Y70.37		Local broadcasting
		(By production process)
Y70.40		Broadcasting production
		(By live broadcasting)
Y70.42		Direct broadcasting
		Live programmes Y70.48.70
		(By technical means)
Y70.44		Satellite broadcasting
		(By programmes)
Y70.48		Broadcasting programmes
		Radio programmes Y70.50.40/70
		Television programmes Y70.70.40/70
		(By exchange)
Y70.48.10		Programme exchange
		(By content)
Y70.48.50		Programme content
		UF Broadcasting content
		Communication content
		(By type)
Y70.48.70		Live programmes
Y70.50		Radio
		Educational radio J55.07.02
		Radio engineering Y80.40
		Radio listeners Y95.30.10
		(By ownership)
Y70.50.40		Commercial radio
		(By programme)
Y70.50.40/70		Radio programmes

Y65/79		**Communication Media** (cont.)
Y70		**Mass Media** (cont.)
	Y70.30/90	Broadcasting (cont.)
	Y70.50.45	Radio news
	Y70.50.55	Radio drama
	Y70.50.60	Radio serials
	Y70.50.65	Radio games
	Y70.70	Television
		UF Telecast
		Educational television J55.07.03
		Teleconferencing Y55.20.70
		Televiewing Y45.50.20
		Televiewers Y95.30.20
		Television advertising Y60.60.50
		Television engineering Y80.45
		(By ownership)
	Y70.70.20	Commercial television
		(By production process)
	Y70.70.30	Television production
		(By channels)
	Y70.70.35	Television channels
		(By programme)
	Y70.70.40/70	Television programmes
	Y70.70.45	Television news
	Y70.70.50	Television documentaries
	Y70.70.55	Television drama
	Y70.70.60	Television serials
	Y70.70.65	Television games
		(By film)
	Y70.70.80	Television films
		Video recordings Z15.88
		For type of film combine with descriptors appearing under Films at W90

Y80		**Communication Technology**
		(By theory)
	Y80.10	Communication and information theory
		Cybernetics H38
	Y80.10.10	Information theory
	Y80.10.30	Messages
	Y80.10.35	Codes
	Y80.10.35C	Coding
	Y80.10.35D	Decoding
	Y80.10.50	Modulation
	Y80.10.60/80	Signal processing and detection
		UF Reception (signal)
	Y80.10.65	Signals
	Y80.10.70	Radiowave interference
		UF Jamming
		Noise (electrical)
	Y80.10.70K	Interference suppression
		(By systems)
	Y80.30	Telecommunication
		UF Telecommunication engineering
		Teleprocessing H93.40
		Underwater communication G52.10
	Y80.30.03	Communication systems
	Y80.30.05	Communication networks
	Y80.30.10	Telephone engineering
		UF Telephony
		Telephone Y50.30
	Y80.30.20/30	Data transmission

Y80		**Communication Technology** (cont.)
	Y80.30	Telecommunication (cont.)
	Y80.30.25	Telegraphy
	Y80.30.25C	Telex
	Y80.30.25M	Teleprinters
	Y80.30.30	Telephotography
		UF Facsimile transmission
	Y80.30.35	Telemetry
	Y80.30.40	Mobile communication
	Y80.30.45	Space communication
	Y80.40	Radio engineering
		Radio Y70.50
		Radio navigation H55.35
		Radio receivers Y80.70.30C
		Radio transmitters Y80.70.10C
		Radio waves C11.50.60
	Y80.40.10	Allocation of frequencies
	Y80.40.60	Radio stations
	Y80.40.65	Radio studios
	Y80.45	Television engineering
		Television Y70.70
		Television cameras Y80.70.40
		Television receivers Y80.70.30D
		Television transmitters Y80.70.10D
	Y80.45.10	Cable television
	Y80.45.10C	Closed circuit television
	Y80.45.20	Colour television
	Y80.45.60	Television stations
	Y80.45.65	Television studios
	Y80.50	Radar
		Radar meteorology D64.70
		Radar navigation H55.40
	Y80.60	Recording engineering
		Phonorecord industry Y90.65
		Recordings Z15.80/89
	Y80.60.10	Sound recording
	Y80.60.20	Video recording
	Y80.60.20B	Telerecording
		UF Optical television recording
		Kinerecording
		(By equipment)
	Y80.60.40	Recording equipment
	Y80.60.40A	Tape recorders
	Y80.60.40C	Video recorders
	Y80.60.40H	Record players
		UF Gramophones
		Phonograms
		(By equipment)
	Y80.65/80	Communication engineering equipment
		Electroacoustic devices G29.70
		Recording equipment Y80.60.40
	Y80.70.05	Antennas
	Y80.70.10	Transmitters
	Y80.70.10C	Radio transmitters
	Y80.70.10D	Television transmitters
	Y80.70.10R	Repeaters
	Y80.70.30	Receivers
	Y80.70.30C	Radio receivers
		UF Radio sets
	Y80.70.30D	Television receivers
		UF Television sets

Y80		**Communication Technology** (cont.)
	Y80.65/80	Communication engineering equipment (cont.)
	Y80.70.40	Television cameras
	Y80.80	Telecommunication links
	Y80.80.10	Transmission lines
	Y80.80.30	Waveguides
	Y80.80.40	Radio links
		UF Television links
	Y80.80.50	Communication satellites
		UF Direct diffusion satellites
		Distribution satellites
		Satellite links
		Television relay satellites

Y90		**Communication Industry**
		Film industry W91
		Postal services Y50.50
	Y90.10/40	Book industry
	Y90.20/29	Publishing
		Micropublishing W67.70
		The Press Y70.05/25
		Publishers Y25.20
		(By subject of publication)
	Y90.21.40	Music publishing
		(By technical process)
	Y90.22.10	Book production
		Printing W55/64
	Y90.22.40	Editing
	Y90.22.45	Proof reading
		(By output and sales)
	Y90.24.05	Book availability
		UF Book shortage
	Y90.24.10	Book output
	Y90.24.10K	Information explosion
	Y90.24.20	Book costs
		Cheap editions Z15.37.10H
	Y90.24.40	Circulation figures
		(By administrative and legal consideration)
	Y90.26.10	Royalties
	Y90.26.20	Copyright deposit
	Y90.26.40	ISBN
		UF International standard book number
	Y90.26.44	ISSN
		UF International standard serial number
	Y90.30	Bookselling
		UF Bookshops
		Book distribution Z10.10.20
		Booksellers Y25.28
	Y90.50	Telecommunication industry
	Y90.55	Television and radio industry
	Y90.65	Phonorecord industry

Y95		**Communication Users**
		Communication psychology Y38
		Feedback (communication) Y44.30.20
		Information users Z72.30
	Y95.10	General public
	Y95.10.20	Untapped public

Y95	**Communication Users** (cont.)
Y95.15	Public opinion
Y95.15.05	Public taste
Y95.15.30	Public opinion polls
Y95.30	Audiences
	UF Listeners
	Spectators
	Viewers
Y95.30.10	Radio listeners
Y95.30.20	Televiewers
Y95.30.25	Listening groups
Y95.30.30	Fans (supporters)
	(By characteristics)
Y95.30.40	Audience composition
Y95.30.42	Audience participation
Y95.30.44	Audience reaction
	(By measurement and research)
Y95.30.50	Audience rating
Y95.30.55	Audience research

Z	**INFORMATION LIBRARIES AND ARCHIVES**
	Summary

Z08	**Information**
Z10	**Information transfer**
Z15	**Information materials**
Z15.01/59	**Bookform materials**
Z15.60/99	**Non-book materials**
Z18	**Bibliology**
Z20/84	**Library and information science**
Z24	**Information/library history**
Z26	**Information/library research**
Z28	**Information/library philosophy, policy and development**
Z30	**Information/library planning and administration**
Z32	**Information/library facilities**
Z34	**Information/library personnel**
Z36	**Information/library profession**
Z38	**Information/library training**
Z40/56	**Information/library operations**
Z42	**Library housekeeping operations**
Z45/56	**Information processing**
Z48	**Document description**
Z50	**Index languages**
Z52	**Information storage devices**
Z54	**Information retrieval**
Z56	**Information systems evaluation**
Z58	**Information/library stock**
Z60/70	**Information/library systems**
Z62	**Libraries**
Z65	**Information services**
Z68	**Information systems**
Z72	**Information use**
Z73/75	**Library use promotion**
Z85/99	**Archives**
Z92	**Records management**
Z93	**Archive operations**
Z95/97	**Records**
Z98	**Archive agencies**

Z08   **Information**

(By subject of information)

Z08.10	Scientific information
	UF Science information
	Technical information
	Scientific information systems Z68.50
	Scientific libraries Z62.68.10
	Scientific terminology Y46.20.80
	Technical writing Y45.30.30
Z08.10.10	Science popularization
Z08.10.30	Scientific publications
Z08.10.30P	Scientific periodicals

For individual scientific and technical subjects combine 'Scientific information' with descriptor for the subject, e.g.
'Engineering information'—'Engineering' & 'Scientific information'
For specific information and library techniques, use terms in the 'Library and Information Science' section.

Z08.20	Educational information
	Educational publications J55.03
	Educational terminology X46.20.60
Z08.30	Social science information

For other subjects combine 'Information' with descriptor for specific subject.

Z10   **Information Transfer**

UF Flow of information
Information communication
Information flow
Information use Z72
News flow Y70.10.30

Z10.03	Access to information
Z10.05	Free flow of information
	Right to information M94.60
Z10.10	Dissemination of information
	Current dissemination of information Z54.25
	Selective dissemination of information Z68.30.10D
Z10.10.10	Dissemination of knowledge
Z10.10.20	Book distribution
Z10.10.40	International circulation of materials
Z10.30	Information exchange
Z10.30.10	Exchange of ideas
Z10.30.30	Exchange of publications
Z10.50	Information sources
	Guides to information sources Z15.20.35
	Information materials Z15
	Information services Z65
	Libraries Z62
	Resource centres J55.20
	Source materials Z15.15.03

Z15   **Information Materials**

UF Documents
Data medium
Recorded information

Z15.01/59   **Bookform Materials**

UF Print media
Publications
Volumes
Textual media

Z15	**Information Materials** (cont.)
Z15.01/59	**Bookform Materials** (cont.)

	(By document parts)
Z15.10	Document parts
	Abstracts Z15.20.60
	Bibliographic data Z48.10.10
	UF Title pages
	Introduction (book)
	Contents page
	Chapters
	Appendices
Z15.10.20	Articles
Z15.10.25	Text
Z15.10.40	Citations
	(By physical parts and features of documents)
Z15.10.60	Format
Z15.10.63	Pages
Z15.10.65	Covers (document)
Z15.10.65B	Bindings
Z15.10.70	Spines (book)
	(By primary and secondary nature)
Z15.15	Primary documents
	SN An original document which is not the result of a documentation
	process
	Archive records Z97
	Correspondence Z15.42.30
	Manuscripts Z15.42.10
	Monographs Z15.22
	Newspapers Z15.30.40
	Patents A67.10
	Periodicals Z15.30.50
	Standards A63
	Specifications A63.50
	Records Z95/97
Z15.15.03	Source materials
	Source documents
Z15.15.05	Reports
	Law reports M46.20
Z15.15.05A	Annual reports
Z15.15.05B	Technical reports
Z15.15.05D	Project reports
Z15.15.05E	Progress reports
Z15.15.05H	Expert reports
Z15.15.05J	Mission reports
Z15.15.05L	Country reports
Z15.15.05R	Interim reports
Z15.15.05T	Final reports
Z15.15.10	Dictionaries
	UF Lexicons
Z15.15.11	Glossaries
Z15.15.12	Encyclopaedias
Z15.15.18	Directories
Z15.15.34	Conference papers
	UF Meeting papers
Z15.15.36	Albums
Z15.15.40	Guides
	UF Handbooks
	Manuals
Z15.15.40B	Maintenance handbooks
Z15.15.42	Guidebooks
Z15.15.50	Tables
	UF Scheduled information
Z15.15.50D	Data books

Z15		**Information Materials** (cont.)
Z15.01/59		**Bookform Materials** (cont.)
	Z15.15	Primary documents (cont.)
	Z15.15.50	Tables (cont.)
	Z15.15.50D	Data books (cont.)
	Z15.15.50DF	Formularies
	Z15.15.50S	Statistical data
		UF Numerical data
	Z15.15.80	Trade literature
	Z15.15.91	Biographies
	Z15.20	Secondary documents
		SN A document containing data or information about primary documents
		Adaptations Z15.37.50
		Catalogues Z52.80
		Indexes Z52.01/99
		Translations Z15.37.30
	Z15.20.10	Bibliographies
	Z15.20.10A	Bibliographies of bibliographies
	Z15.20.10C	International bibliographies
	Z15.20.10D	National bibliographies
	Z15.20.10G	Special bibliographies
	Z15.20.30	Literature reviews
		UF Annual reviews of the literature
		Reviews of the literature
		State-of-the-art reviews
	Z15.20.35	Guides to information sources
	Z15.20.50	Abstract journals
		UF Indexing journals
	Z15.20.60	Abstracts
	Z15.20.60A	Author abstracts
	Z15.20.60C	Indicative abstracts
	Z15.20.60D	Informative abstracts
	Z15.20.63	Synopses
	Z15.20.65	Epitomes
	Z15.20.68	Digests
	Z15.20.70	Anthologies
	Z15.20.72	Excerpts
		UF Extracts
		Quotations
		Abstracts Z15.20.60
	Z15.20.75	Concordances
	Z15.20.77	Inventories
		(By frequency of publication)
	Z15.22	Monographs
		Books Z15.36
	Z15.22.10	Compendia
	Z15.22.20	Composite works
	Z15.27	Multivolume publications
	Z15.28	Series
	Z15.30	Serials
	Z15.30.01	Daily publications
	Z15.30.02	Weekly publications
	Z15.30.04	Monthly publications
	Z15.30.06	Quarterly publications
	Z15.30.08	Yearbooks
		UF Annuals
	Z15.30.10	Calendars
	Z15.30.40	Newspapers
	Z15.30.50	Periodicals
		UF Bulletins

Z15		**Information Materials** (cont.)
Z15.01/59		**Bookform Materials** (cont.)
	Z15.30	Serials (cont.)
	Z15.30.50	Periodicals (cont.)

Journals
Magazines
Newsletters
Proceedings
Transactions
Abstract journals Z15.20.50
Educational periodicals J55.03.30
Information bulletins Z74.10.20B
Scientific periodicals Z08.10.30P

	Z15.30.50H	Popular periodicals
	Z15.30.50K	Comics
		(By physical form)
	Z15.35.02	Hard copy
	Z15.35.30	Pamphlets UF Brochures
	Z15.35.32	Leaflets
	Z15.35.40	Forms (blank)
	Z15.36	Books

Antiquarian books Z15.48.30
Children's books J55.03.01
Monographs Z15.22
Textbooks J55.03.04

	Z15.36.10	Pocket books
	Z15.36.15	Paperbacks
	Z15.36.20	Oversize books
	Z15.36.30	Art books
	Z15.36.35	Large print books
	Z15.36.50	New books
	Z15.36.60	Second-hand books
		(By relation to first issue)
	Z15.37.10	Editions
	Z15.37.10A	First editions
	Z15.37.10C	New editions
	Z15.37.10F	Abridged editions
	Z15.37.10H	Cheap editions
	Z15.37.10R	Reprints
	Z15.37.30	Translations
	Z15.37.50	Adaptations
		(By degree of publication)

	Z15.40.30	Semi-published documents
		        Reports Z15.15.05
		        Theses J40.21.12C
		        Trade literature Z15.15.80

	Z15.40.30C	Preprints
	Z15.40.30F	Separates UF Offprints
	Z15.42	Unpublished documents *Reports Z15.15.05*
	Z15.42.10	Manuscripts
	Z15.42.30	Correspondence UF Letters
		(By availability) *Rare books Z15.48.30R*
	Z15.44.10	In-print publications
	Z15.44.20	Out-of-print publications

Z15		**Information Materials** (cont.)
Z15.01/59		**Bookform Materials** (cont.)
		(By publishing body)
	Z15.46.20	Official publications
		UF Government documents
	Z15.46.40	Commercial publications
	Z15.46.60	Privately printed documents
		(By date of documents)
	Z15.48.30	Antiquarian books
	Z15.48.30B	Incunabula
	Z15.48.30R	Rare books
		(By permanence of value)
	Z15.50	Ephemera
		(By conditions of use)
	Z15.52.10	Reference materials
	Z15.52.30	Restricted documents
		UF Censored documents
		Classified documents (confidential)
		Confidential documents
		Secret documents
		Security restricted documents
		(By purpose)
	Z15.54.50	Therapeutic documents
		UF Bibliotherapy
	Z15.58	*(By subject)*
		*Educational publications J55.03
		*Library publications Z74.10
		*Scientific publications Z08.10.30
	Z15.58.10	Fiction stock
	Z15.58.20	Non-fiction stock
Z15.60/99		**Non-Book Materials**
	Z15.62.10	Cuttings
		UF Clippings
	Z15.62.10A	Press cuttings
	Z15.62.30	Tablets (documents)
	Z15.65/89	Audiovisual materials
		*Audiovisual aids J55.05.14A
		*Audiovisual archives Z97.30
	Z15.70/79	Visual materials
		*Television Y70.70
		*Video recordings Z15.88
		(By opaque materials)
		*Tables Z15.15.50
		*Maps H34.10
	Z15.72.10	Charts
	Z15.72.10F	Flow charts
	Z15.72.15	Plans
	Z15.72.20	Globes
	Z15.72.25	Relief maps
	Z15.72.30	Drawings
	Z15.72.40	Pictures
	Z15.72.42	Reproductions (pictures)
	Z15.72.45	Prints
	Z15.72.47	Posters
	Z15.72.47B	Photoposters
	Z15.72.49	Photographs
	Z15.72.60	Photocopies
	Z15.72.65	Diagrams
	Z15.72.72	Technical drawings
	Z15.72.74	Graphs

Z15		**Information Materials** (cont.)
Z15.60/99		**Non-Book Materials** (cont.)
	Z15.65/89	Audiovisual materials (cont.)
	Z15.70/79	Visual materials (cont.)
		(By transparencies)
	Z15.75	Transparencies
		Films W90
	Z15.75.10	Film strips
	Z15.75.30	Photographic slides
		UF Slides
	Z15.75.30C	Colour slides
		(By size)
	Z15.77	Microforms
		UF Microrecords
		Microphotography W67
	Z15.77.10	Microfilms
	Z15.77.15	Microfiche
	Z15.77.20	Microcards
	Z15.77.25	Extreme reduction microforms
		UF PCMI
	Z15.77.40	Computer output microform
		UF COM
		COM catalogue Z52.80.30
	Z15.78	Audio materials
		Radio Z70.50
		Sound recordings Z15.86
	Z15.80/89	Recordings
		Recording equipment Y80.60.40
		(By form of equipment)
	Z15.81	Cylinder recordings
	Z15.82	Disc recordings
		UF Gramophone records
		Phonograph records
		Video discs Z15.88.10
	Z15.82.20	Long playing records
	Z15.83	Magnetic tape recordings
		UF Tape recordings
		Phonotapes Z15.86.10
		Video tape recordings Z15.88.20
	Z15.84	Cassette recordings
		Sound cassettes Z15.86.50
		Video cassettes Z15.88.50
		(By audiovisual characteristics)
	Z15.86	Sound recordings
		Sound recording Y80.60.10
	Z15.86.10	Phonotapes
		SN Sound recordings on magnetic tape
		UF Audio tapes
	Z15.86.20	Talking books
	Z15.86.30	Stereophonic recordings
	Z15.86.50	Sound cassettes
	Z15.88	Video recordings
		Video recording Y80.60.20
	Z15.88.10	Video discs
	Z15.88.20	Video tape recordings
	Z15.88.50	Video cassettes
	Z15.90	Machine-readable materials
		Data bases Z52.10.70
		Machine-readable archives Z97.60
	Z15.90.40	Programmed materials

Z18		**Bibliology**

UF Bibliography (study of books)
Bibliographic services Z65.40
Bibliography compilation Z54.20
Bibliographies Z15.20.10
Palaeography U78
Epigraphy U76

Z18.10	Book collecting
Z18.20	Analytical bibliography
Z18.20.10	Historical bibliography
	Antiquarian books Z15.48.30
Z18.30	Bibliometrics

SN Study and measurements of the properties of documents and their use
Book availability Y90.24.05
Book costs Y90.24.20
Book distribution Z10.10.20
Book output Y90.24.10

Z18.30.05	Currency of documents
Z18.30.10	Obsolescence
Z18.30.10B	Book use frequency
Z18.30.20	Information scatter
	UF Bradford's law of scatter

Z20/84   Library and Information Science

(By constituent disciplines)
Use for general works only

Z22.10	Information science

SN The science concerned with creation management and exploitation of recordable knowledge (Wersig)

Z22.20	Library science

SN The branch of learning concerned with collecting, storing and distributing written or printed records by means of libraries and of the management of libraries (Wersig)

Z22.30	Informatics

SN The science concerned with the study of problems connected with processes of specialised information and documentation (Wersig)

Z22.40	Documentation

SN The continuous and systematic processing of documents or data including location, identification, 'acquisition' analysis, storage, retrieval, circulation and preservation for the specialised information of users (Wersig)

Z24		**Information/Library History**
	Z24.10	History of libraries

Z26	**Information/Library Research**

(By subject of research)
Z26.30.30   Classification research

For other specific library and documentation problems combine 'Information/library research' with terms for research problem

(By methods)
For research methods use terms in Section A70/99 Research

Z26.70	**Comparative Librarianship**

Z28	**Information/Library Philosophy, Policy and Development** (†)

Z28.10	Information/library philosophy
	UF Library philosophy
Z28.20	Information/library policy

Z20/84	**Library and Information Science** (cont.)
Z28	**Information/Library Philosophy, Policy and Development** (cont.)

Z28.20	Information/library policy (cont.)
Z28.20.10	Information/library aims UF Information/library goals Library aims
Z28.20.20	Information/library role UF Library role
Z28.40	Information/library development UF Library development

Z30

Information/Library Planning and Administration (†)

SN Includes planning, administration and management at the international, national and individual library level

(By planning)

Z30.01/29	Information/library planning UF Library planning *Information/library policy Z28.20*
	(By problems)
Z30.05.05	Information/library needs UF Library demand Library needs
Z30.05.10	Information/library resources *Information/library facilities Z32* *Information/library stock Z58* *Information/library personnel Z34*
Z30.05.25	Information/library cooperation UF Information/library coordination International/library cooperation
Z30.05.30	Information/library integration UF Library integration
Z30.05.35	Information/library centralization UF Library centralization
Z30.05.40	Information/library decentralization UF Library decentralization
Z30.05.45	Library location
Z30.05.50	Information/library standards UF Library standards
Z30.05.55	Information/library statistics UF Library statistics
	(By programmes)
Z30.15	Information/library programmes UF Library programmes
	(By economics)
Z30.30/49	Information/library economics UF Library economics
	(By finance)
Z30.40	Information/library finance UF Library finance
Z30.40.20	Information/library financing UF Library financing
Z30.40.30	Information/library budgets UF Library budgets
Z30.40.40	Information/library income UF Library income
Z30.40.40C	Library charges *Loan charges Z42.62*
Z30.40.50	Information/library expenditure UF Library expenditure
	(By administration)
Z30.50/99	Information/library administration UF Library administration

Z20/84		**Library and Information Science** (cont.)
Z30		**Information/Library Planning and Administration** (cont.)
	Z30.50/99	Information/library administration (cont.)

(By organisations)

	Z30.60	Information/library organizations
	Z30.60.10	International information/library organizations
	Z30.60.20	National information/library organizations
	Z30.60.30	Government information/library organizations
	Z30.60.30L	Local government information/library organizations
		UF Local government library authorities
	Z30.60.60	Private information/library organizations
		Information/library professional associations Z36.60

(By activities)

	Z30.65	Information/library legislation
		UF Library legislation
		Library law
	Z30.70/99	Information/library management
		UF Library management
		Library use promotion Z73/75
	Z30.73	Library rules and regulations
		Loan fines Z42.62.10
		Loan period Z42.67
	Z30.73.10	Library admission
	Z30.73.20	Library hours of opening
	Z30.75	Library maintenance services
	Z30.77	Library transport
	Z30.79	Library removals

Z32		**Information/Library Facilities**

(By buildings)

	Z32.10	Library buildings

(By architecture and design)
Combine with terms from Construction engineering section G56/60

(By specific buildings, rooms and parts)

	Z32.10.10	Library stacks
	Z32.10.15	Library carrels

For others combine with terms from appropriate schedules, e.g.
Branch library buildings (Branch libraries & Library buildings)

(By services)
Combine with terms from Construction engineering schedules, for example:
Library lighting systems (Library buildings & Lighting)
Library heating systems (Library buildings & Heating systems)

(By equipment)

	Z32.50/90	Information/library equipment
		Archive equipment Z89.40
	Z32.60/90	Library equipment
	Z32.65	Library furniture
	Z32.65.10	Library shelving
	Z32.65.30	Library counters
	Z32.65.50	Library display cases
	Z32.70	Library vehicles
		Mobile libraries Z62.72.70
		Library transport Z30.77
	Z32.70.20	Library conveyors
	Z32.70.40	Library trolleys

Z34		**Information/Library Personnel**

(By executive officers)

	Z34.10	Information/library administrators
		UF Directors (documentation systems)
		Chief librarians
		Heads of departments (libraries)

Z20/84		**Library and Information Science** (cont.)
Z34		**Information/Library Personnel** (cont.)
	Z34.10	Information/library administrators (cont.)

(By professional staff)

	Z34.20/50	Information/library professional personnel
	Z34.24	Information scientists
	Z34.26	Documentalists
	Z34.30	Librarians

                    Academic librarians J35.05.02
                    School librarians J35.05.04
                    Teacher librarians J35.05.06

	Z34.30.10	Public librarians
	Z34.30.20	Children's librarians
	Z34.30.25	Reference librarians
	Z34.30.30	Special librarians
	Z34.30.35	Information officers

(By special characteristics)

	Z34.30.60	Part-time librarians
	Z34.30.70	Women librarians
	Z34.30.70B	Married women librarians

(By specific role)

	Z34.35	Indexers
	Z34.35.10	Cataloguers
	Z34.35.30	Classifiers
	Z34.40	Abstractors
	Z34.45	Classificationists
	Z34.50	Bibliographers

(By support personnel)

	Z34.60	Information/library support personnel

                    Computer personnel H97.50

	Z34.60.20	Translators
	Z34.60.50	Library technicians

(By non-professional personnel)

	Z34.80	Non-professional information/library personnel
	Z34.80.10	Library assistants
	Z34.80.20	Information/library clerical personnel
	Z34.80.50	Information/library manual personnel
	Z34.80.50B	Library porters

(By recruitment and conditions of service)
Combine with terms in the Labour section Q50/59, for example:
Librarian recruitment (Librarians & Recruitment)
Librarians conditions of employment (Librarians & Conditions of employment)
Librarians salaries (Librarians & Salaries)

Z36		**Information/Library Profession**

        UF Information science profession
            Library profession

(By status)

	Z36.30	Information/library professional status

        UF Information scientists professional status
            Documentalists professional status
            Librarians professional status

(By associations)

	Z36.60	Information/library professional associations
	Z36.60.10	Library Associations

Z20/84   **Library and Information Science** (cont.)
Z38   **Information/Library Training**

UF Documentation training
Information science training
Library training
Archive science training Z90.70

(By institutions)
Z38.20   Information/library schools
UF Information science schools
Library schools

(By qualifications)
Z38.30   Information/library qualifications
UF Information science qualifications
Library qualifications
Z38.30.50   Information/library degrees

(By training courses and methods)
Z38.50   Information/library courses

For other methods combine with descriptors in J. Education

Z40/56   **Information/Library Operations**
Library Housekeeping Operations
Z42   *(By mechanization)*

Z42.03   Library automation
SN Automation of library housekeeping operations
UF Computerized libraries
Acquisition systems automation Z42.05.05
Loans records automation Z42.70.50
Periodical circulation automation Z42.45.50

For automation of other housekeeping processes combine 'Library automation' with terms for the process

(By specific operation)
Z42.05   Acquisition systems
Acquisitions Z58.10.10
Z42.05.05   Acquisition systems automation
(By policy)
Z42.05.10   Acquisition policy
(By process)
Z42.05.20   Book selection
Z42.05.20M   Stock revision
Z42.05.35   Book ordering
UF Document ordering
Exchange of publications Z10.30.30
Z42.05.35A   Approval ordering
Z42.05.35P   Periodical acquisition systems
UF Periodical subscriptions
Z42.05.70   Gifts (acquisition)

Z42.10   Document processing
SN Excludes processing of contents
For this see Information processing Z45/56
UF Book processing
Z42.10.10   Accessioning
Z42.10.30   Document preparation
SN Includes labelling, etc.
UF Book processing (physical)
Document processing (physical)
Z42.10.40   Shelving (operation)
Z42.10.45   Filing
Z42.10.60   Stock-taking (document)
UF Book stock taking
Document stock taking
Z42.10.80   Document withdrawal
UF Book withdrawal
Document discarding

Z20/84		**Library and Information Science** (cont.)
Z40/56		**Information/Library Operations** (cont.)
Z42		**Library Housekeeping Operations** (cont.)
	Z42.10	Document processing (cont.)
	Z42.10.80	Document withdrawal (cont.)

Document disposal
Document weeding
Records disposal Z92.50.50

	Z42.30	Document storage

UF Book storage
Library stacks Z32.10.10
Library shelving Z32.65.10

	Z42.35	Document maintenance

UF Book maintenance
Binding W64

	Z42.35.10	Document preservation

UF Book preservation

	Z42.35.10B	Document losses

UF Book losses
Book thefts

	Z42.40/79	Library circulation work

UF Circulation work

	Z42.45	Periodical circulation
	Z42.45.50	Periodical circulation automation
	Z42.50/90	Loans services

UF Book loan services
Lending services (libraries)
Loans (library)
Loans work

(By authors rights)

	Z42.51	Public lending right

(By type of service)

	42.52	Internal loans
	Z42.54	Inter-library loans

UF External loans

	Z42.56	Postal loans

(By processes)

	Z42.60	Borrower registration
	Z42.62	Loan charges
	Z42.62.10	Loan fines
	Z42.65	Loan reservations
	Z42.67	Loan period
	Z42.67.10	Loan renewal
	Z42.67.30	Overdue loans

(By records and control)

	Z42.70	Loan records

UF Charging systems (loans)
Circulation control
Loan control

	Z42.70.10	Punched card loan records
	Z42.70.20	Photocharging
	Z42.70.50	Loan records automation
Z45/56		**Information Processing**

UF Information handling
Information storage and retrieval
Information work

(By automation)

	Z47	Information processing automation

UF Computerized documentation
Computerized information processing
SN Use for general works on the automation of information storage
and retrieval

Z20/84	**Library and Information Science** (cont.)
Z40/56	**Information/Library Operations** (cont.)
Z45/56	**Information Processing** (cont.)

For the computerization of individual operations in this subject field combine 'Information processing automation' with the descriptor for the operation, except where the concept is already pre-coordinated, for example:
Automatic generation of index languages Z50.95.60
Automatic indexing Z48.50/52

Z47.10	Computer-assisted compilation
	Computerized catalogues Z52.80.10
	Computerized indexes Z52.10.60
Z47.30	On-line information processing
	On-line searching Z54
	On-line information systems Z68.18

Z48	**Document Description**
Z48.02	Abstracting
	Abstracts Z15.20.60
Z48.04/59	Indexing
	Indexes Z52.01/99
Z48.05/24	Cataloguing
	Author cataloguing Z48.25.10
	Catalogues Z52.80
	Name cataloguing Z48.27.20
	Title cataloguing Z48.30.10
	Subject cataloguing Z48.42
Z48.10	Descriptive cataloguing
	UF Author/title descriptive cataloguing
Z48.10.05/15	Bibliographic description
	(By control and standards)
Z48.10.06	Bibliographic control
Z48.10.08	Bibliographic standards
Z48.10.08B	ISBD
	UF International Standard Bibliographic Description
Z48.10.08BM	ISBD (M)
Z48.10.08BN	ISBD (NBM)
Z48.10.08BS	ISBD (S)
	(By data)
Z48.10.10	Bibliographic data
	Author headings Z48.10.20A
Z48.10.10C	Collation
Z48.10.10K	Imprint
Z48.10.10T	Titles
Z48.10.20	Cataloguing rules
Z48.10.20A	Author headings
	UF Corporate authors
	Personal authors
Z48.10.20P	Pseudonyms
Z48.10.40	Annotated cataloguing
Z48.12	Simplified cataloguing
Z48.14	Centralized cataloguing
Z48.15	Cooperative cataloguing
	UF Shared cataloguing
Z48.17	Cataloguing-in-source
	UF Pre-natal cataloguing
	Cataloguing-in-publication
Z48.20	Re-cataloguing
	(By indexing and cataloguing by author, title and subject)
Z48.25	Author indexing
Z48.25.10	Author cataloguing
	Author catalogues Z52.80.40

Z20/84	**Library and Information Science** (cont.)
Z40/56	**Information/Library Operations** (cont.)
Z48	**Document Description** (cont.)

Z48.04/59	Indexing (cont.)
Z48.27	Name indexing
Z48.27.20	Name cataloguing
Z48.30	Title indexing
	Title indexes Z52.45
Z48.30.10	Title cataloguing
Z48.35	Bibliographic coupling
Z48.35.10	Citation indexing
	Citation indexes Z52.47
Z48.40/50	Subject indexing
	Abstracting Z48.02
	Subject indexes Z52.55/99
Z48.42	Subject cataloguing
	(By process)
Z48.44	Content analysis
	UF Concept analysis
	Document analysis
	Information analysis
	Subject analysis
Z48.48	Classifying
	UF Classification
Z48.48.60	Re-classifying
Z48.50/52	Automatic indexing
	UF Automatic classification
	Automatic indexes
	Machine indexing
	Automatic translation X54.10
	Computer linguistics X15
	Automatic generation of index languages Z50.95.60
Z48.51	Automatic text analysis
	UF Automatic extraction
	Automatic abstracting
	Natural language processing
	Text processing
	(By statistical methods)
Z48.52	Statistical linguistics (indexing)
	UF Matrix analysis (language analysis)
	Term frequency (occurrence)
Z48.52.15	Term co-occurrence
Z48.52.50	Associative indexing
	UF Latent class analysis
	Matrix eigen value analysis
Z48.52.50C	Clustering
Z48.52.50D	Clumping
	(By file management)
Z48.54	File management (index)
	UF Index production (physical)
Z48.54.12	Posting
Z48.54.14	Sorting
Z48.54.16	Filing (index)
Z48.54.20	File guidance (index)
Z48.54.25	Collating
	UF File merging
Z48.54.30	Cumulating
Z48.54.50	File maintenance (index)
	UF File updating
	(By indexing characteristics)
Z48.55.10	Indexing exhaustivity
Z48.55.20	Indexing specificity
Z48.55.20D	Depth indexing

Z20/84   **Library and Information Science** (cont.)

Z40/56   **Information/Library Operations** (cont.)

Z48   **Document Description** (cont.)

	Z48.04/59	Indexing (cont.)
	Z48.55.50	Generic posting
	Z48.55.70	Indexing consistency

Z50   **Index Languages**

(By basic type)

Z50.01/15	Controlled languages
Z50.05	Classification systems

(By specificity)

Z50.05.10	Broad classification systems
Z50.05.15	Close classification systems

(By basic type)

Z50.05.20   Hierarchical classification systems
UF Enumerative classification systems
Monohierarchical classification systems

List individual systems, alphabetically, e.g.

Z50.05.20D	Dewey Decimal Classification
Z50.05.20L	Library of Congress Classification
Z50.05.30/40	Analytico-synthetic classification systems

UF Polyhierarchical classification systems
Synthetic classification systems

List individual systems, alphabetically, e.g.

Z50.05.30U   UDC
UF Universal Decimal Classification

(By facet systems)

Z50.05.40   Faceted classification systems

List individual systems alphabetically, e.g.

Z50.05.40B	Bliss Classification System
Z50.05.40C	Colon classification
Z50.07	Alphabetical subject heading lists
Z50.08	Term lists
Z50.08.20	Uniterms
Z50.10	Thesauri

UF Descriptor languages

Z50.10.10	Alphabetical thesauri
Z50.10.30	Systematic thesauri
Z50.10.40	Classification/thesaurus systems
Z50.10.50	Compressed vocabularies
Z50.10.60	Macrothesauri
Z50.10.65	Microthesauri
Z50.10.70	Monolingual thesauri
Z50.10.72	Multilingual thesauri
Z50.12	Authority lists
Z50.14	Switching languages
Z50.16	Natural language systems
Z50.18	Free language systems

(By index language by element)

Z50.26/94   Index language elements
Linguistics X02/54

Z50.27   Recall oriented devices
Hierarchical relations Z50.56
Terminological control Z50.48

Z50.28   Precision oriented devices
Compound terms Z50.35.40
Coordination Z50.74
Link indicators Z50.77
Operator systems Z50.62

Z20/84   **Library and Information Science** (cont.)
Z40/56   **Information/Library Operations** (cont.)
Z50   **Index Languages** (cont.)

Z50.26/94	Index language elements (cont.)
Z50.28	Precision oriented devices (cont.)

*Relational indexing Z50.62.10
*Role indicators Z50.64
*Vocabulary specificity Z50.45.10
*Weights Z50.68

Z50.30/59	Index language vocabularies
Z50.31	Concepts (index language)
Z50.31.10	Isolates
Z50.35	Index terms
	UF Descriptors
	Keywords
	Preferred terms
Z50.35.10	Subject headings
Z50.35.10A	Sub-headings
Z50.35.20	Bound terms
Z50.35.25	Abbreviations
Z50.35.25A	Acronyms
Z50.35.30	Homographs
Z50.35.35	Identifiers
Z50.35.35C	Proprietary names
Z50.35.40	Compound terms
	UF Combined terms
	Pre-coordinated terms
Z50.35.45	Synthesised terms
Z50.35.50	Modifier terms
Z50.35.50A	Qualifiers
Z50.35.60	Semantic factoring
Z50.37	Lead-in terms
	UF Entry terms
	Non-descriptors
Z50.41	Blank words
	UF Common function words
Z50.43	Scope notes
	(By characteristics)
Z50.45.10	Vocabulary specificity
Z50.45.30	Term frequency (use)
	(By processes)
Z50.48	Terminological control
	UF Vocabulary control
Z50.48.05	Synonym control
Z50.48.20	Wordform confounding
	UF Wordform control
Z50.48.20C	Truncation
	UF Word stems
Z50.50/84	Term interrelations
Z50.52/69	Semantic relations
Z50.53	Paradigmatic relations
Z50.54	Classes (terms)
Z50.54.10	Main classes
Z50.55	Equivalence relations
Z50.55.10	Synonyms
Z50.55.10B	Quasi-synonyms
	UF Near synonyms
Z50.56	Hierarchical relations
	UF Generic relations
	Genus/species relations

Z20/84	**Library and Information Science** (cont.)
Z40/56	**Information/Library Operations** (cont.)
Z50	**Index Languages** (cont.)

Z50.26/94	Index language elements (cont.)
Z50.50/84	Term interrelation (cont.)
Z50.52/69	Semantic relations (cont.)
Z50.56	Hierarchical relations (cont.)
Z50.56.10	Superordination
Z50.56.10B	Broader terms
Z50.56.20	Subordination
Z50.56.20B	Narrower terms
Z50.56.30	Polyhierarchical relations
Z50.56.60	Tree structures
Z50.57	Non-hierarchical relations
	UF Associative relations
Z50.57.05	Related terms
Z50.57.10	Part-whole relations
Z50.59	Graphic displays
	UF Arrowgraphs
Z50.60	Facet analysis
Z50.60.10	Facets
Z50.60.40	Arrays
Z50.62	Operator systems
Z50.62.10	Relational indexing
Z50.64	Role indicators
Z50.66	Literary warrant
Z50.68	Weights
Z50.70/79	Syntactic relations
	UF Syntagmatic relations
Z50.72/75	Logical relations
	UF Boolean relations
Z50.73	'Or' relation
	UF Sum
	Union relation
Z50.74	Coordination (concept)
	UF 'And' relation
	Product relation
Z50.74.10	Post-coordination
Z50.74.20	Pre-coordination
Z50.74.20A	Strings (words)
Z50.74.20C	Citation order
	UF Preferred order
Z50.74.20E	Multiple entry
Z50.74.20EC	Chain procedure
Z50.74.20EP	Permutation
Z50.74.20ER	Rotation (indexes)
Z50.75	'Not' relation
	UF Difference relation
	Negation
Z50.77	Link indicators
Z50.78	Phase relations
Z50.79	Partition
	UF Splitting (document)
Z50.82	Cross references
	UF Syndesis
Z50.82.50	Reference codes
	UF Cross-reference codes
Z50.85	Index language codes
Z50.85.20	Notation
	UF Class numbers
Z50.85.20A	Expressive notation

Z20/84	**Library and Information Science** (cont.)
Z40/56	**Information/Library Operations** (cont.)
Z50	**Index Languages** (cont.)

Z50.26/94	Index language elements (cont.)
Z50.85	Index language codes (cont.)
Z50.85.20	Notation (cont.)
Z50.85.20A	Expressive notation (cont.)
Z50.85.20AC	Hierarchical notation
Z50.85.20C	Ordinal notation
Z50.85.20F	Retroactive notation
Z50.85.20H	Numeric notation
Z50.85.20J	Alphabetic notation
Z50.85.20K	Mixed notation
Z50.85.20M	Mnemonic notation
Z50.85.20R	Hospitality (notation)
Z50.85.20RA	Interpolation (index language)
	UF Intercalation
Z50.85.40	Call numbers
	UF Location numbers
	Shelf marks
	Shelf numbers
Z50.90	Index language order
	Citation order Z50.74.20C
Z50.90.10	Collocation
	UF Helpful order
Z50.90.30	Filing order
Z50.90.30A	Alphabetization
	(By compilation)
Z50.95	Index language compilation
Z50.95.20	Thesaurus compilation
	Computer-assisted compilation Z47.10
	(By automation)
Z50.95.60	Automatic generation of index languages

Z52	**Information Storage Devices**
Z52.01/99	Indexes
	UF Information files
	(By physical form)
Z52.10.05	Shelf as index
Z52.10.07	Shelf arrangement
	Call numbers Z50.85.40
Z52.10.07G	Shelf guides
Z52.10.20	Visible indexes
Z52.10.30	Printed indexes
Z52.10.60	Computerized indexes
	UF Printed indexes (computer produced)
	Articulated indexes Z52.65.40
	KWAC indexes Z52.65.55
	KWIC indexes Z52.65.50
	KWOC indexes Z52.65.53
	Permuted indexes Z52.65.35
	PRECIS indexes Z52.65.30
Z52.10.70	Data bases
	(By purpose)
Z52.15.10	Book indexes
	SN Indexes to books
	Concordances Z15.20.75
Z52.15.20	Periodical indexes
	UF Abstract journal indexes
Z52.15.30	Cumulative indexes

Z20/84   **Library and Information Science** (cont.)
Z40/56   **Information/Library Operations** (cont.)
Z52   **Information Storage Devices** (cont.)

Z52.01/99	Indexes (cont.)	
	(By arrangement)	
Z52.20	File organization (index)	
Z52.20.10	Inverted file	
	UF Term entry	
Z52.20.30	Item entry	
	(By elements)	
Z52.25	Index entries	
	UF Catalogue entries	
	Surrogates	
Z52.25.10	Unit entries	
Z52.25.30	Main entries	
Z52.25.40	Added entries	
	(By author and subject)	
Z52.40	Author indexes	
	Author catalogue Z52.80.40	
Z52.42	Name indexes	
	Name catalogues Z52.80.35	
Z52.45	Title indexes	
	KWAC indexes Z52.65.55	
	KWIC indexes Z52.65.50	
	KWOC indexes Z52.65.53	
	Title catalogues Z52.80.38	
Z52.47	Citation indexes	
Z52.55/99	Subject indexes	
	Subject catalogues Z52.80.50/70	
	(By type of index language)	
Z52.60/70	Pre-coordinate indexes	
Z52.62	Classified indexes	
	Classified catalogues Z52.80.60	
Z52.65	Alphabetical subject indexes	
Z52.65.10	Relative indexes	
	UF Indexes to classification systems	
Z52.65.20	Chain indexes	
Z52.65.30	PRECIS indexes	
Z52.65.35	Permuted indexes	
Z52.65.40	Articulated indexes	
Z52.65.45	Rotated indexes	
Z52.65.50	KWIC indexes	
Z52.65.53	KWOC indexes	
Z52.65.55	KWAC indexes	
Z52.70	Alphabetico-classed indexes/catalogues	
Z52.75	Coordinate indexes	
	UF Post-coordinate subject indexes	
Z52.75.10	Manual coordinate indexes	
Z52.75.10D	Dual dictionaries	
Z52.75.30	Punched card coordinate indexes	
	UF Edge punched indexes	
Z52.75.30C	Optical coincidence systems	
	(By catalogues)	
Z52.80	Catalogues	
Z52.80.05	Library catalogues	
	(By automation)	
Z52.80.10	Computerized catalogues	
	UF Computerized library catalogues	
Z52.80.10C	Library catalogue convertion	

Z20/84		**Library and Information Science** (cont.)
Z40/56		**Information/Library Operations** (cont.)
Z52		**Information Storage Devices** (cont.)
	Z52.01/99	Indexes (cont.)
	Z52.80	Catalogues (cont.)
		(By physical form)
	Z52.80.15	Card catalogues
	Z52.80.15C	Catalogue cards
	Z52.80.15E	Card catalogue cabinets
	Z52.80.18	Printed catalogues
		UF Bookform catalogues
	Z52.80.25	Sheaf catalogues
	Z52.80.30	COM catalogues
		UF Computer output microform catalogues
	Z52.80.30B	Microfilm catalogues
	Z52.80.30E	Microfiche catalogues
		(By title author and subject)
	Z52.80.35	Name catalogues
	Z52.80.38	Title catalogues
	Z52.80.40	Author catalogues
	Z52.80.50/70	Subject catalogues
		Alphabetico-classed indexes/catalogues Z52.70
	Z52.80.60	Classified catalogues
	Z52.80.70	Alphabetical subject catalogues
		UF Subject headings catalogues
	Z52.80.75	Dictionary catalogues
		(By application)
	Z52.80.90	Union catalogues
	Z52.80.90P	Union catalogue of periodicals
	Z52.80.95	Shelf lists

Z54		**Information Retrieval**
		(By services given)
	Z54.10	Reference work
		UF Assistance to readers
		Enquiry work
		Reference services Z65.20
	Z54.15	Literature searches
	Z54.20	Bibliography compilation
	Z54.25	Current dissemination of information
		Abstracting and indexing services Z68.30
		Accession lists Z74.10.20A
		Selective dissemination of information Z68.30.10D
	Z54.40	Data retrieval
		(By techniques)
	Z54.60/99	Searching
		(By type)
	Z54.62.05	Random searching
	Z54.62.05B	Browsing
	Z54.62.20	Retrospective searching
	Z54.62.30	Natural language searching
		Truncation Z50.48.20C
	Z54.62.30B	Text searching
		UF Text retrieval
		(By accessibility)
	Z54.65.05	Batch searching
	Z54.65.10	On-line searching
		(By questions)
	Z54.70	Search questions
	Z54.75	Search profiles

Z20/84		**Library and Information Science** (cont.)
Z40/56		**Information/Library Operations** (cont.)
Z54		**Information Retrieval** (cont.)
	Z54.60/99	Searching (cont.)
		(By process)
	Z54.80	Search process
	Z54.80.10	Query formulation
		UF Profile compilation
	Z54.80.30	Search strategies
		UF Search order
		Logical relations Z50.72/75
	Z54.80.30B	Contextual searching
	Z54.80.30C	Search cut-off
	Z54.80.30R	Search revision
	Z54.80.30RF	Relevance feedback
		(By output)
		Information systems evaluation Z56
	Z54.90	Search output
	Z54.90.10	Ranked output
	Z54.90.60	Post-search editing

Z56		**Information Systems Evaluation**
		UF Information systems testing
	Z56.10	Recall
	Z56.20	Silence (recall)
	Z56.40	Precision
	Z56.40F	False-drops
		(By ratios)
	Z56.60	Performance ratios
		UF Fall-out ratio
		Miss ratio
		Noise ratio
		Novelty ratio
		Output ratio
		Pertinence ratio
	Z56.60P	Precision ratio
	Z56.60R	Recall ratio
	Z56.70	Generality number

Z58		**Information/Library Stock**
		Information materials Z15
	Z58.10	Library stock
		UF Library materials
	Z58.10.10	Acquisitions
		UF Accessions
	Z58.10.40	Library collections
	Z58.10.40A	Private collections (library)
	Z58.10.40D	Special collections (library)

For library materials by subject, combine with appropriate terms in the whole thesaurus.

Z60/70		**Information/Library Systems**
	Z61	Information/library networks

Z62		**Libraries**
		(By services)
	Z62.05	Library services
		(By type of library)
	Z62.10	International libraries
	Z62.13	National libraries

Z20/84		**Library and Information Science** (cont.)
Z60/70		**Information/Library Systems** (cont.)
Z62		**Libraries** (cont.)
	Z62.13	National libraries (cont.)
	Z62.13.10	Depository libraries
	Z62.15/17	Government libraries
	Z62.16	Central government libraries
	Z62.16.20	Legislature libraries
	Z62.16.40	Government department libraries
	Z62.17	State libraries
		UF Province libraries
	Z62.20	Armed forces libraries
	Z62.26	Public libraries
		SN A library which serves the population of a community or region free of charge or for a nominal fee
		UF Local authority libraries
	Z62.26.10	Regional libraries
	Z62.26.20	County libraries
	Z62.26.30	Rural libraries
	Z62.26.40	Municipal libraries
		UF City libraries
	Z62.26.60	District libraries
	Z62.28	Public/academic libraries
	Z62.30	Educational libraries
	Z62.30.10	Academic libraries
	Z62.30.10A	University libraries
		For others combine with terms under Higher Education J70.08
	Z62.30.30	School libraries
		Children's libraries Z62.70.10
	Z62.30.30C	Primary school libraries
	Z62.30.30E	Secondary school libraries
		For others combine with terms for type of school at J70.07
	Z62.35	Institutional libraries
	Z62.35.10	Hospital libraries
	Z62.35.10D	Medical hospital libraries
	Z62.35.30	Prison libraries
	Z62.35.40	Ship libraries
	Z62.35.50	Libraries for the blind
		For others combine 'Institutional libraries' with descriptor for specific user
	Z62.40/59	Special libraries
		Information services Z65
	Z62.42	Private libraries
	Z62.44	Religious institution libraries
		UF Cathedral libraries
	Z62.46	Learned libraries
		UF Learned society libraries
		Professional bodies libraries
		Scholarly libraries
	Z62.48	Research libraries
	Z62.50	Industrial libraries
	Z62.52	Business libraries
		UF Commercial libraries
		Marketing libraries
	Z62.52.40	Newspaper libraries
		(By economic basis)
	Z62.56	Philanthropic libraries
	Z62.58	Subscription libraries
		UF Rental libraries
		Self-supporting libraries

Z20/84	**Library and Information Science** (cont.)
Z60/70	**Information/Library Systems** (cont.)
Z62	**Libraries** (cont.)

Z62.40/59	Special libraries (cont.)
	(By type of stock)
Z62.60	Document centres
Z62.63	Film libraries
Z62.64	Phonorecord libraries UF Record libraries
Z62.65	Map libraries
Z62.66	Program libraries
	(By subject)
Z62.68.10	Scientific libraries
Z62.68.20A	Agricultural libraries
Z62.68.20E	Engineering libraries
Z62.68.20M	Medical libraries
Z62.68.30	Law libraries
Z62.68.40	Art libraries
	For others combine 'Libraries' with term for specific subject
	(By user)
Z62.70.10	Children's libraries
	(By conditions of use)
Z62.72.30	Reference libraries
Z62.72.30D	Reading rooms

Z62.72.50	Lending libraries
	    UF Copying libraries
	        Postal libraries

Z62.72.70	Mobile libraries
	    UF Bibliobus
	        Book mobiles

	(By parts of whole system)
Z62.74.10	Headquarters libraries
Z62.74.20	Branch libraries
	(By size)
Z62.76.10	Large libraries
Z62.76.20	Medium size libraries
Z62.76.30	Small libraries
	(By experimental libraries)
Z62.78.10	Pilot libraries

Z65	**Information Services**

	UF Documentation services
	    Information Bureaux
	    Information centres
	Special libraries Z62.40/59

Z65.10	Enquiry services UF Advisory services

Z65.20	Reference services
	    UF Readers advisory services
	        Readers guidance services
	    Reference work Z54.10

Z65.30	Referral centres
Z65.35	Clearing houses
Z65.40	Bibliographic services *Bibliography compilation Z54.20*
Z65.40.10	Literature review services
Z65.50	Translation services *Translations Z15.37.30*

Z20/84   **Library and Information Science** (cont.)
Z60/70   **Information/Library Systems** (cont.)
Z68   **Information Systems**

	UF Documentation systems
Z68.10	International information systems
Z68.15	National information systems
	(By automation)
Z68.18	On-line information systems
	On-line information processing Z47.30
	On-line searching Z54.65.10
	(By function)
Z68.20	Information analysis centres
Z68.25	Data centres
	UF Data information systems
Z68.28	Data banks
Z68.30	Abstracting and indexing services
Z68.30.10	Current awareness services
Z68.30.10D	Selective dissemination of information
Z68.30.30	Retrospective search services
	Retrospective searching Z54.62.20
Z68.30.45	Card services
Z68.30.50	Tape services
	(By subject)
Z68.50	Scientific information systems
Z68.50.10	Agricultural information systems
Z68.50.20	Engineering information systems
Z68.50.50	Medical information systems
Z68.50.50R	Medical records information systems
Z68.65	Legal information systems
Z68.70	Management information systems

For others combine 'Information systems' with descriptor for subject covered.

Z72   **Information Use**

	UF Library use
	Book use frequency Z18.30.10B
	Information transfer Z10
	(By user)
Z72.30	Information users
Z72.30.10	Library users
	UF Borrowers
	Readers (library)
	Borrower registration Z42.60
	(By user needs and habits)
Z72.40	Information user needs
	UF User demand
	Information demand
	User needs
	User satisfaction
	(By user habits)
Z72.50	Information user habits
	UF User attitudes
	User behaviour
	Information gathering habits
	(By information exchange persons and groups)
Z72.50.50	Gatekeepers
Z72.50.55	Invisible colleges
	(By user studies)
Z72.60	Information user studies
	UF User analysis

Z20/84		**Library and Information Science** (cont.)
Z72		**Information Use** (cont.)

                             (By user instruction)

Z72.70   Information user instruction
                              Reading guidance Z75.20.10

                             (By relation with information/library staff)

Z72.82   Information scientist-user relationship

Z72.84   Documentalist-user relationship

Z72.86   Librarian-user relationship

Z73/75   **Library Use Promotion**

Z74.10   Library publicity

Z74.10.10   Library exhibitions

Z74.10.20   Library publications

Z74.10.20A   Accession lists

Z74.10.20B   Information bulletins

Z74.20   Library public relations

Z75   Library extension work
                              UF Library cultural activities
                              Cultural activities T78
                              Discussion groups Y55.05
                              Lectures J50.11
                              Play reading W83.60

Z75.20   Reading promotion

Z75.20.10   Reading guidance

Z75.20.20   Story hours

Z75.50   Library theatres

Z75.55   Library cinemas

Z85/99   **Archives**

                             UF Archive science

                             (By history)

Z86.10   History of archives

                             (By research)

Z86.20   Archive research

                             (By policy and development)

Z87   Archive policy

Z87.30   Archive development

                             (By planning and administration)

Z88.10   Archive planning

Z88.60   Archive administration

Z88.60.10   Archive legislation

                             (By facilities)

Z89   Archive facilities

Z89.10   Archive repositories
                                UF Archive depositories

Z89.20   Records centres

Z89.40   Archive equipment

                             (By personnel)

Z90   Archive personnel

Z90.10   Archivists

Z90.40   Records managers

Z90.50   Manuscript curators

                             (By profession and training)

Z90.60   Archive profession

Z90.70   Archive science training

Z85/99   **Archives** (cont.)

Z92   **Records Management**

SN That area of general administrative management concerned with
achieving economy and efficiency in the creation use and
maintenance, and disposition of records
UF Mail management
Paperwork management

(By special subjects)
Z92.10   Files administration

Z92.20   Correspondence management

(By techniques)
Z92.40   Records appraisal

Z92.50   Records disposition
Z92.50.10   Disposition schedules
Z92.50.50   Records disposal

Z93   **Archive Operations**

SN Operations on non-current records retained as archives

Z93.10   Archive records preservation

Z93.60   Archive finding aids
UF Calendars
Archive registers
For other storage aids use terms in Z52 'Information storage devices', for
example, 'Indexes', 'Catalogues'.

For records management and archive operations in common with information
and library process, use terms in schedules Z40/59 'Information/library
operations', for example:
'Document processing', 'Accessioning', 'Loans systems', 'Indexing',
'Cataloguing', 'Classification', 'Information retrieval'.

Z95/97   **Records**

SN All recorded information regardless of media or characteristics,
made or received and maintained by an organisation or
institution in pursuance of its legal obligation or in
the transaction of its business.
Correspondence Z15.42.30
Educational records J40.26
Manuscripts Z15.42.10

Z96.05   Official records

(By arrangement)
Z96.10   Records file
Z96.10.10   Case files

(By currency)
Z96.30   Current records

Z96.35   Semi-current records

Z96.70   Non-current records

Z97   Archive records
SN Non-current records of an organisation or institution
preserved because of their continuing value
UF Archive documents
Archive holdings
Permanent records
Textual archives

Z97.10   Personal papers
UF Private papers

(By non-textual archives)
Z97.30   Audiovisual archives
Z97.30.10   Cartographic archives
Z97.30.20   Photographic archives
Z97.60   Machine-readable archives
UF Data archives

Z85/99		**Archives** (cont.)
Z98		**Archive Agencies**
	Z98.10	Public archives
	Z98.15	International archives
	Z98.20	National archives
	Z98.25	Government archives

                                                        UF Central government archives
                                                               Federal archives
      Official archives
      Regional government archives
      (By type of government)

	Z98.25.70	Local government archives

                   UF Municipal archives

	Z98.50	Private archives

      UF Academic archives
      Church archives
      Industrial archives

	Z98.50.30	Business archives

PERMUTED INDEX

Church administration
Communication administration
Cultural administration
Cultural planning and administration
Economic administration
Economic planning and administration
Educational administration
Educational planning and administration
Environmental planning administration
Files administration
Financial administration
Information/library administration
Judicial control of administration
Museum administration
Museum planning and administration
Public administration
Science administration
Science planning and administration
Social science administration
Social welfare administration
Administration of justice
Educational administrative bodies
Administrative law
Administrative reform
Administrative sciences
Administrative structure
Educational administrative structure
Administrative tribunals
Teacher -administrator relationship
Administrators
Cultural administrators
Educational administrators
Information/library administrators
Admissibility of evidence
Admission
Educational admission
Library admission
Admission criteria
Adolescence
Adolescent psychology
Adolescents
Adopted children
Adoption
Adriatic Sea
Adsorption
Adult basic education
Adult education
Polyvalent adult education
Adult education institutions
Adult education programmes
Adult educators
Adult learning
Adult literacy
Adult psychology
Adult students
Adults
Young adults
Advertising
Press advertising
Radio advertising
Television advertising
Advertising agencies
Legal advice
Educational advisers
Advisory committees
Advocacy
Aegean Sea
Aerial ecosystems
Aerial photography
Aerial sports

Aerial surveying
Aerobiology
Aerodynamics
Aerosols
Aerospace engineering
Aerospace industry
Aerospace medicine
Aerospace navigation
Aesthetics
Afars and Issas
Salt affected soils
Affective psychology
Affective psychoses
Affluent societies
Afghanistan
Africa
Central Africa
East Africa
English speaking Africa
French speaking Africa
North Africa
Southern Africa
West Africa
Africa South of the Sahara
African art
African cultures
African history
African languages
Central African Republic
South African Republic
Afrikaans
After-school activities
Gulf of Aqaba
Age
Bronze age
Iron age
Minimum marriage age
Old age
School-leaving age
Stone age
Terrestrial age
Age composition
Age differences
Age distribution
Age groups
School -age population
Generations (age)
Ageing
Advertising agencies
Archive agencies
News agencies
Cleaning agents
Cultural agents
Theatre agents
Cleaning agents technology
Processing agents technology
Cultural agents training
Geological ages
Middle ages
War aggression
Aggressiveness
Aggressor nations
Agnosticism
Agrarian structure
Agreements
Bilateral agreements
Collective agreements
Cultural agreements
Economic agreements
Reciprocal agreements

Agricultural biology
Agricultural buildings
Agricultural chemistry
Agricultural colleges
Agricultural cooperatives
Agricultural development
Agricultural economics
Agricultural education
Agricultural engineering
Agricultural enterprises
Agricultural extension
Agricultural genetics
Agricultural information systems
Agricultural innovations
Agricultural land
Agricultural libraries
Agricultural machinery
Agricultural planning
Agricultural policy
Agricultural production
Agricultural products
Agricultural research
Agricultural training
Agricultural workers
Agriculture
Subsistence agriculture
Agroclimatology
Agronomy
Development aid
Economic aid
Financial aid
First aid
Foreign aid
Legal aid
Right to legal aid
State aid
Teacher aides
Archive finding aids
Audiovisual aids
Hearing aids
Sensory aids
Tactile aids
Teaching aids
Sensory aids (teaching)
Aims
Cultural aims
Educational aims
Information/library aims
Social welfare aims
Air
Law of the air
Air conditioning
Air forces
Air masses
Air pollution
Air pollution legislation
Air pollution treatment
Air safety
Open air schools
Territorial air space
Open air theatre
Air traffic
Air transport
Air warfare
Aircraft
Aircraft engineering
Aircraft engines
Airports
Gulf of Alaska
Alaska Coastal Waters

Albania
Albanian
Alboran Sea
Albums
Alchemy
Alcohol education
Alcoholic drinks
Alcoholism
Algae
Aquatic algae
Marine algae
Algebra
Boolean algebra
Linear algebra
Matrix algebra
Algeria
Algorithms
Alicyclic compounds
Social alienation
Non-aligned countries
Aliphatic compounds
Alkalinity
Alkaloids
Alkanes
Alkenes
Alkynes
Allergies
Alliances
Resource allocation
Allocation of frequencies
Alloys
Aluminium alloys
Chromium alloys
Copper alloys
Iron alloys
Nickel alloys
Initial teaching alphabet
Letters (alphabet)
Alphabetic notation
Alphabetical subject catalogues
Alphabetical subject heading lists
Alphabetical subject indexes
Alphabetical thesauri
Alphabetico-classed indexes/catalogues
Alphabetization
Alphabets
Altaic languages
Aluminium
Aluminium alloys
Amateur actors
Amateur choirs
Amateur musical performances
Amateur musicians
Amateur orchestras
Amateur photography
Amateur sportsmen
Amateur status
Amateur theatre
Amateurism
Amateurs
Ambition
Land amelioration
Amenities
Amenities conservation
Amenities destruction
America
Central America
Latin America
North America
South America

United States of America
Latin American art
Latin American cultures
North American cultures
American history
Latin American history
North American history
North American Indian culture
Central American Indian languages
North American Indian languages
South American Indian languages
North American Indians
South American Indians
American Samoa
Amerindian languages
Amharic
Amino resins
Amnesia
Amnesty
Amorphous state
Amphibia
Amplifiers
Anaesthesiology
Anaesthetics
Analogue computers
Differential analysers
Digital differential analysers
Analysis
Automatic text analysis
Biochemical analysis
Causal analysis
Chemical analysis
Chromatographic analysis
Colorimetric analysis
Comparative analysis
Content analysis
Contextual analysis
Cost/benefit analysis
Cross-cultural analysis
Cross-national analysis
Data analysis
Discriminant analysis
Ecological analysis
Economic analysis
Error analysis
Facet analysis
Factor analysis
Fourier analysis
Functional analysis
Gas analysis
Gravimetric analysis
Harmonic analysis
Historical analysis
Input-output analysis
Instrumental analysis
Interaction process analysis
Linguistic analysis
Literary analysis
Mathematical analysis
Multivariate analysis
Network analysis
Numerical analysis
Optical chemical analysis
Photoelastic stress analysis
Polarographic analysis
Potentiometric analysis
Qualitative analysis
Quantitative analysis
Radiochemical analysis
Regression analysis

Role analysis
Sea water analysis
Semantic analysis
Socio-economic analysis
Spectrochemical analysis
Speech analysis
Statistical analysis
Stress analysis
Structural analysis
Survey analysis
Syntactic analysis
Systematic chemical analysis
Systems analysis
Thermal chemical analysis
Trace analysis
Typological analysis
Variance analysis
Volumetric analysis
Water analysis
X-ray analysis
X-ray chemical analysis
Information analysis centres
Sampling (chemical analysis)
Analytical bibliography
Analytical geometry
Analytical jurisprudence
Analytico-synthetic classification systems
Anarchism
Anarchy
Anatomical systems
Anatomy
Animal anatomy
Human anatomy
Plant anatomy
Regional anatomy
Ancient art
Ancient Asiatic religions
Ancient cities
Ancient civilizations
Ancient history
Ancient religions
Ancient scripts
Ancient theatre
Andaman languages
Andaman Sea
Andorra
Anemometers
Anger
Angiospermae
Angola
Saint Kitts-Nevis-Anguilla
Anhydrite
Animal anatomy
Animal behaviour
Animal breeding
Animal development
Animal ecology
Animal genetics
Animal growth
Animal husbandry
Animal life
Animal metabolism
Animal migration
Animal morphology
Animal oils
Vegetable and animal oils technology
Animal products
Animal resources
Animal sports
Animal taxonomy

Animals
Aquatic animals
Domestic animals
Game animals
Laboratory animals
Marine animals
Wild animals
Animation culturelle
Animism
Annam-Muong
Annamese
Anniversary celebrations
Annotated cataloguing
Annual reports
Antarctic Ocean
Antarctic Regions
Antennas
Anthologies
Anthropoda
Anthropogeography
Anthropology
Cultural and social anthropology
Anti-militarism
Antibiotics
Antibodies
Anticurriculum movement
Anticyclones
Antigens
Antigua
Netherlands Antilles
Antimony
Antiquarian books
Antiquarian law
Antiques
Antiquities
Antiquity
Antisemitism
Antisocial behaviour
Anxiety
Anxiety states
Apartments
Apathy
Fluid apertures
Aphotic regions
Apiculture
Appeal courts
Appeals (legal)
Domestic appliances
Computer applications
Applied psychology
Applied research
Appointment to job
Investment appraisal
Records appraisal
Appreciation
Apprentice training schools
Apprentices
Apprenticeship
Approval ordering
Least squares approximation
Approximation theory
Aptitude
Aptitude tests
Aquaculture
Marine aquaculture
Aquatic algae
Aquatic animals
Aquatic drift
Aquatic ecosystems
Aquatic environment

Aquatic microorganisms
Aquatic plants
Aquatic sports
Aquifers
Arab art
Arab countries
Arab culture
United Arab Emirates
Arab history
Libyan Arab Republic
Syrian Arab Republic
Yemen Arab Republic
Saudi Arabia
Arabian Sea
Arabic
Arable farming
Arable land
Arabs
Arafura Sea
Arbitration
Industrial arbitration
International arbitration
Archaeological dating
Archaeological excavations
Archaeological field work
Archaeological interpretation
Archaeological museums
Archaeological objects
Archaeological sites
Archaeological sociology
Archaeological structures
Archaeological surveying
Archaeologists
Archaeology
Archaeometry
East India Archipelago seas
Archipelagos
Architect restorers
Architects
Landscape architects
Architecture
Interior architecture
Museum architecture
Naval architecture
Architecture education
Archive administration
Archive agencies
Archive development
Archive equipment
Archive facilities
Archive finding aids
Archive legislation
Archive operations
Archive personnel
Archive planning
Archive policy
Archive profession
Archive records
Archive records preservation
Archive repositories
Archive research
Archive science training
Archives
Audiovisual archives
Business archives
Cartographic archives
Government archives
History of archives
Information, libraries and archives
International archives

299

Local government archives		Prehistoric art	
Machine-readable archives		Preservation of works of art	
National archives		Psychology of art	
Photographic archives		Religious art	
Private archives		Representative works of art	
Public archives		Slav art	
Archivists		Sociology of art	
Arctic cultures		Works of art	
Arctic Ocean		Art books	
Arctic Regions		Art collections	
Depressed areas		Art criticism	
Educational priority areas		Art education	
Industrial areas		Art galleries	
Intertidal areas		Art glass	
Mangrove areas		Art history	
Metropolitan areas		Art imitations	
Residential areas		Art libraries	
Rural areas		Art metalwork	
Seismic areas		Art museums	
Shopping areas		Art styles	
Urban areas		Arthritis	
Water recreational areas		Articles	
Development areas (urban planning)		Articulated indexes	
Geographical areas and countries		Articulation	
Arenaceous rocks		Artificial intelligence	
Argentina		Artificial limbs	
Argillaceous rocks		Artificial organs	
Argon		Artificial placentas	
Arid zones		Artificial satellites	
Aristocracy		Artistic creation	
Arithmetic		Artistic cultures	
Digital arithmetic		Artistic design	
Armament process		Right to artistic freedom	
Armed forces		Artistic property	
Armed forces libraries		Artists	
Armenian		Visual artists	
Armenian SSR		Young artists	
Armies		Arts	
Armoured vehicles		Fine arts	
Arms control		Graphic arts	
Arms race		Patronage of the arts	
Arms sales		Performing arts	
Aromatic compounds		Plastic arts	
Shelf arrangement		Reproductive arts	
Arrays		Textile arts	
Arrest		Visual arts	
Warrant of arrest		Arts centres	
Arsenic		Liberal arts colleges	
Arson		Arts films	
African art		Shelf as index	
Ancient art		Asbestos	
Arab art		Ascension Island	
Asian art		Asceticism	
Avant-garde art		Ashes	
Byzantine art		Asia	
Ceramic art		South Asia	
Chinese art		South East Asia	
Classical art		Asian art	
Commercial art		Asian cultures	
Contemporary art		Central Asian cultures	
European art		Asian history	
Experimental art		Eurasian and North Asian languages	
Folk art		South and South-East Asian languages	
Islamic art		Asians	
Latin American art		Ancient Asiatic religions	
Medieval art		Cultural aspect	
Modern art		Asphalts	
Native art		Aspiration	
Oceanic art		Assamese	
Pop art		Assassination	

301

International auxiliary lingua
Book availability
Avalanches
Avant-garde art
Averages
Civil aviation
UNESCO awards and honours
Current awareness services
Axiology
Azerbaijani
Azores
Sea of Azov
Aztecs
Bachelors degrees
Educational background
Backward students
Backwardness
Bacteria
Bacterial diseases
Bacteriology
Baffin Bay
Bahamas
Bahrain
Bail
Ecological balance
Energy balance
Water balance
Balance of payments
Balance of trade
Balearic Sea
Bali Sea
Ball games
Ballet
Classical ballet
Modern ballet
Ballet music
Ballistics
Secret ballot
Baltic culture
Baltic languages
Baltic Sea
Banda Sea
Bangladesh
Bank rate
Bankruptcy
Banks
Data banks
Banks Islands
Bantu languages
Bantuide languages
Barbados
Barents Sea
Collective bargaining
Barium
Barometers
Language barriers
Tariff barriers
Saint Barthelemy
Ocean wave base
Data bases
Bases (chemical)
Adult basic education
Basic personality
Basic science education
Basic training
Basins
Drainage basins
River basins
Basque language
Bass Strait

Batch searching
Bathyal zone
Bathymeters
Bathymetric charts
Bathymetry
Bathyspheres
Bathythermographs
Batteries
Baffin Bay
Hudson Bay
Bay of Bengal
Bay of Biscay
Bay of Fundy
Bays
Right to vote and be elected
Beach sand
Beaches
Particle beams
Data bearing media
Beaufort Sea
Sugar beet
Equality before the law
Behaviour
Animal behaviour
Antisocial behaviour
Community behaviour
Cultural behaviour
Group behaviour
Innovation behaviour
Language behaviour
Mass behaviour
Moral behaviour
Political behaviour
Religious behaviour
Sexual behaviour
Social behaviour
Student behaviour
Teacher behaviour
Behavioural disorders
Behavioural sciences
Behaviourism
Belgium
Belief
Religious belief
Believers
Belize
Belligerents
Green belts
Radiation belts
Cost /benefit analysis
Cultural benefits
Fringe benefits
Bay of Bengal
Bengali
Benin (Peoples Republic)
Benthic zone
Libyan -Berber languages
Bering Sea
Bermuda
Beryllium
Best sellers
Beverages
Bhutan
Bibliographers
Bibliographic control
Bibliographic coupling
Bibliographic data
Bibliographic description
Bibliographic services
Bibliographic standards

Botany
Experimental botany
Gulf of Bothnia
Botswana
Drift bottles
Boulders
Bound terms
Boundaries
Boundary layer flow
Boundary layers
Bouvet Island
Boys
Boys schools
Brackish water
Brackish water environment
Brahmanism
Braille system
Brain
Brain deterioration
Brain drain
Brain research
Brain surgery
Brakes
Branch libraries
Brass
Brass instruments
Brazil
Brazing
Breadwinners
Nervous breakdown
Circuit breakers
Animal breeding
Breton
Bricks
Bridges
Brief preparation
Bristol Channel
British Solomon Islands
Broad classification systems
Broadcasters
Broadcasting
Commercial broadcasting
Direct broadcasting
Local broadcasting
National broadcasting
Satellite broadcasting
Broadcasting legislation
Broadcasting organizations
Broadcasting production
Broadcasting programmes
Broader terms
Broken families
Bromide
Bronchitis
Bronze
Bronze age
Browsing
Brunei
Police brutality
Bryophyta
Bubbles
Buddhism
Buddhists
State budget
Budgetary control
Educational budgetary control
Budgets
Cultural budgets
Educational budgets
Household cultural budgets

Information/library budgets
Science budgets
Time budgets
Nation building
Building costs
Building design
Building maintenance
Building materials
Building operations
Building services
Building standards
Building stones
Buildings
Agricultural buildings
Cinema buildings
Educational buildings
Library buildings
Museum buildings
Recreational buildings
Religious buildings
School buildings
Scientific buildings
Theatre buildings
Structural elements (buildings)
Water services (buildings)
Built environment
Bulgaria
Bulgarian
Bulk matter physics
Information bulletins
Buoyancy
Buoys
Oceanographic buoys
Bureaucracy
Burma
Burmese
Tibeto -Burmese languages
Burundi
Show business
Business archives
Business economics
Business formation
Business libraries
Business management
Trial by jury
Byelorussian
Byelorussian SSR
Byzantine art
Byzantine history
Cabinet
Card catalogue cabinets
Submarine cable laying
Cable television
Electric cables
Cadmium
Turks and Caicos Islands
Calcium
Calculating machines
Calculus
Differential calculus
Integral calculus
Variational calculus
New Caledonia
Calendars
Calibration
Gulf of California
Call numbers
Calligraphy
Calories
Cambodian

304

Camels
Trial in camera
Cameras
Film cameras
Television cameras
Underwater cameras
Cameroon
Literacy campaigns
Mass communication campaigns
Camping
Camping sites
Concentration camps
Holiday camps
University campuses
Canada
Panama Canal Zone
Canals
Irrigation canals
Canary Islands
Cancer
Sugar cane
Canteens
Canton and Enderby Islands
Canyons
Submarine canyons
Capacitors
Cinema capacity
Theatre capacity
Cape Verde Islands
Capillarity
Capillary conductivity
Capillary flow
Capillary fringe
Capillary water
Capital
Capital flow
Capital gains
Capital intensive industries
Capital raising
Capitalism
Capitalist systems
Ice caps
Capstans
Carbohydrates
Carbon
Carbon dioxide
Carbonaceous rocks
Carbonate minerals
Carbonate rocks
Carbonyl compounds
Card catalogue cabinets
Card catalogues
Punched card coordinate indexes
Card games
Punched card loan records
Card services
Cardiovascular diseases
Cardiovascular systems
Catalogue cards
Magnetic cards
Punched cards
Day· care
Foster care
Residential child care
Career development
Caribbean
Caribbean Sea
Monte Carlo methods
Caroline Islands
Carpentry

Carpets
Library carrels
Cartographic archives
Cartography
Cartoons
Case files
Case law
Case studies
Library display cases
Cash flow
Caspian Sea
Cassette recordings
Sound cassettes
Video cassettes
Open cast mining
Caste
Casting
Catalan
Card catalogue cabinets
Catalogue cards
Library catalogue conversion
Cataloguers
Catalogues
Alphabetical subject catalogues
Alphabetico-classed
  indexes catalogues
Author catalogues
Card catalogues
Classified catalogues
COM catalogues
Computerized catalogues
Dictionary catalogues
Library catalogues
Microfiche catalogues
Microfilm catalogues
Name catalogues
Printed catalogues
Sheaf catalogues
Subject catalogues
Title catalogues
Union catalogues
Union catalogues of periodicals
Cataloguing
Annotated cataloguing
Author cataloguing
Centralized cataloguing
Cooperative cataloguing
Descriptive cataloguing
Name cataloguing
Re -cataloguing
Simplified cataloguing
Subject cataloguing
Title cataloguing
Cataloguing rules
Cataloguing-in-source
Catalysis
Catering
Educational catering
Catering education
Hotel and catering industry
Catharsis
Catholic schools
Catholicism
Caucasian languages
Hamito-Semitic and Caucasian languages
Causal analysis
Causality
Cause and effect
Caves
Cavitation

Cayman Islands
Ceilings
Celebes Sea
Anniversary celebrations
Celestial mechanics
Cell biology
Cells
Electrolytic cells
Fuel cells
Solar cells
Celtic languages
Cement
Cement and concrete technology
Cemeteries
Cenozoic period
Censorship
Census
Central Africa
Central African Republic
Central America
Central American Indian languages
Central Asian cultures
Central European cultures
Central government
Central government cultural
    organizations
Central government libraries
Central government organizations
Central heating
Central tendency
Centralization
Information.library centralization
Centralized cataloguing
Arts centres
Community centres
Computation centres
Cultural centres
Cultural development centres
Curriculum study centres
Data centres
Document centres
Holiday centres
Information analysis centres
Medical centres
Multimedia resource centres
Records centres
Recreational centres
Referral centres
Research centres
Resource centres
Socio-cultural centres
Sports centres
Teacher centres
Training centres
Urban centres
Centrifuges
Ceram Sea
Ceramic art
Ceramics
Ceramics technology
Cereals
Ceremonies
Educational ceremonies
Religious ceremonies
Educational certificates
Teacher certification
Cesium
Chad
Chain indexes
Chain procedure
Food chains

Thermistor chains
Chalk
Chalkboards
Single chamber legislature
Two -chamber legislature
Attitude change
Cultural change
Language change
Opinion change
Personality change
Resistance to change
Role change
Social change
Sociology of change
Technological change
Environmental changes
Changing society
Bristol Channel
English Channel
Mozambique Channel
Channel flow
Channel islands
Channels
Television channels
Communication channels of flow
Character
Musical character
National character
Character recognition equipment
Managerial characteristics
Characterology
Electric charge
Library charges
Loan charges
Museum charges
Charters
Charts
Bathymetric charts
Flow charts
Cheap editions
Chemical analysis
Optical chemical analysis
Systematic chemical analysis
Thermal chemical analysis
X-ray chemical analysis
Sampling (chemical analysis)
Chemical bonds
Chemical diffusion
Chemical effects
Chemical elements
Chemical engineering equipment
Chemical engineering processes
Chemical equilibrium
Chemical industry
Chemical kinetics
Chemical laboratories
Chemical laboratory equipment
Chemical mechanics
Chemical oceanography
Chemical properties
Chemical radicals
Chemical reactions
Chemical reactors
Chemical research
Chemical statics
Chemical structure
Chemical technology
Chemical thermodynamics
Chemical variables measurement
Absorption (chemical)

Bases (chemical)
Separation (chemical)
Synthesis (chemical)
                Chemical/biological warfare
                Chemicals
                Chemistry
Agricultural chemistry
Colloid chemistry
Crystal chemistry
Experimental chemistry
Inorganic chemistry
Mixed-phase chemistry
Organic chemistry
Physical chemistry
Polymer chemistry
Preparative chemistry
Radiation chemistry
Reaction chemistry
Soil chemistry
Solution chemistry
Surface chemistry
Water chemistry
                Chemistry education
Rights of the child
                Child actors
Residential child care
                Child psychology
Parent -child relationship
                Child welfare
                Child workers
                Childhood
Early childhood
                Children
Adopted children
Deserted children
Handicapped children
Ill-treated children
Only children
Pre-school children
Socially disadvantaged children
                Childrens books
                Childrens films
                Childrens librarians
                Childrens libraries
                Chile
                Chimneys
                China
Indo -China
East China sea
South China Sea
                Chinese
                Chinese art
                Chiropody
                Chloride
Polyvinyl chloride
                Choice
Occupational choice
                Choirs
Amateur choirs
                Cholera
                Choreographers
                Choreography
                Christianity
                Christians
                Christmas Island
                Chromatographic analysis
                Chromium
                Chromium alloys
                Chromosomes

Chronology
Chukchi Sea
Church
Church administration
Church and education
Church and state
Cinema
Cinema attendance
Cinema buildings
Cinema capacity
Cinema management
Library cinemas
Cinematography
Circuit breakers
Closed circuit television
Circuits
Computer circuits
Integrated circuits
Logic and switching circuits
Printed circuits
Atmospheric circulation
Ocean circulation
Periodical circulation
Periodical circulation automation
Circulation figures
International circulation of materials
Library circulation work
Circuses
Citation indexes
Citation indexing
Citation order
Citations
Ancient cities
Citizenship
Civic education
Civil and political rights
Civil aviation
Civil defence
Civil disturbances
Civil engineering
Civil law
Civil servants
Civil service
Civil war
Rights of civilians
Civilization
Leisure civilization
Civilization crises
Ancient civilizations
Clans
Middle class
Ruling class
Social class
Upper class
Working class
Class conflict
Class consciousness
Working class cultures
Class differentiation
Class size
Alphabetico-classed indexes/catalogues
Literacy classes
Main classes
School classes
Transition classes
Classes (terms)
Classical art
Classical ballet
Classical mechanics
Classical music

Energy conservation
Environmental conservation
Resource conservation
Soil conservation
Water conservation
Conservation of nature
Conservation techniques
Conservatism
Indexing consistency
Remote consoles
Tidal constant
Soil constituents
Constitutional history
Constitutional law
Constitutions
Housing construction
Underwater construction
Construction engineering
Construction equipment
Construction industry
Consumer education
Consumer protection
Consumer societies
Consumers
Consumption
Cultural consumption
Energy consumption
Water consumption
Consumption tax
Personal contact
Electric contacts
Containers
Contemporary art
Contemporary culture
Contemporary literature
Contemporary music
Contemporary society
Contempt of court
Cultural content
Programme content
Content analysis
Contextual analysis
Contextual searching
Continental drift
Continental geography
Continental shelf
Continental slope
Continents
Continuum mechanics
Contraception
Marriage contract
Contract law
Contracts
Voluntary contribution
Arms control
Automatic control
Bibliographic control
Biological control
Birth control
Budgetary control
Communication control
Drug control
Educational budgetary control
Electrical variables control
Emission control
Environmental planning control
Flood control
Flow control
Food control
Government control

Humidity control
Magnetic variables control
Management control
Mechanical variables control
Noise control
Numerical control
Optical variables control
Pest control
Pollution control
Pressure control
Price control
Process control
Quality control
Remote control
Right to natural resources control
River control
Sediment control
Social control
Speed control
Synonym control
Temperature control
Terminological control
Thermal variables control
Weed control
Workers control
Control equipment
Electric control equipment
Control groups
Judicial control of administration
Control of specific variables
Control systems
Control technology
Control theory
Controlled languages
Controlled peace
Conurbations
Convection
Conventional weapons
Conventions
Convents
Convergence (mathematics)
Conversation
Conversation instruction
Direct energy conversion
Energy conversion
Library catalogue conversion
Magnetohydrodynamic conversion
Thermionic conversion
Thermoelectric conversion
Converters
Data converters
Conveyors
Library conveyors
Conviction (legal)
Cook Island
Cooking
Cooling
Cooling systems
Cooperation
Cultural cooperation
Educational cooperation
Information/library cooperation
International cooperation
Museum cooperation
Regional cooperation
Scientific cooperation
University cooperation
Cooperative cataloguing
Cooperative education
Cooperatives

311

Agricultural cooperatives
Coordinate indexes
Manual coordinate indexes
Pre-coordinate indexes
Punched card coordinate indexes
Coordination
Educational coordination
Post-coordination
Pre-coordination
Research coordination
Coordination (concept)
Coordination compounds
Copper
Copper alloys
Hard copy
Copyright
Copyright deposit
Copyright transfer
Coral reefs
Coral Sea
Earths core
Magnetic cores
Cores (electric)
Solar corona
Corporal punishment
Right to habeas corpus
Correlation
Correspondence
Correspondence courses
Correspondence management
Corrosion
Electrochemical corrosion
Water corrosion
Corruption
Political corruption
Cosmic matter
Cosmic radiation
Cosmology
Social cost
Cost accounting
Cost effectiveness
Cost of living
Cost reduction
Cost/benefit analysis
Costa Rica
Costs
Book costs
Building costs
Cultural costs
Educational costs
Fixed costs
Variable costs
Press councils
Research councils
Works councils
Right to counsel
Counsel (legal)
Counselling
Counter-cultures
Library counters
Arab countries
Developed countries
Developing countries
Donor countries
Geographical areas and countries
Least developed countries
Mediterranean countries
Neutral countries
Non-aligned countries
Recessing countries

Recipient countries
War-devastated countries
Country programming
Country reports
Countryside
Access to countryside
Countryside conservation
County libraries
Bibliographic coupling
UNESCO coupons
Accelerated courses
Correspondence courses
Credit courses
Education courses
Educational courses
Elective courses
Industrial training courses
Information/library courses
Orientation courses
Part-time courses
Post-graduate courses
Programmed courses
Refresher courses
Sandwich courses
Short courses
Training courses
University courses
Contempt of court
Supreme court
Court rules and procedures
Courts
Appeal courts
Criminal courts
Higher courts
International courts
Juvenile courts
Lower courts
Covers (document)
Craft systems
Craftsmen
Artistic creation
Cultural creation
Creative role
Creative thinking
Creative writing
Creativity
Credit
Credit courses
Creep
Crematoria
Ocean wave crest
Crime
Transnational crime
Crime victims
War crimes
Criminal courts
Criminal investigation
Criminal law
Criminals
War criminals
Criminology
Civilization crises
Cultural crises
Moral crises
Political crises
Ecological crisis
Admission criteria
Art criticism
Literary criticism
Serbo-Croatian

Crops
Grain crops
Red Cross
Cross-cultural analysis
Cross-disciplinary curriculum
Cross-national analysis
Cross-references
Cruelty
Educational cruises
Earths crust
Crustacea
Santa Cruz Islands
Cryogenics
Cryptography
Crystal atomic structure
Crystal chemistry
Crystal defects
Crystal examination
Crystal growth
Crystal microstructure
Crystal structure
Crystalline state
Crystallization
Crystallography
X-ray crystallography
Crystals
Liquid crystals
Cuba
Priests (cultic)
Cultivation
Cults
Cultural accounting
Cultural action
Socio-cultural action
Cultural activities
Socio-cultural activities
Cultural administration
Cultural administrators
Cultural agents
Cultural agents training
Cultural agreements
Cultural aims
Cross-cultural analysis
Cultural and social anthropology
Cultural aspect
Cultural assimilation
Cultural associations
Cultural atlases
Cultural attendance
Cultural behaviour
Cultural benefits
Cultural budgets
Household cultural budgets
Cultural centres
Socio-cultural centres
Cultural change
Socio-cultural clubs
Cultural conditions
Cultural conflict
Cultural consumption
Cultural content
Cultural cooperation
Cultural costs
Cultural creation
Cultural crises
Cultural demand
Cultural democracy
Cultural demonstrations
Cultural development
Cultural development centres

Cultural differentiation
Cultural diplomacy
Cultural disadvantage
Cultural discoveries
Cultural discrimination
Cultural dynamics
Cultural economics
Cultural education
Cultural elite
Cultural environment
Cultural equilibrium
Cultural equipment
Cultural events
Cultural exchange
Cultural exhibitions
Cultural expenditure
Cultural facilities
Cultural factors
Cultural finance
Cultural financing
Cultural geography
Cultural goods
Cultural heritage
Cultural history
Cultural identity
Right to cultural identity
Cultural indicators
Cultural industry
Cultural inequality
Cultural innovations
Cultural integration
Cultural interaction
Cultural isolation
Cultural legislation
Cultural level
Cultural life
Cultural management
Cultural minorities
Cultural models
Cultural nationalism
Cultural needs
Cultural objectives
Regional government cultural organizations
Central government cultural organization
Cultural organizations
Government cultural organizations
International cultural organizations
Local government cultural organizations
National cultural organizations
Private cultural organizations
Regional cultural organizations
Cultural participation
Right to cultural participation
Cultural personnel
Cultural personnel training
Cultural philosophy
Cultural planners
Cultural planning
Cultural planning and administration
Cultural plans
Cultural pluralism
Cultural policy
Cultural productions
Cultural programmes
Cultural property
Movable cultural property
Presentation of cultural property
Preservation of cultural property
Cultural relations
Cultural reproduction

313

Cultural research
Cultural resources
Cultural revolution
Cultural rights
Cultural situation
Cultural sociology
Cultural statistics
Cultural studies
Theoretical cultural studies
Cultural supply
Cultural systems
Cultural tourism
Cultural users
Cultural values
Culturalism
Culturally disadvantaged
Culture
Access to culture
Arab culture
Baltic culture
Concept of culture
Contemporary culture
Democratization of culture
Dissemination of culture
Freshwater fish culture
Mass culture
North American Indian culture
Slav culture
Universal culture
Culture nationalism
Culture of poverty
Culture of work
Animation culturelle
African cultures
Arctic cultures
Artistic cultures
Asian cultures
Central Asian cultures
Central European cultures
Counter -cultures
Disappearing cultures
Dominant cultures
Elite cultures
Established cultures
European cultures
Folk cultures
Iberian cultures
Latin American cultures
Literary cultures
Living cultures
Minority cultures
National cultures
New cultures
North American cultures
Oceanic cultures
Scientific cultures
Spontaneous cultures
Traditional cultures
Working class cultures
Culturology
Cumulating
Cumulative indexes
Cuneiform writing
Manuscript curators
Museum curators
Currency
Currency devaluation
Currency of documents
Current awareness services
Current dissemination of information

Electric current measurement
Ocean current measurement
Current meters
Current records
Non -current records
Semi -current records
Electric currents
Ocean currents
Tidal currents
Water currents
Wind driven currents
Curriculum
Cross-disciplinary curriculum
Integrated curriculum
Pre-primary curriculum
Primary school curriculum
Secondary school curriculum
Teacher training curriculum
University curriculum
Vocational school curriculum
Curriculum development
Curriculum evaluation
Curriculum guides
Curriculum planning
Curriculum research
Curriculum study centres
Curriculum subjects
Tidal curve
Cushitic Languages
Non -custodial punishment
Remand in custody
Customary law
Food customs
Customs and traditions
Customs duties
Customs policy
Search cut-off
Cuttings
Press cuttings
Cybernetics
Hydrological cycle
Life cycle
Tidal cycle
Cyclones
Cylinder recordings
Cyprus
Cytogenetics
Czech
Czechoslovakia
Daily
Daily publications
Dairy farming
Dairy products
Damage
Water damage
Dams
Dance
Folk dance
Modern dance
National dance
Dance music
Dancers
Dangerous materials
Danish
Dardic languages
Darghi
Data
Bibliographic data
Climatic data
Geographical data

314

Geological data
Hydrological data
Meteorological data
Oceanographic data
Statistical data
Survey data
Data analysis
Data banks
Data bases
Data bearing media
Data books
Data centres
Data collection
Data communication equipment
Data converters
Data exchange
Data handling
Data preparation
Data preparation equipment
Data processing
Data retrieval
Data sampling
Sampled data systems
Data transmission
Dating
Archaeological dating
Radiocarbon dating
Davis Strait
Day care
Day Nurseries
Daylight
Rio de la Plata
De-schooling
Disposal of the dead
Dead languages
Dead Sea
Deaf
Education of the deaf
Deaf and dumb
Deafness
Death
Death penalty
Death rate
Debates (teaching method)
Public debt
Debts
Ocean wave decay
Decentralization
Information/library decentralization
Urban decentralization
Decentralized government
Dewey decimal classification
Deciphering
Decision
Decision making
Decision theory
Legal decisions
Decoding
Decolonization
Decomposition reactions
Decontamination
Population decrease
Decrees
Deduction
Deep sea
Deep sea fishing
Speech defective
Crystal defects
Vision defects
Defence

Civil defence
Non-violent defence
Self -defence (war)
Defendants
Mental deficiency
Deflation
Deformation
Elastic deformation
Plastic deformation
Degradation
Degrees
Bachelors degrees
Doctoral degrees
Information/library degrees
Masters degrees
Dehydration
Deism
Delegation of authority
Delinquency
Juvenile delinquency
Deltas
Demand
Cultural demand
Educational demand
Supply and demand
Water demineralization
Democracy
Cultural democracy
Representative democracy
Democratic Kampuchea
Korea (Democratic Peoples Republic)
German Democratic Republic
Lao Peoples Democratic Republic
Madagascar (Democratic Republic)
Yemen (Peoples Democratic Republic)
Democratization
Democratization of culture
Democratization of education
Demography
Demolition
Demonology
Demonstrations
Cultural demonstrations
Demonstrations (lessons)
Denmark
Denominational schools
Density
Fluid density
Population density
Sea water density
Density measurement
Fluid density measurement
Sea water density measurement
Dental diseases
Dental inspection
Dentistry
Deontology
Government department libraries
Government departments
Dependency relationship
Deportation
Copyright deposit
Depository libraries
Clastic deposits
Fossil fuel deposits
Metallic deposits
Mineral deposits
Non-metalliferous
mineral deposits
Salt deposits
Submarine mineral deposits

Depreciation
Depressed areas
Depression
Economic depression
Manic -depressive psychoses
Parental deprivation
Depth indexing
Depth measurement
Depth psychology
Depth recorders
Desalination
Bibliographic description
Document description
Job description
Descriptive cataloguing
Descriptive linguistics
Descriptive statistics
Desegregation
Desert science
Desert soils
Deserted children
Deserts
Design
Artistic design
Building design
Computer-assisted design
Environmental design
Fashion design
Housing design
Industrial design
Landscape design
Logic design
Open plan design
Statistical design
Street furniture design
Urban design
Graphic designers
Amenities destruction
Destructive testing
Non -destructive testing
Signal processing and detection
Detectives
Light detectors
Radiation detectors
Detention
Detergents
Deterioration
Brain deterioration
Environmental deterioration
Soil deterioration
Determinants
Right of self -determination
Wage determination
Determinism
Currency devaluation
War -devastated countries
Developed countries
Least developed countries
Late developers
Developing countries
Development
Agricultural development
Animal development
Archive development
Book development
Career development
Communication development
Community development
Cultural development
Curriculum development

Economic and social development
Education and development
Educational development
Emotional development
Experimental development
Human resources development
Individual development
Industrial development
Information/library development
Language development
Mental development
Moral development
Motor development
Museum development
Museum policy and development
National development
Personality development
Physiological development
Plant development
Political development
Process development
Product development
Research and development
Resource development
Right to economic development
Rural development
Scientific development
Social science development
Thought process development
Urban development
Water resources development
Development aid
Development areas (urban planning)
Cultural development centres
Development education
Development planning
Development plans
Development policy
Development programmes
Development projects
Development strategies
Developmental psychology
Sexual deviance
Social deviance
Standard deviation
Computer storage devices
Dielectric devices
Display devices
Electroacoustic devices
Electrochemical devices
Electromechanical devices
Inflatable devices
Information storage devices
Literary devices
Magnetic devices
Magnetostrictive devices
Optical devices
Optoelectronic devices
Photoelectric devices
Piezoelectric devices
Precision oriented devices
Recall oriented devices
Safety devices
Thermoelectric devices
Warning devices
Dew
Dewey decimal classification
Comparative and diachronic linguistics
Medical diagnosis
Diagrammatical teaching

Rational processes disorders
Sleep disorders
Spastic disorders
Speech disorders
Family disorganization
Social disorganization
Dispatching
Statistical dispersion
Dispersion and surface physics
Dispersion physics
Dispersions
Disphotic regions
Library display cases
Display devices
Graphic displays
Displays (computer)
Records disposal
Sewage disposal and handling
Waste disposal and handling
Disposal of the dead
Records disposition
Disposition schedules
International disputes
Labour disputes
Dissatisfaction
Dissemination of culture
Dissemination of information
Current dissemination of information
Selective dissemination of information
Dissemination of knowledge
Energy dissipation
Dissociation reactions
Marriage dissolution
Dissolved gases
Distance measurement
Distillation
Age distribution
Book distribution
Electric power distribution
Film distribution
Income distribution
Labour distribution
Population distribution
Sex distribution
Temperature distribution
Water distribution
Statistical distributions
Distributive education
District heating
District libraries
Atmospheric disturbances
Civil disturbances
Emotional disturbances
Solar disturbances
Diurnal variations
Diversification of education
Voltage dividers
Diving
Diving equipment
Divorce
Docks
Doctoral degrees
Economic doctrines
Political doctrines
Religious doctrines
Document centres
Document description
Document losses
Document maintenance
Document parts

Document preparation
Document preservation
Document processing
Document storage
Document withdrawal
Covers (document)
Stock-taking (document)
Documentalist-user relationship
Documentalists
Television documentaries
Documentary films
Documentary history
Documentation
Program and systems documentation
Currency of documents
Primary documents
Privately printed documents
Restricted documents
Secondary documents
Semi-published documents
Therapeutic documents
Unpublished documents
Tablets (documents)
Dogmatism
Dolomite
Domestic animals
Domestic appliances
Domestic engineering
Domestic safety
Domestic science
Domestic science education
Domestic violence
Dominant cultures
Dominica
Dominican Republic
Donor countries
Doors
Brain drain
Drainage
Land drainage
Drainage basins
Drainage engineering
Drama
Radio drama
Television drama
Drama education
Dramatic presentation (teaching method)
Dramatization
Dravidian languages
Drawing
Technical drawing
Drawings
Technical drawings
Dredging
Aquatic drift
Continental drift
Drift bottles
Alcoholic drinks
Wind driven currents
Drop-out problem
Drop-out rate
School drop-outs
Social drop-outs
Drops
False drops
Drought
Drug addiction
Drug control
Drug education
Drug psychotherapy

Drugs
Narcotic drugs
Dry farming
Drying
Dual dictionaries
Dual enrolment
Ducts
Deaf and dumb
Dunes
Duplicating
Dust
Dutch
Duties
Customs duties
Role duties
Dyes
Dyes technology
Dynamic oceanography
Dynamics
Atmospheric dynamics
Cultural dynamics
Flight dynamics
Fluid dynamics
Group dynamics
Population dynamics
Social dynamics
Dysentry
Dyslexia
Dyslexic
Early childhood
Earth (planet)
Earth sciences
Earthing
Earthquake engineering
Earthquakes
Submarine earthquakes
Rare earths
Earths core
Earths crust
Earths structure
Far East
Middle East
East Africa
South East Asia
South and South -East Asian languages
East China sea
East India Archipelago seas
East Siberian Sea
Easter Island
Eastern Europe
Eastern Hemisphere
Ecclesiastical law
Echinodermata
Echo sounders
Echo sounding
Solar eclipses
Ecological analysis
Ecological balance
Ecological crisis
Ecological relationships
Ecological research
Marine ecological zones
Ecology
Animal ecology
Human ecology
Plant ecology
Ecomuseums
Econometrics
Economic administration
Economic agreements

Economic aid
Economic analysis
Socio -economic analysis
Economic and social development
Economic competition
Economic concentration
Economic conditions
Economic depression
Right to economic development
Economic doctrines
Economic equilibrium
Economic evaluation
Socio -economic factors
Economic fluctuations
Economic forecasting
Economic geography
Economic geology
Economic growth
Economic history
Socio -economic indicators
Economic legislation
Economic life
Economic models
Economic planning
Economic planning and administration
Economic policy
Economic power
Economic psychology
Economic resources
Social and economic rights
Economic sanctions
Economic sociology
Socio -economic status
Economic structure
Economic surveys
Economic systems
International economic systems
Economic theory
Economic value
Economics
Agricultural economics
Business economics
Cultural economics
Housing economics
Industrial economics
Information library economics
Labour economics
Land economics
Museum economics
Rural economics
Social welfare economics
Transport economics
Economics education
Economics of communication
Economics of education
Economics of research
Economics of scale
Economics of science
Economics research
Economists
Collectivist economy
Free market economy
Mixed economy
National economy
Planned economy
Regional economy
Ecosystems
Aerial ecosystems
Aquatic ecosystems
Marine ecosystems

Terrestrial ecosystems
Ecuador
Ecumenical movement
Editing
Historical editing
Post-search editing
Editions
Abridged editions
Cheap editions
First editions
New editions
Editors
Educability
Education
Access to education
Adult basic education
Adult education
Agricultural education
Alcohol education
Architecture education
Art education
Basic science education
Biology education
Catering education
Chemistry education
Church and education
Civic education
Commercial education
Community education
Comparative education
Compensatory education
Compulsory education
Computer science education
Consumer education
Cooperative education
Cultural education
Democratization of education
Development education
Distributive education
Diversification of education
Domestic science education
Drama education
Drug education
Economics education
Economics of education
Engineering education
Environmental education
Equal education
Evaluation of education
Exceptional student education
Extension education
Family education
Free education
General education
General technical education
Geography education
Geology education
Handicrafts education
Health education
Higher education
Higher technical education
History education
Home education
Humanities education
Hydrology education
Industry and education
Informal education
Intercultural education
International education
Language education

Legal education
Leisure and education
Life-long education
Lower secondary education
Management education
Mass education
Mathematics education
Medical education
Mens education
Middle secondary education
Migrant education
Military education
Moral education
Music education
Non-formal education
Nutrition education
Oceanography education
Out-of-school education
Parent education
Physical education
Physics education
Political science education
Polyvalent adult education
Population education
Pre-primary education
Pre-school education
Pre-university science education
Pre-vocational education
Primary education
Principles of education
Private education
Psychology education
Public education
Quality of education
Recurrent education
Refugee education
Religious education
Right to education
Role of education
Rural education
Safety education
Science education
Secondary education
Sex education
Social science education
Special education
Speech education
State and education
State responsibility for education
Statistics education
Technical education
Upper secondary education
Urban education
Veterinary education
Vocational education
Womens education
Workers education
Education and development
Education and employment
Local government education authorities
Education courses
Education for peace
Adult education institutions
Education of the blind
Education of the deaf
Adult education programmes
Special education teachers
Educational administration
Educational administrative bodies

Educational administrative structure
Educational administrators
Educational admission
Educational advisers
Educational aims
Educational assessment
Educational assistance
Educational associations
Educational attendance
Educational background
Educational biographies
Government educational bodies
International educational bodies
National educational bodies
Regional educational bodies
Self-governing educational bodies
Educational budgetary control
Educational budgets
Educational buildings
Educational catering
Educational ceremonies
Educational certificates
Educational collections
Educational cooperation
Educational coordination
Educational costs
Educational courses
Educational cruises
Educational demand
Educational development
Educational discrimination
Educational environment
Educational equipment
Educational exchanges
Educational exhibitions
Educational expenditure
Educational experiments
Educational facilities
Educational fees
Educational films
Educational finance
Educational financial management
Educational financial resources
Educational financing
Educational forecasting
Educational foundations
Educational games
Educational goals
Educational grants
Educational grouping
Educational guidance
Educational guidance personnel
Educational history
Educational income
Educational information
Educational innovations
Educational input
Educational inspection
Educational institutions
Educational integration
Educational journeys
Educational laboratories
Educational laboratory equipment
Educational laboratory personnel
Educational leave
Educational legislation
Educational levels
Educational libraries
Educational management
Educational manpower

Educational measurement
Educational missions
Educational models
Educational needs
Educational opportunities
Private educational organizations
Educational output
Educational periodicals
Educational personnel
Paraprofessional educational personnel
Educational personnel training
Educational philosophy
Educational planners
Educational planning
Educational planning and administration
Educational plans
Educational policy
Educational population
Educational priority areas
Educational programmes
Museum educational programmes
Educational projects
Educational psychology
Educational psychosociology
Educational publications
Educational radio
Educational records
Educational reform
Educational research
Educational resources
Educational rules
Mobile educational services
Educational sociology
Educational standards
Educational statistics
Educational strategies
Educational supervision
Educational support personnel
Educational systems
Educational systems and institutions
Educational technicians
Educational technology
Educational television
Educational term
Educational terminology
Educational testing
Educational theory
Educational time-tables
Educational toys
Educational transfers
Educational trends
Educational visits
Educational wages
Educational walks
Educational wastage
Educational welfare
Educational workshops
Educational year
Educationally disadvantaged
Educationally subnormal
Teacher educator training
Adult educators
Teacher educators
Cause and effect
Right to an effective remedy
Cost effectiveness
Biological effects
Chemical effects
Electromechanical effects
Human activities effects

321

Physiological effects
Psychological effects
Radiation effects
Tidal effects
Ego
Egocentrism
Egypt
Egyptian religion
Egyptology
Eigenvalues
Eire
El Salvador
Elastic deformation
Elasticity
Elderly
Rights of the elderly
Right to vote and be elected
Elections
Elective courses
Electoral systems
Electric cables
Electric charge
Electric conductors
Electric connectors
Electric contacts
Electric control equipment
Electric current measurement
Electric currents
Electric discharges
Electric fields
Electric generators
Electric heating
Electric lighting
Electric machines
Electric motors
Electric potential
Electric power distribution
Electric power generation
Electric power stations
Electric power systems
Electric power transmission
Electric power transmission lines
Electric reactors
Electric wiring
Cores (electric)
Windings (electric)
Electrical conductivity
Electrical energy
Electrical engineering
Electrical equipment
Electrical faults
Electrical industry
Electrical installations
Electrical instruments
Electrical insulation
Electrical measurements
    and instruments
Electrical properties of substances
Electrical protection gear
Electrical resistance measurement
Electrical safety
Electrical variables control
Electricity
Atmospheric electricity
Static electricity
Electroacoustic devices
Electroacoustics
Electroanalysis
Electrochemical corrosion
Electrochemical devices
Electrochemical reactions

Electrochemistry
Electrodes
Electrodynamics
Electrolysis
Electrolytes
Electrolytic cells
Electrolytic tanks
Electromagnetic waves
Electromagnetism
Electromechanical devices
Electromechanical effects
Electron diffraction
Electron microscopes
Electron physics
Electron tubes
Electronic engineering
Electronic equipment
Electronic music
Electrons
Electrostatics
Electrotherapy
Elementary particles
Chemical elements
Index language elements
Musical elements
Trace elements
Structural elements (buildings)
Elevators
Elimination reactions
Elite
Cultural elite
Power elite
Elite cultures
Gilbert and Ellice Islands
Embargoes
Embarrassment
Embryology
Embryos
Emergency powers
Emigration
United Arab Emirates
Automobile emission
Emission control
Emotional development
Emotional disturbances
Emotional immaturity
Emotional maturity
Emotions
Empire
Empiricism
Self-employed
Employees
Employers
Employers organizations
Employment
Conditions of employment
Education and employment
Full employment
Full-time employment
Labour and employment
Part-time employment
Student employment
Teacher conditions of employment
Womens employment
Youth employment
Employment abroad
Employment opportunities
Employment policy
Employment services

323

Environmental planning
Environmental planning
   administration
Environmental planning control
Environmental planning legislation
Environmental planning policy
Environmental planning processes
Environmental quality
Right to environmental quality
Environmental sciences
Environmentalists
Enzymes
Ephemera
Epidemics
Epidemiology
Epigraphy
Epilepsy
Epistemology
Epitomes
Epoxy resins
Equal education
Equal opportunity
Equal pay
Equal representation
Equal rights of men and women
Equality before the law
Equality of states
Equations
Differential equations
Integral equations
Non-linear equations
Partial differential equations
Equatorial Guinea
Equatorial zones
Equestrian sports
Chemical equilibrium
Cultural equilibrium
Economic equilibrium
International equilibrium
Phase equilibrium
Population equilibrium
Social equilibrium
Equipment
Acoustic equipment
Archive equipment
Character recognition equipment
Chemical engineering equipment
Chemical laboratory equipment
Communication engineering equipment
Computer graphic equipment
Computer peripheral equipment
Construction equipment
Control equipment
Cultural equipment
Data communication equipment
Data preparation equipment
Diving equipment
Educational equipment
Educational laboratory equipment
Electric control equipment
Electrical equipment
Electronic equipment
Excavating equipment
Heating equipment
Hydraulic equipment
Information/library equipment
Laboratory equipment
Leisure equipment
Library equipment
Lifting equipment
Medical equipment

Microform equipment
Military equipment
Mining equipment
Museum equipment
Oceanographic equipment
Office equipment
Photographic equipment
Printing equipment
Recording equipment
Scientific equipment
Sports equipment
Teaching materials and equipment
Therapeutic equipment
Equivalence between diplomas
Equivalence relations
Ergonomics
Erosion
Coastal erosion
Soil erosion
Probable error
Standard error
Error analysis
Errors
Volcanic eruptions
Escalators
Eskimo languages
Eskimos
Esoteric practices
Esperanto
Espionage
Essays
Established cultures
Self-esteem
Ester polymers
Estimation
Estonian
Estonian SSR
Estuaries
Ethers
Ethics
Communication ethics
Medical ethics
Political ethics
Press ethics
Teacher professional ethics
Ethics of science
Ethiopia
Ethnic groups
Ethnic minorities
Ethnocentrism
Ethnographic films
Ethnographic museums
Ethnography
Ethnolinguistics
Ethnology
Ethnopsychology
Etiquette
Etymology
Eugenics
Euphoria
Euphotic regions
Eurasian and North Asian
   languages
Europe
Eastern Europe
Western Europe
European art
European cultures
Central European cultures
European history
Indo-European languages

Euthanasia
Eutrophication
Evaluation
Curriculum evaluation
Economic evaluation
Information systems evaluation
Job evaluation
Evaluation of education
Evaporation
Evaporation technology
Evapotranspiration
Evening schools
Cultural events
Population events
Everyday life
Evidence
Admissibility of evidence
Evidence gathering
Evolution
Crystal examination
Examination boards
Examination marks
Examination standards
Examinations
Entrance examinations
External examinations
Internal examinations
Oral examinations
Practical examinations
Written examinations
Excavating equipment
Excavation
Underwater excavation
Archaeological excavations
Exceptional schools
Exceptional student education
Exceptional students
Excerpts
Cultural exchange
Data exchange
Foreign exchange
Information exchange
Ion exchange
Programme exchange
Exchange of ideas
Exchange of publications
Exchange programmes
Exchange rates
Exchange reactions
Heat exchangers
Educational exchanges
Student exchanges
Executive functions (psychology)
Executive government
Executive power
Supervisory and executive programs
Exercise
Indexing exhaustivity
Exhibitions
Cultural exhibitions
Educational exhibitions
Library exhibitions
Travelling exhibitions
Exile
Existentialism
Exobiology
Exogenous processes
Exosphere
Expanded towns
Urban expansion

Expectation
Scientific expeditions
Expenditure
Cultural expenditure
Educational expenditure
Information/library expenditure
Public expenditure
Scientific expenditure
Experience
Religious experience
Experimental art
Experimental biology
Experimental botany
Experimental chemistry
Experimental development
Experimental geology
Experimental groups
Experimental methods
Experimental physics
Experimental projects
Experimental psychology
Experimental schools
Experimental zoology
Experimentation
Experiments
Educational experiments
Experiments (lessons)
Expert missions
Expert reports
Exploitation
Exploration
Geographical exploration
Ocean exploration
Resource exploration
Space exploration
Information explosion
Explosions
Nuclear explosions
Explosives
Explosives technology
Exports,imports
Mass media exposure
Expression
Oral expression
Physical expression
Right to freedom of expression
Expressive notation
Agricultural extension
University extension
Extension education
Library extension work
External examinations
Extra-sensory perception
Underwater oil and gas extraction
Extraction technology
Extractive industries
Extractive metallurgy
Extradition
Extreme reduction microforms
Facet analysis
Faceted classification systems
Facets
Archive facilities
Cultural facilities
Educational facilities
Information,library facilities
Museum facilities
Recreational facilities
Research facilities
Scientific facilities

Sports facilities
Tourist facilities
Factor analysis
Semantic factoring
Cultural factors
Social factors
Socio-economic factors
Factors of production
Factory management
Factory workers
Faeroe Islands
Faeroese
Failure
Right to a fair hearing
Fun fairs
Fairy tales
Falkland Islands
Radioactive fallout
False drops
Broken families
One-parent families
Problem families
Family
Joint family
Nuclear family
Family disorganization
Family education
Family environment
Family influence
Family law
Family life
Family planning
Family rights
Family role
Family size
Famine
Fans
Fans (supporters)
Far East
Farmers
Arable farming
Dairy farming
Dry farming
Mixed farming
Stock farming
Farming systems
Fascism
Fashion
Fashion design
Fast reactors
Fast-response computer systems
Fasting
Fathers
Fathometers
Fatigue
Faults
Electrical faults
Fauna
Most favoured nation
Fear
Feasts
Water features
German Federal Republic
Federalism
Federation
Relevance feedback
Feedback (communication)
Feedback (learning)
Fees
Educational fees

Feldspar
Fellowships
Research fellowships
Female
Fens
Fermentation
Ferrous metals
Non -ferrous metals
Fertility
Soil fertility
Fertilizers
Festivals
Film festivals
Musical festivals
Pop festivals
Religious festivals
Fetishism
Feudalism
Fibres
Synthetic fibres
Fiction
Science fiction
Science fiction films
Fiction stock
Non -fiction stock
Quantum field theory
Field work
Archaeological field work
Electric fields
Gas fields
Oil fields
Playing fields
Circulation figures
Fiji Islands
Inverted file
Records file
File guidance (index)
File maintenance (index)
File management (index)
File organization (computer)
File organization (index)
Case files
Files administration
Filing
Filing (index)
Filing order
Film actors
Film cameras
Film clubs
Film directors
Film distribution
Film festivals
Film industry
Film libraries
Film music
Film producers
Film production statistics
Film scripts
Film sets
Film strips
Film-makers
Film-making
Film-making training
Films
Arts films
Childrens films
Comedy films
Documentary films
Educational films
Ethnographic films

Full-length films
Historical films
Magnetic films
Musical comedy films
News films
Political films
Romance films
Science fiction films
Short films
Surface films
Television films
Thin films
Thriller films
War films
Filtration
Final reports
Finance
Communication finance
Cultural finance
Educational finance
Housing finance
Information/library finance
Land and property finance
Local finance
Museum finance
Public finance
Regional finance
Research finance
Science finance
Social welfare finance
Financial administration
Financial aid
Financial institutions
Educational financial management
Financial markets
Financial policy
Financial resources
Educational financial resources
Financial statements
Financial support
Financing
Communication financing
Cultural financing
Educational financing
Information library financing
Museum financing
Science financing
Position finding
Archive finding aids
Fine arts
Loan fines
Finishing (process)
Finland
Gulf of Finland
Finnish
Fire
Fire insurance
Fire protection
Forest fires
First aid
First editions
Fiscal policy
Fish
Freshwater fish
Marine fish
Freshwater fish culture
Fisheries
Fishery resources
Coastal fishing
Deep sea fishing

Freshwater fishing
Sea fishing
Fishing gear
Fishing industry
Fishing operations
Fishing rights
Fishing vessels
Nuclear fission
Fixation
Fixed costs
Fjords
Flags
Flannelgraphs
High rise flats
Flemish
Flight dynamics
Floating ice
Floats
Flood control
Floods
Ocean floor
Floors
Flora
Flores Sea
Flotation
Flow
Boundary layer flow
Capillary flow
Capital flow
Cash flow
Channel flow
Communication
channels of flow
Laminar flow
News flow
Turbulent flow
Flow charts
Flow control
Flow in pipes
Flow measurement and instruments
Free flow of information
Flowers
Flowmeters
Economic fluctuations
Fluid apertures
Fluid density
Fluid density measurement
Fluid dynamics
Fluid handling
Fluid measurement and instruments
Fluid mechanical properties
Fluid mechanics
Fluid physics
Fluid power engineering
Fluid pressure
Fluid waves
Fluids
Polyvinyl fluoride
Fluorine
Foams
Problem focused research
Fog
Folk art
Folk cultures
Folk dance
Folk literature
Folk medicine
Folk music
Folk songs
Folklore
Folklore troupes

Food
Frozen food
Synthetic food
Food chains
Food control
Food customs
Food industry
Food preservation
Food production
Food resources
Food shortages
Food technology
Forage
Force
Force measurement
Air forces
Armed forces
Peace-keeping forces
Armed forces libraries
Forecasting
Economic forecasting
Educational forecasting
Hydrological forecasting
Science forecasting
Weather forecasting
Foreign aid
Foreign exchange
Foreign industries
Foreign investment
Foreign languages
Foreign literature
Foreign policy
Foreign relations
Foreign students
Foreign workers
Foreigners
Forensic medicine
Forest engineering
Forest fires
Forest industry
Forest management
Forest products
Forest protection
Forest resources
Forestry
Forests
Tropical forests
Non-formal education
Formal language
Format
Business formation
Image formation
Atmospheric formations
Formosan
Land forms
Musical forms
Sixth forms
Forms (blank)
Literary forms and genres
Formularies
Query formulation
Fortune-telling
Fossil fuel deposits
Fossils
Foster care
Educational foundations
Research foundations
Foundry practice
Fourier analysis
Fourier transforms

Fracture
France
Francium
Fraud
Free education
Free flow of information
Free language systems
Free market economy
Right to free movement of persons
Free trade
Free-will
Academic freedom
Religious freedom
Right to artistic freedom
Right to freedom from inhuman treatment
Right to freedom of expression
Right to freedom of residence
Freedom of speech
Freedom of the press
Right to freedom of thought
Freemasonry
Freezers
Freezing
Freight transport
French
French Guiana
French Polynesia
French speaking Africa
Allocation of frequencies
Frequency
Book use frequency
Ocean wave frequency
Wave frequency
Term frequency (use)
Freshwater
Freshwater fish
Freshwater fish culture
Freshwater fishing
Friction
Tidal friction
Friendship
Capillary fringe
Fringe benefits
Ocean wave front
Frontal systems
Frost
Frozen food
Fruit
Frustration
Fuel cells
Fossil fuel deposits
Nuclear fuel processing
Fuel resources
Fuel technology
Fuels
Gas fuels
Nuclear fuels
Full employment
Full-length films
Full-time employment
Fumes
Fun fairs
Functional analysis
Functional literacy
Functionalism
Functions (mathematics)
Executive functions (psychology)
Fundamental research
Bay of Fundy
Fungi

Furnaces
Furniture
Library furniture
School furniture
Street furniture design
Furniture manufacture
Further training
Fuses
Nuclear fusion
Fusion reactors
Wallis and Futuna Islands
Future
Future society
Futurology
Gabon
Gaelic
Irish Gaelic
Capital gains
Galapagos Islands
Galaxies
Art galleries
Gallium
Gambia
Gambling
Game animals
Game theory
Academic games
Ball games
Card games
Educational games
Indoor games
Olympic games
Radio games
Television games
War games
Gamma rays
Gangs
Generation gap
Technological gap
Avant-garde art
Gardening
Botanical gardens
Public gardens
Zoological gardens
Manufactured gas
Natural gas
Gas analysis
Underwater oil and gas extraction
Gas fields
Gas fuels
Gas industry
Gas physics
Natural gas production
Gas resources
Gas supply
Gas technology
Gas turbine power stations
Gas turbines
Gases
Dissolved gases
Liquefaction of gases
Gasoline
Gatekeepers
Evidence gathering
Gauges
Rain gauges
Tide gauges
Electrical protection gear
Fishing gear
Gears

Gels
Gems
Genealogy
General education
General public
General purpose computers
General technical education
Generality number
Electric power generation
Solar power generation
Generation gap
Automatic generation of index languages
Generations (age)
Electric generators
Report generators
Generic posting
Genes
Soil genesis
Genetic psychology
Genetics
Agricultural genetics
Animal genetics
Human genetics
Plant genetics
Geniuses
Genocide
Literary forms and genres
Geochemistry
Geochronology
Geodesy
Geodynamics
Geoelectricity
Geographers
Geographical areas and countries
Geographical data
Geographical exploration
Geographical research
Geography
Continental geography
Cultural geography
Economic geography
Global geography
Historical geography
Human geography
Local geography
National geography
Physical geography
Political geography
Regional geography
Geography education
Geological ages
Geological data
Geologists
Geology
Economic geology
Engineering geology
Experimental geology
Marine geology
Mining geology
Petroleum geology
Physical geology
Submarine geology
Geology education
Geomagnetism
Geomathematics
Geometry
Analytical geometry
Differential geometry
Geomorphology
Geophysical measurements and instruments

Geophysical prospecting
Geophysicists
Geophysics
Marine geophysics
Georgian
Georgian SSR
Geothermal energy
Geothermal power stations
Geriatric psychology
Geriatrics
German
German Democratic Republic
German Federal Republic
Germanic Languages
Germanium
Gerontology
Gesture
Ghana
Gibraltar
Strait of Gibraltar
Gifted students
Gifts
Gifts (acquisition)
Gilbert and Ellice Islands
Gill nets
Gipsies
Girls
Girls schools
Glaciation
Glaciers
Glaciology
Glass
Art glass
Stained glass
Glass blowing
Glass technology
Glassware
Global geography
Globes
Glossaries
Gneiss
Goal setting
Goals
Educational goals
God
Gold
Cultural goods
Governing boards
Self-governing educational bodies
Non-self-governing territories
Government
Central government
Decentralized government
Executive government
Local government
Municipal government
Regional government
Self-government
World government
Government archives
Local government archives
Government control
Regional government cultural organizations
Central government cultural organizations
Government cultural
 organizations
Local government cultural
 organizations
Government department libraries
Government departments
Local government education authorities
Government educational bodies

Local government information/library
 organizations
Government information/library
 organizations
Government libraries
Central government libraries
Government organizations
Central government organizations
Local government organizations
Regional government organizations
Government policy
Non-governmental organizations
Grabs
Middle grade personnel
Post-graduate courses
Graduates
Grain crops
Grammar
Grandparents
Granite
Grants
Educational grants
Personal grants
Research grants
Travel grants
Graph theory
Graphic arts
Graphic designers
Graphic displays
Computer graphic equipment
Graphical methods
Graphology
Graphonomy
Graphs
Grasses
Grasslands
Gratuities
Gravels
Gravimeters
Gravimetric analysis
Gravitation
Grazing land
Great Australian Bight
Greece
Greek (classical)
Greek (modern)
Green belts
Greenland
Greenland Sea
Grenada
Grinding
Gross national product
Ground support systems
Groundwater
Group behaviour
Group communication
Group dynamics
Peer-group relationship
Group selection
Group size
Group theory
Group training
Group work (social work)
Group work (teaching method)
Ability grouping
Educational grouping
Groups
Age groups
Control groups
Discussion groups
Ethnic groups
Experimental groups

Listening groups
Majority groups
Minority groups
Play groups
Pressure groups
Racial groups
Rights of special groups
Small groups
Training groups
Working groups
Growth
Animal growth
Crystal growth
Economic growth
Ocean wave growth
Plant growth
Growth rate
Guadeloupe
Guam
Guatemala
Guerilla activities
French Guiana
Educational guidance
Reading guidance
School-leaving guidance
Vocational guidance
File guidance (index)
Educational guidance personnel
Guidebooks
Guides
Curriculum guides
Shelf guides
Teacher guides
Guides to information sources
Guinea
Equatorial Guinea
Gulf of Guinea
Papua New Guinea
Guinea-Bissau
Gujurati
Gulf of Aden
Gulf of Agaba
Gulf of Alaska
Gulf of Boni
Gulf of Bothnia
Gulf of California
Gulf of Finland
Gulf of Guinea
Gulf of Iran
Gulf of Mexico
Gulf of Oman
Gulf of Riga
Gulf of St. Lawrence
Gulf of Suez
Gulf of Thailand
Gulf of Tomini
Gulf States
Gulfs
Gullies
Guns
Guyana
Gymnasia
Gymnastics
Gymnospermae
Gynaecology
Gypsum
Lime and gypsum technology
Gyroscopes
Right to habeas corpus
Reading habit

Habitats
Habits
Information user habits
Speech habits
Hadal regions
Haemic and lymphatic systems
Haemic and lymphatic systems diseases
Hafnium
Haiti
Music-hall
Concert halls
Halmahra Sea
Halogens
Hamitic languages
Hamito-Semitic and Caucasian languages
Hamito-Semitic languages
Water hammer
Second-hand books
Maintenance handbooks
Handedness
Handicapped
Mentally handicapped
Multiply handicapped
Physically handicapped
Rights of the handicapped
Handicapped children
Handicaps
Physical handicaps
Handicrafts
Handicrafts education
Handiness
Data handling
Fluid handling
Materials handling
Sewage disposal and handling
Waste disposal and handling
Handwriting
Handwriting instruction
Happiness
Harbour and coastal engineering
Harbours
Hard copy
Hardness
Water hardness
Computer hardware
Hardwood
Harmonic analysis
Harvesting
Incitement to hate and violence
Hatred
Hawaii
Hawaiian
Hay
Radiation hazards
Hazards accidents and disasters
Head
Head of state
Alphabetical subject heading lists
Author headings
Sub-headings
Subject headings
Headquarters libraries
Headstart
Health
Mental health
Public health
Right to health
Health education
Health services
School health services

Hearing
Right to a fair hearing
Hearing aids
Hearings
Heart
Heart diseases
Heat
Latent heat
Specific heat
Terrestrial heat
Heat conduction
Heat engines
Heat exchangers
Heat pumps
Waste heat recovery
Heat storage
Heat transfer
Heat treatment
Heating
Central heating
District heating
Electric heating
Process heating
Solar heating
Heating equipment
Heating systems
Hebrew
New Hebrides
Ocean wave height
Saint Helena
Helicopters
Helium
Eastern Hemisphere
Northern hemisphere
Southern Hemisphere
Western Hemisphere
Heraldry
Herbicides
Heredity
Cultural heritage
Natural heritage
Heterocyclic compounds
Heuristic method (teaching)
Hi-jacking
Hibernation
Hierarchical classification systems
Hierarchical notation
Hierarchical relations
Non -hierarchical relations
Hieroglyphics
High energy physics
High pressure techniques
High rise flats
High temperature techniques
High temperatures
Higher courts
Higher education
Higher mental processes
Higher technical education
Higher technical personnel
Hiking
Hills
Himalayan States
Hindi
Hinduism
Hindus
Hindustani
Histology
Plant histology

Historians
Historic monuments
Historical analysis
Historical bibliography
Historical editing
Historical films
Historical geography
Historical method
Historical museums
Historical research
Historical systems of law
Historical writing
Historiography
History
African history
American history
Ancient history
Arab history
Art history
Asian history
Australasian history
Byzantine history
Communication history
Constitutional history
Cultural history
Documentary history
Economic history
Educational history
European history
Information/library history
Latin American history
Legal history
Literary history
Medieval history
Modern history
Natural history
North American history
Objective history
Oral history
Philosophy of history
Political history
Quantitative history
Religious history
Russian history
Social history
History and associated studies
History education
Natural history museums
History of archives
History of libraries
History of psychology
History of science
Hobbies
Hoists
Scholarship -holders
Hostage -holding
Black holes
Holiday camps
Holiday centres
Holiday schools
Holidays
School holidays
Holidays abroad
Holography
Acoustic holography
Holy See
Home education
Home ownership
Home trade
Homelessness

333

Individual study
Individualism
Individuality
Individualized instruction
Indo-China
Indo-European languages
Indoctrination
Indonesia
Indonesian
Indoor games
Inductors
Industrial arbitration
Industrial areas
Industrial conciliation
Industrial design
Industrial development
Industrial economics
Industrial enterprises
Industrial libraries
Industrial management
Industrial planning
Industrial plant
Industrial policy
Industrial pollution
Industrial psychology
Industrial societies
Post -industrial societies
Industrial sociology
Industrial towns
Industrial training
Industrial training courses
Industrialization
Non -industrialized people
Non -industrialized societies
Industries
Capital intensive industries
Extractive industries
Foreign industries
Indigenous industries
Labour intensive industries
Manufacturing industries
Service industries
Aerospace industry
Book industry
Chemical industry
Clothing industry
Communication industry
Construction industry
Cultural industry
Electrical industry
Engineering industry
Film industry
Fishing industry
Food industry
Forest industry
Gas industry
Hotel and catering industry
Location of industry
Metal industry
Motor industry
Oil industry
Paper industry
Phonorecord industry
Power industry
Shipbuilding industry
Telecommunication industry
Television and radio industry
Textile industry
Tourist industry
Water supply industry

Industry and education
Ineducable
Cultural inequality
Social inequality
Inertial navigation
Infectious diseases
Statistical inference
Inferiority complex
Infiltration
Inflatable devices
Inflation
Family influence
Interpersonal influence
Social influence
Influenza
Informal education
Informatics
Information
Access to information
Current dissemination of information
Dissemination of information
Educational information
Free flow of information
Right to information
Scientific information
Selective dissemination of information
Social science information
Information analysis centres
Information bulletins
Information exchange
Information explosion
Information materials
Information officers
Information processing
On-line information processing
Information processing automation
Information retrieval
Information scatter
Information science
Library and information science
Information scientist-user relationship
Information scientists
Information services
Information sources
Guides to information sources
Information storage devices
Information systems
Agricultural information systems
Engineering information systems
International information systems
Legal information systems
Management information systems
Medical information systems
Medical records information systems
National information systems
On-line information systems
Scientific information systems
Information systems evaluation
Information theory
Communication and information theory
Information transfer
Information use
Information user habits
Information user instruction
Information user needs
Information user studies
Information users
Information/library administration
Information/library administrators
Information/library aims

Information/library budgets
Information/library centralization
Information/library clerical personnel
Information/library cooperation
Information/library courses
Information/library decentralization
Information/library degrees
Information/library development
Information/library economics
Information/library equipment
Information/library expenditure
Information/library facilities
Information/library finance
Information/library financing
Information/library history
Information/library income
Information/library integration
Information/library legislation
Information/library management
Information/library manual personnel
Information/library needs
Information/library networks
Information/library operations
Local government information/library organizations
International information/library organizations
Government information/library organizations
National information/library organizations
Private information/library organizations
Information/library organizations
Non-professional information/library personnel
Information/library personnel
Information/library philosophy
Information/library planning
Information/library planning and
  administration
Information/library policy
Information/library profession
Information/library professional
  associations
Information/library professional
  personnel
Information/library professional status
Information/library programmes
Information/library qualifications
Information/library research
Information/library resources
Information/library role
Information/library schools
Information/library standards
Information/library statistics
Information/library stock
Information/library support personnel
Information/library systems
Information/library training
Information, libraries and archives
Informative abstracts
Infrared radiation
Transport infrastructure
Inheritance law
Inhibitions
Inhuman treatment
Right to freedom from inhuman treatment
Initial teaching alphabet
Scientific initiation
Initiation rites
Injunctions
Injuries
Inks
Seto Naikai Inland Sea
West Scotland Inland Sea
Inland water transport

Right to presumption of innocence
Innovation behaviour
Innovations
Agricultural innovations
Cultural innovations
Educational innovations
Scientific innovations
Teaching method innovations
Inorganic chemistry
Inorganic compounds
Inorganic polymers
Educational input
Input-output analysis
Input-output programs
Sit-ins
Teach-ins (teaching method)
Insects
Inspection
Dental inspection
Educational inspection
Labour inspection
Medical inspection
Inspiration
Electrical installations
Instincts
Technological institutes
University institutes
Religious institution libraries
Institutional libraries
Institutionalization
Institutions
Adult education institutions
Educational institutions
Educational systems and institutions
Financial institutions
Political institutions
Religious institutions
Scientific institutions
Social science institutions
Audiovisual instruction
Computer-assisted instruction
Conversation instruction
Handwriting instruction
Individualized instruction
Information user instruction
Language of instruction
Listening instruction
Mother tongue instruction
Multimedia instruction
Programmed instruction
Reading instruction
Remedial instruction
Spelling instruction
Vocabulary instruction
Instructional programmes
Meteorological
  measurements and instruments
Astronomical
  measurements and instruments
Hydrological
  measurements and instrument
Instrumental analysis
Instrumental music
Instrumentalists
Instruments
Acoustic measurements and instruments
Brass instruments
Dimensional
  measurements and instruments
Electrical instruments
Electrical
  measurements and instruments
Flow measurement and instruments

Fluid measurement and instruments
Geophysical measurements and instruments
Indicating instruments
International instruments
Keyboard instruments
Magnetic measurements and instruments
Measurement and instruments
Mechanical measurements and instruments
Medical instruments
Musical instruments
Navigational instruments
Oceanographic instruments
Optical measurements and instruments
Particle measurements and instruments
Percussion instruments
Pressure measurement and instruments
Radiation measurement and instruments
Recording instruments
String instruments
Surgical instruments
Surveying instruments
Temperature measurement and instruments
Thermal measurements and instruments
Time measurement and instruments
Wind instruments
Insubordination
Electrical insulation
Sound insulation
Thermal insulation
Insurance
Accident insurance
Fire insurance
Life insurance
Intaglio printing
Integral calculus
Integral equations
Integrated circuits
Integrated curriculum
Integration
Cultural integration
Educational integration
Information/library integration
Racial integration
Social integration
Intellectual property
Right of intellectual property
Intelligence
Artificial intelligence
Intelligence quotient
Intelligence tests
Intelligentsia
Capital intensive industries
Labour intensive industries
Inter-library loans
Cultural interaction
Social interaction
Interaction process analysis
Interception of communication
Intercultural education
Interdisciplinary
Interdisciplinary research
Interdisciplinary science
and technology
Interest
Interest (learning)
Student interests
Interethnic relations
Computer interfaces
Interference
Radio wave interference
Interference suppression
Interferometry

Intergovernment organizations
Intergroup relations
Interim reports
Interior architecture
Internal combustion engines
Internal examinations
Internal loans
Internal migration
Internal politics
Internal waves
Internalization
International arbitration
International archives
International assistance
International auxiliary lingua
International bibliographies
International book year
International circulation of materials
International competition
International conferences
International conflict
International cooperation
International courts
International cultural organizations
International disputes
International economic systems
International education
International educational bodies
International entente
International equilibrium
International information systems
International information/library organizations
International instruments
International languages
International law
Private international law
Public international law
International libraries
International monetary systems
International movement of persons
International organizations
International politics
International relations
International schools
International standards
International technology transfer
International tension
International trade
International training programmes
International transport
International understanding
International universities
International voluntary services
Internationalism
Internment
Interpersonal attraction
Interpersonal communication
Interpersonal conflict
Interpersonal influence
Interpersonal relations
Interplanetary matter
Interpolation
Interpolation (index language)
Archaeological interpretation
Interpreters
Interpreting
Term interrelations
Interrogation
Interstellar space
Intertidal areas
Intertidal environment
Interviewing for job

337

Joint management
Joint stock companies
Joints
Jordan
Journalism
Journalist schools
Journalist training
Journalists
Abstract journals
Educational journeys
Judaism
Judges
Value judgment
Judgments
Judicial control of administration
Judicial power
Judiciary
Independent judiciary
Jungle
Junior colleges (USA)
Juries
Analytical jurisprudence
Trial by jury
Justice
Administration of justice
Right to justice
Social justice
Juvenile courts
Juvenile delinquency
Democratic Kampuchea
Kannada
Kara Sea
Karst
Kashmiri
Kattegat
Kazakh
Kazakh SSR
Kechua
Peace-keeping forces
Kenya
Kermadec Islands
Keyboard instruments
Keyboards
Mon-Khmer languages
Khoin languages
Kidnapping
Relief in kind
Kinematics
Chemical kinetics
United Kingdom
Kinship
Saint Kitts-Nevis-Anguilla
Knowledge
Dissemination of knowledge
Sociology of knowledge
Structure of knowledge
Hong Kong
Korea (Democratic Peoples Republic)
Korea (Republic)
Korean
Krypton
Kurdish
Kushan
Kuwait
KWAC indexes
KWIC indexes
KWOC indexes
Rio de la Plata
Laboratories
Chemical laboratories

Educational laboratories
Language laboratories
Medical laboratories
Museum laboratories
Oceanographic laboratories
School laboratories
Laboratory animals
Laboratory equipment
Chemical laboratory equipment
Educational laboratory equipment
Educational laboratory personnel
Labour
Compulsory labour
Labour and employment
Labour conflict
Labour disputes
Labour distribution
Labour economics
Labour inspection
Labour intensive industries
Labour law
Labour market
Labour migration
Labour mobility
Labour movement
Labour planning
Labour policy
Labour productivity
Labour relations
Labour shortages
Labour supply
Labour systems
Labour turnover
Labrador Sea
Laccadive Sea
Lagoons
River and lake engineering
Lakes
Laminar flow
Tidal lamination
Agricultural land
Arable land
Grazing land
Land amelioration
Land and property finance
Land drainage
Land economics
Land forms
Land ice
Land pollution
Land reclamation
Land reform
Land resources
Land subsidence
Land tenure
Land transport
Land use
Land value
Land vehicles
Land warfare
Landlords
Landscape
Landscape architects
Landscape design
Landscape protection
Landslides
Basque language
Colloquial language
Formal language
Malay language

342

Private information/library organizations
Information /library organizations
Non-professional
information/library personnel
Information /library personnel
Information /library philosophy
Information /library planning
Information/library planning and administration
Information /library policy
Library porters
Information /library profession
Information/library professional associations
Information/library professional personnel
Information /library professional status
Information /library programmes
Library public relations
Library publications
Library publicity
Information /library qualifications
Library removals
Information /library research
Information /library resources
Information /library role
Library rules and regulations
Information /library schools
Library science
Library services
Library shelving
Library stacks
Information /library standards
Information /library statistics
Library stock
Information /library stock
Information /library support personnel
Information /library systems
Library technicians
Library theatres
Information /library training
Library transport
Library trolleys
Library use promotion
Library users
Library vehicles
Library work (study method)
Private collections (library)
Special collections (library)
Libyan Arab Republic
Libyan-Berber languages
Lichens
Liechtenstein
Life
Animal life
Community life
Cultural life
Economic life
Everyday life
Family life
Literary life
Marine life
Occupational life
Plant life
Political life
Prison life
Quality of life
Right to life
Social life
Theatrical life
Life cycle
Life insurance
Life sciences
Life styles

Life support systems
Life-long education
Lifting equipment
Light
Light absorption
Light detectors
Light pens
Lighthouses
Lighting
Electric lighting
Street lighting
Lightning
Ligurian Sea
Limbs
Artificial limbs
Lime
Lime and gypsum technology
Limestone
Limnology
Lincoln Sea
On -line information processing
On -line information systems
Line Islands
On -line searching
On -line systems
Linear algebra
Non -linear equations
Electric power
transmission lines
Transmission lines
International auxiliary lingua
Linguistic analysis
Linguistic research
Linguistic theory
Linguistic unification
Linguistics
Comparative and
diachronic linguistics
Computer linguistics
Descriptive linguistics
Statistical linguistics
Statistical linguistics (indexing)
Morphology (linguistics)
Linguists
Link Indicators
Radio links
Telecommunication links
Lipids
Liquefaction of gases
Liquefaction technology
Liquid crystals
Liquid level measurement
Liquid structure
Liquidations
Liquidity
Liquids
Physics of liquids
Radio listeners
Listening
Listening groups
Listening instruction
Accession lists
Alphabetical subject
heading lists
Authority lists
Shelf lists
Term lists
Literacy
Adult literacy
Functional literacy
Literacy campaigns
Literacy classes

343

Literacy methodology
Literacy programmes
Post-literacy programmes
Literacy promotion
Literacy workers
Literary analysis
Literary composition
Literary criticism
Literary cultures
Literary devices
Literary forms and genres
Literary history
Literary life
Literary philosophy
Literary prizes
Literary property
Literary research
Literary style
Literary warrant
Literary works
Representative literary works
New literates
Literature
Contemporary literature
Folk literature
Foreign literature
Modern literature
Popular literature
Trade literature
Literature review services
Literature reviews
Literature searches
Lithium
Lithography
Lithuanian
Lithuanian SSR
Littoral zone
Right to live in peace
Live programmes
Liver diseases
Livestock
Cost of living
Standard of living
Living conditions
Living cultures
Right to adequate living standards
Living substances
Teaching load
Loams
Loan charges
Loan fines
Loan period
Loan records
Punched card loan records
Loan records automation
Loan renewal
Loan reservations
Loan services
Loans
Inter-library loans
Internal loans
Overdue loans
Postal loans
Student loans
Local broadcasting
Local communities
Local finance
Local geography
Local government
Local government archives

Local government cultural organizations
Local government education authorities
Local government information/library
    organizations
Local government organizations
Local press
Library location
Location of industry
Lockouts
Locks (waterways)
Locomotives
Locomotory system diseases
Locomotory systems
Locusts
Loess
Logic
Mathematical logic
Logic and switching circuits
Logic design
Logical relations
Military logistics
Life-long education
Long playing records
Long range planning
Lord Howe Island
Water loss
Document losses
Love
Low achievers
Low pressure systems
Low temperatures
Lower atmosphere
Lower courts
Lower house
Lower secondary education
Lubricants
Lubrication
Lubrication systems
Saint Lucia
Luminescence
Luxembourg
Lycees
Haemic and lymphatic systems
Haemic and lymphatic systems diseases
Lynching
ISBD(M)
Macao
Macedonian
Machine oriented languages
Man-machine systems
Machine tools
Machine typesetting
Machine-readable archives
Machine-readable materials
Agricultural machinery
Textile machinery
Machines
Calculating machines
Electric machines
Teaching machines
Machining
Macroeconomics
Macromolecules
Macros
Macrothesauri
Madagascar (Democratic Republic)
Man-made disasters
Madeira
Magic
Magistrates
Magnesium

Magnetic cards
Magnetic cores
Magnetic devices
Magnetic discs
Magnetic films
Magnetic measurements and
    instruments
Magnetic navigation
Magnetic properties of substances
Magnetic tape recordings
Magnetic tapes
Magnetic variables control
Magnetism
Magnetochemistry
Magnetohydrodynamic conversion
Magnetohydrodynamics
Magnetosphere
Magnetostrictive devices
Mahayana
Main classes
Main entries
Water mains
Maintenance
Building maintenance
Document maintenance
File maintenance (index)
Maintenance handbooks
Library maintenance services
Political majorities
Majority groups
Makassar Strait
Film -makers
Decision making
Film -making
Iron and steel making
Peace -making
Policy making
Speech -making
Film -making training
Malacca Strait
Maladjusted
Maladjustment
Malagasy
Malaria
Malawi
Malay language
Malaya
Malayalam
Malayo-Polynesian languages
Malaysia
Maldives
Male
Mali
Malnutrition
Malta
Mammals
Man
Prehistoric man
Man-machine systems
Man-made disasters
Management
Business management
Cinema management
Computer management
Correspondence management
Cultural management
Educational financial management
Educational management
Environmental management
Factory management
Forest management

Industrial management
Information/library management
Joint management
Middle management
Office management
Personnel management
Production management
Project management
Records management
Research management
Resource management
Stage management
Theatre management
Top management
Water resources management
File management (index)
Management audit
Management control
Management education
Management information systems
Management operations
Management techniques
Management theory
Managerial characteristics
Managerial services
Managers
Records managers
Manganese
Mangrove areas
Manic-depressive psychoses
Manihiki Islands
Manners
Manometers
Manpower
Educational manpower
Manpower needs
Manual coordinate indexes
Information/library manual personnel
Manual workers
Clothing manufacture
Furniture manufacture
Toy manufacture
Manufactured gas
Manufacturing industries
Manuscript curators
Manuscripts
Maori
Map libraries
School mapping
Maps
Climatic maps
Hydrogeological maps
Metallogenic maps
Mineral maps
Quarternary maps
Relief maps
Soil maps
Tectonic maps
Vegetation maps
Marathi
Marble
Mariana Islands
Marine algae
Marine animals
Marine aquaculture
Marine biology
Marine ecological zones
Marine ecosystems
Marine engineering
Marine engines

Marine environment
Marine fish
Marine geology
Marine geophysics
Marine life
Marine microorganisms
Marine navigation
Marine plants
Marine pollution
Marine resources
Marine safety
Marine traffic
San Marino
Marital status
Labour market
Free market economy
Market research
Market structure
Marketing
Markets
Financial markets
Markov processes
Examination marks
Trade marks
Marls
Sea of Marmara
Marriage
Consent to marriage
Minimum marriage age
Marriage contract
Marriage dissolution
Mixed marriages
Married men
Married women
Married women librarians
Married women teachers
Married women workers
Right to marry
Marshall Islands
Marshes
Saint Martin
Martinique
Masers
Mass
Atomic mass
Mass behaviour
Mass communication
Mass communication campaigns
Mass communication programmes
Mass culture
Mass education
Mass media
Mass media exposure
Mass production
Mass society
Mass spectroscopy
Mass transfer
Weight (mass)
Air masses
Water masses
Masters degrees
Materialism
Materials
Audio materials
Audiovisual materials
Bookform materials
Building materials
Composite materials
Dangerous materials
Information materials

International circulation of materials
Machine-readable materials
Non-book materials
Porous materials
Programmed materials
Raw materials
Reading materials
Reference materials
Source materials
Visual materials
Teaching materials and equipment
Materials handling
Materials science
Materials testing
Mathematical analysis
Mathematical logic
Mathematical models
Mathematical physics
Mathematical programming
Mathematical sciences
Mathematics
Combinatorial mathematics
Modern mathematics
Statistical mathematics
Mathematics education
Convergence (mathematics)
Functions (mathematics)
Series (mathematics)
Matrix algebra
Cosmic matter
Interplanetary matter
Organic matter
States of matter
Bulk matter physics
Condensed matter physics
Maturity
Emotional maturity
Mauritania
Mauritius
School meals
Measles
Atmospheric humidity measurement
Atmospheric pressure measurement
Chemical variables measurement
Density measurement
Depth measurement
Distance measurement
Educational measurement
Electric current measurement
Electrical resistance measurement
Fluid density measurement
Force measurement
Liquid level measurement
Moisture measurement
Noise measurement
Ocean current measurement
Ocean wave measurement
pH measurement
Position measurement
Precipitation measurement
Rotation measurement
Salinity measurement
Sea level measurement
Sea water density measurement
Sea water pressure measurement
Sea water temperature measurement
Strain measurement
Tide measurement
Units of measurement
Vacuum measurement

Velocity measurement
Vibration measurement
Voltage measurement
Volume measurement
Weight measurement
Wind measurement
Measurement and instruments
Flow measurement and instruments
Fluid measurement and instruments
Pressure measurement and instruments
Radiation measurement and instruments
Temperature measurement and instruments
Time measurement and instruments
Measurement tolerances
Oceanographic measurements
Sea water acoustic measurements
Sea water measurements
Sea water optical measurements
Meteorological measurements and instruments
Astronomical measurements and instruments
Hydrological measurements and instruments
Acoustic measurements and instruments
Dimensional measurements and instruments
Electrical measurements and instruments
Geophysical measurements and instruments
Magnetic measurements and instruments
Mechanical measurements and instruments
Optical measurements and instruments
Particle measurements and instruments
Thermal measurements and instruments
Post-war measures
Safety measures
Meat
Mechanical components
Mechanical engineering
Mechanical measurements and
    instruments
Mechanical music
Fluid mechanical properties
Mechanical properties of substances
Mechanical sports
Mechanical strength
Mechanical transmission systems
Mechanical variables control
Stress (mechanical)
Mechanics
Celestial mechanics
Chemical mechanics
Classical mechanics
Continuum mechanics
Fluid mechanics
Rock mechanics
Soil mechanics
Statistical mechanics
Wave mechanics
Mechanics of solids
Mechanization
Communication media
Data bearing media
Mass media
Mass media exposure
Mediation
Medical centres
Medical diagnosis
Medical education
Medical equipment
Medical ethics
Medical hospital libraries
Medical information systems
Medical inspection
Medical instruments

Medical laboratories
Medical libraries
Medical personnel
Medical profession
Medical records information
    systems
Medical research
Medical sciences
Medical specialities
Medical technology
Medical treatment
Medicinal plants
Aerospace medicine
Clinical medicine
Folk medicine
Forensic medicine
Preventive medicine
Sports medicine
Systems of medicine
Veterinary medicine
Medieval art
Medieval history
Mediterranean Countries
Mediterranean Sea
Medium size libraries
Meetings
Committee meetings
Public meetings
Melancholia
Melanesia
Melanesian
Melting
Member states
Structural members
Members of parliament
Memorization
Memory
Memory disorders
Men
Married men
Equal rights of men and women
Men students
Menopause
Mens education
Menstruation
Mental deficiency
Mental development
Mental diseases
Mental health
Higher mental processes
Mental strain
Mentally disadvantaged
Mentally handicapped
Mentally ill
Rights of the mentally ill
Mercury
Mergers
Mesolithic period
Mesosphere
Mesozoic period
Messages
Messianism
Nutrition and metabolic diseases
Metabolism
Animal metabolism
Plant metabolism
Metal industry
Metal mining
Metal refining
Metal removal
Metal treatment

347

Metallic deposits
Non -metalliferous mineral deposits
Metalliferous minerals
Non -metalliferous minerals
Metallogenic maps
Metallography
Metalloids
Metallurgical engineering
Metallurgy
Extractive metallurgy
Physical metallurgy
Powder metallurgy
Production metallurgy
Vacuum metallurgy
Metals
Ferrous metals
Non-ferrous metals
Non -metals
Precious metals
Art metalwork
Metalworking
Metamorphic rocks
Metaphysics
Computer metatheory
Metazoa
Meteorites
Meteorological data
Meteorological measurements and
instruments
Meteorological observatories
Meteorological satellites
Meteorology
Radar meteorology
Meteors
Current meters
Sound velocity meters
Historical method
Sight method
Direct method (teaching)
Heuristic method (teaching)
Project method (teaching)
Teaching method innovations
Debates (teaching method)
Discussions (teaching method)
Dramatic
presentation (teaching method)
Group work (teaching method)
Library work (study method)
Play (teaching method)
Questioning (teaching method)
Teach-ins (teaching method)
Methodology
Literacy methodology
Methods
Activity methods
Experimental methods
Graphical methods
Iterative methods
Learning methods
Monte Carlo methods
Numerical methods
Research methods
Self-teaching methods
Statistical methods
Study methods
Teaching methods
Training methods
Organization and methods study
Metric system
Metropolitan areas
Mexico

Gulf of Mexico
Mica
Microanalysis
Microbiology
Microcards
Microchemistry
Microclimatology
Microeconomics
Microfiche
Microfiche catalogues
Microfilm catalogues
Microfilms
Computer output microform
Microform equipment
Microforms
Extreme reduction microforms
Micronesia
Micronesian
Microorganisms
Aquatic microorganisms
Marine microorganisms
Micropalaeontology
Microphones
Microphotography
Micropublishing
Microscopes
Electron microscopes
Microscopy
Crystal microstructure
Microteaching
Microthesauri
Microwaves
Middle ages
Middle class
Middle East
Middle grade personnel
Middle management
Middle secondary education
Midway Islands
Migrant education
Migrants
Animal migration
Internal migration
Labour migration
Population migration
Rural migration
Seasonal migration
Migration policy
Militarism
Anti -militarism
Military education
Military engineering
Military equipment
Military law
Military logistics
Military operations
Military personnel
Military strategy
Milk
Milky Way
Millenarianism
Mime
Miming
Mind
Philosophy of mind
Mineral deposits
Non-metalliferous mineral deposits
Submarine mineral deposits
Mineral maps
Mineral resources
Mineralogy

Minerals
Carbonate minerals
Clay minerals
Metalliferous minerals
Non-metalliferous minerals
Silica minerals
Sulphate minerals
Miniature painting
Minicomputers
Minimization
Minimum marriage age
Minimum wages
Mining
Coal mining
Metal mining
Open cast mining
Underground mining
Mining equipment
Mining geology
Mining operations
Mining safety
Mining services
Prime minister
Ministers
Ministers of religion
Cultural minorities
Ethnic minorities
Language minorities
Political minorities
Racial minorities
Religious minorities
Minority cultures
Minority groups
Saint Pierre and Miquelon Islands
Mirrors
Misconduct
Missiles
Mission reports
Missionary work
Missions
Educational missions
Expert missions
Mist
Mixed economy
Mixed enterprises
Mixed farming
Mixed marriages
Mixed notation
Mixed race
Mixed-phase chemistry
Mixing technology
Mixtures
Language mixtures
Mnemonic notation
Mobile communication
Mobile educational services
Mobile homes
Mobile libraries
Mobile schools
Labour mobility
Social mobility
Student mobility
Synoptic modelling
Models
Cultural models
Economic models
Educational models
Mathematical models
Simulation models
Modern art

Modern ballet
Modern dance
Modern history
Modern languages
Modern law
Modern literature
Modern mathematics
Modern music
Modern religions
Greek (modern)
Modernization
Weather modification
Modifier terms
Modulation
Moisture
Soil moisture
Moisture measurement
Moldavian SSR
Molecular biology
Molecular physics
Molecular structure
Molecules
Mollusca
Molucca Sea
Molybdenum
Momentum
Mon-Khmer languages
Monaco
Monarchy
Monetary policy
Monetary systems
International monetary systems
Money
Mongolia
Mongolian languages
Mongols
Monitorial systems
Monitoring
Environmental monitoring
Monks
Monographs
Monolingual
Monolingual thesauri
Monopolies
Monorail
Monte Carlo methods
Montessori system
Monthly
Monthly publications
Montserrat
Monuments
Historic monuments
Preservation of monuments
Moods
Moon
Moraines
Moral behaviour
Moral concepts
Moral crises
Moral development
Moral education
Moral order
Moral problems
Moral values
Morbidity
Mores
Morocco
Animal morphology
Plant morphology
Morphology (linguistics)

Mortality
Mortgages
Mosaics
Moslem law
Moslems
Mosques
Most favoured nation
Mother tongue
Mother tongue instruction
Mothers
Unmarried mothers
Working mothers
Ocean wave motion
Motivation
Achievement motivation
Motor development
Motor industry
Motor processes
Motor vehicles
Electric motors
Hydraulic motors
Mountains
Movable cultural property
Anticurriculum movement
Ecumenical movement
Labour movement
Restriction on movement
Womens liberation movement
International movement of persons
Right to free movement of persons
Movement studies
Liberation movements
Political movements
Protest movements
Religious movements
Revolutionary movements
Sciosophic movements
Student movements
Youth movements
Prime movers
Mozambique
Mozambique Channel
Multiaccess systems
Multiculturalism
Multilingual
Multilingual thesauri
Multilingualism
Multimedia
Multimedia instruction
Multimedia resource centres
Multiparty systems
Multiple entry
Multiply handicapped
Multiprocessing systems
Multiracial societies
Multisensory learning
Multivariate analysis
Multivolume publications
Munda languages
Municipal government
Municipal libraries
Annam -Muong
Murals
Musee imaginaire
Museobuses
Museographers
Museography
Museology
Museum activities
Museum administration

Museum architecture
Museum attendance
Museum buildings
Museum charges
Museum collections
Museum cooperation
Museum curators
Museum development
Museum economics
Museum educational programmes
Museum equipment
Museum facilities
Museum finance
Museum financing
Museum laboratories
Museum legislation
Museum objects
Museum personnel
Museum planning
Museum planning and administration
Museum policy
Museum policy and development
Museum programmes
Museum reorganization
Museum statistics
Museum techniques
Museum training
Museum users
Museum visits
Museums
Archaeological museums
Art museums
Ethnographic museums
Historical museums
National museums
Natural history museums
Regional museums
School museums
Science museums
Specialized museums
Music
Abstract music
Ballet music
Classical music
Concrete music
Contemporary music
Dance music
Electronic music
Film music
Folk music
Instrumental music
Mechanical music
Modern music
National music
Pop music
Popular music
Religious music
Sound and music
Traditional music
Vocal music
Music education
Music publishing
Music scores
Music-hall
Musical character
Musical comedy
Musical comedy films
Musical composition
Musical concerts
Musical elements

Musical festivals
Musical forms
Musical instruments
Musical performances
Amateur musical performances
Musical theory
Musicians
Amateur musicians
Pop musicians
Musicology
Mutation
Mutiny
Myriapoda
Mysticism
Mythology
Seto Naikai Inland Sea
Name catalogues
Name cataloguing
Name indexes
Name indexing
Proprietary names
Namibia
Code Napoleon
Narcotic drugs
Narrower terms
Natality
Most favoured nation
Nation building
National accounting
Cross -national analysis
National archives
National bibliographies
National broadcasting
National character
National consciousness
National cultural organizations
National cultures
National dance
National development
National economy
National educational bodies
National geography
National identity
National income
National information systems
National information/library
  organizations
National libraries
National museums
National music
National parks
National policy
National press
National prestige
Gross national product
National school types
National stereotype
National theatre
Nationalism
Cultural nationalism
Culture nationalism
Nationality
Right to nationality
Nationality discrimination
Nationalization
Nations
Aggressor nations
Native art
Natives
Natural disasters
Natural environment

Natural gas
Natural gas production
Natural heritage
Natural history
Natural history museums
Natural language searching
Natural language systems
Natural law
Natural resins
Natural resources
Right to natural resources control
Natural selection
Naturalization
Conservation of nature
Human nature
Nature reserves
Naturopathy
Nauru Island
Naval architecture
Naval warfare
Navies
Navigation
Aerospace navigation
Inertial navigation
Magnetic navigation
Marine navigation
Radar navigation
Radio navigation
Satellite navigation
Sonar navigation
Underwater navigation
Navigational instruments
Nazism
ISBD (NBM)
Nebulae
People-in -need
Needlework
Needs
Cultural needs
Educational needs
Housing needs
Human needs
Information user needs
Information/library needs
Manpower needs
Social needs
Negative peace
Neighbourhoods
Neighbouring rights
Neocolonialism
Neolithic period
Neon
Neoplasms
Nepal
Nepali
Neritic province
Nervous breakdown
Nervous system diseases
Nervous systems
Netherlands
Netherlands Antilles
Gill nets
Seine nets
Trawl nets
Network analysis
Communication networks
Computer networks
Hydrological networks
Information/library networks
Railway networks

Nursing
Nutrients
Nutrition
Nutrition and metabolic diseases
Nutrition education
Nuts
Nylon
Oases
Obesity
Conscientious objection
Objective history
Cultural objectives
Archaeological objects
Museum objects
Obligation
Observation
Observatories
Astronomical observatories
Meteorological observatories
Seismological observatories
Obsessional neuroses
Obsolescence
Obstetrics
Occult
Occupational choice
Occupational diseases
Occupational life
Occupational psychology
Occupational qualifications
Occupational safety
Occupational sociology
Occupational status
Occupational therapy
Occupations
Professional occupations
Occupied territories
Term co-occurrence
Antarctic Ocean
Arctic Ocean
Atlantic Ocean
Indian Ocean
North Atlantic Ocean
North Pacific Ocean
Pacific Ocean
South Atlantic Ocean
South Pacific ocean
Ocean circulation
Ocean current measurement
Ocean currents
Ocean exploration
Ocean floor
Ocean stations
Ocean stratification
Ocean structure
Atlantic Ocean Territories
Indian Ocean Territories
Ocean variability
Ocean wave action
Ocean wave base
Ocean wave crest
Ocean wave decay
Ocean wave energy
Ocean wave frequency
Ocean wave front
Ocean wave growth
Ocean wave height
Ocean wave length
Ocean wave measurement
Ocean wave motion
Ocean wave profile

Ocean wave velocity
Ocean waves
Oceania
Oceanic art
Oceanic cultures
Austronesian and Oceanic languages
Oceanic province
Oceanic stratosphere
Oceanic troposphere
Oceanographers
Oceanographic buoys
Oceanographic data
Oceanographic equipment
Oceanographic instruments
Oceanographic laboratories
Oceanographic measurements
Oceanographic research
Oceanographic samplers
Oceanography
Chemical oceanography
Dynamic oceanography
Physical oceanography
Oceanography education
Oceanologists
Oceans
Run-off
Search cut-off
Offences
Political offences
Sexual offences
Office equipment
Office management
Office services
Office workers
Information officers
Law officers
Training officers
Patent offices
Official publications
Official records
Underwater oil and gas extraction
Oil fields
Oil industry
Oil painting
Oil pollution
Oil resources
Animal oils
Vegetable oils
Vegetable and animal oils technology
Sea of Okhotsk
Old age
Old peoples clubs
Oligarchy
Olympic games
Oman
Gulf of Oman
Ombudsman
Restriction on movement
On-line information processing
On-line information systems
On-line searching
On-line systems
One-parent families
One-party systems
One-teacher schools
One-way communication
Only children
Ontology
Opacity
Open air schools

Open air theatre
Open cast mining
Open plan design
Open spaces
Open universities
Library hours of opening
Opera
Opera houses
Operating systems (computer)
Shelving (operation)
Operational planning
Archive operations
Building operations
Fishing operations
Information library operations
Library housekeeping operations
Management operations
Military operations
Mining operations
Printing operations
Operations research
Operator systems
Ophthalmology
Opinion
Public opinion
Opinion change
Public opinion polls
Educational opportunities
Employment opportunities
Equal opportunity
Legitimate opposition
Political opposition
Oppression
Resistance to oppression
Right to resist oppression
Optical chemical analysis
Optical coincidence systems
Optical devices
Sea water optical measurements
Optical measurements and
    instruments
Sea water optical properties
Optical properties of substances
Optical variables control
Optics
Atmospheric optics
Particle optics
Quantum optics
Optimism
Optimization
Population optimum
Opting out
Optoelectronic devices
Oracy
Oral composition
Oral examinations
Oral expression
Oral history
Oral reading
Oral tradition
Oral work
Orchestras
Amateur orchestras
Youth orchestras
Birth order
Citation order
Filing order
Index language order
Moral order
Approval ordering
Book ordering
Religious orders

Superior orders
Ordinal notation
Iron ores
Local government organizations
Organ transplantation
International
information/library organizations
Organic chemistry
Organic complex compounds
Organic compounds
Organic matter
Organic psychoses
Government
information/library organizations
National
information/library organizations
Regional government
cultural organizations
Central government
cultural organizations
Private information/library organizations
File organization (computer)
File organization (index)
Organization and methods study
Organizations
Broadcasting organizations
Central government organizations
Communication organizations
Cultural organizations
Employers organizations
Government cultural organizations
Government organizations
Information library organizations
Intergovernment organizations
International cultural organizations
International organizations
Local government cultural organizations
Local government organizations
National cultural organizations
Non-governmental organizations
Parent-teacher organizations
Private cultural organizations
Private educational organizations
Private organizations
Regional cultural organizations
Regional government organizations
Regional organizations
Scientific organizations
Social science organizations
Social welfare organizations
Student organizations
Voluntary organizations
Voluntary welfare organizations
War relief organizations
Womens organizations
Youth organizations
Organometallic compounds
Artificial organs
Oriental languages
Orientation courses
Precision oriented devices
Recall oriented devices
Machine oriented languages
Problem oriented languages
Procedure oriented languages
Orifices
Social origin
Oriya
Ornithology
Orphans
Orthopaedics
Oscillators

Osmosis
Osteopathy
Opting out
Drop -out problem
Drop -out rate
Out-of-print publications
Out-of-school education
Out-of-school youth
Outdoor pursuits
Book output
Educational output
Ranked output
Search output
Input -output analysis
Computer output microform
Input -output programs
School drop -outs
Social drop -outs
Overachievers
Overdue loans
Overemployment
Overpopulation
Oversize books
Overspill towns
Overtime
Home ownership
Private ownership
Public ownership
Oxidation
Oxygen
Ozone
Ozonosphere
Pacific Ocean
North Pacific Ocean
South Pacific ocean
Pacifism
Packaging
Paediatrics
Pagans
Pages
Pain
Paint technology
Painters
Painting
Miniature painting
Oil painting
Rock painting
Restoration of paintings
Paints
Pakistan
Palaces
Palaeobiochemistry
Palaeobotany
Palaeoclimatology
Palaeoecology
Palaeogeography
Palaeogeology
Palaeography
Palaeohydrology
Palaeolithic period
Palaeontology
Invertebrate palaeontology
Vertebrate palaeontology
Palaeosiberian languages
Palaeozoic period
Palestine
Palmistry
Pampas
Pamphlets
Panama
Panama Canal Zone

Panjabi
Pantomime
Paper
Printing paper
Paper industry
Paper technology
Paperbacks
Conference papers
Personal papers
Papua New Guinea
Papuan languages
Paradigmatic relations
Paraguay
Parallel processing systems
Paramedical personnel
Non -parametric statistics
Paranoia
Paraprofessional educational personnel
Parapsychology
Parasites
Parasitology
Parazoa
Parent attitude
Parent education
One -parent families
Parent participation
Parent responsibility
Parent role
Parent-child relationship
Parent-school relationship
Parent-teacher organizations
Parent-teacher relationship
Parental deprivation
Parents
Parks
National parks
Members of parliament
Parliamentary systems
Parochial schools
Parole
Part-time courses
Part-time employment
Part-time librarians
Part-time teachers
Part-whole relations
Partial differential equations
Partial sight
Partially sighted
Participation
Audience participation
Community participation
Cultural participation
Parent participation
Political participation
Right to cultural participation
Social participation
Student participation
Teacher participation
Workers participation
Youth participation
Public participation in planning
Particle accelerators
Particle beams
Particle measurements and instruments
Particle optics
Particle physics
Elementary particles
Political parties
Partition
Partnerships
Document parts

Reciprocating parts
One -party systems
Two -party systems
Northwest Passage
Passive resistance
Social passivity
Pastoral work
Patent offices
Patenting
Patents
Pathology
Patients
Rights of hospital patients
Patriotism
Patronage of the arts
Pattern recognition
Equal pay
Balance of payments
Peace
Controlled peace
Education for peace
Negative peace
Positive peace
Right to live in peace
Peace research
Peace treaties
Peace-keeping forces
Peace-making
Peaceful coexistence
Peat
Peat soils
Peer-group relationship
Pelagic zone
Death penalty
Peninsulas
Light pens
Pensions
People
Aboriginal people
Coloured people
Non-industrialized people
Semitic people
White people
People-in-need
Old peoples clubs
Lao Peoples Democratic Republic
Yemen (Peoples Democratic Republic)
Benin (Peoples Republic)
Congo (Peoples Republic)
Korea (Democratic Peoples Republic)
Perception
Extra-sensory perception
Perception of the environment
Percolation
Percussion instruments
Performance
Performance ratios
Amateur musical performances
Musical performances
Theatrical performances
Performers
Performing arts
Cenozoic period
Loan period
Mesolithic period
Mesozoic period
Neolithic period
Palaeolithic period
Palaeozoic period
Precambrian period
Probation period

Quarternary period
Tertiary period
Periodical acquisition systems
Periodical circulation
Periodical circulation automation
Periodical indexes
Periodical press
Periodicals
Educational periodicals
Popular periodicals
Scientific periodicals
Union catalogues of periodicals
Rest periods
Study periods
Computer peripheral equipment
Perjury
Permafrost
Permeability
Permutation
Permuted indexes
Persian
Personal contact
Personal grants
Personal papers
Personal property law
Personal social services
Personality
Basic personality
Personality change
Personality development
Personality disorders
Information/library
professional personnel
Personnel
Academic teaching personnel
Archive personnel
Communication personnel
Computer personnel
Cultural personnel
Educational guidance personnel
Educational laboratory personnel
Educational personnel
Educational support personnel
Higher technical personnel
Information/library
clerical personnel
Information/library
manual personnel
Information/library personnel
Information/library
support personnel
Medical personnel
Middle grade personnel
Military personnel
Museum personnel
Non-professional
information/library personnel
Paramedical personnel
Paraprofessional
educational personnel
Professional personnel
Scientific personnel
Social science personnel
Television and radio personnel
Television and
radio technical personnel
Personnel management
Personnel records
Personnel selection
Communication personnel training
Cultural personnel training
Educational personnel training

Scientific personnel training
Television and radio personnel training
Illegitimate persons
International movement of persons
Religious persons
Right to free movement of persons
Sick persons
Persuasion
Peru
Pessimism
Pest control
Pesticides
Pests
Right of petition
Petitioning
Petrochemicals
Petrochemicals technology
Petrochemistry
Petroleum
Petroleum geology
Petroleum production
Petroleum products
Petroleum technology
Petrology
pH
pH measurement
Pharmaceutical technology
Pharmacology
Pharmacy
Mixed -phase chemistry
Phase equilibrium
Phase relations
Phase transformations
Solid state phase transformations
Physics of energy phenomena
Philanthropic libraries
Philatelic service
Philippine Sea
Philippines
Philology
Philosophical schools
Philosophy
Cultural philosophy
Educational philosophy
Information/library philosophy
Literary philosophy
Political philosophy
Science philosophy
Social welfare philosophy
Philosophy of action
Philosophy of history
Philosophy of mind
School phobia
Phobias
Phonetic writing
Phonetics
Phonology
Phonorecord industry
Phonorecord libraries
Phonotapes
Phosphorus
Photocharging
Photochemical reactions
Photochemistry
Photocomposition
Photocopies
Photocopying
Photoelastic stress analysis
Photoelectric devices
Photoelectricity
Photogrammetry
Photographers

Photographic archives
Photographic equipment
Photographic slides
Photographs
Photography
Aerial photography
Amateur photography
Underwater photography
Photometry
Photons
Photoperiodism
Photoposters
Photosensitivity
Photosynthesis
Physical chemistry
Physical education
Physical expression
Physical geography
Physical geology
Physical handicaps
Physical metallurgy
Physical oceanography
Physical properties
Physical sciences
Physical standards
Physically disadvantaged
Physically handicapped
Physicians
Physics
Atmospheric physics
Atomic physics
Bulk matter physics
Colloid physics
Condensed matter physics
Dispersion and surface physics
Dispersion physics
Electron physics
Experimental physics
Fluid physics
Gas physics
High energy physics
Ion physics
Mathematical physics
Molecular physics
Neutron physics
Nuclear physics
Particle physics
Plasma physics
Radiation physics
Semiconductor physics
Soil physics
Solid state physics
Statistical physics
Surface physics
Theoretical physics
Vacuum physics
Wave physics
Physics education
Physics of energy phenomena
Physics of liquids
Physics of solids
Transport processes (physics)
Physiognomy
Physiological development
Physiological effects
Physiological psychology
Physiology
Human physiology
Plant physiology
Physiotherapy
Phytochemistry

357

Phytogeography
Phytopathology
Phytoplankton
Phytotrons
Picketing
Pictographic scripts
Pictures
Reproductions (pictures)
Saint Pierre and Miquelon Islands
Piers
Piezoelectric devices
Piezoelectricity
Pilgrimages
Pilipino
Pilot libraries
Pilot projects
Pipes
Flow in pipes
Pitcairn Islands
Pitot tubes
Artificial placentas
Plains
Coastal plains
Submarine plains
Plaintiffs
Open plan design
Earth (planet)
Planetaria
Planets
Plankton
Plankton recorders
Planned economy
Planners
Communication planners
Cultural planners
Educational planners
Environmental planners
Communication planners training
Planning
Agricultural planning
Archive planning
Communication planning
Cultural planning
Curriculum planning
Development planning
Economic planning
Educational planning
Environmental planning
Family planning
Industrial planning
Information/library planning
Labour planning
Long range planning
Museum planning
Operational planning
Programme planning
Public participation in planning
Regional planning
Research planning
Rural planning
Science planning
Social planning
Social science planning
Social welfare planning
Strategic planning
Transport planning
Urban planning
Visual planning
Environmental planning administration
Information/library planning and administration

Social science planning and administration
Communication planning and administration
Cultural planning and administration
Economic planning and administration
Educational planning and administration
Museum planning and administration
Science planning and administration
Environmental planning control
Environmental planning legislation
Environmental planning policy
Environmental planning processes
Development areas (urban planning)
Plans
Cultural plans
Development plans
Educational plans
Industrial plant
Plant adaptation
Plant anatomy
Plant development
Plant ecology
Plant genetics
Plant growth
Plant histology
Plant life
Plant metabolism
Plant morphology
Plant physiology
Plant resources
Plant transpiration
Planting
Plants
Aquatic plants
Marine plants
Medicinal plants
Wild plants
Plasma physics
Plastic arts
Plastic deformation
Plastic surgery
Plasticity
Plastics
Polymer and plastics technology
Rio de la Plata
Plateaus
Platinum
Play
Play (teaching method)
Play groups
Play reading
Record players
Playgrounds
Role playing
Playing fields
Long playing records
School plays
Pleadings
Pleasure
Pluralingual
Pluralism
Cultural pluralism
Social pluralism
Plutonic rocks
Plutonium
Pneumonia
Pocket books
Poetry
Spoken poetry
Poisons
Poland

Polar regions
Polarization
Polarographic analysis
North Pole
South Pole
Polemology
Police
Police activities
Police brutality
Police power
Policy
Acquisition policy
Agricultural policy
Archive policy
Communication policy
Cultural policy
Customs policy
Development policy
Economic policy
Educational policy
Employment policy
Environmental planning policy
Financial policy
Fiscal policy
Foreign policy
Government policy
Housing policy
Incomes policy
Industrial policy
Information/library policy
Labour policy
Language policy
Migration policy
Monetary policy
Museum policy
National policy
Population policy
Price policy
Research policy
Science policy
Social policy
Social science policy
Transport policy
Wages policy
Welfare policy
Museum policy and development
Policy making
Poliomyelitis
Polish
Polishes
Political action
Right to political asylum
Political attitude
Political behaviour
Political conflict
Political corruption
Political crises
Political development
Political doctrines
Political ethics
Political films
Political geography
Political history
Political institutions
Political leadership
Political life
Political majorities
Political minorities
Political movements

Political offences
Political opposition
Political participation
Political parties
Political philosophy
Political power
Political reform
Political representation
Civil and political rights
Political science
Political science education
Political sociology
Political support
Political systems
Political theory
Political trials
Politicians
Politics
Internal politics
International politics
Public opinion polls
Pollutants
Pollution
Air pollution
Industrial pollution
Land pollution
Marine pollution
Oil pollution
Radioactive pollution
River pollution
Soil pollution
Visual pollution
Water pollution
Pollution control
Air pollution legislation
Air pollution treatment
Polonium
Polyesters
Polyethylene
Polygamy
Polyhierarchical relations
Polymer and plastics technology
Polymer chemistry
Polymerization
Polymers
Ester polymers
Inorganic polymers
Polynesia
French Polynesia
Polynesian
Malayo-Polynesian languages
Polynomials
Polypropylene
Polystyrene
Polytechnic schools (USSR)
Polytechnics
Polyurethanes
Polyvalent adult education
Polyvinyl chloride
Polyvinyl fluoride
Ponds
Swimming pools
Poor
Pop art
Pop festivals
Pop music
Pop musicians
Popular literature
Popular music
Popular periodicals

Popular theatre
Popularization
Science popularization
Population
Educational population
Rural population
School-age population
Urban population
World population
Population decrease
Population density
Population distribution
Population dynamics
Population education
Population equilibrium
Population events
Population increase
Population legislation
Population migration
Population optimum
Population policy
Population problems
Population programmes
Population projection
Population research
Indigenous populations
Pornography
Porosity
Porous materials
Library porters
Ports
Portugal
Portuguese
Portuguese Timor
Position finding
Position measurement
Positioning
Positive peace
Positivism
Post-coordination
Post-graduate courses
Post-industrial societies
Post-literacy programmes
Post-search editing
Post-war measures
Postage stamps
Postal loans
Postal services
Posters
Posting
Generic posting
Potassium
Electric potential
Scientific potential
Potentiometric analysis
Pottery
Poverty
Culture of poverty
Powder metallurgy
Powders
Abuse of power
Economic power
Executive power
Judicial power
Legislative power
Police power
Political power
Steam power
Water power
Wind power

Electric power distribution
Power elite
Fluid power engineering
Solar power engineering
Electric power generation
Solar power generation
Power industry
Power reactors
Diesel power stations
Electric power stations
Gas turbine power stations
Geothermal power stations
Hydroelectric power stations
Nuclear power stations
Steam power stations
Thermal power stations
Tidal power stations
Wind power stations
Electric power systems
Electric power transmission
Electric power transmission lines
Emergency powers
Separation of powers
PPBS
Practical astronomy
Practical examinations
Practical studies
Practical training
Practice
Foundry practice
Religious practice
Legal practice and procedure
Practice teaching
Esoteric practices
Prayer
Pre-coordinate indexes
Pre-coordination
Pre-primary curriculum
Pre-primary education
Pre-primary school teachers
Pre-primary teacher training
Pre-school children
Pre-school education
Pre-service teacher training
Pre-university science education
Pre-vocational education
Preaching
Precambrian period
Precious metals
Precipitation
Precipitation measurement
PRECIS indexes
Precision
Precision engineering
Precision oriented devices
Precision ratio
Tidal prediction
Prefabrication
Pregnancy
Prehistoric art
Prehistoric man
Prehistoric religions
Prehistory
Prejudice
Racial prejudice
Brief preparation
Data preparation
Document preparation
Data preparation equipment
Preparative chemistry

Thought process development
Process heating
Sensory process psychology
Finishing (process)
Chemical engineering processes
Diazo processes
Endogenous processes
Environmental planning processes
Exogenous processes
Higher mental processes
Learning processes
Markov processes
Motor processes
Printing processes
Random processes
Social processes
Textile processes
Transport processes (physics)
Rational processes disorders
Data processing
Document processing
Information processing
Nuclear fuel processing
On-line information processing
Processing agents technology
Signal processing and detection
Information processing automation
Parallel processing systems
Program processors
Film producers
Television and radio producers
Theatre producers
Gross national product
Product development
Production
Agricultural production
Book production
Broadcasting production
Factors of production
Food production
Large scale production
Mass production
Natural gas production
Petroleum production
Speech production
Television production
Textbook production
Theatrical production
Production engineering
Production management
Production metallurgy
Film production statistics
Book production training
Cultural productions
Productivity
Labour productivity
Products
Agricultural products
Animal products
Dairy products
Forest products
Petroleum products
Volcanic products
Archive profession
Information/library profession
Legal profession
Medical profession
Teaching profession
Information/library professional associations
Professional associations

Teacher professional ethics
Non-professional information/library personnel
Professional occupations
Information/library professional personnel
Professional personnel
Professional standards
Teacher professional standards
Professional status
Information/library professional status
Professional training
Ocean wave profile
Search profiles
Soil profiles
Profits
Program and systems documentation
Program libraries
Program processors
Program testing
Programme content
Programme exchange
Programme planning
Programmed courses
Programmed instruction
Programmed materials
Programmes
Accelerated programmes
Adult education programmes
Broadcasting programmes
Communication programmes
Communication research programmes
Cultural programmes
Development programmes
Educational programmes
Exchange programmes
Information/library programmes
Instructional programmes
International training programmes
Literacy programmes
Live programmes
Mass communication programmes
Museum educational programmes
Museum programmes
Population programmes
Post-literacy programmes
Radio programmes
Reading programmes
Research programmes
Scientific programmes
Social programmes
Television programmes
Computer programming
Country programming
Mathematical programming
Complete computer programs
Input-output programs
Supervisory and executive programs
Time-sharing programs
Utility programs
Progress
Scientific progress
Social progress
Student progress
Progress reports
Project management
Project method (teaching)
Project reports
Population projection
Enrolment projections
Projectors
Slide projectors

Development projects
Educational projects
Experimental projects
Pilot projects
Research projects
Student projects
Non-proliferation treaties
Library use promotion
Literacy promotion
Reading promotion
Social promotion
Teacher promotion
Promotion (job)
Proof reading
Propaganda
War propaganda
Sound wave propagation
Wave propagation
Properties
Acoustic properties
Chemical properties
Dielectric properties
Fluid mechanical properties
Nuclear structure and properties
Physical properties
Rock properties
Sea water acoustic properties
Sea water optical properties
Sea water properties
Soil properties
Thermodynamic properties
Water properties
Electrical properties of substances
Magnetic properties of substances
Mechanical properties of substances
Optical properties of substances
Thermal properties of substances
Artistic property
Cultural property
Intellectual property
Literary property
Movable cultural property
Presentation of cultural property
Preservation of cultural property
Right of intellectual property
Right to property
Land and property finance
Property law
Personal property law
Real property law
Prophets
Proportional representation
Proprietary names
Nuclear propulsion
Prose
Public prosecutors
Geophysical prospecting
Prosperity
Prosthetics
Coastal protection
Consumer protection
Fire protection
Forest protection
Landscape protection
Radiation protection
Social protection
Theft protection
Wildlife protection
Electrical protection gear
Protectionism

Protective clothing
Protectorates
Proteins
Social protest
Protest movements
Protestantism
Protons
Protozoa
Proverbs
Neritic province
Oceanic province
Pseudonyms
Psychiatry
Psychoanalysis
Psychodrama
Psychohistory
Psychokinesis
Psycholinguistics
Psychological effects
Psychological research
Psychological schools
Psychological tests
Stress (psychological)
Psychologists
Psychology
Adolescent psychology
Adult psychology
Affective psychology
Applied psychology
Child psychology
Clinical psychology
Communication psychology
Comparative psychology
Depth psychology
Developmental psychology
Economic psychology
Educational psychology
Experimental psychology
Genetic psychology
Geriatric psychology
History of psychology
Individual psychology
Industrial psychology
Occupational psychology
Physiological psychology
Sensory process psychology
Social psychology
Psychology education
Psychology of art
Psychology of religion
Executive functions (psychology)
Psychometrics
Psychopathology
Psychophysiology
Psychoses
Affective psychoses
Manic-depressive psychoses
Organic psychoses
Educational psychosociology
Psychosomatic disorders
Psychosomatics
Psychotechnics
Psychotherapy
Drug psychotherapy
Pteridophyta
Puberty
General public
Untapped public
Public administration
Public archives

Public debt
Public education
Public enquiries
Public enterprises
Public expenditure
Public finance
Public gardens
Public health
Public housing
Public image
Public international law
Public law
Public lending right
Public liaison
UNESCO public liaison
Public librarians
Public libraries
Public meetings
Public opinion
Public opinion polls
Public ownership
Public participation in planning
Public prosecutors
Public relations
Library public relations
Public sector
Public speaking
Public taste
Public transport
Public utilities
Public works
Public/academic libraries
College publications
Commercial publications
Daily publications
Educational publications
Exchange of publications
In-print publications
Library publications
Monthly publications
Multivolume publications
Official publications
Out-of-print publications
Quarterly publications
School publications
Scientific publications
UNESCO publications
Weekly publications
Publicity
Library publicity
Semi-published documents
Publishers
Publishers training
Publishing
Music publishing
Puerto Rico
Pulsars
Pumping stations
Pumps
Heat pumps
Punched card coordinate indexes
Punched card loan records
Punched cards
Punched tapes
Punishment
Corporal punishment
Non-custodial punishment
School punishments
Puppets
Purchasing

Purification
General purpose computers
Special purpose computers
Outdoor pursuits
Pushto
Pyrometallurgy
Pyrometers
Qatar
Qualifications
Information/library qualifications
Occupational qualifications
Teacher qualifications
Qualifiers
Qualitative analysis
Quality
Environmental quality
Right to environmental quality
Quality control
Quality of education
Quality of life
Quality of water
Quantitative analysis
Quantitative history
Quantity
Quantum field theory
Quantum optics
Quantum theory
Quarantine
Quarrying
Quarterly
Quarterly publications
Quarternary maps
Quarternary period
Quartz
Quasars
Quasi-synonyms
Query formulation
Questioning (teaching method)
Questionnaires
Search questions
Queueing theory
Intelligence quotient
Rabies
Race
Arms race
Mixed race
Race relations
Racial conflict
Racial discrimination
Racial groups
Racial integration
Racial minorities
Racial prejudice
Racial segregation
Racial tolerance
Racialism
Racism
Radar
Radar meteorology
Radar navigation
Radiation
Atmospheric radiation
Cosmic radiation
Infrared radiation
Solar radiation
Ultraviolet radiation
Radiation belts
Radiation chemistry
Radiation detectors
Radiation effects

Radiation hazards
Radiation measurement and
    instruments
Radiation physics
Radiation protection
Radiation technology
Radiative transfer
Radicalism
Chemical radicals
Radio
Commercial radio
Educational radio
Radio advertising
Television and radio directors
Radio drama
Radio engineering
Radio games
Television and radio industry
Radio links
Radio listeners
Radio navigation
Radio news
Television and radio personnel
Television and radio personnel training
Television and radio producers
Radio programmes
Radio receivers
Radio serials
Radio stations
Radio studios
Television and radio technical personnel
Radio transmitters
Radio wave interference
Radio waves
Radioactive fallout
Radioactive pollution
Radioactive tracers
Radioactive wastes
Radioactivity
Radioastronomy
Radiobiology
Radiocarbon dating
Radiochemical analysis
Radiochemistry
Radiography
Radioisotopes
Radiolysis
Radiotelephone
Radiotherapy
Radium
Radon
Rail safety
Rail traffic
Railway engineering
Railway networks
Railway stations
Railway tracks
Railway transport
Underground railways
Rain
Rain gauges
Capital raising
Random processes
Random searching
Random walk
Tidal range
Long range planning
Ranked output
Rare books
Rare earths
Attendance rate

Bank rate
Birth rate
Death rate
Drop-out rate
Growth rate
Exchange rates
Ratification
Audience rating
Ratio
Precision ratio
Recall ratio
Teacher-student ratio
Rational processes disorders
Rationalism
Rationalization
Enrolment ratios
Performance ratios
Raw materials
X-ray analysis
X-ray chemical analysis
X-ray crystallography
X-ray diffraction
X-ray spectroscopy
Gamma rays
X-rays
Re-cataloguing
Re-classifying
Audience reaction
Reaction chemistry
Addition reactions
Chemical reactions
Combination reactions
Decomposition reactions
Dissociation reactions
Electrochemical reactions
Elimination reactions
Exchange reactions
Nuclear reactions
Photochemical reactions
Rearrangement reactions
Redox reactions
Replacement reactions
Ring closure reactions
Nuclear reactor components
Nuclear reactor safety
Nuclear reactor theory
Chemical reactors
Electric reactors
Fast reactors
Fusion reactors
Nuclear reactors
Power reactors
Thermal reactors
Machine-readable archives
Machine-readable materials
Learning readiness
Reading readiness
Reading
Oral reading
Play reading
Proof reading
Silent reading
Speed reading
Reading ability
Reading guidance
Reading habit
Reading instruction
Reading materials
Reading problems
Reading programmes

Disphotic regions
Euphotic regions
Hadal regions
Polar regions
Research registers
Borrower registration
Regression analysis
Regulations
Library rules and regulations
Rehabilitation
Rehearsal
Related terms
NOT relation
OR relation
Relational indexing
Cultural relations
Equivalence relations
Foreign relations
Hierarchical relations
Interethnic relations
Intergroup relations
International relations
Interpersonal relations
Labour relations
Library public relations
Logical relations
Non-hierarchical relations
Paradigmatic relations
Part-whole relations
Phase relations
Polyhierarchical relations
Public relations
Race relations
Semantic relations
Syntactic relations
Diplomatic relations suspension
Dependency relationship
Documentalist-user relationship
Information scientist-user relationship
Librarian-user relationship
Parent-child relationship
Parent-school relationship
Parent-teacher relationship
Peer-group relationship
School-community relationship
School-student relationship
Teacher-administrator relationship
Teacher-student relationship
Ecological relationships
Relative indexes
Relativity
Relays
Press releases
Relevance feedback
Reliability
War relief
Relief in kind
Relief maps
War relief organizations
Relief printing
Disaster relief work
Religion
Egyptian religion
Ministers of religion
Psychology of religion
Sociology of religion
Ancient Asiatic religions
Ancient religions
Modern religions
Prehistoric religions

Primitive religions
Religious art
Religious behaviour
Religious belief
Religious buildings
Religious ceremonies
Religious communities
Religious conflict
Religious discrimination
Religious doctrines
Religious education
Religious experience
Religious festivals
Religious freedom
Religious history
Religious institution libraries
Religious institutions
Religious leaders
Religious minorities
Religious movements
Religious music
Religious orders
Religious persons
Religious practice
Religious reform
Religious systems
Remand in custody
Remedial instruction
Right to an effective remedy
Remote access
Remote consoles
Remote control
Metal removal
Library removals
Loan renewal
Urban renewal
Renewal theory
Rented housing
Rents
Museum reorganization
Repair workshops
War reparations
Repeaters
Repertory theatre
Repetitive work
Replacement reactions
Right of reply
Report generators
Report writing
Reports
Annual reports
Country reports
Expert reports
Final reports
Interim reports
Law reports
Mission reports
Progress reports
Project reports
Technical reports
Archive repositories
Equal representation
Political representation
Proportional representation
Representative democracy
Representative literary works
Representative works of art
Reprints
Reprisals
Cultural reproduction

Reproduction (biological)
Reproductions (pictures)
Reproductive arts
Reprography
Reptiles
Union of Soviet Socialist Republics
Job requirements
Water requirements
Rescue
Research
Agricultural research
Applied research
Archive research
Audience research
Biological research
Botanical research
Brain research
Chemical research
Classification research
Communication research
Conflict research
Cultural research
Curriculum research
Ecological research
Economics of research
Economics research
Educational research
Fundamental research
Geographical research
Historical research
Hydrological research
Information library research
Interdisciplinary research
Linguistic research
Literary research
Market research
Medical research
Oceanographic research
Operations research
Peace research
Population research
Problem focused research
Psychological research
Reading research
Scientific research
Social science research
Sociology of research
Research and development
Research centres
Research coordination
Research councils
Research facilities
Research fellowships
Research finance
Research foundations
Research grants
Research libraries
Research management
Research methods
Research planning
Research policy
Research priorities
Research programmes
Communication research programmes
Research projects
Research registers
Research results
Scientific research results
Research ships
Research strategy

Research techniques
Research training
Research trends
Research work
Research workers
Loan reservations
Nature reserves
Reservoirs
Right to freedom of residence
Residential areas
Residential child care
Residential social work
Amino resins
Epoxy resins
Natural resins
Silicon resins
Right to resist oppression
Passive resistance
Thermal resistance
Electrical resistance measurement
Resistance to change
Resistance to oppression
Resistors
Conflict resolution
Resource allocation
Resource centres
Multimedia resource centres
Resource conservation
Resource development
Resource exploration
Resource management
Resources
Animal resources
Coal resources
Cultural resources
Economic resources
Educational financial resources
Educational resources
Energy resources
Financial resources
Fishery resources
Food resources
Forest resources
Fuel resources
Gas resources
Human resources
Information library resources
Land resources
Marine resources
Mineral resources
Natural resources
Oil resources
Plant resources
Soil resources
Water resources
Right to natural resources control
Human resources development
Water resources development
Water resources management
Respiratory diseases
Respiratory systems
Response
Fast-response computer systems
Responsibility
Parent responsibility
Social responsibility
State responsibility
Teacher responsibility
State responsibility for education
Rest

Right to rest and leisure
Rest periods
Restaurants
Restoration
Restoration of paintings
Architect restorers
Restraint systems
Restricted documents
Restriction on movement
Research results
Scientific research results
Retail trade
Retention
Retirement
Teacher retirement
Retraining
Data retrieval
Information retrieval
Retroactive notation
Retrospective search services
Retrospective searching
Investment return
Reunion Islands
Literature review services
Book reviews
Literature reviews
Search revision
Stock revision
Revolt
Revolution
Cultural revolution
Revolutionary movements
Rewards
School rewards
Rhenium
Rheology
Southern Rhodesia
Nursery rhymes
Rhythm
Costa Rica
Puerto Rico
Submarine ridges
Gulf of Riga
Public lending right
Right of assembly
Right of association
Right of intellectual property
Right of petition
Right of reply
Right of self-determination
Right to a fair hearing
Right to adequate living standards
Right to an effective remedy
Right to artistic freedom
Right to communicate
Right to confidentiality
Right to counsel
Right to cultural identity
Right to cultural participation
Right to die
Right to dignity
Right to economic development
Right to education
Right to environmental quality
Right to free movement of persons
Right to freedom from inhuman
    treatment
Right to freedom of expression
Right to freedom of residence
Right to freedom of thought
Right to habeas corpus

Right to health
Right to information
Right to justice
Right to legal aid
Right to life
Right to live in peace
Right to marry
Right to nationality
Right to natural resources control
Right to non-discrimination
Right to political asylum
Right to presumption of innocence
Right to privacy
Right to property
Right to resist oppression
Right to rest and leisure
Right to social security
Right to social welfare
Right to vote and be elected
Right to work
Civil and political rights
Collective human rights
Cultural rights
Family rights
Fishing rights
Human rights
Neighbouring rights
Recognition rights
Role rights
Social and economic rights
Territorial rights
Trade union rights
Womens rights
Rights and privileges
Rights of accused
Rights of authors
Rights of civilians
Rights of hospital patients
Equal rights of men and women
Rights of prisoners
Rights of soldiers
Rights of special groups
Rights of states
Rights of students
Rights of the child
Rights of the elderly
Rights of the handicapped
Rights of the mentally ill
Rights of war prisoners
Rights of war wounded
Human rights violation
Ring closure reactions
Rio de la Plata
Riots
Tidal rise
High rise flats
Risk
Rites
Initiation rites
Rituals
River and lake engineering
River basins
River control
River pollution
Rivers
Discharge of rivers
Road engineering
Road safety
Road traffic
Road transport

Social	science development
	Science education
Basic	science education
Computer	science education
Domestic	science education
Political	science education
Pre-university	science education
Social	science education
	Science fiction
	Science fiction films
	Science finance
	Science financing
	Science forecasting
Social	science information
Social	science institutions
	Science museums
	Science of science and technology
Social	science organizations
Social	science personnel
	Science philosophy
	Science planning
Social	science planning
Social	science planning and administration
	Science planning and administration
	Science policy
Social	science policy
	Science popularization
Social	science research
	Science statistics
Archive	science training
Administrative	sciences
Behavioural	sciences
Earth	sciences
Environmental	sciences
Life	sciences
Mathematical	sciences
Medical	sciences
Physical	sciences
Social	sciences
Space	sciences
	Scientific activities
	Scientific buildings
	Scientific communities
	Scientific cooperation
	Scientific cultures
	Scientific development
	Scientific discoveries
	Scientific equipment
	Scientific expeditions
	Scientific expenditure
	Scientific facilities
	Scientific information
	Scientific information systems
	Scientific initiation
	Scientific innovations
	Scientific institutions
	Scientific libraries
	Scientific organizations
	Scientific periodicals
	Scientific personnel
	Scientific personnel training
	Scientific potential
	Scientific programmes
	Scientific progress
	Scientific publications
	Scientific research
	Scientific research results
	Scientific terminology
Information	scientist-user relationship
	Scientists

Information	scientists
Social	scientists
	Sciosophic movements
	Scope notes
Music	scores
	Scotland
West	Scotland Inland Sea
	Scripts
Ancient	scripts
Film	scripts
Ideographic	scripts
Pictographic	scripts
	Scriptures
	Scriptwriters
	Sculptors
	Sculpture
Adriatic	Sea
Aegean	Sea
Alboran	Sea
Andaman	Sea
Arabian	Sea
Arafura	Sea
Balearic	Sea
Bali	Sea
Baltic	Sea
Banda	Sea
Barents	Sea
Beaufort	Sea
Bering	Sea
Bismarck	Sea
Black	Sea
Caribbean	Sea
Caspian	Sea
Celebes	Sea
Ceram	Sea
Chukchi	Sea
Coral	Sea
Dead	Sea
Deep	sea
East China	sea
East Siberian	Sea
Flores	Sea
Greenland	Sea
Halmahra	Sea
Ionian	Sea
Irish	Sea
Java	Sea
Kara	Sea
Labrador	Sea
Laccadive	Sea
Laptev	Sea
Law of the	sea
Ligurian	Sea
Lincoln	Sea
Mediterranean	Sea
Molucca	Sea
North	Sea
Norwegian	Sea
Philippine	Sea
Red	Sea
Savu	Sea
Seto Naikai Inland	Sea
Solomon	Sea
South China	Sea
Sulu	Sea
Tasman	Sea
Timor	Sea
Tyrrhenian	Sea
West Scotland Inland	Sea
White	Sea

Yellow Sea
Sea fishing
Deep sea fishing
Sea ice
Sea level
Sea level measurement
Sea of Azov
Sea of Japan
Sea of Marmara
Sea of Okhotsk
Sea transport
Sea water
Sea water acoustic measurements
Sea water acoustic properties
Sea water analysis
Sea water composition
Sea water density
Sea water density measurement
Sea water measurements
Sea water optical measurements
Sea water optical properties
Sea water pressure
Sea water pressure measurement
Sea water properties
Sea water temperature
Sea water temperature measurement
Seals
Search and seizure
Search cut-off
Post -search editing
Search output
Search process
Search profiles
Search questions
Search revision
Retrospective search services
Search strategies
Search warrants
Literature searches
Searching
Batch searching
Contextual searching
Natural language searching
On-line searching
Random searching
Retrospective searching
Text searching
Seas
East India Archipelago seas
Seasonal migration
Seasons
Seaweeds
Second homes
Second language
Second-hand books
Secondary documents
Secondary education
Lower secondary education
Middle secondary education
Upper secondary education
Secondary school curriculum
Secondary school leaving
Secondary school libraries
Secondary school teachers
Secondary teacher training
Secret ballot
Secret societies
Sectarianism
Private sector
Public sector

Sects
Collective security
Right to social security
Social security
State security
Sediment
Sediment control
Sediment transport
Sedimentary rocks
Sedimentation
Sedimentology
Holy See
Seeds
Seepage
Racial segregation
Seine nets
Seiners
Seismic areas
Seismicity
Seismological observatories
Seismology
Seismometers
Search and seizure
Book selection
Competitive selection
Group selection
Natural selection
Personnel selection
Student selection
Selective dissemination of information
Selenium
Self-defence (war)
Right of self-determination
Self-discipline
Self-employed
Self-esteem
Self-governing educational bodies
Non -self-governing territories
Self-government
Self-teaching methods
Best sellers
Semantic analysis
Semantic factoring
Semantic relations
Semantics
Semi-current records
Semi-published documents
Semi-skilled workers
Semiconductor physics
Semiconductors
Semimicroanalysis
Seminars
Semiology
Semisolids
Hamito -Semitic and Caucasian languages
Semitic languages
Hamito -Semitic languages
Semitic people
Senegal
Sensation
Smell (sense)
Sensorimotor activities
Sensors
Sensory aids
Sensory aids (teaching)
Extra -sensory perception
Sensory process psychology
Sensory system diseases
Sensory systems
Prison sentences

373

Residential social work
Voluntary social work
Group work (social work)
Social workers
Social workers training
Socialism
Vietnam (Socialist Republic)
Union of Soviet Socialist Republics
Socialization
Socially disadvantaged
Socially disadvantaged children
Affluent societies
Consumer societies
Industrial societies
Learned societies
Multiracial societies
Non-industrialized societies
Post-industrial societies
Secret societies
Society
Changing society
Contemporary society
Future society
Mass society
Society Islands
Socio-cultural action
Socio-cultural activities
Socio-cultural centres
Socio-cultural clubs
Socio-economic analysis
Socio-economic factors
Socio-economic indicators
Socio-economic status
Sociodrama
Sociography
Sociolinguistics
Sociologists
Sociology
Archaeological sociology
Cultural sociology
Economic sociology
Educational sociology
Industrial sociology
Occupational sociology
Political sociology
Rural sociology
Student sociology
Urban sociology
Sociology of art
Sociology of change
Sociology of communication
Sociology of knowledge
Sociology of law
Sociology of leisure
Sociology of religion
Sociology of research
Sociology of science
Sociometry
Sodium
Computer software
Softwood
Soil chemistry
Soil compaction
Soil conservation
Soil constituents
Soil deterioration
Soil erosion
Soil fertility
Soil genesis
Soil maps

Soil mechanics
Soil moisture
Soil physics
Soil pollution
Soil profiles
Soil properties
Soil resources
Soil science
Soil surveys
Soil temperature
Soil water
Soils
Clay soils
Desert soils
Peat soils
Salt affected soils
Sandy soils
Saturated soils
Unsaturated soils
Volcanic soils
Solar cells
Solar corona
Solar disturbances
Solar eclipses
Solar heating
Solar power engineering
Solar power generation
Solar radiation
Solar stills
Solar system
Rights of soldiers
Solid solutions
Solid state phase transformations
Solid state physics
Solidification
Solids
Mechanics of solids
Physics of solids
Solitary confinement
Solomon Islands
British Solomon Islands
Solomon Sea
Sols
Solubility
Solutes
Solution chemistry
Solutions
Solid solutions
Solvents
Problem solving
Somali
Somalia
Sonar
Sonar navigation
Songs
Folk songs
Sorption
Sorption technology
Sorrow
Sorting
Underwater sound
Sound and music
Sound cassettes
Sound insulation
Sound recording
Sound recordings
Sound velocity
Sound velocity meters
Sound wave propagation
Echo sounders

Stamp collecting
Postage stamps
Standard deviation
Standard error
Standard of living
Standardization
Standards
Bibliographic standards
Building standards
Educational standards
Examination standards
Information/library standards
International standards
Physical standards
Professional standards
Right to adequate living standards
Teacher professional standards
Teaching standards
Standing water
Stars
State
Amorphous state
Church and state
Crystalline state
Head of state
Unitary state
State aid
State and education
State budget
State libraries
Solid state phase transformations
Solid state physics
State responsibility
State responsibility for education
State security
State succession
Statelessness
Financial statements
Anxiety states
Equality of states
Gulf States
Himalayan States
Member states
Newly-independent states
Rights of states
United States of America
States of matter
Static electricity
Statics
Chemical statics
Diesel power stations
Electric power stations
Gas turbine power stations
Geothermal power stations
Hydroelectric power stations
Nuclear power stations
Ocean stations
Pumping stations
Radio stations
Railway stations
Space stations
Steam power stations
Television stations
Thermal power stations
Tidal power stations
Wind power stations
Statistical analysis
Statistical data
Statistical design
Statistical dispersion

Statistical distributions
Statistical inference
Statistical linguistics
Statistical linguistics (indexing)
Statistical mathematics
Statistical mechanics
Statistical methods
Statistical physics
Statistical tests
Statistics
Communication statistics
Cultural statistics
Descriptive statistics
Educational statistics
Film production statistics
Information/library statistics
Museum statistics
Non-parametric statistics
Science statistics
Statistics education
Statistics presentation
Amateur status
Information/library
professional status
Legal status
Marital status
Occupational status
Professional status
Social status
Socio-economic status
Teacher status
Statutes
Statutory bodies
Steam engineering
Steam power
Steam power stations
Steam turbines
Iron and steel making
Steels
Stainless steels
Stencil printing
Steppe
Stereochemistry
Stereophonic recordings
National stereotype
Stills
Solar stills
Stimulus
Fiction stock
Information/library stock
Library stock
Non-fiction stock
Joint stock companies
Stock farming
Stock revision
Stock-taking (document)
Stone age
Building stones
Storage
Digital storage
Document storage
Heat storage
Water storage
Computer storage devices
Information storage devices
Romance stories
Storms
Story hours
Story telling
Mental strain
Strain measurement

Bass Strait
Davis Strait
Hudson Strait
Makassar Strait
Malacca Strait
Singapore Strait
Strait of Gibraltar
Straits
Strategic planning
Strategies
Communication strategies
Development strategies
Educational strategies
Search strategies
Teaching strategies
Military strategy
Research strategy
Ocean stratification
Social stratification
Stratigraphy
Stratosphere
Oceanic stratosphere
Straw
Streamflow
Streams
Underground streams
Street furniture design
Street lighting
Mechanical strength
Stress (mechanical)
Stress (psychological)
Stress analysis
Photoelastic stress analysis
Strikes
Teacher strikes
String instruments
Strings (terms)
Film strips
Strontium
Structural analysis
Structural elements (buildings)
Structural engineering
Structural members
Structuralism
Administrative structure
Agrarian structure
Atomic structure
Chemical structure
Crystal atomic structure
Crystal structure
Earths structure
Economic structure
Educational administrative structure
Liquid structure
Market structure
Molecular structure
Ocean structure
Social structure
Nuclear structure and properties
Structure of knowledge
Structures
Archaeological structures
Hydraulic structures
Tree structures
Student assistants
Student attitude
Student behaviour
Exceptional student education
Student employment

Student exchanges
Student housing
Student interests
Student leisure
Student loans
Student mobility
Student movements
Student organizations
Student participation
Student progress
Student projects
Teacher -student ratio
School -student relationship
Teacher -student relationship
Student selection
Student sociology
Student teachers
Student transportation
Student unrest
Students
Adult students
Backward students
Exceptional students
Foreign students
Gifted students
Men students
Rights of students
Women students
Students (college)
Case studies
Cultural studies
History and associated studies
Information user studies
Movement studies
Practical studies
Social studies
Theoretical cultural studies
Radio studios
Television studios
Study
Compulsory study
Independent study
Individual study
Organization and
methods study
Voluntary study
Work study
Curriculum study centres
Library work (study method)
Study methods
Study periods
Study tours
Literary style
Art styles
Life styles
Sub-headings
Subconscious
Subcultures
Subject catalogues
Alphabetical subject catalogues
Subject cataloguing
Alphabetical subject heading lists
Subject headings
Subject indexes
Alphabetical subject indexes
Subject indexing
Curriculum subjects
Sublimation
Submarine cable laying
Submarine canyons
Submarine earthquakes

Submarine geology
Submarine mineral deposits
Submarine plains
Submarine ridges
Submarine topography
Submarine valleys
Submarine volcanoes
Submarines
Educationally subnormal
Subordination
Subroutines
Subscription libraries
Subscriptions
Land subsidence
Subsidies
Subsistence agriculture
Electrical properties of substances
Living substances
Magnetic properties of substances
Mechanical properties of substances
Optical properties of substances
Thermal properties of substances
Substations
Substructures
Suburbs
Subventions
Subversive activities
Social success
State succession
Sudan
Sudanic languages
Gulf of Suez
Suffering
Womens suffrage
Sugar beet
Sugar cane
Suicide
Sulphate minerals
Sulphur
Sulu Sea
Summer schools
Summons
Sun
Sunlight
Superconductivity
Superconductors
Superior orders
Superiority complex
Superordination
Superstition
Superstructures
Supervision
Educational supervision
School supervision
Teacher supervision
Supervisors
Supervisory and executive programs
Supply
Cultural supply
Gas supply
Labour supply
Teacher supply
Water supply
Supply and demand
Water supply industry
Financial support
Political support
Educational support personnel
Information/library support personnel
Ground support systems

Life support systems
Fans (supporters)
Interference suppression
Supreme court
Surf
Surface chemistry
Surface films
Surface physics
Dispersion and surface physics
Surface tension
Surface water
Surfaces
Surgery
Brain surgery
Plastic surgery
Surges
Surgical instruments
Surinam
Volcano surveillance
Survey analysis
Survey data
Surveying
Aerial surveying
Archaeological surveying
Hydrographic surveying
Surveying instruments
Surveys
Economic surveys
Sample surveys
Soil surveys
Diplomatic relations suspension
Suspensions
Swahili
Swamps
Swaziland
Sweden
Swedish
Swimming
Swimming pools
Switches
Switchgear
Logic and switching circuits
Switching languages
Switching theory
Switzerland
Symbiosis
Symbolic languages
Symbolic learning
Symbols
Symmetrical conflict
Symposia
Symptoms of disease
Synecology
Synonym control
Synonyms
Quasi -synonyms
Synopses
Synoptic modelling
Syntactic analysis
Syntactic relations
Syntax
Synthesis (chemical)
Synthesised terms
Analytico-synthetic classification systems
Synthetic fibres
Synthetic food
Synthetic rubber
Syrian Arab Republic
Analytico-synthetic classification systems
Bliss classification system

Braille   system
Metric   system
Montessori   system
Solar   system
Digestive   system diseases
Locomotory   system diseases
Nervous   system diseases
Sensory   system diseases
Systematic chemical analysis
Systematic thesauri
Systemology
Acquisition   systems
Agricultural information   systems
Anatomical   systems
Astronomical bodies and   systems
Broad classification   systems
Capitalist   systems
Cardiovascular   systems
Classification   systems
Classification/thesaurus   systems
Close classification   systems
Communication   systems
Control   systems
Cooling   systems
Craft   systems
Cultural   systems
Digestive   systems
Economic   systems
Educational   systems
Electoral   systems
Electric power   systems
Endocrine   systems
Engineering information   systems
Faceted classification   systems
Farming   systems
Fast-response computer   systems
Free language   systems
Frontal   systems
Ground support   systems
Haemic and lymphatic   systems
Heating   systems
Hierarchical classification   systems
Information   systems
Information/library   systems
International economic   systems
International information   systems
International monetary   systems
Irrigation   systems
Labour   systems
Legal information   systems
Legal   systems
Life support   systems
Locomotory   systems
Low pressure   systems
Lubrication   systems
Man-machine   systems
Management information   systems
Mechanical transmission   systems
Medical information   systems
Medical records information   systems
Monetary   systems
Monitorial   systems
Multiaccess   systems
Multiparty   systems
Multiprocessing   systems
National information   systems
Natural language   systems
Nervous   systems
On-line information   systems
On-line   systems

One-party   systems
Operator   systems
Optical coincidence   systems
Parallel processing   systems
Parliamentary   systems
Periodical acquisition   systems
Political   systems
Presidential   systems
Real-time   systems
Religious   systems
Respiratory   systems
Restraint   systems
Sampled data   systems
School   systems
Scientific information   systems
Sensory   systems
Social   systems
Teaching   systems
Time-sharing   systems
Two-party   systems
Urogenital   systems
Writing   systems
Operating   systems (computer)
Systems analysis
Educational   systems and institutions
Acquisition   systems automation
Haemic and lymphatic   systems diseases
Program and   systems documentation
Information   systems evaluation
Historical   systems of law
Systems of medicine
Tables
Educational time -tables
Tablets (documents)
Taboos
Tacheometry
Tactile aids
Tagalog
Tahitian
Taiga
Taiwan
Stock -taking (document)
Talent
Fairy   tales
Talking books
Tamil
Electrolytic   tanks
Water   tanks
Tantalum
Tanzania (United Republic)
Taoism
Tape recorders
Magnetic   tape recordings
Video   tape recordings
Tape services
Magnetic   tapes
Punched   tapes
Tapestry
Tariff barriers
Tariffs
Tasman Sea
Tasmania
Tasmanian languages
Taste
Public   taste
Consumption   tax
Income   tax
Taxation
Taxonomy
Animal   taxonomy

Botanical taxonomy
Teach-ins (teaching method)
Teacher aides
Teacher associations
Teacher attitude
Teacher authority
Teacher behaviour
Teacher centres
Teacher certification
Teacher conditions of employment
Teacher dismissal
Teacher educator training
Teacher educators
Teacher guides
Teacher leave
Teacher librarians
Parent-teacher organizations
Teacher participation
Teacher professional ethics
Teacher professional standards
Teacher promotion
Teacher qualifications
Teacher recruitment
Parent-teacher relationship
Teacher responsibility
Teacher retirement
Teacher role
Teacher salaries
One-teacher schools
Teacher shortage
Teacher sick leave
Teacher status
Teacher strikes
Teacher supervision
Teacher supply
Teacher trade unions
Teacher training
In-service teacher training
Pre-primary teacher training
Pre-service teacher training
Primary teacher training
Secondary teacher training
Special teacher training
Vocational teacher training
Teacher training curriculum
Teacher training schools
Teacher-administrator relationship
Teacher-student ratio
Teacher-student relationship
Teachers
Itinerant teachers
Married women teachers
Part-time teachers
Pre-primary school teachers
Primary school teachers
Secondary school teachers
Special education teachers
Student teachers
Visiting teachers
Vocational school teachers
Women teachers
Teaching
Automatic teaching
Diagrammatical teaching
Language teaching
Practice teaching
Sleep teaching
Team teaching
Teaching abroad
Teaching aids

Initial teaching alphabet
Teaching load
Teaching machines
Teaching materials and equipment
Teaching method innovations
Debates (teaching method)
Discussions (teaching method)
Dramatic presentation (teaching method)
Group work (teaching method)
Play (teaching method)
Questioning (teaching method)
Teach-ins (teaching method)
Teaching methods
Self-teaching methods
Academic teaching personnel
Teaching profession
Teaching skills
Teaching standards
Teaching strategies
Teaching systems
Direct method (teaching)
Heuristic method (teaching)
Project method (teaching)
Sensory aids (teaching)
Team teaching
Technetium
Technical assistance
Technical colleges
Technical drawing
Technical drawings
Technical education
General technical education
Higher technical education
Higher technical personnel
Television and radio technical personnel
Technical reports
Technical training
Technical writing
Technicians
Educational technicians
Library technicians
Techniques
Computer techniques
Conservation techniques
High pressure techniques
High temperature techniques
Management techniques
Museum techniques
Research techniques
Technocracy
Technological change
Technological gap
Technological institutes
Technologists
Technology
Adhesives technology
Cement and concrete technology
Ceramics technology
Chemical technology
Cleaning agents technology
Coal technology
Communication technology
Control technology
Diffusion of technology
Dyes technology
Educational technology
Evaporation technology
Explosives technology
Extraction technology
Food technology

Fuel technology
Gas technology
Glass technology
Implantation of technology
Interdisciplinary science and technology
Isotope technology
Laundry technology
Leather technology
Lime and gypsum technology
Liquefaction technology
Medical technology
Mixing technology
Paint technology
Paper technology
Petrochemicals technology
Petroleum technology
Pharmaceutical technology
Polymer and plastics technology
Processing agents technology
Radiation technology
Rubber technology
Science and technology
Science of science and technology
Separation technology
Sorption technology
Space technology
Textile technology
Underwater technology
Vegetable and animal oils technology
Wood technology
Technology transfer
Horizontal technology transfer
International technology transfer
Vertical technology transfer
Technology transfer services
Tectonic maps
Tectonics
Teflon
Teleclubs
Telecommunication
Telecommunication industry
Telecommunication links
Teleconferencing
Telegraphy
Telegu
Telemetry
Teleology
Telepathy
Telephone
Telephone engineering
Telephotography
Teleprinters
Teleprocessing
Telerecording
Telescopes
Astronomical telescopes
Televiewers
Televiewing
Television
Cable television
Closed circuit television
Colour television
Commercial television
Educational television
Television advertising
Television and radio directors
Television and radio industry
Television and radio personnel
Television and radio personnel training
Television and radio producers

Television and radio technical personnel
Television cameras
Television channels
Television documentaries
Television drama
Television engineering
Television films
Television games
Television news
Television production
Television programmes
Television receivers
Television serials
Television stations
Television studios
Television transmitters
Telex
Fortune -telling
Story telling
Tellurium
Temperate zones
Temperature
Atmospheric temperature
Body temperature
Sea water temperature
Soil temperature
Water temperature
Temperature control
Temperature distribution
Sea water temperature measurement
Temperature measurement and instruments
Temperature probes
High temperature techniques
High temperatures
Low temperatures
Temples
Tenancy
Central tendency
International tension
Surface tension
Tensors
Land tenure
Educational term
Term co-occurrence
Term frequency (use)
Term interrelations
Term lists
Computer terminals
Termination of service
Terminological control
Terminology
Communication terminology
Educational terminology
Scientific terminology
Termites
Bound terms
Broader terms
Compound terms
Index terms
Lead-in terms
Modifier terms
Narrower terms
Related terms
Synthesised terms
Classes (terms)
Strings (terms)
Terrestrial age
Terrestrial ecosystems
Terrestrial environment
Terrestrial heat

Terrestrial rotation
Territorial air space
Territorial rights
Territorial waters
Atlantic Ocean Territories
Indian Ocean Territories
Non-self-governing territories
Occupied territories
Trust territories
Terrorism
Tertiary period
Testing
Destructive testing
Educational testing
Materials testing
Non-destructive testing
Program testing
Tests
Achievement tests
Aptitude tests
Intelligence tests
Psychological tests
Reading tests
Statistical tests
Tetanus
Text
Automatic text analysis
Text searching
Textbook production
Textbooks
Textile arts
Textile industry
Textile machinery
Textile processes
Textile technology
Textiles
Thai languages
Thailand
Gulf of Thailand
Thallium
Thallophyta
Theatre
Amateur theatre
Ancient theatre
Commercial theatre
National theatre
Open air theatre
Popular theatre
Repertory theatre
Total theatre
Traditional theatre
Travelling theatre
Theatre agents
Theatre attendance
Theatre buildings
Theatre capacity
Theatre directors
Theatre management
Theatre producers
Lecture theatres
Library theatres
Theatrical companies
Theatrical life
Theatrical performances
Theatrical production
Theft
Theft protection
Theocracy
Theology
Theoretical cultural studies

Theoretical physics
Theory
Approximation theory
Automata theory
Communication and information theory
Control theory
Decision theory
Economic theory
Educational theory
Game theory
Graph theory
Group theory
Information theory
Legal theory
Linguistic theory
Management theory
Musical theory
Nuclear reactor theory
Number theory
Political theory
Probability theory
Quantum field theory
Quantum theory
Queueing theory
Renewal theory
Sampling theory
Schools of legal theory
Set theory
Switching theory
Therapeutic documents
Therapeutic equipment
Therapy
Occupational therapy
Speech therapy
Theravada
Thermal chemical analysis
Thermal conductivity
Thermal diffusion
Thermal diffusivity
Thermal engineering
Thermal insulation
Thermal measurements and instruments
Thermal power stations
Thermal properties of substances
Thermal reactors
Thermal resistance
Thermal springs
Thermal variables control
Thermionic conversion
Thermistor chains
Thermistors
Thermochemistry
Thermoclines
Thermocouples
Thermodynamic properties
Thermodynamics
Atmospheric thermodynamics
Chemical thermodynamics
Thermoelectric conversion
Thermoelectric devices
Thermoelectricity
Thermometers
Thesauri
Alphabetical thesauri
Monolingual thesauri
Multilingual thesauri
Systematic thesauri
Thesaurus compilation
Classification /thesaurus systems
Theses

Thin films
Thinking
Creative thinking
Thorium
Right to freedom of thought
Thought process development
Communication (thought transfer)
Thriller films
Thrillers
Tibet
Tibetan
Sino -Tibetan languages
Tibeto-Burmese languages
Tidal constant
Tidal currents
Tidal curve
Tidal cycle
Tidal effects
Tidal energy
Tidal friction
Tidal lamination
Tidal power stations
Tidal prediction
Tidal range
Tidal rise
Tidal waters
Tide gauges
Tide measurement
Tides
Wind tides
Tiles
Time
Leisure time
School time
Working time
Leisure time activities
Time budgets
Part -time courses
Full -time employment
Part -time employment
Part -time librarians
Time measurement and instruments
Time series
Real -time systems
Part -time teachers
Time-sharing programs
Time-sharing systems
Educational time-tables
Portuguese Timor
Timor Sea
Tin
Titanium
Title catalogues
Title cataloguing
Title indexes
Title indexing
Titles
Tobacco
Trinidad and Tobago
Togo
Tokelau Islands
Tolerance
Racial tolerance
Measurement tolerances
Sao Tome and Principe
Gulf of Tomini
Tonga
Mother tongue
Mother tongue instruction
Machine tools

Top management
Topography
Submarine topography
Topology
Tornadoes
Torso
Torts
Torture
Total theatre
Totalitarianism
Totemism
Touch
Tourism
Cultural tourism
Weekend tourism
Tourist accommodation
Tourist facilities
Tourist industry
Study tours
Water towers
Town reconstruction
Towns
Expanded towns
Industrial towns
New towns
Overspill towns
Small towns
Toxicology
Toy manufacture
Toys
Educational toys
Trace analysis
Trace elements
Radioactive tracers
Tracking
Railway tracks
Trade
Balance of trade
Free trade
Home trade
International trade
Retail trade
Wholesale trade
Trade literature
Trade marks
Trade union rights
Trade unions
Teacher trade unions
Tradesmen
Oral tradition
Written tradition
Traditional cultures
Traditional music
Traditional theatre
Traditionalism
Customs and traditions
Traffic
Air traffic
Marine traffic
Rail traffic
Road traffic
Urban traffic
Tragedy
Trainees
Sports trainers
Training
Agricultural training
Archive science training
Basic training
Book production training

Communication personnel training
Communication planners training
Cultural agents training
Cultural personnel training
Educational personnel training
Film-making training
Further training
Group training
In-service teacher training
In-service training
Industrial training
Information/library training
Job training
Journalist training
Museum training
Practical training
Pre-primary teacher training
Pre-service teacher training
Primary teacher training
Professional training
Publishers training
Research training
Scientific personnel training
Secondary teacher training
Social workers training
Special teacher training
Teacher educator training
Teacher training
Technical training
Television and radio
personnel training
Vocational teacher training
Vocational training
Training abroad
Training centres
Training courses
Industrial training courses
Teacher training curriculum
Training groups
Training methods
Training officers
International training programmes
Apprentice training schools
Teacher training schools
Trains
Traits
Transcription
Transducers
Pressure transducers
Copyright transfer
Energy transfer
Heat transfer
Horizontal technology transfer
Information transfer
International technology transfer
Mass transfer
Radiative transfer
Technology transfer
Vertical technology transfer
Transfer (job)
Technology transfer services
Communication (thought transfer)
Educational transfers
Phase transformations
Solid state phase transformations
Transformers
Transforms
Fourier transforms
Transistors
Transition classes
Transition from school to work

Translation
Automatic translation
Translation services
Translations
Translators
Transliteration
Data transmission
Electric power transmission
News transmission
Transmission lines
Electric power transmission lines
Mechanical transmission systems
Transmitters
Radio transmitters
Television transmitters
Transnational crime
Transnational enterprises
Transparencies
Transparency
Plant transpiration
Organ transplantation
Transport
Air transport
Freight transport
Inland water transport
International transport
Land transport
Library transport
Private transport
Public transport
Railway transport
Road transport
Rural transport
Sea transport
Sediment transport
Urban transport
Water transport
Transport economics
Transport engineering
Transport infrastructure
Transport planning
Transport policy
Transport processes (physics)
Transport safety
Student transportation
Travel
Travel abroad
Travel grants
Travelling exhibitions
Travelling theatre
Trawl nets
Trawlers
Ill-treated children
Treaties
Non-proliferation treaties
Peace treaties
Air pollution treatment
Heat treatment
Inhuman treatment
Medical treatment
Metal treatment
Right to freedom
from inhuman treatment
Sewage treatment
Shock treatment
Waste treatment
Water treatment
Tree structures
Trees
Educational trends
Enrolment trends

Research trends
Trespass
Trial by jury
Trial in camera
Trials
Political trials
Triangulation
Tribal conflict
Tribalism
Tribes
Tribology
Administrative tribunals
Trigonometry
Trinidad and Tobago
Library trolleys
Tropical diseases
Tropical forests
Tropical zones
Troposphere
Oceanic troposphere
Folklore troupes
Truancy
Truces
Trucks
Truncation
Trust territories
Trusts
Truth
Tsunami
Tuamotu Islands
Tuberculosis
Electron tubes
Pitot tubes
Tubuai Islands
Tundra
Tungsten
Tungus
Tunisia
Tunnels
Turbidimetry
Gas turbine power stations
Turbines
Gas turbines
Steam turbines
Water turbines
Turbulence
Turbulent flow
Turkey
Turkish
Turks and Caicos Islands
Labour turnover
Tutorials
Tutoring
Two-chamber legislature
Two-party systems
Two-way communication
National school types
Machine typesetting
Typhoid
Typhoons
Typological analysis
Typology
Tyranny
Tyrrhenian Sea
UDC
Uganda
Virgin Islands (UK)
Ukrainian
Ukrainian SSR
Ultimatum

Ultrasonics
Ultraviolet radiation
Uncertainty
Unconscious
Unconventional warfare
Underdevelopment
Underemployment
Undergraduates
Underground mining
Underground press
Underground railways
Underground streams
Underprivileged youth
International understanding
Underwater cameras
Underwater communication
Underwater construction
Underwater excavation
Underwater navigation
Underwater oil and gas extraction
Underwater photography
Underwater salvage
Underwater sound
Underwater technology
Unemployed
Unemployment
Youth unemployment
UNESCO awards and honours
UNESCO clubs
UNESCO coupons
UNESCO public liaison
UNESCO publications
UNESCO voluntary assistance
Linguistic unification
Union catalogues
Union catalogues of periodicals
Union of Soviet Socialist Republics
Trade union rights
Teacher trade unions
Trade unions
Unit entries
Unitary state
United Arab Emirates
United Kingdom
Tanzania (United Republic)
United States of America
Uniterms
Units of measurement
Academic unity
Universal culture
Universe
Universities
International universities
Open universities
University campuses
University colleges
University cooperation
University courses
University curriculum
University extension
University institutes
University libraries
Pre-university science education
Unmarried
Unmarried mothers
Unpublished documents
Social unrest
Student unrest
Youth unrest
Unsaturated soils

Untapped public
Unwritten languages
Upper atmosphere
Upper class
Upper house
Upper secondary education
Upper Volta
Uralic languages
Uranium
Urban areas
Urban centres
Urban decentralization
Urban design
Urban development
Urban education
Urban environment
Urban expansion
Urban planning
Development areas (urban planning)
Urban population
Urban renewal
Urban sociology
Urban spaces
Urban sprawl
Urban traffic
Urban transport
Urban warfare
Urban youth
Urbanization
Urdu
Urogenital diseases
Urogenital systems
Uruguay
Junior colleges (USA)
Virgin Islands (USA)
Information use
Land use
Book use frequency
Library use promotion
Term frequency (use)
Information user habits
Information user instruction
Information user needs
Documentalist -user relationship
Information scientist -user relationship
Librarian -user relationship
Information user studies
Communication users
Cultural users
Information users
Library users
Museum users
Polytechnic schools (USSR)
Public utilities
Utility programs
Water utilization
Utopia
Vaccination
Vacuum engineering
Vacuum measurement
Vacuum metallurgy
Vacuum physics
Vagrants
Validity
Valleys
Submarine valleys
Value
Economic value
Land value
Value judgment

Cultural values
Moral values
Social values
Valves
Vanadium
Vandalism
Vaporization
Water vapour
Vapours
Variability
Ocean variability
Variable costs
Control of specific variables
Electrical variables control
Magnetic variables control
Mechanical variables control
Optical variables control
Thermal variables control
Chemical variables measurement
Variance analysis
Variational calculus
Diurnal variations
Language varieties
Variety shows
Vectors
Vegetable and animal oils technology
Vegetable oils
Vegetables
Vegetation
Vegetation maps
Road vehicle engineering
Vehicles
Armoured vehicles
Land vehicles
Library vehicles
Motor vehicles
Road vehicles
Space vehicles
Velocity
Ocean wave velocity
Sound velocity
Velocity measurement
Sound velocity meters
Venereal diseases
Venezuela
Venturimeters
Non -verbal communication
Verbal learning
Cape Verde Islands
Verification
Vernacular languages
Vertebrata
Vertebrate palaeontology
Vertical technology transfer
Blood vessels
Fishing vessels
Veterinary education
Veterinary medicine
Vibration measurement
Vibrations
Virtue and vice
Crime victims
Video cassettes
Video clubs
Video discs
Video recorders
Video recording
Video recordings
Video tape recordings
Videotelephone

Sea water analysis
Water balance
Water chemistry
Sea water composition
Water conservation
Water consumption
Water corrosion
Water currents
Water damage
Water demineralization
Sea water density
Sea water density measurement
Water discharge
Water distribution
Brackish water environment
Water features
Water hammer
Water hardness
Water law
Water level
Water loss
Water mains
Water masses
Sea water measurements
Sea water optical measurements
Sea water optical properties
Water pollution
Water power
Water pressure
Sea water pressure
Sea water pressure measurement
Water properties
Sea water properties
Water recreational areas
Water requirements
Water resources
Water resources development
Water resources management
Water sampling
Water services (buildings)
Water shortages
Water sources
Water storage
Water supply
Water supply industry
Water tanks
Water temperature
Sea water temperature
Sea water temperature measurement
Water towers
Water transport
Inland water transport
Water treatment
Water turbines
Water utilization
Water vapour
Water waves
Water yield
Waterfalls
Waterlogging
Alaska Coastal Waters
Coastal waters
Regime of waters
Territorial waters
Tidal waters
Watersheds
Waterway engineering
Locks (waterways)
Ocean wave action
Ocean wave base

Ocean wave crest
Ocean wave decay
Ocean wave energy
Wave frequency
Ocean wave frequency
Ocean wave front
Ocean wave growth
Ocean wave height
Radio wave interference
Ocean wave length
Ocean wave measurement
Wave mechanics
Ocean wave motion
Wave physics
Ocean wave profile
Wave propagation
Sound wave propagation
Wave recorders
Ocean wave velocity
Absorption (wave)
Waveguides
Wavelength
Electromagnetic waves
Fluid waves
Internal waves
Ocean waves
Radio waves
Water waves
Milky Way
One-way communication
Two-way communication
Wealth
Weapons
Conventional weapons
Nuclear weapons
Wear
Weather
Weather forecasting
Weather modification
Weed control
Weekend tourism
Weekly
Weekly publications
Weight (mass)
Weight measurement
Weights
Weirs
Welding
Child welfare
Educational welfare
Right to social welfare
Social welfare
Social welfare administration
Social welfare aims
Social welfare economics
Social welfare finance
Social welfare organizations
Voluntary welfare organizations
Social welfare philosophy
Social welfare planning
Welfare policy
Wells
Welsh
West Africa
West Scotland Inland Sea
Western Europe
Western Hemisphere
Western Samoa
Wetlands
White collar workers

White people
White Sea
Part -whole relations
Wholesale trade
Widowers
Widows
Wild animals
Wild plants
Wildlife
Wildlife protection
Will
Free -will
Winches
Wind
Wind driven currents
Wind instruments
Wind measurement
Wind power
Wind power stations
Wind tides
Windings (electric)
Windows
Winter sports
Wire ropes
Electric wiring
Witchcraft
Document withdrawal
Witnesses
Women
Equal rights of men and women
Married women
Working women
Women librarians
Married women librarians
Women students
Women teachers
Married women teachers
Married women workers
Womens education
Womens employment
Womens liberation movement
Womens organizations
Womens rights
Womens suffrage
Wood
Wood technology
Woodcarving
Woodworking
Wordform confounding
Blank words
Archaeological field work
Community work
Culture of work
Disaster relief work
Field work
Library circulation work
Library extension work
Missionary work
Oral work
Pastoral work
Press work
Reference work
Repetitive work
Research work
Residential social work
Right to work
Social work
Transition from school to work
Voluntary social work
Written work

Group work (social work)
Library work (study method)
Group work (teaching method)
Work attitude
Work study
Group work (social work)
Work-to-rule
Workers
Agricultural workers
Child workers
Factory workers
Foreign workers
Itinerant workers
Literacy workers
Manual workers
Married women workers
Office workers
Research workers
Semi-skilled workers
Skilled workers
Social workers
White collar workers
Young workers
Workers control
Workers education
Workers participation
Social workers training
Working class
Working class cultures
Working conditions
Working groups
Working mothers
Working time
Working women
Composite works
Literary works
Public works
Representative literary works
Works councils
Works of art
Preservation of works of art
Representative works of art
Workshops
Educational workshops
Printing workshops
Repair workshops
School workshops
World government
World population
World war
Rights of war wounded
War wounded
Writers
Writing
Creative writing
Cuneiform writing
Historical writing
Letter writing
Phonetic writing
Report writing
Technical writing
Writing systems
Written examinations
Written languages
Written tradition
Written work
X-ray analysis
X-ray chemical analysis
X-ray crystallography
X-ray diffraction

X-ray spectroscopy
X-rays
Xenon
Xerography
Educational year
International book year
Yearbooks
Yearly
Yellow Sea
Yemen (Peoples Democratic Republic)
Yemen Arab Republic
Water yield
Yoruba
Young adults
Young artists
Young workers
Youth
Out-of-school youth
Rural youth
Underprivileged youth
Urban youth
Youth activities
Youth clubs
Youth employment
Youth hostels
Youth leaders
Youth movements
Youth orchestras
Youth organizations
Youth participation
Youth unemployment
Youth unrest

Yttrium
Yugoslavia
Zaire
Zambia
New Zealand
Zinc
Zirconium
Abyssal zone
Bathyal zone
Benthic zone
Littoral zone
Panama Canal Zone
Pelagic zone
Arid zones
Climatic zones
Coastal zones
Cold zones
Equatorial zones
Humid zones
Marine ecological zones
Temperate zones
Tropical zones
Zoochemistry
Zoogeography
Zoohistology
Zoological gardens
Zoology
Experimental zoology
Zoopathology
Zoophysiology
Zooplankton
Zoroastrianism

HIERARCHICAL DISPLAY
OF THESAURUS TERMS

All the hierarchical chains contained in the Thesaurus are arranged in alphabetical order of the top term of their hierarchy. These top terms (TT) are given in the Alphabetical Thesaurus so that the latter can be used in conjunction with the hierarchical display. A term can appear in more than one hierarchical chain and also more than once in any particular hierarchy, e.g. the term 'Rights of war wounded' appears in two hierarchies with top terms 'Humanitarian law' and 'Rights and privileges' and appears twice in the latter hierarchy, as illustrated by the following:

Alphabetical Thesaurus   *Hierarchies*

Rights of war wounded   Humanitarian law   Rights and privileges
BT Humanitarian law   ...   ...
    Rights of soldiers   . *Rights of war wounded*   . Human rights
    Rights of special groups   ...
TT Humanitarian law   . . Rights of special groups
    Rights and privileges   ...
RT War wounded   . . . Rights of soldiers
                                                          ...
                                                . . . . *Rights of war wounded*
                                            . . . Rights of students
                                                         ...
                                            . . . Rights of the elderly
                                                         ...
                                            . . . *Rights of war wounded*

Ability
. Reading ability

Absorption (wave)
. Light absorption

Achievement
. Academic achievement

Administrative sciences
. Administration
. . Archive administration
. . . Archive legislation
. . Church administration
. . Communication administration
. . . Communication legislation
. . . . Broadcasting legislation
. . . . Copyright
. . Cultural administration
. . . Museum administration
. . . . Museum reorganization
. . Educational administration
. . . Educational cooperation
. . . . University cooperation
. . . Educational coordination
. . . Educational legislation
. . . Educational supervision
. . . . Educational inspection
. . . . School supervision
. . . . Teacher supervision
. . Financial administration
. . . Accounting
. . . . Auditing
. . . . Cost accounting
. . . . Cultural accounting
. . . . . Cultural budgets
. . . . . . Household cultural budgets
. . . . . Cultural expenditure
. . . Business formation
. . . . Mergers
. . . Capital raising
. . . . Investment appraisal
. . . Educational financial management
. . . . Educational expenditure
. . . . . Educational wages
. . . . . . Teacher salaries
. . . . . Teacher salaries
. . . . Educational income
. . . . Educational fees
. . Information/library administration
. . . Information/library legislation
. . . Information/library management
. . Public administration
. . . Administration of justice
. . . . Legal practice and procedure
. . . . . Advocacy
. . . . . Brief preparation
. . . . . Court rules and procedures
. . . . . . Bail
. . . . . . Contempt of court
. . . . . . Remand in custody
. . . . . Evidence
. . . . . . Witnesses
. . . . . Hearings
. . . . . Legal advice
. . . . . Legal decisions
. . . . . . Appeals (legal)
. . . . . . Decrees
. . . . . . Injunctions

Administrative sciences (cont.)
. . . . Judgments
. . . . Acquittal
. . . . Conviction (legal)
. . . . Decrees
. . . . . . Mediation
. . . . Arbitration
. . . . Industrial arbitration
. . . . . . Conciliation
. . . . Industrial conciliation
. . . . Industrial arbitration
. . . . . . Industrial conciliation
. . . . Industrial arbitration
. . . . . Pleadings
. . . . . Summons
. . . . . Trials
. . . . . . Political trials
. . . . . . Trial by jury
. . . . . . Trial in camera
. . . Economic administration
. . . Educational administration
. . . . Educational cooperation
. . . . . University cooperation
. . . . Educational coordination
. . . . Educational legislation
. . . . Educational supervision
. . . . . Educational inspection
. . . . . School supervision
. . . . . Teacher supervision
. . . Environmental planning administration
. . . Social welfare administration
. . Science administration
. . Social science administration
. Management
. . Business management
. . . Financial administration
. . . . Accounting
. . . . . Auditing
. . . . . Cost accounting
. . . . . Cultural accounting
. . . . . . Cultural budgets
. . . . Household cultural budgets
. . . . . . Cultural expenditure
. . . . Business formation
. . . . . Mergers
. . . . Capital raising
. . . . . Investment appraisal
. . . . Educational financial management
. . . . . Educational expenditure
. . . . . . Educational wages
. . . . Teacher salaries
. . . . . . Teacher salaries
. . . . . Educational income
. . . . . Educational fees
. . . Industrial management
. . . . Factory management
. . . . Production management
. . . . . Process development
. . . . . Product development
. . . Marketing
. . . Personnel management
. . . . Recruitment
. . . . . Appointment to job
. . . . . Personnel selection
. . . . . . Group selection
. . . . . . Interviewing for job
. . . . . Teacher recruitment
. . Computer management
. . Cultural management
. . . Cinema management
. . . Theatre management
. . . . Stage management

Administrative sciences (cont.)
. . Educational management
. . . Educational financial management
. . . . Educational expenditure
. . . . . Educational wages
. . . . . . Teacher salaries
. . . . . Teacher salaries
. . . . Educational income
. . . . . Educational fees
. . Environmental management
. . . Environmental conservation
. . . . Amenities conservation
. . . . . Conservation of nature
. . . . . . Countryside conservation
. . . . Landscape protection
. . . . . . Nature reserves
. . . . . . Wildlife protection
. . . . . Countryside conservation
. . . . . . Landscape protection
. . . . . Noise control
. . . . Conservation of nature
. . . . . Countryside conservation
. . . . . . Landscape protection
. . . . . Nature reserves
. . . . . Wildlife protection
. . . Environmental monitoring
. . . Environmental planning
. . . . Environmental planning processes
. . . . . Amenities conservation
. . . . . . Conservation of nature
. . . . Countryside conservation
. . . . Landscape protection
. . . . Nature reserves
. . . . Wildlife protection
. . . . . . Countryside conservation
. . . . Landscape protection
. . . . . . Noise control
. . . . . Environmental design
. . . . . . Landscape design
. . . . . . Urban design
. . . . Street furniture design
. . . . . . Visual planning
. . . . Regional planning
. . . . Rural planning
. . . . . Countryside conservation
. . . . . Landscape protection
. . . . Transport planning
. . . . Urban planning
. . . . . Town reconstruction
. . . . . Urban decentralization
. . . . . Urban design
. . . . . . Street furniture design
. . . . . Urban development
. . . . . Urban expansion
. . . . . . Urban sprawl
. . . . . Urban renewal
. . . Noise control
. . . Pollution control
. . Forest management
. . Industrial management
. . . Factory management
. . . Production management
. . . . Process development
. . . . Product development
. . Information/library management
. . Joint management
. . Office management
. . Personnel management
. . . Recruitment
. . . . Appointment to job
. . . . Personnel selection
. . . . . Group selection

Administrative sciences (cont.)
. . . . . Interviewing for job
. . . . Teacher recruitment
. . Production management
. . . Process development
. . . Product development
. . Records management
. . . Correspondence management
. . . Files administration
. . . Records appraisal
. . . Records disposition
. . . . Records disposal
. . Research management
. . . Research coordination
. . . Research planning
. . Resource management
. . . Resource allocation
. . . Resource conservation
. . . . Conservation of nature
. . . . . Countryside conservation
. . . . . . Landscape protection
. . . . . Nature reserves
. . . . . Wildlife protection
. . . . Energy conservation
. . . . Soil conservation
. . . . Water conservation
. . . Resource development
. . . . Human resources development
. . . . Water resources development
. . . Water resources management
. . . . Hydrological forecasting
. . . . Water conservation
. . . . Water resources development
. . . . Water utilization

Administrative structure
. Educational administrative structure
. . Examination boards
. . Governing boards
. . Self-governing educational bodies

Admission
. Educational admission
. . Enrolment
. . . Dual enrolment
. . Readmission
. . Student selection
. . . Competitive selection
. Library admission

Age
. School-leaving age
. Terrestrial age

Agreements
. Collective agreements
. Cultural agreements
. Economic agreements
. International instruments
. . Bilateral agreements
. . Cultural agreements
. . Economic agreements
. . Reciprocal agreements
. . Treaties
. . . Non-proliferation treaties
. . . Peace treaties

Agricultural land
. Arable land
. Grazing land

Aims
. Cultural aims
. . Cultural democracy
. Educational aims
. . Educational goals
. Information/library aims
. Social welfare aims

Alloys
. Aluminium alloys
. Chromium alloys
. Copper alloys
. . Brass
. . Bronze
. Iron alloys
. . Steels
. . . Stainless steels
. Nickel alloys

Amateurs
. Amateur actors
. Amateur musicians
. Amateur sportsmen

Amenities
. Countryside
. Cultural heritage
. Cultural property
. . Monuments
. . . Historic monuments
. . Movable cultural property
. . Works of art
. . . Representative works of art
. Landscape
. Natural heritage
. Open spaces
. . Countryside
. . Green belts
. . Parks
. . . National parks
. . . Public gardens
. . . . Botanical gardens
. . . . Zoological gardens
. . Playgrounds
. . Playing fields
. . Urban spaces

Analysis
. Causal analysis
. Chemical analysis
. . Biochemical analysis
. . Chemical variables measurement
. . . Moisture measurement
. . . pH measurement
. . Chromatographic analysis
. . Electroanalysis
. . . Polarographic analysis
. . . Potentiometric analysis
. . Gas analysis
. . Gravimetric analysis
. . Instrumental analysis
. . Microanalysis
. . Optical chemical analysis

Analysis (cont.)
. . . Colorimetric analysis
. . . Spectrochemical analysis
. . Qualitative analysis
. . Quantitative analysis
. . Radiochemical analysis
. . Semimicroanalysis
. . Systematic chemical analysis
. . . Sampling (chemical analysis)
. . . . Water sampling
. . Thermal chemical analysis
. . Trace analysis
. . Volumetric analysis
. . Water analysis
. . . Sea water analysis
. . . Water sampling
. . X-ray chemical analysis
. Comparative analysis
. Content analysis
. Cross-cultural analysis
. Cross-national analysis
. Data analysis
. Ecological analysis
. Economic analysis
. . Cost/benefit analysis
. . Input-output analysis
. . Socio-economic analysis
. Historical analysis
. Linguistic analysis
. . Contextual analysis
. . Semantic analysis
. . Speech analysis
. . Statistical linguistics
. . . Statistical linguistics (indexing)
. . . . Associative indexing
. . . . . Clumping
. . . . . Clustering
. . . . . Discriminant analysis
. . Syntactic analysis
. Literary analysis
. Mathematical analysis
. . Calculus
. . . Differential calculus
. . . Integral calculus
. . . Variational calculus
. . Eigenvalues
. . Fourier analysis
. . Functional analysis
. . . Harmonic analysis
. . Numerical analysis
. . . Approximation theory
. . . . Least squares approximation
. . . Error analysis
. . . Graphical methods
. . . Interpolation
. . . Iterative methods
. . . Monte Carlo methods
. . . Numerical methods
. . Series (mathematics)
. . Transforms
. . . Fourier transforms
. Network analysis
. Role analysis
. Statistical analysis
. . Correlation
. . Economic analysis
. . . Cost/benefit analysis
. . . Input-output analysis
. . . Socio-economic analysis
. . Multivariate analysis
. . . Discriminant analysis
. . . Factor analysis

397

Analysis (cont.)
. . Optimization
. . Variance analysis
. Structural analysis
. Survey analysis
. Systems analysis
. Typological analysis

Anatomical systems
. Cardiovascular systems
. . Blood vessels
. . Heart
. Digestive systems
. Endocrine systems
. Haemic and lymphatic systems
. Locomotory systems
. Nervous systems
. . Brain
. . Sensory systems
. . . Hearing
. . . Sight
. . . Smell (sense)
. . . Taste
. . . Touch
. Respiratory systems
. Urogenital systems

Animals
. Amphibia
. Aquatic animals
. . Fish
. . . Freshwater fish
. . . Marine fish
. . . Shellfish
. . . . Crustacea
. . Marine animals
. . . Marine fish
. . . Shellfish
. . . . Crustacea
. . . Zooplankton
. . Shellfish
. . . Crustacea
. . Zooplankton
. Birds
. Camels
. Domestic animals
. . Livestock
. Insects
. Laboratory animals
. Mammals
. . Camels
. . Primates
. . . Human species
. Reptiles
. Wild animals
. . Game animals

Antiquities
. Antiques
. Archaeological objects
. Historic monuments
. Works of art
. . Representative works of art

Aptitude
. Skill
. . Teaching skills

Aquaculture
. Freshwater fish culture
. Marine aquaculture

Archaeological interpretation
. Archaeological dating
. . Radiocarbon dating
. Archaeological sociology
. Archaeometry
. . Archaeological dating
. . . Radiocarbon dating

Archive agencies
. Government archives
. . Local government archives
. International archives
. National archives
. Private archives
. . Business archives
. Public archives

Archive facilities
. Archive equipment
. Archive repositories
. Records centres

Archive operations
. Archive records preservation

Armament process
. Arms race
. Arms sales

Armed forces
. Air forces
. Armies
. Navies
. Peace-keeping forces

Art styles
. Byzantine art
. Classical art
. Folk art
. Native art
. Pop art
. Religious art
. . Iconography
. . Islamic art

Astronomical bodies and systems
. Cosmic matter
. . Interplanetary matter
. . . Asteroids
. . . Comets
. . . Meteorites
. . . Meteors
. Galaxies
. . Milky Way
. Solar system
. Universe

Attitude
. Intolerance

399

Behaviour (cont.)
. . . . . Labour conflict
. . . . . . Labour disputes
. . . . Lockouts
. . . . Sit-ins
. . . . Strikes
. . . . Teacher strikes
. . . . Work-to-rule
. . . . . Racial conflict
. . . . . Role conflict
. . . . . Tribal conflict
. . . Interpersonal relations
. . . . Documentalist-user relationship
. . . . Friendship
. . . . Information scientist-user relationship
. . . . Interpersonal attraction
. . . . . Friendship
. . . . . Love
. . . . Interpersonal conflict
. . . . . Aggressiveness
. . . . . Hatred
. . . . . Hostility
. . . . Interpersonal influence
. . . . . Dependency relationship
. . . . Librarian-user relationship
. . . . Love
. . . . Parent-child relationship
. . . . Parent-school relationship
. . . . Parent-teacher relationship
. . . . Parental deprivation
. . . . Peer-group relationship
. . . . Personal contact
. . . . School-student relationship
. . . . . School phobia
. . . . . Truancy
. . . . Sociability
. . . . Teacher-administrator relationship
. . . . Teacher-student relationship
. . Social participation
. . . Community participation
. . . Cultural participation
. . . Youth participation
. . Social responsibility
. . Socialization
. . . Internalization
. Student behaviour
. . Student attitude
. . Student participation
. Teacher behaviour
. . Teacher attitude
. . Teacher participation

Behavioural sciences
. Psychology
. . Affective psychology
. . . Opinion
. . . . Public opinion
. . Applied psychology
. . . Communication psychology
. . . Economic psychology
. . . Educational psychology
. . . . Child psychology
. . . . Educational psychosociology
. . . Indoctrination
. . . Industrial psychology
. . . Psychiatry
. . . . Clinical psychology
. . . . . Psychoanalysis
. . . . . Psychotherapy
. . . . . . Drug psychotherapy
. . . . . . Hypnotherapy

Behavioural sciences (cont.)
. . . . . . Occupational therapy
. . . . . . Psychodrama
. . . . . . Shock treatment
. . . . . . Sociodrama
. . . . Psychopathology
. . . Psycholinguistics
. . . . Language behaviour
. . . Psychology of art
. . . Psychology of religion
. . . Psychotechnics
. . . Social psychology
. . . . Communication psychology
. . . . Educational psychosociology
. . . . Ethnopsychology
. . . . Industrial psychology
. . . . Occupational psychology
. . . . . Industrial psychology
. . Clinical psychology
. . . Psychoanalysis
. . . Psychotherapy
. . . . Drug psychotherapy
. . . . Hypnotherapy
. . . . Occupational therapy
. . . . Psychodrama
. . . . Shock treatment
. . . . Sociodrama
. . Comparative psychology
. . Depth psychology
. . . Subconscious
. . . . Hypnosis
. . . . Inhibitions
. . . Unconscious
. . . . Sleep
. . Developmental psychology
. . . Adolescent psychology
. . . Adult psychology
. . . Child psychology
. . . Emotional development
. . . . Emotional immaturity
. . . . Emotional maturity
. . . Geriatric psychology
. . . Individual development
. . . Mental development
. . . . Language development
. . . . Thought process development
. . . Moral development
. . . Personality development
. . . . Emotional immaturity
. . . . Personality change
. . Individual psychology
. . Parapsychology
. . . Extra-sensory perception
. . . . Psychokinesis
. . . . Telepathy
. . Physiological psychology
. . . Psychosomatics
. . Sensory process psychology
. . Sociometry

Belief
. Religious belief
. Superstition
. Uncertainty

Biological control
. Pest control
. Weed control

Biomes
. Marine ecological zones
. . Abyssal zone
. . Aphotic regions
. . Bathyal zone
. . Benthic zone
. . Brackish water environment
. . Disphotic regions
. . Euphotic regions
. . Hadal regions
. . Intertidal environment
. . Littoral zone
. . Mangrove areas
. . Pelagic zone
. . . Neritic province
. . . Oceanic province

Book output
. Information explosion

Book production
. Textbook production

Broadcasting production
. Television production

Budgetary control
. Educational budgetary control

Budgets
. Cultural budgets
. . Household cultural budgets
. Educational budgets
. Information/library budgets
. Science budgets
. State budget

Building services
. Air conditioning
. Electrical installations
. Heating systems
. . Central heating
. . District heating
. . Electric heating
. . Solar heating
. Lighting
. . Electric lighting
. . Street lighting
. Water services (buildings)

Buildings
. Agricultural buildings
. Apartments
. . High rise flats
. Archive repositories
. Educational buildings
. . Educational laboratories
. . . Language laboratories
. . . School laboratories
. . . . Language laboratories
. . Educational libraries
. . . Academic libraries
. . . . University libraries
. . . School libraries
. . . . Primary school libraries

Buildings (cont.)
. . . . Secondary school libraries
. . Educational workshops
. . . School workshops
. . Lecture theatres
. . School buildings
. . . School laboratories
. . . . Language laboratories
. . . School libraries
. . . . Primary school libraries
. . . . Secondary school libraries
. . . School museums
. . . School workshops
. . . Swimming pools
. . Swimming pools
. . University campuses
. Historic monuments
. Houses
. Library buildings
. Monuments
. . Historic monuments
. Museum buildings
. Palaces
. Railway stations
. Recreational buildings
. . Cinema buildings
. . Concert halls
. . Opera houses
. . Theatre buildings
. Religious buildings
. . Mosques
. . Shrines
. . Temples
. Scientific buildings

Buoys
. Oceanographic buoys

Career development
. Promotion (job)
. . Teacher promotion
. Transfer (job)
. . Educational transfers

Chemical structure
. Atomic structure
. . Crystal atomic structure
. Molecular structure
. . Chemical bonds
. . Stereochemistry

Chemistry
. Agricultural chemistry
. Biochemistry
. . Human biochemistry
. . Palaeobiochemistry
. . Phytochemistry
. . Zoochemistry
. Chemistry of elements and compounds
. . Inorganic chemistry
. . Organic chemistry
. . Polymer chemistry
. Experimental chemistry
. . Chemical analysis
. . . Biochemical analysis
. . . Chemical variables measurement
. . . . Moisture measurement
. . . . pH measurement

Committees
. Advisory committees

Communication control
. Censorship

Communication media
. Exhibitions
. . Cultural exhibitions
. . . Art galleries
. . . Cultural demonstrations
. . Educational exhibitions
. . Library exhibitions
. . Travelling exhibitions
. Information materials
. . Bookform materials
. . . Adaptations
. . . Books
. . . . Antiquarian books
. . . . . Incunabula
. . . . . Rare books
. . . . Art books
. . . . Childrens books
. . . . Fiction stock
. . . . Forms (blank)
. . . . Large print books
. . . . New books
. . . . Out-of-print publications
. . . . Oversize books
. . . . Pamphlets
. . . . Paperbacks
. . . . Pocket books
. . . . Second-hand books
. . . Commercial publications
. . . Editions
. . . . Abridged editions
. . . . Cheap editions
. . . . First editions
. . . . New editions
. . . Educational publications
. . . . Childrens books
. . . . College publications
. . . . Educational periodicals
. . . . Reading materials
. . . . School publications
. . . . Teacher guides
. . . . Textbooks
. . . Ephemera
. . . Forms (blank)
. . . Hard copy
. . . In-print publications
. . . Leaflets
. . . Library publications
. . . . Accession lists
. . . . Information bulletins
. . . Monographs
. . . . Compendia
. . . . Composite works
. . . . Reports
. . . . . Annual reports
. . . . . Country reports
. . . . . Expert reports
. . . . . Final reports
. . . . . Interim reports
. . . . . Law reports
. . . . . Mission reports
. . . . . Progress reports
. . . . . Project reports
. . . . . Technical reports
. . . Multivolume publications

Communication media (cont.)
. . . Music scores
. . . Non-fiction stock
. . . Official publications
. . . Out-of-print publications
. . . Pamphlets
. . . Primary documents
. . . . Albums
. . . . Archive records
. . . . . Audiovisual archives
. . . . . . Cartographic archives
. . . . . . Photographic archives
. . . . . Correspondence
. . . . . Machine-readable archives
. . . . . Manuscripts
. . . . . Personal papers
. . . . Biographies
. . . . . Educational biographies
. . . . Codes of rules
. . . . . Cataloguing rules
. . . . Conference papers
. . . . Correspondence
. . . . Dictionaries
. . . . Directories
. . . . Encyclopaedias
. . . . Glossaries
. . . . Guidebooks
. . . . Inventories
. . . . Manuscripts
. . . Monographs
. . . . Compendia
. . . . Composite works
. . . . Reports
. . . . . Annual reports
. . . . . Country reports
. . . . . Expert reports
. . . . . Final reports
. . . . . Interim reports
. . . . . Law reports
. . . . . Mission reports
. . . . . Progress reports
. . . . . Project reports
. . . . . Technical reports
. . . Newspapers
. . . Patents
. . . Periodicals
. . . . Abstract journals
. . . . Educational periodicals
. . . . Information bulletins
. . . . Popular periodicals
. . . . Scientific periodicals
. . . Records
. . . . Archive records
. . . . . Audiovisual archives
. . . . . . Cartographic archives
. . . . . . Photographic archives
. . . . . Correspondence
. . . . . Machine-readable archives
. . . . . Manuscripts
. . . . . Personal papers
. . . . Current records
. . . . Educational records
. . . . Manuscripts
. . . . Non-current records
. . . . Official records
. . . . Personnel records
. . . . Semi-current records
. . . Reports
. . . . Annual reports
. . . . Country reports
. . . . Expert reports
. . . . Final reports

404

Communication media (cont.)
. . . . Documentary films
. . . . Educational films
. . . . Ethnographic films
. . . . Full-length films
. . . . Historical films
. . . . Musical comedy films
. . . . News films
. . . . Political films
. . . . Romance films
. . . . Science fiction films
. . . . Short films
. . . . Television films
. . . . Thriller films
. . . . War films
. . . . . Globes
. . . . . Graphs
. . . . . Maps
. . . . . . Climatic maps
. . . . . . Hydrogeological maps
. . . . . . Metallogenic maps
. . . . . . Mineral maps
. . . . . . Quarternary maps
. . . . . . Soil maps
. . . . . . Tectonic maps
. . . . . . Vegetation maps
. . . . . Microforms
. . . . . . Computer output microform
. . . . . . Extreme reduction microforms
. . . . . . Microcards
. . . . . . Microfiche
. . . . . . Microfilms
. . . . . Photocopies
. . . . . Photographs
. . . . . Pictures
. . . . . Plans
. . . . . . Development plans
. . . . . . Educational plans
. . . . . Posters
. . . . . . Photoposters
. . . . . Prints
. . . . . Relief maps
. . . . . Transparencies
. . . . . . Film strips
. . . . . . Films
. . . . Arts films
. . . . Childrens films
. . . . Comedy films
. . . . Documentary films
. . . . Educational films
. . . . Ethnographic films
. . . . Full-length films
. . . . Historical films
. . . . Musical comedy films
. . . . News films
. . . . Political films
. . . . Romance films
. . . . Science fiction films
. . . . Short films
. . . . Television films
. . . . Thriller films
. . . . War films
. . . . . . Microfilms
. . . . . . Microforms
. . . . Computer output microform
. . . . Extreme reduction microforms
. . . . Microcards
. . . . Microfiche
. . . . Microfilms
. . . . . . Photographic slides
. . . . Colour slides
. . . . . . Video recordings

Communication media (cont.)
. . . . . . Video cassettes
. . . . . . Video discs
. . . . . . Video tape recordings
. . . Cuttings
. . . . Press cuttings
. . . Drawings
. . . . Cartoons
. . . . Technical drawings
. . . Machine-readable materials
. . . . Data bases
. . . . Machine-readable archives
. . . . Programmed materials
. . . Tablets (documents)
. Mass media
. . Broadcasting
. . . Commercial broadcasting
. . . . Commercial radio
. . . . Commercial television
. . Direct broadcasting
. . Local broadcasting
. . National broadcasting
. . Radio
. . . Educational radio
. . Satellite broadcasting
. . Television
. . . Cable television
. . . . Closed circuit television
. . . Colour television
. . . Commercial television
. . . Educational television
. . Cinema
. . . Library cinemas
. . Press
. . . Local press
. . . National press
. . . Newspaper press
. . . Periodical press
. . . Underground press
. Multimedia
. Signs
. Speech
. . Conversation
. . Public speaking
. Symbols

Communication planning and administration
. Communication administration
. . Communication legislation
. . . Broadcasting legislation
. . . Copyright
. Communication planning
. Economics of communication

Communication process
. Communication (thought transfer)
. Communication skills
. . Acting
. . . Miming
. . Gesture
. . Listening
. . Miming
. . Non-verbal communication
. . . Miming
. . Reading
. . . Oral reading
. . . Silent reading
. . . Speed reading
. . Singing
. . Speech

Communication process (cont.)
- . . . Conversation
- . . . Public speaking
- . . Watching
- . . . Televiewing
- . . Writing
- . . . Creative writing
- . . . . Oral composition
- . . . Handwriting
- . . . . Calligraphy
- . . . Historical writing
- . . . . Historical editing
- . . . Letter writing
- . . . Literary composition
- . . . . Creative writing
- . . . . . Oral composition
- . . . Report writing
- . . . Technical writing
- . Group communication
- . . Discussion groups
- . . Meetings
- . . . Committee meetings
- . . . Conferences
- . . . . International conferences
- . . . . Press conferences
- . . . Public meetings
- . . . Symposia
- . Information transfer
- . . Dissemination of information
- . . . Book distribution
- . . . Current dissemination of information
- . . . . Selective dissemination of information
- . . . International circulation of materials
- . . Information exchange
- . . . Exchange of ideas
- . . . Exchange of publications
- . . News flow
- . Interpersonal communication
- . Mass communication
- . . Advertising
- . . . Press advertising
- . . . Radio advertising
- . . . Television advertising
- . . Popularization
- . . . Science popularization
- . . Propaganda
- . . . War propaganda
- . . Public relations
- . . . Library public relations
- . . . Public liaison
- . . . . UNESCO public liaison
- . . . . . Anniversary celebrations
- . . . . . Philatelic service
- . . . . . UNESCO awards and honours
- . . . . . . Literary prizes
- . . . . . UNESCO clubs
- . . . . . UNESCO coupons
- . . . . . UNESCO publications
- . . . . . UNESCO voluntary assistance
- . . Publicity
- . . . Library publicity
- . One-way communication
- . Two-way communication

Communication users
- . Audiences
- . . Fans (supporters)
- . . Listening groups
- . . Radio listeners
- . . Televiewers
- . General public

Communication users (cont.)
- . . Untapped public

Computer applications
- . Computer-assisted design
- . Computer-assisted instruction
- . Computer linguistics
- . Information processing automation
- . . Automatic generation of index languages
- . . Automatic indexing
- . . . Automatic text analysis
- . . . Statistical linguistics (indexing)
- . . . . Associative indexing
- . . . . . Clumping
- . . . . . Clustering
- . . . . . Discriminant analysis
- . . Computer-assisted compilation
- . . . Computerized catalogues
- . . . . COM catalogues
- . . . . . Microfiche catalogues
- . . . . . Microfilm catalogues
- . . . Computerized indexes
- . . . . Articulated indexes
- . . . . KWAC indexes
- . . . . KWIC indexes
- . . . . KWOC indexes
- . . . . Permuted indexes
- . . . . PRECIS indexes
- . . On-line information processing
- . . . On-line searching
- . Library automation
- . . Acquisition systems automation
- . . Loan records automation
- . . Periodical circulation automation
- . Photocomposition

Computer software
- . Complete computer programs
- . Input-output programs
- . Macros
- . Operating systems (computer)
- . Program processors
- . Program testing
- . Report generators
- . Subroutines
- . Time-sharing programs
- . Utility programs

Computers
- . Analogue computers
- . . Differential analysers
- . Calculating machines
- . Digital computers
- . . General purpose computers
- . . Minicomputers
- . . On-line systems
- . . . On-line information systems
- . . Satellite computers
- . . Special purpose computers
- . . . Digital differential analysers
- . Hybrid computers

Concepts
- . Concepts (index language)
- . . Isolates

Conditions of employment
. Leave
. . Absenteeism
. . Educational leave
. . Sick leave
. . . Teacher sick leave
. . Teacher leave
. . . Teacher sick leave
. Promotion (job)
. . Teacher promotion
. Teacher conditions of employment
. . Teacher dismissal
. . Teacher leave
. . . Teacher sick leave
. . Teacher promotion
. . Teacher retirement
. . Teacher salaries
. . Teacher sick leave
. . Teacher strikes
. . Teaching abroad
. . Teaching load
. Termination of service
. . Dismissal
. . . Teacher dismissal
. . Redundancy
. . Retirement
. . . Teacher retirement
. Transfer (job)
. . Educational transfers
. Wages
. . Educational wages
. . . Teacher salaries
. . Equal pay
. . Minimum wages
. . Salaries
. . . Teacher salaries
. Working time
. . Overtime

Conflict
. Asymmetrical conflict
. Cultural conflict
. International conflict
. . Asymmetrical conflict
. . Cold war
. . Symmetrical conflict
. Interpersonal conflict
. . Aggressiveness
. . Hatred
. . Hostility
. Labour conflict
. . Labour disputes
. . . Lockouts
. . . Sit-ins
. . . Strikes
. . . . Teacher strikes
. . . Work-to-rule
. Political conflict
. Religious conflict
. Social conflict
. . Class conflict
. . Cultural conflict
. . Interpersonal conflict
. . . Aggressiveness
. . . Hatred
. . . Hostility
. . Labour conflict
. . . Labour disputes
. . . . Lockouts
. . . . Sit-ins
. . . . Strikes

Conflict (cont.)
. . . . . Teacher strikes
. . . . Work-to-rule
. . Racial conflict
. . Role conflict
. . Tribal conflict
. Symmetrical conflict
. Tribal conflict

Conflict resolution
. Arbitration
. . Industrial arbitration
. Conciliation
. . Industrial conciliation
. . . Industrial arbitration
. Peace-making

Conservation
. Conservation of nature
. . Countryside conservation
. . . Landscape protection
. . Nature reserves
. . Wildlife protection
. Countryside conservation
. . Landscape protection
. Environmental conservation
. . Amenities conservation
. . . Conservation of nature
. . . . Countryside conservation
. . . . . Landscape protection
. . . . Nature reserves
. . . . Wildlife protection
. . . Countryside conservation
. . . . Landscape protection
. . . Noise control
. . Conservation of nature
. . . Countryside conservation
. . . . Landscape protection
. . . Nature reserves
. . . Wildlife protection
. Preservation of cultural property
. . Preservation of monuments
. . Preservation of works of art
. . . Restoration of paintings
. Resource conservation
. . Conservation of nature
. . . Countryside conservation
. . . . Landscape protection
. . . Nature reserves
. . . Wildlife protection
. . Energy conservation
. . Soil conservation
. . Water conservation

Consumption
. Cultural consumption
. Energy consumption
. Water consumption

Containers
. Water tanks

Contracts
. Marriage contract

Control of specific variables
. Electrical variables control
. Humidity control
. Mechanical variables control
. . Flow control
. . Positioning
. . Pressure control
. . Speed control
. Noise control
. Optical variables control
. Thermal variables control
. . Temperature control

Control systems
. Automatic control
. . Remote control
. Numerical control
. Process control
. Remote control

Coordinate indexes
. Manual coordinate indexes
. . Dual dictionaries
. Punched card coordinate indexes
. . Optical coincidence systems

Corruption
. Political corruption

Costs
. Book costs
. Building costs
. Cultural costs
. Educational costs
. Fixed costs
. Social cost
. Variable costs

Courts
. Administrative tribunals
. Appeal courts
. Criminal courts
. Higher courts
. International courts
. Juvenile courts
. Lower courts
. Supreme court

Criminals
. Gangs
. War criminals

Crystal examination
. X-ray crystallography

Crystal growth
. Crystallization

Crystal structure
. Crystal atomic structure
. Crystal defects
. Crystal microstructure

Crystallography
. X-ray crystallography

Crystals
. Liquid crystals

Cultural activities
. Cultural events
. . Festivals
. . . Film festivals
. . . Musical festivals
. . . Pop festivals
. . . Religious festivals
. Cultural tourism
. Leisure time activities
. . Clubs
. . . Old peoples clubs
. . . School clubs
. . . Socio-cultural clubs
. . . . Book clubs
. . . . Film clubs
. . . . Teleclubs
. . . . Video clubs
. . . Sports clubs
. . . UNESCO clubs
. . . Youth clubs
. . Entertainment
. . . • Cultural events
. . . . Festivals
. . . . . Film festivals
. . . . . Musical festivals
. . . . . Pop festivals
. . . . . Religious festivals
. . . Festivals
. . . . Film festivals
. . . . Musical festivals
. . . . Pop festivals
. . . . Religious festivals
. . . Fun fairs
. . . Performing arts
. . . . Acting
. . . . . Miming
. . . . Ballet
. . . . . Classical ballet
. . . . . Modern ballet
. . . . Cinema
. . . . . Library cinemas
. . . . Circuses
. . . . Concerts
. . . . . Musical concerts
. . . . Dance
. . . . . Ballet
. . . . . . Classical ballet
. . . . . . Modern ballet
. . . . . Folk dance
. . . . . Modern dance
. . . . . National dance
. . . . Mime
. . . . Music-hall
. . . . Musical comedy
. . . . Opera
. . . . Pantomime
. . . . Play reading
. . . . Puppets
. . . . Sound and music
. . . . Spoken poetry
. . . . Theatre
. . . . . Amateur theatre
. . . . . . School plays
. . . . . Ancient theatre

Cultural activities (cont.)
. . . . . Commercial theatre
. . . . . Library theatres
. . . . . National theatre
. . . . . Open air theatre
. . . . . Popular theatre
. . . . . Repertory theatre
. . . . . Total theatre
. . . . . . Traditional theatre
. . . . . . Travelling theatre
. . . . Theatrical performances
. . . . . Dramatization
. . . . Variety shows
. . Hobbies
. . . Amateur photography
. . . Gardening
. . . Stamp collecting
. . Play
. . . Play (teaching method)
. . Sport
. . . Acrobatics
. . . Aerial sports
. . . Animal sports
. . . Aquatic sports
. . . . Swimming
. . . Athletics
. . . Ball games
. . . Combative sports
. . . . Hunting
. . . Equestrian sports
. . . Gymnastics
. . . Hunting
. . . Indoor games
. . . . Card games
. . . . Radio games
. . . . Television games
. . . Mechanical sports
. . . Olympic games
. . . Outdoor pursuits
. . . . Camping
. . . . Hiking
. . . Winter sports
. . Tourism
. . . Cultural tourism
. . . Weekend tourism
. Library extension work
. . Reading promotion
. Museum activities
. . Museum visits
. Socio-cultural activities
. . Socio-cultural clubs
. . . Book clubs
. . . Film clubs
. . . Teleclubs
. . . Video clubs

Cultural and social anthropology
. Ethnography
. . Folk cultures
. . . Folk art
. . . Folk dance
. . . Folk literature
. . . . Fairy tales
. . . . Legends
. . . . Nursery rhymes
. . . . Proverbs
. . . Folk music
. . . . Folk songs
. . . Folklore
. Ethnology
. . Folk cultures

Cultural and social anthropology (cont.)
. . . Folk art
. . . Folk dance
. . . Folk literature
. . . . Fairy tales
. . . . Legends
. . . . Nursery rhymes
. . . . Proverbs
. . . Folk music
. . . . Folk songs
. . . Folklore

Cultural attendance
. Cinema attendance
. Museum attendance
. Theatre attendance

Cultural conditions
. Civilization crises
. . Cultural crises
. Cultural change
. . Cultural innovations
. . Cultural revolution
. . Democratization of culture
. . Disappearing cultures
. Cultural crises
. Cultural differentiation
. . Cultural disadvantage
. . Cultural discrimination
. . Cultural inequality
. Cultural environment
. Cultural isolation
. Cultural needs
. Cultural situation
. Cultural systems
. . Artistic cultures
. . Counter-cultures
. . Culture of poverty
. . Culture of work
. . Disappearing cultures
. . Dominant cultures
. . Elite cultures
. . Established cultures
. . Folk cultures
. . . Folk art
. . . Folk dance
. . . Folk literature
. . . . Fairy tales
. . . . Legends
. . . . Nursery rhymes
. . . . Proverbs
. . . Folk music
. . . . Folk songs
. . . Folklore
. . Literary cultures
. . Living cultures
. . Mass culture
. . Minority cultures
. . Multiculturalism
. . . Biculturalism
. . National cultures
. . New cultures
. . Scientific cultures
. . Spontaneous cultures
. . Subcultures
. . Traditional cultures
. . . Folklore
. . Universal culture
. . Working class cultures

Cultural creation
. Artistic creation
. Cultural innovations

Cultural exchange
. Programme exchange

Cultural planning and administration
. Cultural administration
. . Museum administration
. . . Museum reorganization
. Cultural economics
. . Cultural finance
. . . Cultural accounting
. . . . Cultural budgets
. . . . . Household cultural budgets
. . . . Cultural expenditure
. . . Cultural financing
. . . . Museum financing
. . . . Patronage of the arts
. . . Museum finance
. . . . Museum charges
. . . . Museum financing
. . Museum economics
. . . Museum finance
. . . . Museum charges
. . . . Museum financing
. Cultural planning
. . Museum planning

Cultural users
. Audiences
. . Fans (supporters)
. . Listening groups
. . Radio listeners
. . Televiewers
. Culturally disadvantaged
. . Immigrants
. Library users
. Museum users

Culture
. African cultures
. . African art
. Arab culture
. . Arab art
. Arctic cultures
. Artistic cultures
. Arts
. . African art
. . Ancient art
. . Arab art
. . Asian art
. . . Chinese art
. . Byzantine art
. . Chinese art
. . Classical art
. . Contemporary art
. . . Avant-garde art
. . European art
. . . Slav art
. . Experimental art
. . Folk art
. . Latin American art
. . Medieval art
. . Modern art
. . . Contemporary art
. . . . Avant-garde art

Culture (cont.)
. . Music
. . . Abstract music
. . . Classical music
. . . Concrete music
. . . Electronic music
. . . Folk music
. . . . Folk songs
. . . Instrumental music
. . . Jazz
. . . Mechanical music
. . . Modern music
. . . . Contemporary music
. . . National music
. . . Pop music
. . . Popular music
. . . Religious music
. . . Traditional music
. . . Vocal music
. . . . Songs
. . . . . Folk songs
. . Native art
. . Oceanic art
. . Performing arts
. . . Acting
. . . . Miming
. . . Ballet
. . . . Classical ballet
. . . . Modern ballet
. . . Cinema
. . . . Library cinemas
. . . Circuses
. . . Concerts
. . . . Musical concerts
. . . Dance
. . . . Ballet
. . . . . Classical ballet
. . . . . Modern ballet
. . . . Folk dance
. . . . Modern dance
. . . . National dance
. . . Mime
. . . Music-hall
. . . Musical comedy
. . . Opera
. . . Pantomime
. . . Play reading
. . . Puppets
. . . Sound and music
. . . Spoken poetry
. . . Theatre
. . . . Amateur theatre
. . . . . School plays
. . . . Ancient theatre
. . . . Commercial theatre
. . . . Library theatres
. . . . National theatre
. . . . Open air theatre
. . . . Popular theatre
. . . . Repertory theatre
. . . . Total theatre
. . . . Traditional theatre
. . . . Travelling theatre
. . . Theatrical performances
. . . . Dramatization
. . . Variety shows
. . Pop art
. . Prehistoric art
. . . Rock painting
. . Religious art
. . . Iconography
. . . Islamic art

Culture (cont.)
. . Slav art
. . Visual arts
. . . Fine arts
. . . . Architecture
. . . . . Interior architecture
. . . . . Museum architecture
. . . . Graphic arts
. . . . . Calligraphy
. . . . . Commercial art
. . . . . Drawing
. . . . . . Technical drawing
. . . . . Painting
. . . . . . Miniature painting
. . . . . . Oil painting
. . . . . . Rock painting
. . . . Plastic arts
. . . . . Art glass
. . . . . . Glassware
. . . . . . Stained glass
. . . . . Art metalwork
. . . . . Ceramic art
. . . . . . Pottery
. . . . . Engraving
. . . . . Jewelry
. . . . . Mosaics
. . . . . Sculpture
. . . . . Sigillography
. . . . . Woodcarving
. . . Handicrafts
. . . . Fashion design
. . . . Needlework
. . . . Textile arts
. . . . . Tapestry
. . . Reproductive arts
. . . . Photography
. . . . . Aerial photography
. . . . . Amateur photography
. . . . . Cinematography
. . . . . Microphotography
. . . . . Photocopying
. . . . . . Diazo processes
. . . . . . Xerography
. . . . . Underwater photography
. . . . Printing
. . . . . Printing operations
. . . . . . Composition
. . . . Machine typesetting
. . . . Photocomposition
. . . . . . Press work
. . . . . Printing processes
. . . . . . Illustration printing
. . . . . . Intaglio printing
. . . . . . Lithography
. . . . . . Relief printing
. . . . . . Stencil printing
. . . . Reprography
. . . . . Duplicating
. . . . . Microphotography
. . . . . Photocopying
. . . . . . Diazo processes
. . . . . . Xerography
. Asian cultures
. . Asian art
. . . Chinese art
. . Central Asian cultures
. . . Kushan
. Contemporary culture
. . Contemporary art
. . . Avant-garde art
. . Contemporary literature
. . Contemporary music

Culture (cont.)
. Counter-cultures
. Culture of poverty
. Culture of work
. Disappearing cultures
. Dominant cultures
. Elite cultures
. Established cultures
. European cultures
. . Baltic culture
. . Central European cultures
. . European art
. . . Slav art
. . Iberian cultures
. . Slav culture
. . . Slav art
. Latin American cultures
. . Aztecs
. . Incas
. . Latin American art
. Literary cultures
. Literature
. . Foreign literature
. . Modern literature
. . . Contemporary literature
. Living cultures
. Mass culture
. Minority cultures
. Multiculturalism
. . Biculturalism
. National cultures
. New cultures
. North American cultures
. . North American Indian culture
. Oceanic cultures
. Scientific cultures
. Spontaneous cultures
. Subcultures
. Traditional cultures
. . Folklore
. Universal culture
. Working class cultures

Curriculum
. Cross-disciplinary curriculum
. . Integrated curriculum
. Pre-primary curriculum
. Primary school curriculum
. Secondary school curriculum
. Teacher training curriculum
. University curriculum
. Vocational school curriculum

Curriculum subjects
. Agricultural education
. . Agricultural training
. Catering education
. Civic education
. . Education for peace
. Commercial education
. Computer science education
. Consumer education
. Cultural education
. . Architecture education
. . Art education
. . Drama education
. . Movement studies
. . Music education
. . Speech education
. Development education

Curriculum subjects (cont.)
- Distributive education
- Domestic science education
- Economics education
- Education courses
- Environmental education
- General education
- Handicrafts education
- Health education
- - Alcohol education
- - Drug education
- - Nutrition education
- - Population education
- - Sex education
- History education
- Humanities education
- Language education
- Legal education
- Management education
- Mathematics education
- - Modern mathematics
- - Statistics education
- Medical education
- - Veterinary education
- Military education
- Moral education
- Mother tongue instruction
- - Conversation instruction
- - Handwriting instruction
- - Listening instruction
- - Reading instruction
- - Spelling instruction
- - Vocabulary instruction
- Physical education
- Political science education
- Population education
- Professional training
- - Architecture education
- - Archive science training
- - Communication personnel training
- - - Book production training
- - - Communication planners training
- - - Journalist training
- - - Publishers training
- - - Television and radio personnel training
- - Cultural personnel training
- - - Cultural agents training
- - - Film-making training
- - - Museum training
- - Information/library training
- - Legal education
- - Medical education
- - - Veterinary education
- - Research training
- - Social workers training
- - Teacher training
- - - In-service teacher training
- - - Practice teaching
- - - Pre-primary teacher training
- - - Pre-service teacher training
- - - Primary teacher training
- - - Secondary teacher training
- - - Special teacher training
- - - Teacher educator training
- - - Vocational teacher training
- Psychology education
- Religious education
- Safety education
- Science education
- - Basic science education
- - Biology education
- - Chemistry education

Curriculum subjects (cont.)
- - Geography education
- - Geology education
- - Hydrology education
- - Oceanography education
- - Physics education
- - Pre-university science education
- Social science education
- Technical education
- - Engineering education
- - General technical education
- - Higher technical education
- - Pre-university science education
- - Technical colleges
- - Technical training
- - - Book production training
- - - Group training
- - - Industrial training
- - - Scientific personnel training
- Vocational education
- - Agricultural education
- - - Agricultural training
- - Commercial education
- - Distributive education
- - Film-making training
- - Vocational training
- - - Agricultural training
- - - Basic training
- - - Cooperative education
- - - Job training
- - - Technical training
- - - - Book production training
- - - - Group training
- - - - Industrial training
- - - - Scientific personnel training

Customs and traditions
- Ceremonies
- - Religious ceremonies
- Commemorations
- Fashion
- Feasts
- - Religious festivals
- Festivals
- - Film festivals
- - Musical festivals
- - Pop festivals
- - Religious festivals
- Folk cultures
- - Folk art
- - Folk dance
- - Folk literature
- - - Fairy tales
- - - Legends
- - - Nursery rhymes
- - - Proverbs
- - Folk music
- - - Folk songs
- - Folklore
- Food customs
- Manners
- Mores
- Oral tradition
- Rites
- - Initiation rites
- Rituals
- Taboos

Damage
- Deformation

412

Damage (cont.)
. . Elastic deformation
. . Plastic deformation
. . . Creep
. Fracture
. Water damage

Data
. Bibliographic data
. . Collation
. . Imprint
. . Titles
. Climatic data
. Geographical data
. Geological data
. Hydrological data
. Meteorological data
. Oceanographic data
. Statistical data
. . Census
. Survey data

Data bearing media
. Magnetic cards
. Magnetic cores
. Magnetic discs
. Magnetic films
. Magnetic tapes
. Punched cards
. Punched tapes

Defence
. Non-violent defence

Delinquency
. Juvenile delinquency

Descriptive cataloguing
. Annotated cataloguing

Deterioration
. Brain deterioration
. Corrosion
. . Electrochemical corrosion
. . . Water corrosion
. Environmental deterioration
. . Amenities destruction
. . . Noise
. . . Visual pollution
. . Pollution
. . . Air pollution
. . . Industrial pollution
. . . Land pollution
. . . . Soil pollution
. . . Oil pollution
. . . Radioactive pollution
. . . . Radioactive fallout
. . . Soil pollution
. . . Visual pollution
. . . Water pollution
. . . . Marine pollution
. . . . River pollution
. Soil deterioration

Developed countries
. Donor countries
. Recessing countries

Developing countries
. Least developed countries
. Recipient countries

Development
. Economic and social development
. . Agricultural development
. . Archive development
. . Communication development
. . . Book development
. . . . International book year
. . Cultural development
. . . Cultural action
. . . . Animation culturelle
. . . . Cultural integration
. . . . . Cultural assimilation
. . . . . Enculturation
. . . . Democratization of culture
. . . . Dissemination of culture
. . . . . Cultural education
. . . . . . Architecture education
. . . . . . Art education
. . . . . . Drama education
. . . . . . Movement studies
. . . . . . Music education
. . . . . . Speech education
. . . . Information/library development
. . . . Presentation of cultural property
. . . . . Cultural exhibitions
. . . . . . Art galleries
. . . . . . Cultural demonstrations
. . . . . Museums
. . . . . . Archaeological museums
. . . . . . Ethnographic museums
. . . . . . Historical museums
. . . . . . Musee imaginaire
. . . . . . Museobuses
. . . . . . National museums
. . . . . . Regional museums
. . . . . . School museums
. . . . . . Science museums
. . . . Ecomuseums
. . . . Natural history museums
. . . . . . Specialized museums
. . . . Preservation of cultural property
. . . . . Preservation of monuments
. . . . . Preservation of works of art
. . . . . . Restoration of paintings
. . . . Socio-cultural action
. . . Museum development
. . Economic growth
. . Educational development
. . . Curriculum development
. . . . Anticurriculum movement
. . . . . De-schooling
. . . Educational trends
. . Industrial development
. . Information/library development
. . National development
. . Political development
. . . Decolonization
. . . Democratization
. . . . Democratization of culture
. . . . Democratization of education
. . . Political reform
. . . . Democratization

413

Development (cont.)
. . . . Democratization of culture
. . . . Democratization of education
. . Resource development
. . . Human resources development
. . . Water resources development
. . Rural development
. . Social science development
. . Underdevelopment
. . Urban development
. Physiological development
. . Animal development
. . . Animal growth
. . Embryology
. . Growth
. . . Animal growth
. . . Ocean wave growth
. . . Plant growth
. . Motor development
. . Plant development
. . . Plant growth
. Scientific development
. . Technological change

Diffraction
. Electron diffraction
. Neutron diffraction
. X-ray diffraction

Diplomacy
. Cultural diplomacy

Disarmament
. Arms control

Discoveries
. Cultural discoveries
. Scientific discoveries

Diseases
. Allergies
. Cancer
. Cardiovascular diseases
. . Heart diseases
. Digestive system diseases
. . Dental diseases
. . Liver diseases
. Endocrine diseases
. Haemic and lymphatic systems diseases
. Infectious diseases
. . Bacterial diseases
. . Cholera
. . Diptheria
. . Dysentry
. . Influenza
. . Leprosy
. . Malaria
. . Measles
. . Poliomyelitis
. . Rabies
. . Smallpox
. . Tetanus
. . Tuberculosis
. . Typhoid
. . Venereal diseases
. Locomotory system diseases
. . Arthritis

Diseases (cont.)
. Mental diseases
. . Behavioural disorders
. . . Antisocial behaviour
. . . Apathy
. . . . Social passivity
. . . Maladjustment
. . . Social deviance
. . . . Addiction
. . . . . Alcoholism
. . . . . Drug addiction
. . . . . Gambling
. . . . . Smoking
. . . . Opting out
. . . . Sexual deviance
. . . . Social alienation
. . . . Suicide
. . . Suicide
. . Neuroses
. . . Amnesia
. . . Anxiety states
. . . Emotional disturbances
. . . Hysteria
. . . Mental strain
. . . Nervous breakdown
. . . Obsessional neuroses
. . . Phobias
. . Personality disorders
. . Psychoses
. . . Affective psychoses
. . . . Manic-depressive psychoses
. . . . Melancholia
. . . Organic psychoses
. . . Paranoia
. . . Schizophrenia
. . Psychosomatic disorders
. . Rational processes disorders
. . . Brain deterioration
. . . Memory disorders
. Neoplasms
. . Cancer
. Nervous system diseases
. . Epilepsy
. . Sensory system diseases
. . . Deafness
. . . Dyslexia
. . . Vision defects
. . . . Blindness
. . . . Colour blindness
. . . . Partial sight
. . Spastic disorders
. . Speech disorders
. Nutrition and metabolic diseases
. . Malnutrition
. . Obesity
. Occupational diseases
. Respiratory diseases
. . Asthma
. . Bronchitis
. . Pneumonia
. Skin diseases
. Tropical diseases
. Urogenital diseases
. . Enuresis

Dispersion and surface physics
. Dispersion physics
. . Colloid physics
. Surface physics

Document parts
. Abstracts
. . Author abstracts
. . Indicative abstracts
. . Informative abstracts
. Articles
. Bibliographic data
. . Collation
. . Imprint
. . Titles
. Citations
. Covers (document)
. . Bindings
. Format
. Pages
. Spines (book)
. Text

Earth sciences
. Geography
. . Historical geography
. . Human geography
. . . Anthropogeography
. . . Cultural geography
. . . Economic geography
. . . Political geography
. . Physical geography
. . . Phytogeography
. . . Zoogeography
. . Regional geography
. . . Continental geography
. . . Global geography
. . . Local geography
. . . National geography
. Geology
. . Economic geology
. . . Mining geology
. . . Petroleum geology
. . Engineering geology
. . . Mining geology
. . . Petroleum geology
. . Experimental geology
. . Hydrogeology
. . Marine geology
. . . Submarine geology
. . Palaeogeology
. . Physical geology
. . . Earths structure
. . . . Earths core
. . . . Earths crust
. . . Geodynamics
. . . . Endogenous processes
. . . . . Tectonics
. . . . . . Continental drift
. . . . . . Land subsidence
. . . . . . Landslides
. . . . . Thermal springs
. . . . . Volcanic eruptions
. . . . Exogenous processes
. . . . . Erosion
. . . . . . Coastal erosion
. . . . . . Soil erosion
. . . . . Glaciology
. . . . . Sedimentation
. . . Mineralogy
. . . Petrology
. . Stratigraphy
. . . Geological ages
. . . . Cenozoic period
. . . . Mesozoic period
. . . . Palaeozoic period

Earth sciences (cont.)
. . . . Precambrian period
. . . . Quarternary period
. . . . . Neolithic period
. . . . . Palaeolithic period
. . . . Tertiary period
. Geomorphology
. . Topography
. . . Land forms
. . . . Basins
. . . . . Drainage basins
. . . . . . River basins
. . . . . River basins
. . . . Caves
. . . . Cliffs
. . . . Coasts
. . . . Continents
. . . . Deltas
. . . . Deserts
. . . . Grasslands
. . . . . Pampas
. . . . . Savannah
. . . . . Steppe
. . . . Hills
. . . . . Submarine ridges
. . . . Islands
. . . . . Archipelagos
. . . . . Atolls
. . . . Jungle
. . . . Karst
. . . . Moraines
. . . . Mountains
. . . . . Submarine ridges
. . . . Pampas
. . . . Peninsulas
. . . . Plains
. . . . . Coastal plains
. . . . . Pampas
. . . . . Savannah
. . . . . Steppe
. . . . . Submarine plains
. . . . Plateaus
. . . . Reefs
. . . . . Coral reefs
. . . . Savannah
. . . . Steppe
. . . . Tundra
. . . . Valleys
. . . . . Canyons
. . . . . . Submarine canyons
. . . . . . Submarine valleys
. . . . Wetlands
. . . . . Bogs
. . . . . Fens
. . . . . Marshes
. . . . . Swamps
. . . Landscape
. . . Submarine topography
. . . Water features
. . . . Bays
. . . . . Baffin Bay
. . . . . Bay of Bengal
. . . . . Bay of Biscay
. . . . . Bay of Fundy
. . . . . Great Australian Bight
. . . . . Hudson Bay
. . . . Canals
. . . . . Irrigation canals
. . . . Estuaries
. . . . Fjords
. . . . Lagoons
. . . . Lakes

417

Economics (cont.)
. . Research finance
. . . Research grants
. . Savings
. . Science finance
. . . Science budgets
. . . Science financing
. . . . Research grants
. . . Scientific expenditure
. . Social welfare finance
. Housing economics
. . Housing finance
. . . Mortgages
. . . Rents
. Industrial economics
. Information/library economics
. . Information/library planning
. Labour economics
. Land economics
. . Agrarian structure
. . Land and property finance
. . Land tenure
. . Land use
. Macroeconomics
. Microeconomics
. . Business management
. . . Financial administration
. . . . Accounting
. . . . . Auditing
. . . . . Cost accounting
. . . . . Cultural accounting
. . . . . . Cultural budgets
. . . . Household cultural budgets
. . . . . . Cultural expenditure
. . . . Business formation
. . . . . Mergers
. . . . Capital raising
. . . . . Investment appraisal
. . . . Educational financial management
. . . . . Educational expenditure
. . . . . . Educational wages
. . . . Teacher salaries
. . . . . . Teacher salaries
. . . . . Educational income
. . . . . . Educational fees
. . . Industrial management
. . . . Factory management
. . . . Production management
. . . . . Process development
. . . . . Product development
. . . Marketing
. . . Personnel management
. . . . Recruitment
. . . . . Appointment to job
. . . . . Personnel selection
. . . . . . Group selection
. . . . . . Interviewing for job
. . . . . Teacher recruitment
. Rural economics
. Social welfare economics
. . Social welfare finance
. Trade
. . Home trade
. . . Retail trade
. . . Wholesale trade
. . International trade
. . . Balance of trade
. . . Economic agreements
. . . Exports/imports
. . . Free trade
. . . International competition
. . . Protectionism

Economics (cont.)
. . Marketing
. Transport economics

Ecosystems
. Aerial ecosystems
. Aquatic ecosystems
. . Marine ecosystems
. Terrestrial ecosystems

Editing
. Historical editing

Educational attendance
. Educational term
. Educational year
. Sabbatical leave
. School holidays
. School time

Educational courses
. Accelerated courses
. Correspondence courses
. Credit courses
. Education courses
. Elective courses
. Information/library courses
. Orientation courses
. Part-time courses
. Post-graduate courses
. Programmed courses
. Refresher courses
. Sandwich courses
. Short courses
. Training courses
. . Industrial training courses
. . . Sandwich courses

Educational exchanges
. Student exchanges

Educational grouping
. Ability grouping
. Educational integration
. School classes
. . Literacy classes
. . Sixth forms
. . Transition classes

Educational guidance
. School-leaving guidance
. Vocational guidance

Educational levels
. Higher education
. . Colleges
. . . Liberal arts colleges
. . . Technical colleges
. . . Universities
. . . . Academies of science
. . . . International universities
. . . . Open universities
. . . . Polytechnics
. . . . Technological institutes

419

Educational systems and institutions (cont.)
. . . Adult education
. . . . Adult basic education
. . . . Parent education
. . . . Polyvalent adult education
. . . . Workers education
. . . Coeducation
. . . Exceptional student education
. . . . Migrant education
. . . . Refugee education
. . . . Special education
. . . . . Education of the blind
. . . . . Education of the deaf
. . . Mens education
. . . Womens education
. . Family education
. . Free education
. . Higher education
. . . Colleges
. . . . Liberal arts colleges
. . . . Technical colleges
. . . . Universities
. . . . . Academies of science
. . . . . International universities
. . . . . Open universities
. . . . . Polytechnics
. . . . . Technological institutes
. . . . . University colleges
. . . . . University institutes
. . . . Vocational colleges
. . . . . Agricultural colleges
. . . . . Information/library schools
. . . . . Journalist schools
. . . . . Teacher training schools
. . . . . . Teacher centres
. . Home education
. . Informal education
. . Life-long education
. . . Recurrent education
. . Mass education
. . Mobile educational services
. . . Mobile schools
. . Out-of-school education
. . . Non-formal education
. . Pre-primary education
. . . Day Nurseries
. . . Nursery schools
. . . Play groups
. . Pre-school education
. . Primary education
. . Private education
. . Public education
. . Rural education
. . School systems
. . Secondary education
. . . Comprehensive schools
. . . Lower secondary education
. . . Lycees
. . . Middle secondary education
. . . Sixth forms
. . . Upper secondary education
. . . Volksschule
. . Urban education
. . Youth activities
. . . Youth movements
. . . . Student movements
. . . Youth orchestras

Electric power generation
. Direct energy conversion
. . Batteries

Electric power generation (cont.)
. . . Fuel cells
. . Magnetohydrodynamic conversion
. . Solar power generation
. . Thermionic conversion
. . Thermoelectric conversion

Electric power stations
. Hydroelectric power stations
. . Tidal power stations
. Nuclear power stations
. Thermal power stations
. . Diesel power stations
. . Gas turbine power stations
. . Steam power stations
. . . Geothermal power stations
. Wind power stations

Electric power transmission
. Electric power distribution

Electrolytic cells
. Batteries
. . Fuel cells

Elementary particles
. Electrons
. Neutrons
. Photons
. Protons

Emotions
. Anger
. Anxiety
. Apathy
. . Social passivity
. Boredom
. Depression
. Dissatisfaction
. Embarrassment
. Euphoria
. Fear
. Frustration
. Happiness
. Hatred
. Jealousy
. Laughter
. Love
. Optimism
. Pessimism
. Pleasure
. Satisfaction
. . Job satisfaction
. Sorrow
. Suffering

Employment abroad
. Teaching abroad

Energy
. Electrical energy
. Geothermal energy
. Nuclear energy
. Ocean wave energy
. Solar radiation

Energy (cont.)
. . Sunlight
. Steam power
. Tidal energy
. Water power
. Wind power

Energy conversion
. Direct energy conversion
. . Batteries
. . . Fuel cells
. . Magnetohydrodynamic conversion
. . Solar power generation
. . Thermionic conversion
. . Thermoelectric conversion

Environment
. Cultural environment
. Educational environment
. Human environment
. . Human settlement
. . . Urban areas
. . . . Conurbations
. . . . Development areas (urban planning)
. . . . Industrial areas
. . . . Neighbourhoods
. . . . Residential areas
. . . . Shopping areas
. . . . Suburbs
. . . . Urban centres
. . . Villages
. . Urban environment
. . . Built environment
. Natural environment
. . Aquatic environment
. . . Marine environment
. . . . Intertidal environment
. . Atmosphere
. . . Lower atmosphere
. . . . Ozonosphere
. . . . Stratosphere
. . . . Troposphere
. . . Upper atmosphere
. . . . Exosphere
. . . . Ionosphere
. . . . Magnetosphere
. . . . Mesosphere
. . . . Radiation belts
. . Biosphere
. . Terrestrial environment
. Social environment
. . Cultural environment
. . Family environment

Environmental changes
. Ecological crisis
. Environmental deterioration
. . Amenities destruction
. . . Noise
. . . Visual pollution
. . Pollution
. . . Air pollution
. . . Industrial pollution
. . . Land pollution
. . . . Soil pollution
. . . Oil pollution
. . . Radioactive pollution
. . . . Radioactive fallout
. . . Soil pollution

Environmental changes (cont.)
. . . Visual pollution
. . . Water pollution
. . . . Marine pollution
. . . . River pollution

Environmental sciences
. Ecology
. . Aerobiology
. . Animal ecology
. . Autecology
. . Exobiology
. . Human ecology
. . Hydrobiology
. . . Limnology
. . . Marine biology
. . Palaeoecology
. . Plant ecology
. . . Plant adaptation
. . Synecology
. Environmental engineering
. . Air pollution treatment
. . Noise control
. . Sanitary engineering
. . . Sewage disposal and handling
. . . Waste disposal and handling
. . . . Sewage disposal and handling
. . . . Waste collection
. . . . Waste treatment
. . . . . Sewage treatment
. . Water treatment
. . . Desalination
. . . Water demineralization
. Environmental management
. . Environmental conservation
. . . Amenities conservation
. . . . Conservation of nature
. . . . . Countryside conservation
. . . . . . Landscape protection
. . . . . Nature reserves
. . . . . Wildlife protection
. . . . Countryside conservation
. . . . . Landscape protection
. . . . Noise control
. . . Conservation of nature
. . . . Countryside conservation
. . . . . Landscape protection
. . . . Nature reserves
. . . . Wildlife protection
. . Environmental monitoring
. . Environmental planning
. . . Environmental planning processes
. . . . Amenities conservation
. . . . . Conservation of nature
. . . . . . Countryside conservation
. . . . Landscape protection
. . . . . . Nature reserves
. . . . . . Wildlife protection
. . . . . Countryside conservation
. . . . . . Landscape protection
. . . . . Noise control
. . . . Environmental design
. . . . Landscape design
. . . . Urban design
. . . . . Street furniture design
. . . . Visual planning
. . . Regional planning
. . . Rural planning
. . . . Countryside conservation
. . . . . Landscape protection
. . . Transport planning

Environmental sciences (cont.)
. . . Urban planning
. . . . Town reconstruction
. . . . Urban decentralization
. . . . Urban design
. . . . . Street furniture design
. . . . Urban development
. . . . Urban expansion
. . . . . Urban sprawl
. . . . Urban renewal
. . Noise control
. . Pollution control

Equipment
. Acoustic equipment
. . Electroacoustic devices
. . . Echo sounders
. . . Hearing aids
. . . Hydrophones
. . . Microphones
. . . Piezoelectric devices
. . Sonar
. Archive equipment
. Chemical engineering equipment
. . Autoclaves
. . Centrifuges
. . Chemical reactors
. . Stills
. . . Solar stills
. Communication engineering equipment
. . Antennas
. . Lasers
. . Masers
. . Microphones
. . Receivers
. . . Radio receivers
. . . Television receivers
. . Recording equipment
. . . Record players
. . . Tape recorders
. . . Video recorders
. . Telecommunication links
. . . Communication satellites
. . . Radio links
. . . Transmission lines
. . . Waveguides
. . Teleprinters
. . Television cameras
. . Transmitters
. . . Radio transmitters
. . . Repeaters
. . . Television transmitters
. Computer hardware
. . Computer circuits
. . . Logic and switching circuits
. . Computer peripheral equipment
. . . Character recognition equipment
. . . Computer graphic equipment
. . . . Light pens
. . . . Remote consoles
. . . Data communication equipment
. . . . Computer interfaces
. . . . Computer terminals
. . . Data converters
. . . Data preparation equipment
. . . Displays (computer)
. . . Keyboards
. . . Printers (computer)
. . Computer storage devices
. . . Digital storage
. . . Direct access

Equipment (cont.)
. Construction equipment
. . Excavating equipment
. Control equipment
. . Electric control equipment
. . Hydraulic motors
. Cultural equipment
. . Cultural goods
. . . Books
. . . . Antiquarian books
. . . . . Incunabula
. . . . . Rare books
. . . . Art books
. . . . Childrens books
. . . . Fiction stock
. . . . Forms (blank)
. . . . Large print books
. . . . New books
. . . . Out-of-print publications
. . . . Oversize books
. . . . Pamphlets
. . . . Paperbacks
. . . . Pocket books
. . . . Second-hand books
. . . Leisure equipment
. . . . Sports equipment
. . . Radio receivers
. . . Record players
. . . Recordings
. . . . Cassette recordings
. . . . . Sound cassettes
. . . . . Video cassettes
. . . . Cylinder recordings
. . . . Disc recordings
. . . . . Long playing records
. . . . . Video discs
. . . . Magnetic tape recordings
. . . . . Phonotapes
. . . . . Video tape recordings
. . . . Sound recordings
. . . . . Phonotapes
. . . . . Sound cassettes
. . . . . Stereophonic recordings
. . . . . Talking books
. . . . Video recordings
. . . . . Video cassettes
. . . . . Video discs
. . . . . Video tape recordings
. . . Television receivers
. Domestic appliances
. Educational equipment
. . School furniture
. . Teaching materials and equipment
. . . Teaching aids
. . . . Audiovisual aids
. . . . . Chalkboards
. . . . . Flannelgraphs
. . . . Educational collections
. . . . Educational exhibitions
. . . . Educational films
. . . . Educational laboratory equipment
. . . . Educational radio
. . . . Educational television
. . . . Educational toys
. . . . Educational visits
. . . . . Educational cruises
. . . . . Educational journeys
. . . . . Educational walks
. . . . . Study tours
. . . . . . Educational cruises
. . . . School museums
. . . . Sensory aids (teaching)

Equipment (cont.)

. . . . . Audiovisual aids
. . . . . . Chalkboards
. . . . . . Flannelgraphs
. . . . . Tactile aids
. . . . . . Braille system
. . . . Teaching machines
. . . . . Automatic teaching
. . . . . Computer-assisted instruction
. . . . . Language laboratories
. . . . . Programmed instruction
. Electrical equipment
. . Circuits
. . . Amplifiers
. . . Computer circuits
. . . . Logic and switching circuits
. . . Integrated circuits
. . . Logic and switching circuits
. . . Oscillators
. . . Printed circuits
. . Converters
. . . Inverters
. . Cores (electric)
. . . Magnetic cores
. . Dielectric devices
. . . Capacitors
. . . Electrical insulation
. . . Piezoelectric devices
. . Electric conductors
. . . Superconductors
. . Electric connectors
. . Electric contacts
. . Electric control equipment
. . Electric machines
. . . Electric generators
. . . Electric motors
. . Electric reactors
. . Electric wiring
. . Electrical protection gear
. . . Circuit breakers
. . . Earthing
. . . Fuses
. . Electrochemical devices
. . . Batteries
. . . . Fuel cells
. . . Electrolytic tanks
. . Electrodes
. . Electromechanical devices
. . Inductors
. . Magnetic devices
. . . Magnetic cards
. . . Magnetic cores
. . . Magnetic discs
. . . Magnetic films
. . . Magnetic tapes
. . . Magnetostrictive devices
. . Rectifiers
. . Resistors
. . Switches
. . . Relays
. . Switchgear
. . . Circuit breakers
. . Transformers
. . Voltage dividers
. . Windings (electric)
. Electronic equipment
. . Circuits
. . . Amplifiers
. . . Computer circuits
. . . . Logic and switching circuits
. . . Integrated circuits
. . . Logic and switching circuits

Equipment (cont.)

. . . Oscillators
. . . Printed circuits
. . Electroacoustic devices
. . . Echo sounders
. . . Hearing aids
. . . Hydrophones
. . . Microphones
. . . Piezoelectric devices
. . Electron tubes
. . Lasers
. . Masers
. . Optoelectronic devices
. . . Photoelectric devices
. . . . Solar cells
. . Semiconductors
. . . Thermistors
. . . Transistors
. . Superconductors
. . Thermoelectric devices
. . . Thermocouples
. Heating equipment
. . Boilers
. . Furnaces
. . Heat exchangers
. Hydraulic equipment
. . Compressors
. . Fans
. . Floats
. . Fluid apertures
. . . Ducts
. . . Nozzles
. . . Orifices
. . . Pipes
. . . . Sewers
. . . . Water mains
. . Hydraulic accumulators
. . Hydraulic motors
. . Inflatable devices
. . Pipes
. . . Sewers
. . . Water mains
. . Pumps
. . Valves
. . Water turbines
. Information/library equipment
. . Library equipment
. . . Card catalogue cabinets
. . . Catalogue cards
. . . Library furniture
. . . . Library counters
. . . . Library display cases
. . . . Library shelving
. . . Library vehicles
. . . . Library conveyors
. . . . Library trolleys
. . . . Mobile libraries
. . . Visible indexes
. Leisure equipment
. . Sports equipment
. Lifting equipment
. . Elevators
. . Hoists
. Machine tools
. Machines
. . Agricultural machinery
. . Electric machines
. . . Electric generators
. . . Electric motors
. . Prime movers
. . . Gas turbines
. . . Internal combustion engines

Equipment (cont.)
. . . . Diesel engines
. . . Steam turbines
. . . Turbines
. . . . Gas turbines
. . . . Steam turbines
. . . . Water turbines
. . . Water turbines
. . Textile machinery
. Mechanical components
. . Cooling systems
. . Grabs
. . Joints
. . Lubrication systems
. . Mechanical transmission systems
. . . Brakes
. . . Clutches
. . . Gears
. . Reciprocating parts
. . Ropes
. . . Wire ropes
. . Seals
. . Shafts
. . Springs (components)
. . Valves
. Medical equipment
. . Life support systems
. . Medical instruments
. . . Surgical instruments
. . Therapeutic equipment
. . . Drugs
. . . . Anaesthetics
. . . . Antibiotics
. . . . Narcotic drugs
. Microform equipment
. Military equipment
. . Weapons
. . . Conventional weapons
. . . . Armoured vehicles
. . . . Guns
. . . Missiles
. . . Nuclear weapons
. Mining equipment
. . Pumps
. Museum equipment
. Office equipment
. Photographic equipment
. . Cameras
. . . Film cameras
. . . Television cameras
. . . Underwater cameras
. . Projectors
. . . Slide projectors
. Printing equipment
. . Inks
. . Newsprint
. . Printing paper
. . . Newsprint
. Safety devices
. . Protective clothing
. . Restraint systems
. . Warning devices
. Scientific equipment
. . Instruments
. . . Display devices
. . . . Displays (computer)
. . . Electrical instruments
. . . Gauges
. . . . Rain gauges
. . . . Tide gauges
. . . Indicating instruments
. . . Medical instruments

Equipment (cont.)
. . . . Surgical instruments
. . . Musical instruments
. . . Brass instruments
. . . Keyboard instruments
. . . Percussion instruments
. . . String instruments
. . . Wind instruments
. . . Navigational instruments
. . . . Compasses
. . . . Gyroscopes
. . . Oceanographic instruments
. . . . Bathymeters
. . . . Bathythermographs
. . . . Current meters
. . . . Depth recorders
. . . . Drift bottles
. . . . Echo sounders
. . . . Fathometers
. . . . Flowmeters
. . . . . Anemometers
. . . . . Current meters
. . . . . Pitot tubes
. . . . . Venturimeters
. . . . Plankton recorders
. . . . Salinity recorders
. . . . Sonar
. . . . Sound velocity meters
. . . . Thermistor chains
. . . . Tide gauges
. . . . Wave recorders
. . . Recording instruments
. . . Depth recorders
. . . Plankton recorders
. . . Salinity recorders
. . . Wave recorders
. . . Sensors
. . . . Light detectors
. . . . Radiation detectors
. . . . Temperature probes
. . . Surveying instruments
. . . . Gravimeters
. . . Transducers
. . . . Pressure transducers
. . Laboratory equipment
. . . Chemical laboratory equipment
. . . . Reagents
. . . Educational laboratory equipment
. . Medical equipment
. . . Life support systems
. . . Medical instruments
. . . . Surgical instruments
. . . Therapeutic equipment
. . . . Drugs
. . . . . Anaesthetics
. . . . . Antibiotics
. . . . . Narcotic drugs
. . Oceanographic equipment
. . . Bathyspheres
. . . Capstans
. . . Diving equipment
. . . Floats
. . . Hydrophones
. . . Oceanographic buoys
. . . Oceanographic instruments
. . . . Bathymeters
. . . . Bathythermographs
. . . . Current meters
. . . . Depth recorders
. . . . Drift bottles
. . . . Echo sounders
. . . . Fathometers

Equipment (cont.)
. . . . . Flowmeters
. . . . . . Anemometers
. . . . . . Current meters
. . . . . . Pitot tubes
. . . . . . Venturimeters
. . . . . Plankton recorders
. . . . Salinity recorders
. . . . Sonar
. . . . Sound velocity meters
. . . . Thermistor chains
. . . . Tide gauges
. . . . Wave recorders
. . . Oceanographic samplers
. . . . Plankton recorders
. . . Underwater cameras
. . . Winches
. . . Wire ropes
. Sports equipment

Errors
. Probable error
. Standard error

Esoteric practices
. Mysticism
. Occult
. . Alchemy
. . Astrology
. . Fortune-telling
. . Magic
. . . Demonology
. . . Voodoo
. . . Witchcraft
. . Parapsychology
. . . Extra-sensory perception
. . . . Psychokinesis
. . . . Telepathy
. . Physiognomy
. . . Palmistry
. . Spiritualism
. Sciosophic movements
. Secret societies
. . Freemasonry

Ethics
. Communication ethics
. . Press ethics
. Deontology
. . Medical ethics
. . Press ethics
. . Teacher professional ethics
. Ethics of science
. . Bioethics
. . Medical ethics
. Moral behaviour
. . Misconduct
. Moral concepts
. . Accountability
. . Conscience
. . Discipline
. . . School discipline
. . . Self-discipline
. . Duties
. . . Role duties
. . Obligation
. . Responsibility
. . . Parent responsibility
. . . Social responsibility

Ethics (cont.)
. . . State responsibility
. . . . State responsibility for education
. . . Teacher responsibility
. Moral development
. Moral order
. Moral problems
. . Moral crises
. Moral values
. Political ethics
. Virtue and vice
. . Anger
. . Cruelty
. . . Inhuman treatment
. . . . Torture
. . . Torture
. . Hatred
. . Jealousy
. . Love
. . Sexual deviance
. . Tolerance
. . . Racial tolerance
. . Truth

Evaluation
. Curriculum evaluation
. Economic evaluation
. Evaluation of education
. Information systems evaluation
. Job evaluation

Examinations
. Entrance examinations
. External examinations
. Internal examinations
. Oral examinations
. Practical examinations
. Written examinations
. . Theses

Excavation
. Archaeological excavations

Executive functions (psychology)
. Involuntary actions
. . Habits
. . . Reading habit
. . . Speech habits
. . Handedness
. . Instincts
. . . Hunger
. . . Sexual behaviour
. . . . Sexual deviance
. Voluntary actions
. . Will
. . . Self-discipline

Expenditure
. Cultural expenditure
. Educational expenditure
. . Educational wages
. . . Teacher salaries
. . Teacher salaries
. Information/library expenditure
. Public expenditure
. . Educational expenditure
. . . Educational wages

Expenditure (cont.)
. . . . Teacher salaries
. . . Teacher salaries
. . Information/library expenditure
. Scientific expenditure

Experience
. Religious experience

Experiments
. Educational experiments
. Experiments (lessons)

Expression
. Oral expression
. Physical expression

Family
. Broken families
. Joint family
. Nuclear family
. One-parent families
. Problem families

Faults
. Crystal defects
. Deformation
. . Elastic deformation
. . Plastic deformation
. . . Creep
. Electrical faults
. Fatigue
. Fracture

Fees
. Educational fees

Fertility
. Soil fertility

File management (index)
. Coding
. Collating
. Cumulating
. File guidance (index)
. File maintenance (index)
. Filing (index)
. Posting
. . Generic posting
. Sorting

File organization (index)
. Inverted file
. Item entry

Fishing gear
. Gill nets
. Seine nets
. Trawl nets

Fluid waves
. Water waves
. . Ocean waves
. . . Internal waves
. . . Surf
. . . Tsunami

Forests
. Tropical forests

Frequency
. Book use frequency
. Daily
. Monthly
. Quarterly
. Term frequency (use)
. Wave frequency
. . Ocean wave frequency
. Weekly
. Yearly

Furniture
. Library furniture
. . Library counters
. . Library display cases
. . Library shelving
. School furniture

Gems
. Diamonds

Geographical areas and countries
. Africa
. . Africa South of the Sahara
. . . Central Africa
. . . . Burundi
. . . . Cameroon
. . . . Central African Republic
. . . . Chad
. . . . Congo (Peoples Republic)
. . . . Equatorial Guinea
. . . . Gabon
. . . . Rwanda
. . . . Sao Tome and Principe
. . . . Zaire
. . . East Africa
. . . . Afars and Issas
. . . . Burundi
. . . . Comoro Islands
. . . . Ethiopia
. . . . Kenya
. . . . Madagascar (Democratic Republic)
. . . . Malawi
. . . . Mauritius
. . . . Mozambique
. . . . Reunion Islands
. . . . Rwanda
. . . . Seychelles
. . . . Somalia
. . . . Sudan
. . . . Tanzania (United Republic)
. . . . Uganda
. . . . Zambia
. . . Southern Africa
. . . . Angola
. . . . Botswana

Groups (cont.)
. . International organizations
. . . Intergovernment organizations
. . . International educational bodies
. . . International information/library organizations
. . . Non-governmental organizations
. . Private organizations
. . . Associations
. . . . Clubs
. . . . . Old peoples clubs
. . . . . School clubs
. . . . . Socio-cultural clubs
. . . . . . Book clubs
. . . . . . Film clubs
. . . . . . Teleclubs
. . . . . . Video clubs
. . . . . Sports clubs
. . . . . UNESCO clubs
. . . . . Youth clubs
. . . . Cultural associations
. . . . Educational associations
. . . . . Parent-teacher organizations
. . . . . Teacher associations
. . . . . . Teacher trade unions
. . . . Employers organizations
. . . . Learned societies
. . . . Professional associations
. . . . . Information/library professional associations
. . . . . . Library associations
. . . . . Teacher associations
. . . . . . Teacher trade unions
. . . . Secret societies
. . . . . Freemasonry
. . . . Trade unions
. . . . . Teacher trade unions
. . . Private cultural organizations
. . . . Cultural associations
. . . . Socio-cultural clubs
. . . . . Book clubs
. . . . . Film clubs
. . . . . Teleclubs
. . . . . Video clubs
. . Private educational organizations
. . . . Educational associations
. . . . . Parent-teacher organizations
. . . . . Teacher associations
. . . . . . Teacher trade unions
. . . . Educational foundations
. . . Private enterprises
. . . . Joint stock companies
. . . . Partnerships
. . . Private information/library organizations
. . . Trusts
. . . . Educational foundations
. . . Voluntary organizations
. . . . Voluntary welfare organizations
. . . . . Red Cross
. . . Womens organizations
. . . . Womens liberation movement
. . Regional organizations
. . . Regional cultural organizations
. . . Regional educational bodies
. . Scientific organizations
. . . Scientific institutions
. . Social science organizations
. . . Social science institutions
. . Social welfare organizations
. . . Voluntary welfare organizations
. . . . Red Cross
. . Student organizations
. . Womens organizations
. . . Womens liberation movement

Groups (cont.)
. . Youth organizations
. . . Student organizations
. . . Youth clubs
. Pressure groups
. Racial groups
. . Aboriginal people
. . Asians
. . . Indians
. . Coloured people
. . . Asians
. . . . Indians
. . . Blacks
. . Eskimos
. . Lapps
. . North American Indians
. . Racial minorities
. . Semitic people
. . . Arabs
. . . Jews
. . South American Indians
. . White people
. Small groups
. Working groups
. . Training groups

Guides
. Curriculum guides
. Guides to information sources
. Maintenance handbooks

Gulfs
. Gulf of Aden
. Gulf of Agaba
. Gulf of Alaska
. Gulf of Boni
. Gulf of Bothnia
. Gulf of California
. Gulf of Finland
. Gulf of Guinea
. Gulf of Iran
. Gulf of Mexico
. Gulf of Oman
. Gulf of Riga
. Gulf of St. Lawrence
. Gulf of Suez
. Gulf of Thailand
. Gulf of Tomini

Hazards accidents and disasters
. Accidents
. . Explosions
. . . Nuclear explosions
. . Fire
. . . Forest fires
. Disasters
. . Man-made disasters
. . . Nuclear explosions
. . Natural disasters
. . . Avalanches
. . . Drought
. . . Earthquakes
. . . . Submarine earthquakes
. . . Epidemics
. . . Famine
. . . Floods
. . . Landslides
. . . Volcanic eruptions

Head of state
. Presidency

Health
. Hygiene
. Mental health
. Public health

Heat
. Terrestrial heat

Heat engines
. Gas turbines
. Internal combustion engines
. . Diesel engines
. Steam turbines

Higher mental processes
. Cognition
. . Conceptualization
. . Ideation
. . . Imagination
. . . Inspiration
. . . Intuition
. . Learning
. . . Adult learning
. . . Memorization
. . Memory
. . Thinking
. . . Creative thinking
. . . Reasoning
. . . . Abstract reasoning
. . . . Deduction
. . . . Rationalization
. Intelligence

History and associated studies
. Archaeology
. Chronology
. . Dating
. . . Archaeological dating
. . . . Radiocarbon dating
. . . Radiocarbon dating
. . Geochronology
. Epigraphy
. Genealogy
. Heraldry
. History
. . African history
. . American history
. . . Latin American history
. . . North American history
. . Ancient history
. . Arab history
. . Art history
. . Asian history
. . Australasian history
. . Byzantine history
. . Communication history
. . Constitutional history
. . Cultural history
. . . Art history
. . Documentary history
. . Economic history
. . Educational history
. . European history
. . Historiography

History and associated studies (cont.)
. . . Historical analysis
. . . Historical method
. . . Historical research
. . . Historical writing
. . . . Historical editing
. . History of archives
. . History of psychology
. . History of science
. . Information/library history
. . . History of libraries
. . Latin American history
. . Legal history
. . Literary history
. . Medieval history
. . Modern history
. . Objective history
. . Oral history
. . Philosophy of history
. . Political history
. . . Constitutional history
. . Prehistory
. . . Bronze age
. . . Iron age
. . . Stone age
. . . . Mesolithic period
. . . . Neolithic period
. . . . Palaeolithic period
. . Psychohistory
. . Quantitative history
. . Religious history
. . Russian history
. . Social history
. Numismatics
. Palaeography
. Sigillography

Hospitality (notation)
. Interpolation (index language)

Humanitarian law
. Conduct of war rules
. Rights of civilians
. Rights of war prisoners
. Rights of war wounded
. Truces
. War relief

Humidity
. Atmospheric humidity

Ice
. Floating ice
. Land ice
. Sea ice
. . Icebergs

Identity
. Cultural identity
. . National identity

Ideologies
. Economic doctrines
. . Capitalism
. . Collectivism
. . . Communism

Information storage devices (cont.)
. . . Permuted indexes
. . . PRECIS indexes
. . Cumulative indexes
. . Data bases
. . Name indexes
. . . Name catalogues
. . Periodical indexes
. . Printed indexes
. . . Articulated indexes
. . . Book indexes
. . . Chain indexes
. . . Computerized indexes
. . . . Articulated indexes
. . . . KWAC indexes
. . . . KWIC indexes
. . . . KWOC indexes
. . . . Permuted indexes
. . . . PRECIS indexes
. . . KWAC indexes
. . . KWIC indexes
. . . KWOC indexes
. . . Periodical indexes
. . . Permuted indexes
. . . PRECIS indexes
. . . Rotated indexes
. . Shelf as index
. . Shelf lists
. . Subject indexes
. . . Pre-coordinate indexes
. . . . Alphabetical subject indexes
. . . . . Alphabetical subject catalogues
. . . . . Articulated indexes
. . . . ↓ . Chain indexes
. . . . . KWAC indexes
. . . . . KWIC indexes
. . . . . KWOC indexes
. . . . . Permuted indexes
. . . . . PRECIS indexes
. . . . . Relative indexes
. . . . . Rotated indexes
. . . . Alphabetico-classed indexes/catalogues
. . . . Classified indexes
. . . . . Classified catalogues
. . . Subject catalogues
. . . . Alphabetical subject catalogues
. . . . Alphabetico-classed indexes/catalogues
. . . . Classified catalogues
. . . . Dictionary catalogues
. . Title indexes
. . . KWAC indexes
. . . KWIC indexes
. . . KWOC indexes
. . . Title catalogues
. . Visible indexes

Information use
. Book use frequency

Information users
. Library users

Information/library operations
. Information processing
. . Document description
. . . Abstracting
. . . Bibliographic description
. . . . ISBD
. . . . . ISBD (M)

Information/library operations (cont.)
. . . . . ISBD (NBM)
. . . . . ISBD (S)
. . . Indexing
. . . . Author indexing
. . . . . Author cataloguing
. . . . Bibliographic coupling
. . . . Cataloguing
. . . . . Author cataloguing
. . . . . Cataloguing-in-source
. . . . . Centralized cataloguing
. . . . . Cooperative cataloguing
. . . . . Name cataloguing
. . . . . Re-cataloguing
. . . . . Simplified cataloguing
. . . . . Subject cataloguing
. . . . . Title cataloguing
. . . . Citation indexing
. . . . Name indexing
. . . . . Name cataloguing
. . . . Subject indexing
. . . . . Classifying
. . . . . . Re-classifying
. . . . . Content analysis
. . . . . Subject cataloguing
. . . . Title indexing
. . . . . Title cataloguing
. . Information retrieval
. . . Bibliography compilation
. . . Data retrieval
. . . Literature searches
. . . Reference work
. . . Searching
. . . . Batch searching
. . . . Browsing
. . . . Literature searches
. . . . Natural language searching
. . . . . Contextual searching
. . . . . Text searching
. . . . On-line searching
. . . . Random searching
. . . . . Browsing
. . . . Retrospective searching
. . . . Text searching
. . Translation
. . . Automatic translation
. Library housekeeping operations
. . Accessioning
. . Acquisition systems
. . . Book ordering
. . . . Approval ordering
. . . . Periodical acquisition systems
. . . Book selection
. . . Exchange of publications
. . . Periodical acquisition systems
. . Document maintenance
. . . Document preservation
. . Document processing
. . . Accessioning
. . . Document preparation
. . . Document withdrawal
. . . . Records disposal
. . . Filing
. . . Shelving (operation)
. . . Stock-taking (document)
. . Document storage
. . Library circulation work
. . . Loan services
. . . . Inter-library loans
. . . . Internal loans
. . . . Postal loans
. . . Periodical circulation

436

Information/library philosophy policy and development
. Information/library development
. Information/library philosophy
. Information/library policy
. . Acquisition policy

Information/library planning and administration
. Information/library administration
. . Information/library legislation
. . Information/library management
. Information/library economics
. . Information/library planning
. Information/library planning

Information/library systems
. Information services
. . Bibliographic services
. . . Literature review services
. . Clearing houses
. . Enquiry services
. . Reference services
. . Referral centres
. . Translation services
. Information systems
. . Abstracting and indexing services
. . . Current awareness services
. . . Retrospective search services
. . Data banks
. . Data centres
. . Information analysis centres
. . International information systems
. . Legal information systems
. . Management information systems
. . National information systems
. . On-line information systems
. . Scientific information systems
. . . Agricultural information systems
. . . Engineering information systems
. . . Medical information systems
. . . . Medical records information systems
. Information/library networks
. Libraries
. . Agricultural libraries
. . Armed forces libraries
. . Art libraries
. . Branch libraries
. . Childrens libraries
. . Document centres
. . Educational libraries
. . . Academic libraries
. . . . University libraries
. . . School libraries
. . . . Primary school libraries
. . . . Secondary school libraries
. . Film libraries
. . Government libraries
. . . Central government libraries
. . . . Government department libraries
. . . . Legislature libraries
. . . State libraries
. . Headquarters libraries
. . Institutional libraries
. . . Hospital libraries
. . . . Medical hospital libraries
. . . Libraries for the blind
. . . Prison libraries
. . . Ship libraries
. . International libraries
. . Large libraries
. . Law libraries

Information/library systems (cont.)
. . Lending libraries
. . Map libraries
. . Medical libraries
. . . Medical hospital libraries
. . Medium size libraries
. . Mobile libraries
. . National libraries
. . . Depository libraries
. . Phonorecord libraries
. . Pilot libraries
. . Program libraries
. . Public libraries
. . . County libraries
. . . District libraries
. . . Municipal libraries
. . . Regional libraries
. . . Rural libraries
. . Public/academic libraries
. . Reference libraries
. . Scientific libraries
. . . Agricultural libraries
. . . Engineering libraries
. . . Industrial libraries
. . . Medical libraries
. . . . Medical hospital libraries
. . Small libraries
. . Special libraries
. . . Business libraries
. . . . Newspaper libraries
. . . Government libraries
. . . . Central government libraries
. . . . . Government department libraries
. . . . . Legislature libraries
. . . . State libraries
. . . Industrial libraries
. . . Learned libraries
. . . Philanthropic libraries
. . . Private libraries
. . . Religious institution libraries
. . . Research libraries
. . . Subscription libraries

Innovations
. Educational innovations
. . Curriculum development
. . . Anticurriculum movement
. . . . De-schooling
. . Teaching method innovations
. Scientific innovations
. . Agricultural innovations

Inspection
. Educational inspection
. Labour inspection
. Medical inspection
. . Dental inspection

Insurance
. Accident insurance
. Fire insurance
. Life insurance

Interdisciplinary science and technology
. Computer science
. . Computer metatheory
. . Computer programming
. . Computer techniques

Interdisciplinary science and technology (cont.)
. . . Teleprocessing
. . File organization (computer)
. . Logic design
. Control technology
. Data processing
. . Data analysis
. . Data collection
. . Data exchange
. . Data handling
. . . Data preparation
. . Data retrieval
. Design
. . Artistic design
. . . Fashion design
. . Building design
. . . Housing design
. . . Open plan design
. . Computer-assisted design
. . Environmental design
. . . Landscape design
. . . Urban design
. . . . Street furniture design
. . . Visual planning
. . Fashion design
. . Industrial design
. . Statistical design
. . . Mathematical models
. . . Monte Carlo methods
. . . Sampling theory
. . . Statistical analysis
. . . . Correlation
. . . . Economic analysis
. . . . . Cost/benefit analysis
. . . . . Input-output analysis
. . . . . Socio-economic analysis
. . . . Multivariate analysis
. . . . . Discriminant analysis
. . . . . Factor analysis
. . . . Optimization
. . . . Variance analysis
. . . Time series
. Navigation
. . Aerospace navigation
. . Inertial navigation
. . Magnetic navigation
. . Marine navigation
. . Radar navigation
. . Radio navigation
. . Satellite navigation
. . Sonar navigation
. . Underwater navigation
. . . Sonar navigation
. Surveying
. . Aerial surveying
. . Archaeological surveying
. . Hydrographic surveying
. . . Bathymetry
. . . Sounding
. . . . Echo sounding
. . Photogrammetry
. . Tacheometry
. . Triangulation
. Systemology
. . Systems analysis
. Testing
. . Educational testing
. . Information systems evaluation
. . Materials testing
. . . Destructive testing
. . . Non-destructive testing
. . Program testing

Interference
. Radio wave interference

Invertebrata
. Anthropoda
. . Crustacea
. . Insects
. . Myriapoda
. Metazoa
. . Anthropoda
. . . Crustacea
. . . Insects
. . . Myriapoda
. . Coelenterata
. . Echinodermata
. . Mollusca
. Parazoa
. Protozoa

Ionization
. Atmospheric ionization

Job requirements
. Occupational qualifications
. . Teacher qualifications

Justice
. Social justice

Kinship
. Grandparents
. Parents
. . Fathers
. . Mothers
. . . Unmarried mothers
. . . Working mothers
. Siblings

Labour and employment
. Employment
. . Full employment
. . Full-time employment
. . Overemployment
. . Part-time employment
. . Student employment
. . Underemployment
. . Unemployment
. . Womens employment
. . Youth employment
. Labour
. Labour economics
. Labour relations
. . Labour conflict
. . . Labour disputes
. . . . Lockouts
. . . . Sit-ins
. . . . Strikes
. . . . . Teacher strikes
. . . Work-to-rule
. . Workers participation
. . . Joint management
. . . Workers control
. Occupations
. . Farmers
. . Professional occupations
. . . Archive profession

439

441

Languages (cont.)
. . . Italian
. . . Portuguese
. . . Romanian
. . . Spanish
. . Slavic languages
. . . Bulgarian
. . . Byelorussian
. . . Czech
. . . Kazakh
. . . Polish
. . . Russian
. . . Serbo-Croatian
. . . Slovak
. . . Slovene
. . . Ukrainian
. International languages
. . Esperanto
. . International auxiliary lingua
. Language varieties
. . Colloquial language
. . Computer languages
. . . Machine oriented languages
. . . Problem oriented languages
. . . Procedure oriented languages
. . Dead languages
. . . Greek (classical)
. . . Latin
. . Dialects
. . Foreign languages
. . Formal language
. . Index languages
. . . Controlled languages
. . . . Alphabetical subject heading lists
. . . . Authority lists
. . . . Classification systems
. . . . . Analytico-synthetic classification systems
. . . . . . Faceted classification systems
. . . . Bliss classification system
. . . . Colon classification
. . . . UDC
. . . . . Broad classification systems
. . . . . Close classification systems
. . . . . Hierarchical classification systems
. . . . . . Dewey decimal classification
. . . . . . Library of Congress classification
. . . . Switching languages
. . . . Term lists
. . . . . Uniterms
. . . . Thesauri
. . . . . Alphabetical thesauri
. . . . . Classification/thesaurus systems
. . . . . Compressed vocabularies
. . . . . Macrothesauri
. . . . . Microthesauri
. . . . . Monolingual thesauri
. . . . . Multilingual thesauri
. . . . . Systematic thesauri
. . . Free language systems
. . . Natural language systems
. . Language mixtures
. . Modern languages
. . Mother tongue
. . Spoken language
. . . Spoken poetry
. . Symbolic languages
. . . Signs
. . . Symbols
. . Unwritten languages
. . Vernacular languages
. . Written languages
. Monolingual

Languages (cont.)
. Multilingual
. Oriental languages
. . Eurasian and North Asian languages
. . . Altaic languages
. . . . Azerbaijani
. . . . Mongolian languages
. . . . Tungus
. . . . Turkish
. . . Eskimo languages
. . . Japanese
. . . Korean
. . . Palaeosiberian languages
. . . Uralic languages
. . . . Estonian
. . . . Finnish
. . . . Hungarian
. . . . Lappic
. . . . Samoyedic languages
. . Hamito-Semitic and Caucasian languages
. . . Basque language
. . . Caucasian languages
. . . . Darghi
. . . . Georgian
. . . Hamito-Semitic languages
. . . . Hamitic languages
. . . . . Cushitic Languages
. . . . . . Somali
. . . . . Libyan-Berber languages
. . . . Semitic languages
. . . . . Amharic
. . . . . Arabic
. . . . . Hebrew
. . South and South-East Asian languages
. . . Andaman languages
. . . Annam-Muong
. . . Dravidian languages
. . . . Kannada
. . . . Malayalam
. . . . Tamil
. . . . Telegu
. . . Mon-Khmer languages
. . . . Cambodian
. . . Munda languages
. . . Sino-Tibetan languages
. . . . Chinese
. . . . Thai languages
. . . . . Annamese
. . . . . Laotian
. . . . . Siamese
. . . . . Vietnamese
. . . . Tibeto-Burmese languages
. . . . . Burmese
. . . . . Tibetan
. Pluralingual

Law
. Administration of justice
. . Legal practice and procedure
. . . Advocacy
. . . Brief preparation
. . . Court rules and procedures
. . . . Bail
. . . . Contempt of court
. . . . Remand in custody
. . . Evidence
. . . . Witnesses
. . . Hearings
. . . Legal advice
. . . Legal decisions
. . . . Appeals (legal)

Law (cont.)
. . . . . Decrees
. . . . . Injunctions
. . . . . Judgments
. . . . . . Acquittal
. . . . . . Conviction (legal)
. . . . . . Decrees
. . . . Mediation
. . . . . Arbitration
. . . . . . Industrial arbitration
. . . . . Conciliation
. . . . . . Industrial conciliation
. . . . Industrial arbitration
. . . . . Industrial conciliation
. . . . . Industrial arbitration
. . . . Pleadings
. . . . Summons
. . . . Trials
. . . . . Political trials
. . . . . Trial by jury
. . . . . Trial in camera
. Civil law
. . Commercial law
. . . Company law
. . Communication legislation
. . . Broadcasting legislation
. . . Copyright
. . Contract law
. . Family law
. . Labour law
. . Torts
. . . Liability (legal)
. . . Libel
. . . Trespass
. Comparative law
. International law
. . Private international law
. . . Conflict of laws
. . Public international law
. . . International disputes
. . . International instruments
. . . . Bilateral agreements
. . . . Cultural agreements
. . . . Economic agreements
. . . . Reciprocal agreements
. . . . Treaties
. . . . . Non-proliferation treaties
. . . . . Peace treaties
. . . Law of space
. . . Law of the air
. . . . Territorial air space
. . . Law of the sea
. . . Rights of states
. . . . Equality of states
. . . . Recognition rights
. . . . Sovereignty
. . . . State succession
. . . . Territorial rights
. . . . . Boundaries
. . . . . Territorial air space
. . . . . Territorial waters
. Legal systems
. . Case law
. . Codified law
. . Customary law
. . Ecclesiastical law
. . Historical systems of law
. . . Antiquarian law
. . . Code Napoleon
. . . Moslem law
. . Modern law
. . Primitive law

Law (cont.)
. Legal theory
. . Analytical jurisprudence
. . . Concept of law
. . . Sources of law
. . Schools of legal theory
. Legislation
. . Archive legislation
. . Codes of rules
. . . Cataloguing rules
. . Communication legislation
. . . Broadcasting legislation
. . . Copyright
. . Cultural legislation
. . . Museum legislation
. . Economic legislation
. . Educational legislation
. . Environmental legislation
. . . Air pollution legislation
. . . Environmental planning legislation
. . . Water law
. . Information/library legislation
. . Population legislation
. . Regulations
. . Statutes

Law officers
. Judges
. Juries
. Magistrates
. Public prosecutors

Learning processes
. Assimilation
. Attention
. Comprehension
. Concentration
. Conceptualization
. Feedback (learning)
. Interest (learning)
. . Student interests
. . . After-school activities
. . . . School clubs
. Memorization
. Retention

Learning readiness
. Reading readiness

Library rules and regulations
. Library admission
. Library hours of opening
. Loan fines
. Loan period

Library services
. Library circulation work
. . Loan services
. . . Inter-library loans
. . . Internal loans
. . . Postal loans
. . Periodical circulation
. Library extension work
. . Reading promotion

Library use promotion
. Reading promotion

Life
. Animal life
. Plant life
. Wildlife
. . Wild animals
. . . Game animals
. . Wild plants

Life cycle
. Ageing
. Birth
. Death
. Maturity
. . Emotional maturity
. Puberty

Life sciences
. Anthropology
. Biology
. . Aerobiology
. . Agricultural biology
. . . Agricultural genetics
. . Anatomy
. . . Animal anatomy
. . . Human anatomy
. . . Plant anatomy
. . . Regional anatomy
. . . . Head
. . . . Limbs
. . . . . Artificial limbs
. . . . Torso
. . Biochemistry
. . . Human biochemistry
. . . Palaeobiochemistry
. . . Phytochemistry
. . . Zoochemistry
. . Bioclimatology
. . Biogeochemistry
. . Biometrics
. . Biophysics
. . . Bionics
. . . Human biophysics
. . Botany
. . . Botanical taxonomy
. . . Palaeobotany
. . . Phytochemistry
. . . Phytogeography
. . . Phytopathology
. . . Plant anatomy
. . . Plant ecology
. . . . Plant adaptation
. . . Plant genetics
. . . Plant histology
. . . Plant metabolism
. . . Plant morphology
. . . Plant physiology
. . . . Plant development
. . . . . Plant growth
. . . . . Plant transpiration
. . Cell biology
. . Ecology
. . . Aerobiology
. . . Animal ecology
. . . Autecology
. . . Exobiology
. . . Human ecology

Life sciences (cont.)
. . . Hydrobiology
. . . . Limnology
. . . . Marine biology
. . . Palaeoecology
. . . Plant ecology
. . . . Plant adaptation
. . . Synecology
. . Embryology
. . Evolution
. . . Biogenesis
. . Exobiology
. . Experimental biology
. . . Experimental botany
. . . Experimental zoology
. . Genetics
. . . Agricultural genetics
. . . Animal genetics
. . . Cytogenetics
. . . Human genetics
. . . Mutation
. . . Natural selection
. . . Plant genetics
. . Histology
. . . Plant histology
. . . Zoohistology
. . Human biology
. . . Human anatomy
. . . Human biochemistry
. . . Human biophysics
. . . Human genetics
. . . Human physiology
. . Hydrobiology
. . . Limnology
. . . Marine biology
. . Immunology
. . Microbiology
. . . Bacteriology
. . . . Virology
. . . Virology
. . Molecular biology
. . Neurobiology
. . Palaeontology
. . . Invertebrate palaeontology
. . . Micropalaeontology
. . . Palaeobotany
. . . Vertebrate palaeontology
. . Parasitology
. . Pharmacology
. . Physiology
. . . Human physiology
. . . Plant physiology
. . . . Plant development
. . . . . Plant growth
. . . . Plant transpiration
. . . Psychophysiology
. . . Zoophysiology
. . . . Animal development
. . . . . Animal growth
. . . . Animal metabolism
. . Radiobiology
. . Taxonomy
. . . Animal taxonomy
. . . Botanical taxonomy
. . Zoology
. . . Animal anatomy
. . . Animal breeding
. . . Animal ecology
. . . Animal genetics
. . . Animal metabolism
. . . Animal morphology
. . . Animal taxonomy

Life sciences (cont.)
- . . Entomology
- . . Experimental zoology
- . . Zoochemistry
- . . Zoogeography
- . . Zoohistology
- . . Zoopathology
- . . Zoophysiology
- . . . Animal development
- . . . . Animal growth
- . . . Animal metabolism
- . Medical sciences
- . . Anaesthesiology
- . . Clinical medicine
- . . . Medical diagnosis
- . . . Medical treatment
- . . . . First aid
- . . . . Nursing
- . . . . Therapy
- . . . . . Dietetics
- . . . . . Pharmacy
- . . . . . Physiotherapy
- . . . . . . Electrotherapy
- . . . . . . Radiotherapy
- . . . . . . Psychotherapy
- . . . . . . Drug psychotherapy
- . . . . . . Hypnotherapy
- . . . . . . Occupational therapy
- . . . . . . Psychodrama
- . . . . . . Shock treatment
- . . . . . . Sociodrama
- . . . . . Rehabilitation
- . . . . . Speech therapy
- . . Human biology
- . . . Human anatomy
- . . . Human biochemistry
- . . . Human biophysics
- . . . Human genetics
- . . . Human physiology
- . . Medical specialities
- . . . Aerospace medicine
- . . . Chiropody
- . . . Dentistry
- . . . Forensic medicine
- . . . Geriatrics
- . . . Gynaecology
- . . . Ophthalmology
- . . . Orthopaedics
- . . . Paediatrics
- . . . Sports medicine
- . . . Veterinary medicine
- . . Medical technology
- . . . Bioengineering
- . . . Electrotherapy
- . . . Radiotherapy
- . . Pathology
- . . . Phytopathology
- . . . Psychopathology
- . . . Zoopathology
- . . Preventive medicine
- . . . Epidemiology
- . . . Medical inspection
- . . . . Dental inspection
- . . Psychiatry
- . . . Clinical psychology
- . . . . Psychoanalysis
- . . . . Psychotherapy
- . . . . . Drug psychotherapy
- . . . . . Hypnotherapy
- . . . . . Occupational therapy
- . . . . Psychodrama
- . . . . Shock treatment

Life sciences (cont.)
- . . . . . Sociodrama
- . . . Psychopathology
- . . Surgery
- . . . Brain surgery
- . . . Organ transplantation
- . . . Plastic surgery
- . . Systems of medicine
- . . . Acupuncture
- . . . Folk medicine
- . . . Naturopathy
- . . . Osteopathy
- . Natural history

Literacy
- . Adult literacy
- . Functional literacy

Literary criticism
- . Book reviews

Literary forms and genres
- . Biographies
- . . Educational biographies
- . Comics
- . Correspondence
- . Drama
- . . Comedy
- . . Radio drama
- . . Television drama
- . . Tragedy
- . Fairy tales
- . Fiction
- . . Novels
- . . . Romance stories
- . . . Science fiction
- . . . Thrillers
- . . Romance stories
- . . Science fiction
- . . Thrillers
- . Folk literature
- . . Fairy tales
- . . Legends
- . . Nursery rhymes
- . . Proverbs
- . Poetry
- . . Nursery rhymes
- . . Spoken poetry
- . Popular literature
- . . Best sellers
- . . Romance stories
- . . Science fiction
- . . Thrillers
- . Prose
- . . Articles
- . . Comics
- . . Essays
- . . Fairy tales
- . . Novels
- . . . Romance stories
- . . . Science fiction
- . . . Thrillers
- . Scripts
- . . Film scripts
- . Speeches

Literary works
- . Representative literary works

Loan records
. Loan records automation
. Photocharging
. Punched card loan records

Logic
. Mathematical logic

Maintenance
. Building maintenance
. . Library maintenance services
. Document maintenance
. . Document preservation

Man
. Prehistoric man

Management operations
. Centralization
. . Information/library centralization
. Cooperation
. . Cultural cooperation
. . . Museum cooperation
. . Educational cooperation
. . . University cooperation
. . Information/library cooperation
. . International cooperation
. . . Cultural cooperation
. . . . Museum cooperation
. . . Development aid
. . . . Economic aid
. . . . Financial aid
. . . . Technical assistance
. . . . Voluntary contribution
. . . Educational cooperation
. . . . University cooperation
. . . International assistance
. . . . Development aid
. . . . . Economic aid
. . . . . Financial aid
. . . . . Technical assistance
. . . . . Voluntary contribution
. . . . Foreign aid
. . . . International voluntary services
. . . Scientific cooperation
. . Regional cooperation
. . Scientific cooperation
. Coordination
. . Educational coordination
. . Research coordination
. Decentralization
. . Information/library decentralization
. . Urban decentralization
. Decision making
. Goal setting
. Integration
. . Cultural integration
. . . Cultural assimilation
. . . Enculturation
. . Educational integration
. . Information/library integration
. . Social integration
. . . Cultural integration
. . . . Cultural assimilation
. . . . Enculturation
. . . Racial integration
. . . . Desegregation
. Management control

Management operations (cont.)
. Managerial services
. . Management audit
. Planning
. . Development planning
. . . Agricultural planning
. . . Archive planning
. . . Communication planning
. . . Cultural planning
. . . . Museum planning
. . . Economic planning
. . . . Agricultural planning
. . . . Industrial planning
. . . . . Location of industry
. . . . Labour planning
. . . Educational planning
. . . . Curriculum planning
. . . Environmental planning
. . . . Environmental planning processes
. . . . . Amenities conservation
. . . . . . Conservation of nature
. . . . Countryside conservation
. . . . Landscape protection
. . . . Nature reserves
. . . . Wildlife protection
. . . . . . Countryside conservation
. . . . Landscape protection
. . . . . . Noise control
. . . . . Environmental design
. . . . . . Landscape design
. . . . . . Urban design
. . . . Street furniture design
. . . . . . Visual planning
. . . . Regional planning
. . . . Rural planning
. . . . . Countryside conservation
. . . . . . Landscape protection
. . . Transport planning
. . . Urban planning
. . . . Town reconstruction
. . . . Urban decentralization
. . . . Urban design
. . . . . Street furniture design
. . . . Urban development
. . . . Urban expansion
. . . . . Urban sprawl
. . . . Urban renewal
. . Industrial planning
. . . Location of industry
. . Information/library planning
. . Research planning
. . Science planning
. . Social planning
. . . Cultural planning
. . . . Museum planning
. . . Family planning
. . . Social welfare planning
. . Social science planning
. . Transport planning
. Long range planning
. Operational planning
. Policy making
. PPBS
. Programme planning
. Strategic planning
. Problem setting
. Project management
. Strategies
. . Communication strategies
. . Development strategies
. . . Communication strategies
. . Educational strategies

Management operations (cont.)
. . Military strategy
. . Research strategy
. . Search strategies
. . . Contextual searching
. . . Search cut-off
. . . Search revision
. . . . Relevance feedback
. . Teaching strategies
. Supervision
. . Educational supervision
. . . Educational inspection
. . . School supervision
. . . Teacher supervision

Managerial characteristics
. Authority
. . Teacher authority
. Leadership
. . Political leadership
. Prestige
. . National prestige
. Responsibility
. . Parent responsibility
. . Social responsibility
. . State responsibility
. . . State responsibility for education
. . Teacher responsibility

Marine life
. Marine animals
. . Marine fish
. . Shellfish
. . . Crustacea
. . Zooplankton
. Marine plants
. . Marine algae
. . . Seaweeds
. . Marine microorganisms
. . Phytoplankton
. Plankton
. . Phytoplankton
. . Zooplankton

Marital status
. Married men
. Married women
. . Married women workers
. . . Married women librarians
. . . Married women teachers
. . . Working mothers
. Unmarried
. . Unmarried mothers
. Widowers
. Widows

Market structure
. Economic competition
. . International competition
. Monopolies

Markets
. Financial markets
. Labour market

Marriage
. Mixed marriages
. Polygamy

Marriage dissolution
. Divorce

Materials
. Adhesives
. Animal oils
. Building materials
. . Asbestos
. . Bricks
. . Building stones
. . . Granite
. . . Limestone
. . . Marble
. . . Sandstones
. . . Slates
. . Cement
. . Concrete
. . Thermal insulation
. . Tiles
. . Wood
. . . Hardwood
. . . Softwood
. Ceramics
. . Refractories
. Chemical elements
. . Isotopes
. . . Radioisotopes
. . . . Radioactive tracers
. . Metalloids
. . . Antimony
. . . Arsenic
. . . Boron
. . . Germanium
. . . Polonium
. . . Silicon
. . . Tellurium
. . Metals
. . . Actinium
. . . Aluminium
. . . Antimony
. . . Barium
. . . Beryllium
. . . Bismuth
. . . Boron
. . . Cadmium
. . . Calcium
. . . Cesium
. . . Chromium
. . . Cobalt
. . . Copper
. . . Ferrous metals
. . . . Iron
. . . . Steels
. . . . . Stainless steels
. . . Francium
. . . Gallium
. . . Gold
. . . Hafnium
. . . Indium
. . . Iron
. . . Lead
. . . Lithium
. . . Magnesium
. . . Manganese
. . . Mercury
. . . Molybdenum

Mathematical sciences (cont.)
. . . . Interpolation
. . . . Iterative methods
. . . . Monte Carlo methods
. . . . Numerical methods
. . . Series (mathematics)
. . . Transforms
. . . . Fourier transforms
. . Mathematical logic
. . Modern mathematics
. . Number theory
. . Set theory
. . Statistical mathematics
. . . Probability theory
. . . . Expectation
. . . . . Probable error
. . . . . Risk
. . . . . Standard error
. . . . Game theory
. . . . Random processes
. . . . . Markov processes
. . . . . Queueing theory
. . . . . Random walk
. . . . Renewal theory
. . . . Statistical distributions
. . . . . Averages
. . . . . Central tendency
. . . . . Statistical dispersion
. . . . . . Standard deviation
. . . . . Variability
. . . . . . Ocean variability
. . . Statistical design
. . . . Mathematical models
. . . . Monte Carlo methods
. . . . Sampling theory
. . . . Statistical analysis
. . . . . Correlation
. . . . . Economic analysis
. . . . . . Cost/benefit analysis
. . . . . . Input-output analysis
. . . . . . Socio-economic analysis
. . . . . Multivariate analysis
. . . . . . Discriminant analysis
. . . . . . Factor analysis
. . . . . Optimization
. . . . . Variance analysis
. . . . Time series
. . . Statistical methods
. . . . Decision theory
. . . . Non-parametric statistics
. . . . Statistical inference
. . . . . Estimation
. . . . . Statistical tests
. . Topology
. . . Graph theory
. Statistics
. . Communication statistics
. . Cultural statistics
. . . Film production statistics
. . . Household cultural budgets
. . . Information/library statistics
. . . Museum statistics
. . . Time budgets
. . Descriptive statistics
. . . Statistics presentation
. . Educational statistics
. . Information/library statistics
. . Museum statistics
. . Science statistics
. . Statistical linguistics
. . . Statistical linguistics (indexing)
. . . . Associative indexing

Mathematical sciences (cont.)
. . . . . Clumping
. . . . . Clustering
. . . . . Discriminant analysis
. . Statistical mathematics
. . . Probability theory
. . . . Expectation
. . . . . Probable error
. . . . . Risk
. . . . . Standard error
. . . . Game theory
. . . . Random processes
. . . . . Markov processes
. . . . . Queueing theory
. . . . . Random walk
. . . . Renewal theory
. . . . Statistical distributions
. . . . . Averages
. . . . . Central tendency
. . . . . Statistical dispersion
. . . . . . Standard deviation
. . . . . Variability
. . . . . . Ocean variability
. . . Statistical design
. . . . Mathematical models
. . . . Monte Carlo methods
. . . . Sampling theory
. . . . Statistical analysis
. . . . . Correlation
. . . . . Economic analysis
. . . . . . Cost/benefit analysis
. . . . . . Input-output analysis
. . . . . . Socio-economic analysis
. . . . . Multivariate analysis
. . . . . . Discriminant analysis
. . . . . . Factor analysis
. . . . . Optimization
. . . . . Variance analysis
. . . . Time series
. . . Statistical methods
. . . . Decision theory
. . . . Non-parametric statistics
. . . . Statistical inference
. . . . . Estimation
. . . . . Statistical tests

Measurement and instruments
. Acoustic measurements and instruments
. . Acoustic holography
. . Noise measurement
. . Sea water acoustic measurements
. . Sound velocity meters
. Astronomical measurements and instruments
. . Astronomical telescopes
. . Radioastronomy
. Electrical measurements and instruments
. . Electric current measurement
. . Electrical resistance measurement
. . Voltage measurement
. Fluid measurement and instruments
. . Flow measurement and instruments
. . . Flowmeters
. . . . Anemometers
. . . . Current meters
. . . . Pitot tubes
. . . . Venturimeters
. . Fluid density measurement
. . . Hydrometry
. . . Sea water density measurement
. . Liquid level measurement
. . . Sea level measurement

Measurement and instruments (cont.)
. Radiography
. Telemetry
. Thermal measurements and instruments
. . Temperature measurement and instruments
. . . Pyrometers
. . . Sea water temperature measurement
. . . Temperature probes
. . . Thermistor chains
. . . Thermocouples
. . . Thermometers
. Time measurement and instruments
. . Clocks
. . Radiocarbon dating
. Vacuum measurement
. X-ray analysis
. . X-ray chemical analysis
. . X-ray crystallography
. . X-ray diffraction
. . X-ray spectroscopy

Metabolism
. Animal metabolism
. Plant metabolism

Methodology
. Literacy methodology
. Research methods
. . Causal analysis
. . Comparative analysis
. . Cross-cultural analysis
. . Cross-national analysis
. . Data analysis
. . Experimental methods
. . Historical method
. . Systems analysis
. . Typological analysis
. Research techniques
. . Models
. . . Cultural models
. . . Economic models
. . . Mathematical models
. . . Simulation models
. . . Synoptic modelling

Methods
. Graphical methods
. Learning methods
. . Activity learning
. . Associative learning
. . Multisensory learning
. . Rote learning
. . Sequential learning
. . Symbolic learning
. . Verbal learning
. . Visual learning
. Numerical methods
. Research methods
. . Causal analysis
. . Comparative analysis
. . Cross-cultural analysis
. . Cross-national analysis
. . Data analysis
. . Experimental methods
. . Historical method
. . Systems analysis
. . Typological analysis
. Statistical methods
. . Decision theory

Methods (cont.)
. . Non-parametric statistics
. . Statistical inference
. . . Estimation
. . . Statistical tests
. Study methods
. . Homework
. . Independent study
. . Individual study
. . Library work (study method)
. . Oral work
. . . Oral composition
. . . Oral reading
. . Practical studies
. . . Student projects
. . Self-teaching methods
. . Written work
. Teaching methods
. . Audiovisual instruction
. . Debates (teaching method)
. . Diagrammatical teaching
. . Direct method (teaching)
. . Discussions (teaching method)
. . Experiments (lessons)
. . Group work (teaching method)
. . . Activity methods
. . . Dramatic presentation (teaching method)
. . . Educational games
. . . Heuristic method (teaching)
. . . Play (teaching method)
. . . Project method (teaching)
. . . Role playing
. . . Story telling
. . Individualized instruction
. . Lectures
. . Lessons
. . . Classwork
. . . . Dictation
. . . . Rote learning
. . . Demonstrations (lessons)
. . . Experiments (lessons)
. . . Tutorials
. . Literacy methodology
. . Microteaching
. . Questioning (teaching method)
. . Remedial instruction
. . Sleep teaching
. . Teach-ins (teaching method)
. . Teaching systems
. . . Headstart
. . . Monitorial systems
. . . Montessori system
. . Team teaching
. . Tutoring
. Training methods
. . Practical training
. . . Practice teaching

Microorganisms
. Aquatic microorganisms
. . Marine microorganisms
. Bacteria
. Viruses

Microscopes
. Electron microscopes

Migrants
. Gipsies

Migrants (cont.)
. Nomads

Missions
. Expert missions

Moisture
. Soil moisture
. . Capillary water
. Water vapour

Molecules
. Macromolecules

Monitoring
. Environmental monitoring

Motivation
. Achievement motivation
. Ambition
. Aspiration
. Incentives
. . Rewards
. . . Prizes
. . . . Literary prizes
. . . . UNESCO awards and honours
. . . . . Literary prizes
. . . School rewards

Multimedia instruction
. Audiovisual instruction

Museum collections
. Museum objects

Museum planning and administration
. Museum administration
. . Museum reorganization
. Museum economics
. . Museum finance
. . . Museum charges
. . . Museum financing
. Museum planning

Museum policy and development
. Museum development
. Museum policy

Musical elements
. Rhythm

Natural gas production
. Underwater oil and gas extraction

Needs
. Cultural needs
. Educational needs
. Human needs
. . Clothing
. . . Protective clothing

Needs (cont.)
. . Food
. . . Beverages
. . . . Alcoholic drinks
. . . Cereals
. . . Dairy products
. . . . Milk
. . . Fish
. . . . Freshwater fish
. . . . Marine fish
. . . . Shellfish
. . . . . Crustacea
. . . Frozen food
. . . Fruit
. . . Meat
. . . Nutrients
. . . Synthetic food
. . . Vegetables
. . Housing
. . . Apartments
. . . . High rise flats
. . . Houses
. . . Mobile homes
. . . Private housing
. . . Public housing
. . . Rented housing
. . . Second homes
. . . Slums
. . . Student housing
. . Leisure
. . . Commercialized leisure
. . . Leisure time
. . . . Holidays
. . . . . Holidays abroad
. . . . . School holidays
. . . . Leave
. . . . . Absenteeism
. . . . . Educational leave
. . . . . Sick leave
. . . . . . Teacher sick leave
. . . . . Teacher leave
. . . . . . Teacher sick leave
. . . Student leisure
. . Social needs
. . . Cultural needs
. . . Housing needs
. . . . Housing shortages
. . Travel
. . . Commuting
. . . Educational journeys
. . . Pilgrimages
. . . Travel abroad
. Information/library needs
. . Information user needs
. Social needs
. . Cultural needs
. . Housing needs
. . . Housing shortages
. Water requirements

Nuclear reactor components
. Nuclear fuels
. . Plutonium
. . Uranium

Nuclear reactors
. Fast reactors
. Fusion reactors
. Power reactors
. Thermal reactors

Ocean structure
. Ocean stratification

Orchestras
. Amateur orchestras
. . Youth orchestras

Parallel processing systems
. Multiprocessing systems

Participation
. Audience participation
. Cultural participation
. Parent participation
. Political participation
. Public participation in planning
. Social participation
. . Community participation
. . Cultural participation
. . Youth participation
. Student participation
. Teacher participation
. Youth participation

People
. Adolescents
. Adults
. . Adult students
. . Young adults
. Boys
. Children
. . Adopted children
. . Boys
. . Child actors
. . Child workers
. . . Child actors
. . Girls
. . Handicapped children
. . Only children
. . Orphans
. . Pre-school children
. . Schoolchildren
. . Socially disadvantaged children
. . . Deserted children
. . . Ill-treated children
. . . Orphans
. . . School drop-outs
. Elderly
. Ethnic groups
. . Ethnic minorities
. . Indigenous populations
. . . Natives
. Girls
. Men
. . Fathers
. . Married men
. Non-industrialized people
. . Aboriginal people
. . Eskimos
. . Lapps
. . Nomads
. . North American Indians
. . South American Indians
. Parents
. . Fathers
. . Mothers
. . . Unmarried mothers
. . . Working mothers

People (cont.)
. People-in-need
. . Elderly
. . Handicapped
. . . Handicapped children
. . . Mentally disadvantaged
. . . . Mentally handicapped
. . . . . Backward students
. . . . . Educationally subnormal
. . . . Ineducable
. . . . . Mongols
. . . . . Slow learners
. . . . Mentally ill
. . . . . Maladjusted
. . . Multiply handicapped
. . . Physically disadvantaged
. . . . Physically handicapped
. . . . . Autistic
. . . . . Blind
. . . . . Deaf
. . . . . Dyslexic
. . . . . Multiply handicapped
. . . . . Spastic
. . . . . Speech defective
. . . . . . Deaf and dumb
. . . . Sick persons
. . . . . Mentally ill
. . . . . . Maladjusted
. . . . . Patients
. . Socially disadvantaged
. . . Crime victims
. . . . Ill-treated children
. . . Culturally disadvantaged
. . . . Immigrants
. . . Educationally disadvantaged
. . . . Illiterates
. . . Illegitimate persons
. . . One-parent families
. . . Poor
. . . Problem families
. . . Refugees
. . . Social drop-outs
. . . Socially disadvantaged children
. . . . Deserted children
. . . . Ill-treated children
. . . . Orphans
. . . . School drop-outs
. . . Underprivileged youth
. . . Unemployed
. . . Unmarried mothers
. . . Vagrants
. . . War disadvantaged
. . . . Refugees
. . . . War prisoners
. . . . War wounded
. Racial groups
. . Aboriginal people
. . Asians
. . . Indians
. . Coloured people
. . . Asians
. . . . Indians
. . . Blacks
. . Eskimos
. . Lapps
. . North American Indians
. . Racial minorities
. . Semitic people
. . . Arabs
. . . Jews
. . South American Indians
. . White people

People (cont.)
. Religious persons
. . Believers
. . Buddhists
. . Christians
. . Hindus
. . Jews
. . Ministers of religion
. . Monks
. . Moslems
. . Nuns
. . Pagans
. . Priests (cultic)
. . Prophets
. . Religious leaders
. . Saints
. Women
. . Housewives
. . Married women
. . . Married women workers
. . . . Married women librarians
. . . . Married women teachers
. . . . Working mothers
. . Mothers
. . . Unmarried mothers
. . . Working mothers
. . Women students
. . Working women
. . . Married women workers
. . . . Married women librarians
. . . . Married women teachers
. . . . Working mothers
. . . Women librarians
. . . . Married women librarians
. . . Women teachers
. . . . Married women teachers
. . . Working mothers

Performers
. Actors
. . Amateur actors
. . Child actors
. . Dancers
. . Film actors
. Pop musicians
. Singers
. Sportsmen
. . Amateur sportsmen
. . Sports trainers

Personality
. Character
. . National character

Pests
. Locusts
. Termites

Philology
. Linguistics
. . Comparative and diachronic linguistics
. . . Etymology
. . . Language change
. . . Language varieties
. . . . Colloquial language
. . . . Computer languages
. . . . . Machine oriented languages
. . . . . . Problem oriented languages

Philology (cont.)
. . . . . Procedure oriented languages
. . . . Dead languages
. . . . . Greek (classical)
. . . . . Latin
. . . Dialects
. . . Foreign languages
. . . Formal language
. . . Index languages
. . . . Controlled languages
. . . . . Alphabetical subject heading lists
. . . . . Authority lists
. . . . . Classification systems
. . . . . . Analytico-synthetic classification systems
. . . . Faceted classification systems
. . . . Bliss classification system
. . . . Colon classification
. . . . UDC
. . . . . . Broad classification systems
. . . . . . Close classification systems
. . . . . . Hierarchical classification systems
. . . . . . Dewey decimal classification
. . . . . . Library of Congress classification
. . . . . Switching languages
. . . . . Term lists
. . . . . Uniterms
. . . . . Thesauri
. . . . . . Alphabetical thesauri
. . . . . . Classification/thesaurus systems
. . . . . . Compressed vocabularies
. . . . . . Macrothesauri
. . . . . . Microthesauri
. . . . . . Monolingual thesauri
. . . . . . Multilingual thesauri
. . . . . . Systematic thesauri
. . . . Free language systems
. . . . Natural language systems
. . . Language mixtures
. . . Modern languages
. . . Mother tongue
. . . Spoken language
. . . . Spoken poetry
. . . Symbolic languages
. . . . Signs
. . . . Symbols
. . . Unwritten languages
. . . Vernacular languages
. . . Written languages
. . Computer linguistics
. . Descriptive linguistics
. . . Grammar
. . . . Morphology (linguistics)
. . . . Syntax
. . . Graphonomy
. . . . Deciphering
. . . . Transcription
. . . . Transliteration
. . . Phonetics
. . . . Phonology
. . . . Speech analysis
. . . . Speech production
. . . Semantics
. . . . Semiology
. . Ethnolinguistics
. . Linguistic analysis
. . . Contextual analysis
. . . Semantic analysis
. . . Speech analysis
. . Statistical linguistics
. . . Statistical linguistics (indexing)
. . . . Associative indexing
. . . . . Clumping

455

Philology (cont.)
. . . . . . Clustering
. . . . . . Discriminant analysis
. . . Syntactic analysis
. . Linguistic research
. . . Language collection
. . . Language recording
. . Linguistic theory
. . Psycholinguistics
. . . Language behaviour
. . Sociolinguistics
. . . Ethnolinguistics
. . . Language behaviour
. . . Linguistic unification
. Literature
. . Foreign literature
. . Modern literature
. . . Contemporary literature

Philosophical schools
. Behaviourism
. Determinism
. Empiricism
. Existentialism
. Functionalism
. Humanism
. Idealism
. Individualism
. Materialism
. Pluralism
. . Cultural pluralism
. . Social pluralism
. . . Cultural pluralism
. Positivism
. Rationalism
. Structuralism
. Traditionalism

Philosophy
. Axiology
. Cultural philosophy
. . Concept of culture
. . Culturalism
. . Culturology
. Educational philosophy
. Epistemology
. Information/library philosophy
. Literary philosophy
. Metaphysics
. . Causality
. . Ontology
. . Teleology
. Philosophy of action
. Philosophy of history
. Philosophy of mind
. Political philosophy
. . Political ethics
. . Political theory
. . . Political doctrines
. . . . Anarchism
. . . . Anti-militarism
. . . . Capitalism
. . . . Collectivism
. . . . . Communism
. . . . . Socialism
. . . . Colonialism
. . . . . Neocolonialism
. . . . Conservatism
. . . . Fascism
. . . . Federalism

Philosophy (cont.)
. . . . Feudalism
. . . . Imperialism
. . . . Internationalism
. . . . Isolationism
. . . . Liberalism
. . . . Militarism
. . . . Nationalism
. . . . . Cultural nationalism
. . . . Nazism
. . . . Neutralism
. . . . Pacifism
. . . . Patriotism
. . . . Pluralism
. . . . . Cultural pluralism
. . . . . Social pluralism
. . . . . . Cultural pluralism
. . . . Racism
. . . . Radicalism
. . . . Regionalism
. . . . Separatism
. . . . Totalitarianism
. . . . . Fascism
. . . . . Nazism
. . . . Traditionalism
. . . . Utopia
. Science philosophy
. . Ethics of science
. . . Bioethics
. . . Medical ethics
. Social welfare philosophy
. Truth

Physics
. Astrophysics
. Atmospheric physics
. . Atmospheric acoustics
. . Atmospheric circulation
. . . Wind
. . Atmospheric disturbances
. . . Anticyclones
. . . Low pressure systems
. . . . Cyclones
. . . . . Typhoons
. . . . Storms
. . . . Tornadoes
. . . . . Typhoons
. . Atmospheric dynamics
. . . Atmospheric thermodynamics
. . Atmospheric electricity
. . . Lightning
. . Atmospheric formations
. . . Air masses
. . . Frontal systems
. . Atmospheric ionization
. . Atmospheric optics
. . Atmospheric pressure
. . Atmospheric radiation
. . . Auroras
. . . Daylight
. . . Sky
. . . Sunlight
. . Hydrometeorology
. . . Atmospheric condensation
. . . . Clouds
. . . . Dew
. . . . Fog
. . . . Mist
. . . . Precipitation
. . . . . Rain
. . . . . Snow

Physics (cont.)
. . . Hydrological cycle
. . . Precipitation
. . . . Rain
. . . . Snow
. Atomic physics
. Biophysics
. . Bionics
. . Human biophysics
. Bulk matter physics
. . Condensed matter physics
. . . Physics of liquids
. . . . Hydromechanics
. . . . . Hydrodynamics
. . . . . . Dynamic oceanography
. . . . . Hydrostatics
. . . Physics of solids
. . . . Mechanics of solids
. . . . . Deformation
. . . . . . Elastic deformation
. . . . . . Plastic deformation
. . . . Creep
. . . . . Elasticity
. . . . . Fatigue
. . . . . Fracture
. . . . . Hardness
. . . . . Mechanical strength
. . . . . Plasticity
. . . . . Rock mechanics
. . . . . Soil mechanics
. . . . . Stress (mechanical)
. . . . Solid state physics
. . . . . Semiconductor physics
. . . Rheology
. . Fluid physics
. . . Fluid mechanics
. . . . Fluid dynamics
. . . . . Aerodynamics
. . . . . . Flight dynamics
. . . . Astrodynamics
. . . . . Atmospheric dynamics
. . . . . . Atmospheric thermodynamics
. . . . . Flow
. . . . . . Boundary layer flow
. . . . . . Capillary flow
. . . . . . Channel flow
. . . . Streamflow
. . . . . . Flow in pipes
. . . . . . Laminar flow
. . . . . . Turbulent flow
. . . . . . Vortices
. . . . . Hydrodynamics
. . . . . . Dynamic oceanography
. . . . . Turbulence
. . . . Hydromechanics
. . . . . Hydrodynamics
. . . . . . Dynamic oceanography
. . . . . Hydrostatics
. . . Gas physics
. . . Physics of liquids
. . . . Hydromechanics
. . . . . Hydrodynamics
. . . . . . Dynamic oceanography
. . . . . Hydrostatics
. . Plasma physics
. Experimental physics
. . Cryogenics
. . High pressure techniques
. . High temperature techniques
. Geophysics
. . Geochemistry
. . . Biogeochemistry

Physics (cont.)
. . . Hydrogeochemistry
. . Geodesy
. . Geomagnetism
. . Isostasy
. . Marine geophysics
. . Seismology
. . Terrestrial age
. . Terrestrial heat
. . Terrestrial rotation
. Ion physics
. Molecular physics
. Nuclear physics
. . Nuclear reactions
. . . Nuclear fission
. . . Nuclear fusion
. . Nuclear reactor theory
. . Nuclear structure and properties
. Particle physics
. . Electron physics
. . High energy physics
. . Neutron physics
. . Particle optics
. Physics of energy phenomena
. . Electricity
. . . Atmospheric electricity
. . . . Lightning
. . . Electric charge
. . . Electric currents
. . . . Electric discharges
. . . . . Lightning
. . Electric fields
. . Electric potential
. . Electrical energy
. . Electrodynamics
. . Electrostatics
. . Geoelectricity
. . Photoelectricity
. . Piezoelectricity
. . Thermoelectricity
. . Magnetism
. . . Geomagnetism
. . Mechanics
. . . Chemical mechanics
. . . . Chemical kinetics
. . . . . Catalysis
. . . . . Chemical diffusion
. . . . . . Dialysis
. . . . . . Osmosis
. . . . Chemical reactions
. . . . . Addition reactions
. . . . . . Polymerization
. . . . . Combination reactions
. . . . . Combustion
. . . . . Corrosion
. . . . . . Electrochemical corrosion
. . . . Water corrosion
. . . . . Decomposition reactions
. . . . . . Degradation
. . . . . . Dissociation reactions
. . . . Hydrolysis
. . . . Radiolysis
. . . . . . Fermentation
. . . . . Electrochemical reactions
. . . . . Electrochemical corrosion
. . . . . . Water corrosion
. . . . . Electrolysis
. . . . . Elimination reactions
. . . . . Exchange reactions
. . . . . . Ion exchange
. . . . Photochemical reactions
. . . . . Photosynthesis

459

Political science (cont.)
. . . . . Non-violence
. . . . . Petitioning
. . . . . Pressure groups
. . . . . Protest movements
. . . . Political movements
. . . . . Labour movement
. . . . . Liberation movements
. . . . . . Womens liberation movement
. . . . . Protest movements
. . . . . Revolutionary movements
. . . Political support
. . Political conflict
. . Political crises
. . Political leadership
. . Political parties
. . . Multiparty systems
. . . One-party systems
. . . Two-party systems
. . Political sociology
. . . Political behaviour
. . . . Political attitude
. . . . Political corruption
. . . . Political participation
. . . Political conflict
. . . Political life
. International politics
. . International cooperation
. . . Cultural cooperation
. . . . Museum cooperation
. . . Development aid
. . . . Economic aid
. . . . Financial aid
. . . . Technical assistance
. . . . Voluntary contribution
. . . Educational cooperation
. . . . University cooperation
. . . International assistance
. . . . Development aid
. . . . . Economic aid
. . . . . Financial aid
. . . . . Technical assistance
. . . . . Voluntary contribution
. . . . Foreign aid
. . . . International voluntary services
. . . Scientific cooperation
. . International relations
. . . Foreign relations
. . . International conflict
. . . . Asymmetrical conflict
. . . . Cold war
. . . . Symmetrical conflict
. . . International entente
. . . International equilibrium
. . . International understanding
. . . Peace
. . . . Controlled peace
. . . . Negative peace
. . . . Positive peace
. . . Peaceful coexistence
. . . War
. . . . Civil war
. . . . Self-defence (war)
. . . . War aggression
. . . . . Invasion
. . . . World war
. Political philosophy
. . Political ethics
. . Political theory
. . . Political doctrines
. . . . Anarchism
. . . . Anti-militarism

Political science (cont.)
. . . . Capitalism
. . . . Collectivism
. . . . . Communism
. . . . Socialism
. . . . Colonialism
. . . . . Neocolonialism
. . . . Conservatism
. . . Fascism
. . . Federalism
. . . Feudalism
. . . Imperialism
. . . Internationalism
. . . Isolationism
. . . Liberalism
. . . Militarism
. . . Nationalism
. . . . Cultural nationalism
. . . Nazism
. . . Neutralism
. . . Pacifism
. . . Patriotism
. . . Pluralism
. . . . Cultural pluralism
. . . . Social pluralism
. . . . . Cultural pluralism
. . . Racism
. . . Radicalism
. . . Regionalism
. . . Separatism
. . . Totalitarianism
. . . . Fascism
. . . . Nazism
. . . Traditionalism
. . . Utopia
. Politics

Political systems
. Anarchy
. Democracy
. . Cultural democracy
. . Representative democracy
. . . Parliamentary systems
. . . . Electoral systems
. . . . . Political representation
. . . . . . Disenfranchisement
. . . . . . Equal representation
. . . . . . Proportional representation
. . . . . . Womens suffrage
. . . . . Secret ballot
. Dictatorship
. . Fascism
. . Nazism
. Empire
. Federation
. Member states
. Monarchy
. Non-self-governing territories
. . Colonies
. . Protectorates
. . Trust territories
. Oligarchy
. . Technocracy
. Presidential systems
. Republic
. Self-government
. . Newly-independent states
. Theocracy
. Tyranny
. Unitary state
. World government

Pollutants
. Aquatic microorganisms
. . Marine microorganisms
. Ashes
. Automobile emission
. Bacteria
. Detergents
. Dust
. Fertilizers
. Fumes
. Pesticides
. Petroleum
. Poisons
. Radioactive fallout
. Radioactive wastes
. Sewage
. Smog
. Smoke
. Viruses
. Waste water
. Wastes
. . Radioactive wastes
. . Refuse
. . Sewage
. . Waste water

Polymers
. Inorganic polymers
. Natural resins
. . Rubber
. . . Synthetic rubber
. Plastics
. . Amino resins
. . Epoxy resins
. . Ester polymers
. . Nylon
. . Polyesters
. . Polyethylene
. . Polypropylene
. . Polystyrene
. . Polyurethanes
. . Polyvinyl chloride
. . Polyvinyl fluoride
. . Silicon resins
. . Teflon
. Rubber
. . Synthetic rubber

Population
. Educational population
. . Educational manpower
. . . Educational personnel
. . . . Community leaders
. . . . . Youth leaders
. . . . Educational administrators
. . . . . Educational advisers
. . . . . Educational planners
. . . . Educational support personnel
. . . . . Academic librarians
. . . . . Educational guidance personnel
. . . . . School librarians
. . . . . Teacher librarians
. . . . Paraprofessional educational personnel
. . . . . Educational laboratory personnel
. . . . . Educational technicians
. . . . . Teacher aides
. . . . Teachers
. . . . . Academic teaching personnel
. . . . . Adult educators
. . . . . Itinerant teachers

Population (cont.)
. . . . . Literacy workers
. . . . . Part-time teachers
. . . . . Pre-primary school teachers
. . . . . Primary school teachers
. . . . . Secondary school teachers
. . . . . Special education teachers
. . . . . Student assistants
. . . . . Student teachers
. . . . . Teacher educators
. . . . . Training officers
. . . . . Visiting teachers
. . . . . Vocational school teachers
. . . . . Women teachers
. . . . . . Married women teachers
. . School-age population
. Indigenous populations
. . Natives
. Rural population
. . Rural youth
. School-age population
. Urban population
. . Urban youth
. World population

Population distribution
. Age distribution
. Sex distribution

Population dynamics
. Population decrease
. Population increase

Population events
. Morbidity
. Mortality
. Natality
. Nuptiality

Population migration
. Emigration
. . Brain drain
. Immigration
. Internal migration
. Labour migration
. Nomadism
. Rural migration
. Seasonal migration

Population problems
. Overpopulation
. Population decrease
. Population increase

Post-war measures
. War reparations

Practice
. Practice teaching

Preservation
. Archive records preservation
. Document preservation
. Food preservation

Preservation (cont.)
. Preservation of cultural property
. . Preservation of monuments
. . Preservation of works of art
. . . Restoration of paintings

Prison discharge
. Amnesty
. Parole

Prisoners
. War prisoners

Prisons
. Concentration camps

Production
. Agricultural production
. . Food production
. Large scale production
. Mass production
. Petroleum production
. . Underwater oil and gas extraction

Productivity
. Labour productivity

Products
. Agricultural products
. . Animal products
. . . Animal oils
. . . Dairy products
. . . . Milk
. . . Leather
. . . Meat
. . Crops
. . . Flowers
. . . Forage
. . . Fruit
. . . Grain crops
. . . . Cereals
. . . Grasses
. . . Hay
. . . Medicinal plants
. . . Seeds
. . . Straw
. . . Sugar beet
. . . Sugar cane
. . . Tobacco
. . . Vegetables
. Forest products
. . Wood
. . . Hardwood
. . . Softwood
. Volcanic products

Programmes
. Accelerated programmes
. Broadcasting programmes
. . Live programmes
. . Radio programmes
. . . Radio drama
. . . Radio games
. . . Radio news
. . . Radio serials

Programmes (cont.)
. . Television programmes
. . . Television documentaries
. . . Television drama
. . . Television games
. . . Television news
. . . Television serials
. Communication programmes
. . Communication research programmes
. . Mass communication programmes
. Development programmes
. . Communication programmes
. . . Communication research programmes
. . . Mass communication programmes
. . Cultural programmes
. . . Museum programmes
. . . . Museum educational programmes
. . Educational programmes
. . . Adult education programmes
. . . Exchange programmes
. . . Instructional programmes
. . . International training programmes
. . . Literacy programmes
. . . . Post-literacy programmes
. . . Reading programmes
. . Information/library programmes
. . Population programmes
. . Research programmes
. . Scientific programmes
. . Social programmes
. Educational programmes
. . Adult education programmes
. . Exchange programmes
. . Instructional programmes
. . International training programmes
. . Literacy programmes
. . . Post-literacy programmes
. . Reading programmes
. Information/library programmes
. Research programmes

Progress
. Scientific progress
. Social progress

Properties
. Physical properties
. . Acoustic properties
. . . Sea water acoustic properties
. . . Sound velocity
. . Chemical properties
. . . Acidity
. . . Alkalinity
. . . pH
. . Photosensitivity
. . . Salinity
. . . Solubility
. . Electrical properties of substances
. . . Dielectric properties
. . . . Piezoelectricity
. . . Electrical conductivity
. . . . Superconductivity
. . . Electroacoustics
. . . Electromechanical effects
. . . . Piezoelectricity
. . . Photoelectricity
. . . Piezoelectricity
. . . Thermoelectricity
. . Fluid mechanical properties
. . . Buoyancy

Properties (cont.)
. . . Capillarity
. . . Compressibility
. . . Fluid density
. . . . Sea water density
. . . Viscosity
. . Magnetic properties of substances
. . Mechanical properties of substances
. . . Acoustics
. . . . Atmospheric acoustics
. . . . Electroacoustics
. . . . Noise
. . . . Ultrasonics
. . . . Underwater sound
. . . Fluid mechanical properties
. . . . Buoyancy
. . . . Capillarity
. . . . Compressibility
. . . . Fluid density
. . . . . Sea water density
. . . . Viscosity
. . . Mechanics of solids
. . . . Deformation
. . . . . Elastic deformation
. . . . . Plastic deformation
. . . . . . Creep
. . . . Elasticity
. . . . Fatigue
. . . . Fracture
. . . . Hardness
. . . . Mechanical strength
. . . . Plasticity
. . . . Rock mechanics
. . . . Soil mechanics
. . . . Stress (mechanical)
. . . Vibrations
. . Optical properties of substances
. . . Colour
. . . Light absorption
. . . Luminescence
. . . Opacity
. . . Photosensitivity
. . . Sea water optical properties
. . . Transparency
. . . Visibility
. . Thermal properties of substances
. . . Latent heat
. . . Specific heat
. . . Thermal conductivity
. . . Thermal diffusivity
. . . Thermal resistance
. . Thermodynamic properties
. . Water properties
. . . Acidity
. . . Alkalinity
. . . Diffusivity
. . . pH
. . . Quality of water
. . . Salinity
. . . Sea water properties
. . . . Sea water acoustic properties
. . . . Sea water density
. . . . Sea water optical properties
. . . . Sea water pressure
. . . . Sea water temperature
. . . Surface tension
. . . Taste
. . . Viscosity
. . . Water hardness
. . . Water level
. . . . Sea level
. . . Water pressure

Properties (cont.)
. . . . Sea water pressure
. . . Water temperature
. . . . Sea water temperature
. Shape
. Size
. . Class size
. . Family size
. . School size

Property law
. Inheritance law
. Personal property law
. . Intellectual property
. . . Artistic property
. . . Copyright
. . . Literary property
. . . Patents
. . Trade marks
. Real property law

Psychological effects
. Stress (psychological)

Public law
. Administrative law
. Constitutional law
. Criminal law
. Military law

Punishment
. Corporal punishment
. Death penalty
. Inhuman treatment
. . Torture
. Non-custodial punishment
. . Probation
. . Restriction on movement
. . . Deportation
. . . Exile
. . Social sanctions
. School punishments
. Solitary confinement

Qualifications
. Degrees
. . Bachelors degrees
. . Doctoral degrees
. . Information/library degrees
. . Masters degrees
. Diplomas
. Educational certificates
. Information/library qualifications
. . Information/library degrees
. Occupational qualifications
. . Teacher qualifications
. Teacher qualifications

Quality
. Environmental quality
. Quality of education
. Quality of life
. Quality of water

Radiation
. Atmospheric radiation
. . Auroras
. . Daylight
. . Sky
. . Sunlight
. Cosmic radiation
. Electromagnetic waves
. . Gamma rays
. . Infrared radiation
. . Light
. . . Daylight
. . . Sunlight
. . Radio waves
. . . Microwaves
. . Ultraviolet radiation
. Infrared radiation
. Light
. . Daylight
. . Sunlight
. Radiative transfer
. Radioactivity
. Solar radiation
. . Sunlight
. Ultraviolet radiation

Radiation hazards
. Radioactive fallout
. Radioactive pollution
. . Radioactive fallout
. Radioactive wastes

Radiation technology
. Isotope technology

Ratio
. Performance ratios
. . Precision ratio
. . Recall ratio

Reading problems
. Dyslexia

Records file
. Case files

Recreational facilities
. Leisure equipment
. . Sports equipment
. Open spaces
. . Countryside
. . Green belts
. . Parks
. . . National parks
. . . Public gardens
. . . . Botanical gardens
. . . . Zoological gardens
. . Playgrounds
. . Playing fields
. . Urban spaces
. Playgrounds
. Recreational buildings
. . Cinema buildings
. . Concert halls
. . Opera houses
. . Theatre buildings

Recreational facilities (cont.)
. Recreational centres
. . Camping sites
. . Cultural centres
. . . Arts centres
. . . Cultural development centres
. . . Socio-cultural centres
. . Holiday centres
. . . Holiday camps
. . Sports centres
. . Youth hostels
. Sports facilities
. . Gymnasia
. . Playing fields
. . Sports centres
. . Sports equipment
. . Swimming pools
. Tourist facilities
. . Tourist accommodation
. . . Hotels
. . . Youth hostels
. Water recreational areas

Reform
. Administrative reform
. Educational reform
. . Curriculum development
. . . Anticurriculum movement
. . . . De-schooling
. Land reform
. Law reform
. Political reform
. . Democratization
. . . Democratization of culture
. . . Democratization of education
. Religious reform
. Social reform
. . Land reform

Religion
. Religious systems
. . Agnosticism
. . Ancient religions
. . . Ancient Asiatic religions
. . . . Confucianism
. . . . Shamanism
. . . . Shinto
. . . . Taoism
. . . . Zoroastrianism
. . . Egyptian religion
. . Atheism
. . Deism
. . Humanism
. . Messianism
. . Millenarianism
. . Modern religions
. . . Brahmanism
. . . Buddhism
. . . Christianity
. . . . Catholicism
. . . . Protestantism
. . . Hinduism
. . . Islam
. . . Jainism
. . . Judaism
. . . Mahayana
. . . Sectarianism
. . . Sikhism
. . . Theravada
. . Prehistoric religions

Religion (cont.)
. . Primitive religions
. . . Animism
. . . Fetishism
. . . Totemism

Religious movements
. Ecumenical movement

Religious practice
. Asceticism
. Cults
. Fasting
. Pilgrimages
. Prayer
. Preaching
. Religious ceremonies
. Religious festivals

Reproduction (biological)
. Animal breeding

Research
. Applied research
. . Problem focused research
. . Research and development
. . . Experimental development
. . . . Process development
. . . . Product development
. Archive research
. Communication research
. . Audience research
. Cultural research
. . Cultural studies
. . . Cultural geography
. . . Theoretical cultural studies
. . Literary research
. Economics research
. Educational research
. . Curriculum research
. . . Curriculum evaluation
. . Reading research
. Fundamental research
. Historical research
. Information/library research
. . Classification research
. Interdisciplinary research
. Scientific research
. . Agricultural research
. . Biological research
. . . Botanical research
. . Chemical research
. . Ecological research
. . Geographical research
. . Hydrological research
. . Medical research
. . . Brain research
. . Oceanographic research
. . Research and development
. . . Experimental development
. . . . Process development
. . . . Product development
. Social science research
. . Economics research
. . Market research
. . Population research
. . Psychological research
. . . Conflict research

Research (cont.)
. . . . Peace research
. . . Experimental psychology
. . . Psychological tests
. . . . Educational testing
. . . Psychometrics
. . Sociography

Research facilities
. Laboratories
. . Chemical laboratories
. . Educational laboratories
. . . Language laboratories
. . . School laboratories
. . . . Language laboratories
. . Medical laboratories
. . Museum laboratories
. . . Repair workshops
. . Oceanographic laboratories
. Laboratory equipment
. . Chemical laboratory equipment
. . . Reagents
. . Educational laboratory equipment
. Observatories
. . Astronomical observatories
. . . Planetaria
. . Meteorological observatories
. . Ocean stations
. . Seismological observatories
. Research ships
. Scientific facilities
. . Laboratories
. . . Chemical laboratories
. . . Educational laboratories
. . . . Language laboratories
. . . . School laboratories
. . . . . Language laboratories
. . . Medical laboratories
. . . Museum laboratories
. . . . Repair workshops
. . . Oceanographic laboratories
. . Scientific buildings
. . Scientific equipment
. . . Instruments
. . . . Display devices
. . . . . Displays (computer)
. . . . Electrical instruments
. . . . Gauges
. . . . . Rain gauges
. . . . . Tide gauges
. . . . Indicating instruments
. . . . Medical instruments
. . . . . Surgical instruments
. . . . Musical instruments
. . . . . Brass instruments
. . . . . Keyboard instruments
. . . . . Percussion instruments
. . . . . String instruments
. . . . . Wind instruments
. . . . Navigational instruments
. . . . . Compasses
. . . . . Gyroscopes
. . . . Oceanographic instruments
. . . . . Bathymeters
. . . . . Bathythermographs
. . . . . Current meters
. . . . . Depth recorders
. . . . . Drift bottles
. . . . . Echo sounders
. . . . . Fathometers
. . . . . Flowmeters

Research facilities (cont.)
. . . . . . Anemometers
. . . . . . Current meters
. . . . . . Pitot tubes
. . . . . . Venturimeters
. . . . . Plankton recorders
. . . . . Salinity recorders
. . . . . Sonar
. . . . . Sound velocity meters
. . . . . Thermistor chains
. . . . . Tide gauges
. . . . . Wave recorders
. . . . Recording instruments
. . . . . Depth recorders
. . . . . Plankton recorders
. . . . Salinity recorders
. . . . Wave recorders
. . . . Sensors
. . . . . Light detectors
. . . . . Radiation detectors
. . . . . Temperature probes
. . . . Surveying instruments
. . . . . Gravimeters
. . . . Transducers
. . . . . Pressure transducers
. . . Laboratory equipment
. . . . Chemical laboratory equipment
. . . . . Reagents
. . . . Educational laboratory equipment
. . . Medical equipment
. . . . Life support systems
. . . . Medical instruments
. . . . . Surgical instruments
. . . . Therapeutic equipment
. . . . . Drugs
. . . . . . Anaesthetics
. . . . . . Antibiotics
. . . . . . Narcotic drugs
. . . Oceanographic equipment
. . . . Bathyspheres
. . . . Capstans
. . . . Diving equipment
. . . . Floats
. . . . Hydrophones
. . . . Oceanographic buoys
. . . . Oceanographic instruments
. . . . . Bathymeters
. . . . . Bathythermographs
. . . . . Current meters
. . . . . Depth recorders
. . . . . Drift bottles
. . . . . Echo sounders
. . . . . Fathometers
. . . . . Flowmeters
. . . . . . Anemometers
. . . . . . Current meters
. . . . . . Pitot tubes
. . . . . . Venturimeters
. . . . . Plankton recorders
. . . . . Salinity recorders
. . . . . Sonar
. . . . . Sound velocity meters
. . . . . Thermistor chains
. . . . . Tide gauges
. . . . . Wave recorders
. . . . Oceanographic samplers
. . . . . Plankton recorders
. . . . Underwater cameras
. . . . Winches
. . . . Wire ropes

Research projects
. Experimental projects
. Pilot projects

Research results
. Scientific research results

Research work
. Case studies
. Experimentation
. Exploration
. . Geographical exploration
. . Ocean exploration
. . Resource exploration
. . Space exploration
. Field work
. . Archaeological field work
. . . Archaeological excavations
. . . Archaeological surveying
. . Interviews
. Observation

Resistance to oppression
. Passive resistance

Resource centres
. Multimedia resource centres

Resources
. Cultural resources
. . Cultural facilities
. . . Cultural centres
. . . . Arts centres
. . . . Cultural development centres
. . . . Socio-cultural centres
. . . Cultural equipment
. . . . Cultural goods
. . . . . Books
. . . . . . Antiquarian books
. . . . Incunabula
. . . . Rare books
. . . . . . Art books
. . . . . . Childrens books
. . . . . . Fiction stock
. . . . . . Forms (blank)
. . . . . . Large print books
. . . . . . New books
. . . . . . Out-of-print publications
. . . . . . Oversize books
. . . . . . Pamphlets
. . . . . . Paperbacks
. . . . . . Pocket books
. . . . . . Second-hand books
. . . . . Leisure equipment
. . . . . . Sports equipment
. . . . . Radio receivers
. . . . . Record players
. . . . . Recordings
. . . . . . Cassette recordings
. . . . Sound cassettes
. . . . Video cassettes
. . . . . . Cylinder recordings
. . . . . . Disc recordings
. . . . Long playing records
. . . . Video discs
. . . . . . Magnetic tape recordings
. . . . Phonotapes

467

Resources (cont.)

. . . . Cataloguers
. . . . Classifiers
. . . . Information officers
. . . . Information scientists
. . . . Librarians
. . . . Academic librarians
. . . . Childrens librarians
. . . . Part-time librarians
. . . . Public librarians
. . . . Reference librarians
. . . . School librarians
. . . . Special librarians
. . . . Teacher librarians
. . . . Women librarians
. . . . Married women librarians
. . . . . . Information/library support personnel
. . . . Computer personnel
. . . . Library technicians
. . . . Translators
. . . . . . Non-professional information/library personnel
. . . . . . Information/library clerical personnel
. . . . . . Information/library manual personnel
. . . . Library porters
. . . . Library assistants
. . . . . Military personnel
. . . . . Religious persons
. . . . . . Believers
. . . . . . Buddhists
. . . . . . Christians
. . . . . . Hindus
. . . . . . Jews
. . . . . . Ministers of religion
. . . . . . Monks
. . . . . . Moslems
. . . . . . Nuns
. . . . . . Pagans
. . . . . . Priests (cultic)
. . . . . . Prophets
. . . . . . Religious leaders
. . . . . . Saints
. . . . . Self-employed
. . . . . Social science personnel
. . . . . . Economists
. . . . . . Psychologists
. . . . . . Social scientists
. . . . Sociologists
. . . . . . Social workers
. . . . Youth leaders
. . . . . Specialists
. . . . . . Educational advisers
. . . . . Supervisors
. . . . . White collar workers
. . . . . . Administrators
. . . . Cultural administrators
. . . . Educational administrators
. . . . Educational advisers
. . . . Educational planners
. . . . Information/library administrators
. . . . . . Managers
. . . . Directors
. . . . Film directors
. . . . Television and radio directors
. . . . Theatre directors
. . . . Entrepreneurs
. . . . Middle management
. . . . Top management
. . . . . . Middle grade personnel
. . . . . . Office workers
. . . . Information/library clerical personnel
. . . . . . Professional personnel
. . . . Archaeologists

Resources (cont.)

. . . . Architects
. . . . Architect restorers
. . . . Archive personnel
. . . . Archivists
. . . . Manuscript curators
. . . . Records managers
. . . . . . Artists
. . . . Film-makers
. . . . Film directors
. . . . Film producers
. . . . Musicians
. . . . Amateur musicians
. . . . Composers
. . . . Conductors
. . . . Instrumentalists
. . . . Pop musicians
. . . . Singers
. . . . Theatre directors
. . . . Visual artists
. . . . Graphic designers
. . . . Painters
. . . . Photographers
. . . . Sculptors
. . . . Young artists
. . . . . . Computer personnel
. . . . . . Economists
. . . . . . Historians
. . . . . . Information/library professional personnel
. . . . Abstractors
. . . . Archivists
. . . . Bibliographers
. . . . Classificationists
. . . . Classifiers
. . . . Documentalists
. . . . Indexers
. . . . Cataloguers
. . . . Classifiers
. . . . Information officers
. . . . Information scientists
. . . . Librarians
. . . . Academic librarians
. . . . Childrens librarians
. . . . Part-time librarians
. . . . Public librarians
. . . . Reference librarians
. . . . School librarians
. . . . Special librarians
. . . . Teacher librarians
. . . . Women librarians
. . . . Married women librarians
. . . . . . Journalists
. . . . . . Lawyers
. . . . Counsel (legal)
. . . . Judges
. . . . Public prosecutors
. . . . . . Medical personnel
. . . . Nurses
. . . . Paramedical personnel
. . . . Physicians
. . . . . . Ministers of religion
. . . . . . Museum personnel
. . . . Museographers
. . . . Museum curators
. . . . . . Planners
. . . . Communication planners
. . . . Cultural planners
. . . . Educational planners
. . . . Environmental planners
. . . . . . Politicians
. . . . Members of parliament
. . . . . . Psychologists

470

Rights and privileges (cont.)
- . . . . Right of reply
- . . . . Right to communicate
- . . . Right to freedom of residence
- . . . Right to freedom of thought
- . . . . Religious freedom
- . . Right to justice
- . . . . Equality before the law
- . . . . Legal status
- . . . . Right to a fair hearing
- . . . . Right to an effective remedy
- . . . . Right to habeas corpus
- . . . . Right to presumption of innocence
- . . . . Rights of accused
- . . . . . Right to counsel
- . . . . . Right to legal aid
- . . . Right to life
- . . . Right to nationality
- . . . Right to non-discrimination
- . . . . Equal representation
- . . . . Equal rights of men and women
- . . . . . Womens rights
- . . . . . . Womens suffrage
- . . . . Equality before the law
- . . . Right to political asylum
- . . . Right to privacy
- . . . . Right to confidentiality
- . . . Right to resist oppression
- . . . Right to rest and leisure
- . . . Right to vote and be elected
- . . Collective human rights
- . . . Right of self-determination
- . . . Right to economic development
- . . . Right to environmental quality
- . . . Right to live in peace
- . . . Right to natural resources control
- . . Cultural rights
- . . . Access to culture
- . . . Right of intellectual property
- . . . . Rights of authors
- . . . . . Public lending right
- . . . Right to artistic freedom
- . . . Right to communicate
- . . . Right to cultural identity
- . . . Right to cultural participation
- . . . Right to education
- . . . Right to information
- . . . Right to rest and leisure
- . . Rights of special groups
- . . . Rights of hospital patients
- . . . Rights of prisoners
- . . . Rights of soldiers
- . . . . Rights of war prisoners
- . . . . Rights of war wounded
- . . . Rights of students
- . . . Rights of the child
- . . . . Right to education
- . . . Rights of the elderly
- . . . Rights of the handicapped
- . . . Rights of the mentally ill
- . . . Rights of war prisoners
- . . . Rights of war wounded
- . . . Womens rights
- . . . . Womens suffrage
- . . Social and economic rights
- . . . Family rights
- . . . Right to adequate living standards
- . . . Right to economic development
- . . . Right to environmental quality
- . . . Right to marry
- . . . Right to natural resources control
- . . . Right to property

Rights and privileges (cont.)
- . . . Right to rest and leisure
- . . . Right to social welfare
- . . . . Right to health
- . . . . Right to social security
- . . . Right to work
- . . . Trade union rights
- . Rights of states
- . . Equality of states
- . . Recognition rights
- . . Sovereignty
- . . State succession
- . . Territorial rights
- . . . Boundaries
- . . . Territorial air space
- . . . Territorial waters
- . Role rights

Rocks
- . Boulders
- . Igneous rocks
- . . Plutonic rocks
- . . . Granite
- . . Volcanic rocks
- . Metamorphic rocks
- . . Gneiss
- . . Marble
- . . Slates
- . Sedimentary rocks
- . . Clastic deposits
- . . . Arenaceous rocks
- . . . . Gravels
- . . . . Sands
- . . . . . Beach sand
- . . . . Sandstones
- . . . Argillaceous rocks
- . . . . Clays
- . . . . Marls
- . . . . Shales
- . . . Rudaceous rocks
- . . Non-clastic rocks
- . . . Carbonaceous rocks
- . . . . Bituminous sands
- . . . Carbonate rocks
- . . . . Chalk
- . . . . Limestone

Rural areas
- . Villages

Safety
- . Domestic safety
- . Electrical safety
- . Nuclear reactor safety
- . Occupational safety
- . . Mining safety
- . Transport safety
- . . Air safety
- . . Marine safety
- . . Rail safety
- . . Road safety

Safety measures
- . Fire protection
- . First aid
- . Forest protection
- . Radiation protection
- . Rescue

Satellites
. Artificial satellites
. . Communication satellites
. . Meteorological satellites
. Moon

School-leaving
. Secondary school leaving

Science of science and technology
. History of science
. Science philosophy
. . Ethics of science
. . . Bioethics
. . . Medical ethics
. Science planning and administration
. . Economics of science
. . . Science finance
. . . . Science budgets
. . . . Science financing
. . . . . Research grants
. . . . Scientific expenditure
. . Science administration
. . Science planning
. Sociology of science

Search output
. Ranked output

Search process
. Query formulation
. Search strategies
. . Contextual searching
. . Search cut-off
. . Search revision
. . . Relevance feedback

Sensorimotor activities
. Motor processes
. Perception
. . Perception of the environment

Sensory aids
. Hearing aids
. Sensory aids (teaching)
. . Audiovisual aids
. . . Chalkboards
. . . Flannelgraphs
. . Tactile aids
. . . Braille system

Sex
. Female
. . Girls
. . Women
. . . Housewives
. . . Married women
. . . . Married women workers
. . . . . Married women librarians
. . . . . Married women teachers
. . . . . . Working mothers
. . . Mothers
. . . . Unmarried mothers
. . . . Working mothers
. . . Women students

Sex (cont.)
. . . Working women
. . . . Married women workers
. . . . . Married women librarians
. . . . . Married women teachers
. . . . . . Working mothers
. . . . Women librarians
. . . . . Married women librarians
. . . . Women teachers
. . . . . Married women teachers
. . . . Working mothers
. Male
. . Boys
. . Men
. . . Fathers
. . . Married men

Shortages
. Energy shortages
. Food shortages
. Housing shortages
. Labour shortages
. . Teacher shortage
. Water shortages
. . Drought

Sites
. Archaeological sites

Social dynamics
. Cultural dynamics
. Group dynamics

Social factors
. Cultural factors

Social life
. Community life
. Cultural life
. . Everyday life
. . Life styles
. Family life
. Literary life
. Occupational life
. Prison life
. Theatrical life

Social problems
. Crime
. . Offences
. . . Addiction
. . . . Alcoholism
. . . . Drug addiction
. . . . Gambling
. . . . Smoking
. . . Arson
. . . Blackmail
. . . Civil disturbances
. . . . Civil war
. . . . Guerilla activities
. . . . Incitement to hate and violence
. . . . Revolution
. . . . . Cultural revolution
. . . Riots
. . . Subversive activities
. . . . Sabotage

Social problems (cont.)
- . . . . Terrorism
- . . . Disorderly conduct
- . . . Fraud
- . . . Hi-jacking
- . . . Homicide
- . . . . Assassination
- . . . Hostage-holding
- . . . Kidnapping
- . . . Lynching
- . . . Perjury
- . . . Political offences
- . . . . Assassination
- . . . . Espionage
- . . . . Subversive activities
- . . . . . Sabotage
- . . . Sexual offences
- . . . . Pornography
- . . . Subversive activities
- . . . . Sabotage
- . . . Terrorism
- . . . Theft
- . . . Transnational crime
- . . . Vandalism
- . . . Violence
- . . . . Domestic violence
- . . . War crimes
- . . . . Concentration camps
- . . . . Genocide
- . Disasters
- . . Man-made disasters
- . . . Nuclear explosions
- . . Natural disasters
- . . . Avalanches
- . . . Drought
- . . . Earthquakes
- . . . . Submarine earthquakes
- . . . Epidemics
- . . . Famine
- . . . Floods
- . . . Landslides
- . . . Volcanic eruptions
- . Discrimination
- . . Birth discrimination
- . . Cultural discrimination
- . . Language discrimination
- . . Nationality discrimination
- . . Racial discrimination
- . . . Antisemitism
- . . . Racial segregation
- . . Religious discrimination
- . . Sex discrimination
- . Family disorganization
- . Handicaps
- . . Mental deficiency
- . . . Backwardness
- . . Mental diseases
- . . . Behavioural disorders
- . . . . Antisocial behaviour
- . . . . Apathy
- . . . . . Social passivity
- . . . . Maladjustment
- . . . . Social deviance
- . . . . . Addiction
- . . . . . . Alcoholism
- . . . . . . Drug addiction
- . . . . . . Gambling
- . . . . . . Smoking
- . . . . . Opting out
- . . . . . Sexual deviance
- . . . . . Social alienation
- . . . . . Suicide

Social problems (cont.)
- . . . . Suicide
- . . . Neuroses
- . . . . Amnesia
- . . . . Anxiety states
- . . . . Emotional disturbances
- . . . . Hysteria
- . . . . Mental strain
- . . . . Nervous breakdown
- . . . . Obsessional neuroses
- . . . . Phobias
- . . . Personality disorders
- . . . Psychoses
- . . . . Affective psychoses
- . . . . . Manic-depressive psychoses
- . . . . . Melancholia
- . . . . Organic psychoses
- . . . . Paranoia
- . . . . Schizophrenia
- . . . Psychosomatic disorders
- . . . Rational processes disorders
- . . . . Brain deterioration
- . . . . Memory disorders
- . . Physical handicaps
- . . . Blindness
- . . . Deafness
- . . . Speech disorders
- . Housing
- . . Apartments
- . . . High rise flats
- . . Houses
- . . Mobile homes
- . . Private housing
- . . Public housing
- . . Rented housing
- . . Second homes
- . . Slums
- . . Student housing
- . Old age
- . People-in-need
- . . Elderly
- . . Handicapped
- . . . Handicapped children
- . . . Mentally disadvantaged
- . . . . Mentally handicapped
- . . . . . Backward students
- . . . . . Educationally subnormal
- . . . . . Ineducable
- . . . . . Mongols
- . . . . . Slow learners
- . . . . Mentally ill
- . . . . . Maladjusted
- . . . Multiply handicapped
- . . . Physically disadvantaged
- . . . . Physically handicapped
- . . . . . Autistic
- . . . . . Blind
- . . . . . Deaf
- . . . . . Dyslexic
- . . . . . Multiply handicapped
- . . . . . Spastic
- . . . . . Speech defective
- . . . . . . Deaf and dumb
- . . . . Sick persons
- . . . . Mentally ill
- . . . . . Maladjusted
- . . . . Patients
- . . Socially disadvantaged
- . . . Crime victims
- . . . . Ill-treated children
- . . . Culturally disadvantaged
- . . . . Immigrants

Social problems (cont.)
. . . . Educationally disadvantaged
. . . . Illiterates
. . . Illegitimate persons
. . . One-parent families
. . . Poor
. . . Problem families
. . . Refugees
. . . Social drop-outs
. . . Socially disadvantaged children
. . . . Deserted children
. . . . Ill-treated children
. . . . Orphans
. . . . School drop-outs
. . . Underprivileged youth
. . . Unemployed
. . . Unmarried mothers
. . . Vagrants
. . . War disadvantaged
. . . . Refugees
. . . . War prisoners
. . . . War wounded
. Social conflict
. . Class conflict
. . Cultural conflict
. . Interpersonal conflict
. . . Aggressiveness
. . . Hatred
. . . Hostility
. . Labour conflict
. . . Labour disputes
. . . . Lockouts
. . . . Sit-ins
. . . . Strikes
. . . . . Teacher strikes
. . . . Work-to-rule
. . Racial conflict
. . Role conflict
. . Tribal conflict
. Social deviance
. . Addiction
. . . Alcoholism
. . . Drug addiction
. . . Gambling
. . . Smoking
. . Opting out
. . Sexual deviance
. . Social alienation
. . Suicide
. Social disadvantage
. . Cultural disadvantage
. . Famine
. . Homelessness
. . Hunger
. . Parental deprivation
. . Poverty
. . Slums
. . Unemployment
. Social isolation
. . Cultural isolation
. Social unrest
. . Student unrest
. . Youth unrest

Social processes
. Social action
. . Community action
. . Cultural action
. . . Animation culturelle
. . . Cultural integration
. . . . Cultural assimilation

Social processes (cont.)
. . . . Enculturation
. . . Democratization of culture
. . . Dissemination of culture
. . . . Cultural education
. . . . . Architecture education
. . . . . Art education
. . . . . Drama education
. . . . . Movement studies
. . . . . Music education
. . . . . Speech education
. . . Information/library development
. . . Presentation of cultural property
. . . . Cultural exhibitions
. . . . . Art galleries
. . . . . Cultural demonstrations
. . . . Museums
. . . . . Archaeological museums
. . . . . Ethnographic museums
. . . . . Historical museums
. . . . . Musee imaginaire
. . . . . Museobuses
. . . . . National museums
. . . . . Regional museums
. . . . . School museums
. . . . . Science museums
. . . . . . Ecomuseums
. . . . . . Natural history museums
. . . . . Specialized museums
. . . Preservation of cultural property
. . . . Preservation of monuments
. . . . Preservation of works of art
. . . . . Restoration of paintings
. . . Socio-cultural action
. Social change
. . Cultural change
. . . Cultural innovations
. . . Cultural revolution
. . . Democratization of culture
. . . Disappearing cultures
. . Social disorganization
. . . Family disorganization
. . Social progress
. . Social reform
. . . Land reform

Social science planning and administration
. Social science administration
. Social science planning

Social structure
. Role
. . Creative role
. . Family role
. . . Breadwinners
. . . Housewives
. . . Parent role
. . Information/library role
. . Parent role
. . Teacher role
. Social mobility
. . Social promotion
. Social status
. . Occupational status
. . . Professional status
. . . . Information/library professional status
. . . . Teacher status
. . Socio-economic status
. Social stratification
. . Caste

Social structure (cont.)
. . Elite
. . . Cultural elite
. . . Intelligentsia
. . . Power elite
. . . Ruling class
. . . . Power elite
. . Social class
. . . Middle class
. . . Upper class
. . . . Aristocracy
. . . Working class
. . Social differentiation
. . . Class differentiation
. . . Cultural differentiation
. . . . Cultural disadvantage
. . . . Cultural discrimination
. . . . Cultural inequality
. . . Discrimination
. . . . Birth discrimination
. . . . Cultural discrimination
. . . . Language discrimination
. . . . Nationality discrimination
. . . . Racial discrimination
. . . . . Antisemitism
. . . . . Racial segregation
. . . . Religious discrimination
. . . . Sex discrimination
. . . Social inequality
. . . . Cultural inequality
. . . Social pluralism
. . . . Cultural pluralism

Social welfare
. Educational welfare
. . School health services
. Social services
. . Health services
. . . School health services
. . Personal social services
. . . Child welfare
. . Social security
. . . Legal aid
. . . Pensions
. . . Relief in kind
. Social work
. . Community work
. . . Community action
. . Counselling
. . Day care
. . Disaster relief work
. . Foster care
. . Group work (social work)
. . Residential social work
. . . Residential child care
. . Voluntary social work

Society
. Affluent societies
. Changing society
. Consumer societies
. Contemporary society
. Future society
. Industrial societies
. Mass society
. Multiracial societies
. Non-industrialized societies
. Post-industrial societies

Socio-economic indicators
. Cultural indicators

Sociology
. Archaeological sociology
. Cultural sociology
. . Cultural life
. . . Everyday life
. . . Life styles
. Demography
. Economic sociology
. Educational sociology
. . Educational psychosociology
. . Student sociology
. . . Student unrest
. Industrial sociology
. Occupational sociology
. . Industrial sociology
. . Occupational life
. Political sociology
. . Political behaviour
. . . Political attitude
. . . Political corruption
. . . Political participation
. . Political conflict
. . Political life
. Rural sociology
. . Rural migration
. Social psychology
. . Communication psychology
. . Educational psychosociology
. . Ethnopsychology
. . Industrial psychology
. . Occupational psychology
. . . Industrial psychology
. Sociography
. Sociolinguistics
. . Ethnolinguistics
. . Language behaviour
. . Linguistic unification
. Sociology of art
. Sociology of change
. Sociology of communication
. Sociology of knowledge
. Sociology of law
. Sociology of leisure
. Sociology of religion
. Sociology of research
. Sociology of science
. Student sociology
. . Student unrest
. Urban sociology

Soil properties
. Capillarity
. Permeability
. Porosity

Soils
. Clay soils
. Desert soils
. Laterites
. Loams
. Loess
. Peat soils
. Permafrost
. Salt affected soils
. Sandy soils
. Saturated soils

Soils (cont.)
. Unsaturated soils
. Volcanic soils

Solutes
. Dissolved gases

Sorption
. Absorption (chemical)
. Adsorption

Space
. Interstellar space

Space sciences
. Astronomy
. . Astrophysics
. . Celestial mechanics
. . Cosmology
. . Practical astronomy
. . . Astronomical measurements and instruments
. . . . Astronomical telescopes
. . . . Radioastronomy
. . . Astronomical observatories
. . . . Planetaria
. . Spherical astronomy
. Exobiology

Species
. Human species

Spermatophyta
. Angiospermae
. . Flowers
. Gymnospermae
. Trees

States of matter
. Amorphous state
. Crystalline state
. Dispersions
. . Colloids
. . . Aerosols
. . . Emulsions
. . . Foams
. . . Gels
. . . Sols
. . Suspensions
. Fluids
. . Gases
. . . Air
. . . Argon
. . . Carbon dioxide
. . . Dissolved gases
. . . Gas fuels
. . . . Manufactured gas
. . . . Natural gas
. . . Helium
. . . Hydrogen
. . . Neon
. . . Nitrogen
. . . Oxygen
. . Liquids
. . . Water
. . . . Brackish water

States of matter (cont.)
. . . . Freshwater
. . . . Groundwater
. . . . . Springs
. . . . . . Thermal springs
. . . . . Underground streams
. . . . . Wells
. . . . Running water
. . . . . Canals
. . . . . . Irrigation canals
. . . . . Rivers
. . . . . Springs
. . . . . . Thermal springs
. . . . . Streams
. . . . . . Underground streams
. . . . . Underground streams
. . . . . Waterfalls
. . . . Saline water
. . . . . Brackish water
. . . . . Sea water
. . . . Sea water
. . . . Snowmelt
. . . . Soil water
. . . . . Soil moisture
. . . . . . Capillary water
. . . . Stagnant water
. . . . Standing water
. . . . . Lakes
. . . . . . Lagoons
. . . . . Ponds
. . . . . Reservoirs
. . . . Surface water
. . . . . Canals
. . . . . . Irrigation canals
. . . . . Dams
. . . . . Lakes
. . . . . . Lagoons
. . . . . Oceans
. . . . . . Antarctic Ocean
. . . . . . Arctic Ocean
. . . . . . Atlantic Ocean
. . . . North Atlantic Ocean
. . . . South Atlantic Ocean
. . . . . . Indian Ocean
. . . . . . Pacific Ocean
. . . . North Pacific Ocean
. . . . South Pacific ocean
. . . . . Ponds
. . . . . Reservoirs
. . . . . Rivers
. . . . . Seas
. . . . . . Andaman Sea
. . . . . . Arabian Sea
. . . . . . Baltic Sea
. . . . . . Banda Sea
. . . . . . Barents Sea
. . . . . . Beaufort Sea
. . . . . . Bering Sea
. . . . . . Bismarck Sea
. . . . . . Black Sea
. . . . . . Caribbean Sea
. . . . . . Caspian Sea
. . . . . . Chukchi Sea
. . . . . . Coral Sea
. . . . . . Dead Sea
. . . . . . East China sea
. . . . . . East India Archipelago seas
. . . . Arafura Sea
. . . . Bali Sea
. . . . Banda Sea
. . . . Celebes Sea
. . . . Ceram Sea

States of matter (cont.)

. . . . Flores Sea
. . . . Halmahra Sea
. . . . Java Sea
. . . . Molucca Sea
. . . . Savu Sea
. . . . Sulu Sea
. . . . Timor Sea
. . . . . . East Siberian Sea
. . . . . . Greenland Sea
. . . . . . Irish Sea
. . . . . . Kara Sea
. . . . . . Labrador Sea
. . . . . . Laccadive Sea
. . . . . . Laptev Sea
. . . . . . Lincoln Sea
. . . . . . Mediterranean Sea
. . . . Adriatic Sea
. . . . Aegean Sea
. . . . Alboran Sea
. . . . Balearic Sea
. . . . Ionian Sea
. . . . Ligurian Sea
. . . . Tyrrhenian Sea
. . . . . . North Sea
. . . . . . Norwegian Sea
. . . . . . Philippine Sea
. . . . . . Red Sea
. . . . . . Sea of Azov
. . . . . . Sea of Japan
. . . . . . Sea of Marmara
. . . . . . Sea of Okhotsk
. . . . . . Seto Naikai Inland Sea
. . . . . . Solomon Sea
. . . . . . South China Sea
. . . . . . Tasman Sea
. . . . . . West Scotland Inland Sea
. . . . . . White Sea
. . . . . . Yellow Sea
. . . . . Streams
. . . . . . Underground streams
. . . . Waste water
. . Vapours
. . . Water vapour
. Mixtures
. Semisolids
. Solids
. Solutions
. . Electrolytes
. . Solid solutions

Storage

. Digital storage
. Document storage
. Heat storage
. Water storage

Stress analysis

. Photoelastic stress analysis

Structural elements (buildings)

. Ceilings
. Chimneys
. Doors
. Floors
. Roofs
. Stairs
. Walls
. Windows

Structures

. Archaeological structures
. Hydraulic structures
. . Conduits
. . . Canals
. . . . Irrigation canals
. . . Pipes
. . . . Sewers
. . . . Water mains
. . . Sluices
. . . Spillways
. . Dams
. . Irrigation canals
. . Locks (waterways)
. . Reservoirs
. . Sluices
. . Spillways
. . Water towers
. Substructures
. Superstructures

Students

. Adult students
. Exceptional students
. . Backward students
. . Educationally subnormal
. . Foreign students
. . Geniuses
. . Gifted students
. . Ineducable
. . Late developers
. . Low achievers
. . New literates
. . Overachievers
. . Slow learners
. Men students
. Out-of-school youth
. . Apprentices
. Pre-school children
. Scholarship-holders
. School drop-outs
. Schoolchildren
. Students (college)
. . Graduates
. . Scholarship-holders
. . Student assistants
. . Student teachers
. . Undergraduates
. Trainees
. Women students

Study

. Compulsory study
. Creative writing
. . Oral composition
. Voluntary study

Supply and demand

. Demand
. . Cultural demand
. . Educational demand
. Supply
. . Cultural supply
. . Labour supply
. . . Labour distribution
. . . . Labour migration
. . . . Labour mobility
. . . . Redeployment
. . . Labour shortages

Supply and demand (cont.)
. . . . Teacher shortage
. . . Labour turnover
. . . Manpower
. . . . Educational manpower
. . . . . Educational personnel
. . . . . . Community leaders
. . . . Youth leaders
. . . . . . Educational administrators
. . . . Educational advisers
. . . . Educational planners
. . . . . . Educational support personnel
. . . . Academic librarians
. . . . Educational guidance personnel
. . . . School librarians
. . . . Teacher librarians
. . . . . . Paraprofessional educational personnel
. . . . . . Educational laboratory personnel
. . . . . . Educational technicians
. . . . . . Teacher aides
. . . . . . Teachers
. . . . Academic teaching personnel
. . . . Adult educators
. . . . Itinerant teachers
. . . . Literacy workers
. . . . Part-time teachers
. . . . Pre-primary school teachers
. . . . Primary school teachers
. . . . Secondary school teachers
. . . . Special education teachers
. . . . Student assistants
. . . . Student teachers
. . . . Teacher educators
. . . . Training officers
. . . . Visiting teachers
. . . . Vocational school teachers
. . . . Women teachers
. . . . Married women teachers
. . . Teacher supply
. . . . Teacher shortage

Surface films
. Thin films

Surveys
. Economic surveys
. Sample surveys
. Soil surveys

Symptoms of disease
. Incontinence
. . Enuresis
. Pain
. Shock
. Sleep disorders

Tariff barriers
. Customs duties
. Embargoes
. Tariffs

Taxation
. Consumption tax
. Customs duties
. Income tax

Teaching
. Language teaching
. Teaching skills
. Training
. . Basic training
. . Further training
. . In-service training
. . In-service teacher training
. . Professional training
. . . Architecture education
. . . Archive science training
. . . Communication personnel training
. . . . Book production training
. . . . Communication planners training
. . . . Journalist training
. . . . Publishers training
. . . . Television and radio personnel training
. . . Cultural personnel training
. . . . Cultural agents training
. . . . Film-making training
. . . . Museum training
. . . Information/library training
. . . Legal education
. . . Medical education
. . . . Veterinary education
. . . Research training
. . . Social workers training
. . . Teacher training
. . . . In-service teacher training
. . . . Practice teaching
. . . . Pre-primary teacher training
. . . . Pre-service teacher training
. . . . Primary teacher training
. . . . Secondary teacher training
. . . . Special teacher training
. . . . Teacher educator training
. . . . Vocational teacher training
. . Retraining
. . Technical training
. . . Book production training
. . . Group training
. . . Industrial training
. . . Scientific personnel training
. . Training abroad
. . Vocational training
. . . Agricultural training
. . . Basic training
. . . Cooperative education
. . . Job training
. . . Technical training
. . . . Book production training
. . . . Group training
. . . . Industrial training
. . . . Scientific personnel training

Techniques
. Computer techniques
. . Teleprocessing
. Conservation techniques
. High pressure techniques
. High temperature techniques
. Management techniques
. . Decision theory
. . Forecasting
. . . Economic forecasting
. . . Educational forecasting
. . . Hydrological forecasting
. . . Population projection
. . . Science forecasting
. . . Tidal prediction
. . . Weather forecasting

Techniques (cont.)
. . Futurology
. . Game theory
. . Models
. . . Cultural models
. . . Economic models
. . . Mathematical models
. . . Simulation models
. . . Synoptic modelling
. . Network analysis
. . Operations research
. . . Decision theory
. . . Game theory
. . . Mathematical programming
. . . Network analysis
. . Organization and methods study
. . Queueing theory
. . Research techniques
. . . Models
. . . . Cultural models
. . . . Economic models
. . . . Mathematical models
. . . . Simulation models
. . . . Synoptic modelling
. . Systemology
. . . Systems analysis
. . Systems analysis
. . Work study
. Research techniques
. . Models
. . . Cultural models
. . . Economic models
. . . Mathematical models
. . . Simulation models
. . . Synoptic modelling

Technology
. Agriculture
. . Farming systems
. . . Agronomy
. . . . Arable farming
. . . . Cultivation
. . . . . Dry farming
. . . . . Food production
. . . . . Harvesting
. . . . . Hydrophonics
. . . . . Planting
. . . . Horticulture
. . . Animal husbandry
. . . . Apiculture
. . . . Dairy farming
. . . . Stock farming
. . . Mixed farming
. Catering
. . Educational catering
. . . School meals
. Chemical technology
. . Adhesives technology
. . Cement and concrete technology
. . Ceramics technology
. . Chemical engineering processes
. . . Distillation
. . . Drying
. . . Evaporation technology
. . . Extraction technology
. . . Fluid handling
. . . Liquefaction technology
. . . Mixing technology
. . . Process heating
. . . Purification
. . . . Air pollution treatment

Technology (cont.)
. . . . Decontamination
. . . Separation technology
. . . . Filtration
. . . . Leaching
. . . Sewage treatment
. . . Size enlargement
. . . Size reduction
. . . Sorption technology
. . . Water treatment
. . . . Desalination
. . . . Water demineralization
. . Cleaning agents technology
. . Dyes technology
. . Explosives technology
. . Fuel technology
. . . Coal technology
. . . Gas technology
. . . Petroleum technology
. . . . Petroleum production
. . . . . Underwater oil and gas extraction
. . Glass technology
. . . Glass blowing
. . Lime and gypsum technology
. . Paint technology
. . Petrochemicals technology
. . Petroleum technology
. . . Petroleum production
. . . . Underwater oil and gas extraction
. . Pharmaceutical technology
. . Polymer and plastics technology
. . . Rubber technology
. . Processing agents technology
. . Vegetable and animal oils technology
. Clothing manufacture
. Domestic science
. . Cooking
. . Domestic engineering
. Educational technology
. Engineering
. . Aerospace engineering
. . . Aircraft engineering
. . . Space technology
. . Agricultural engineering
. . Communication technology
. . . Radar
. . . . Radar meteorology
. . . Radio engineering
. . . Recording engineering
. . . . Sound recording
. . . . . Language recording
. . . . Video recording
. . . . . Telerecording
. . . Telecommunication
. . . . Communication networks
. . . . Data transmission
. . . . . Telegraphy
. . . . . Telephotography
. . . . Mobile communication
. . . . Space communication
. . . . Teleconferencing
. . . . Telegraphy
. . . . Telemetry
. . . . Telephone engineering
. . . . Teleprocessing
. . . . Underwater communication
. . . Television engineering
. . Construction engineering
. . . Building operations
. . . . Building maintenance
. . . . . Library maintenance services
. . . . Carpentry

Technology transfer (cont.)
. Implantation of technology
. International technology transfer
. . Technical assistance
. Vertical technology transfer

Technology transfer services
. Patent offices
. Scientific information systems
. . Agricultural information systems
. . Engineering information systems
. . Medical information systems
. . . Medical records information systems

Telephone
. Radiotelephone
. Videotelephone

Temperature
. Atmospheric temperature
. Body temperature
. High temperatures
. Low temperatures
. Soil temperature
. Water temperature
. . Sea water temperature

Terminology
. Communication terminology
. Educational terminology
. Scientific terminology

Tests
. Achievement tests
. Aptitude tests
. Intelligence tests
. Psychological tests
. . Educational testing
. Reading tests
. Statistical tests

Thallophyta
. Algae
. . Aquatic algae
. . . Marine algae
. . . . Seaweeds
. Fungi
. Lichens

Theatrical companies
. Folklore troupes

Theory
. Approximation theory
. . Least squares approximation
. Automata theory
. Communication and information theory
. . Cybernetics
. . . Artificial intelligence
. . . Bionics
. . Information theory
. Computer metatheory
. Control theory
. Economic theory

Theory (cont.)
. . Economic doctrines
. . . Capitalism
. . . Collectivism
. . . . Communism
. . . . Socialism
. . . Feudalism
. . Economic equilibrium
. . Economic fluctuations
. . . Economic depression
. . Economic growth
. . Income distribution
. Educational theory
. Graph theory
. Group theory
. Legal theory
. . Analytical jurisprudence
. . . Concept of law
. . . Sources of law
. . Schools of legal theory
. Linguistic theory
. Management theory
. Musical theory
. Nuclear reactor theory
. Number theory
. Political theory
. . Political doctrines
. . . Anarchism
. . . Anti-militarism
. . . Capitalism
. . . Collectivism
. . . . Communism
. . . . Socialism
. . . Colonialism
. . . . Neocolonialism
. . . Conservatism
. . . Fascism
. . . Federalism
. . . Feudalism
. . . Imperialism
. . . Internationalism
. . . Isolationism
. . . Liberalism
. . . Militarism
. . . Nationalism
. . . . Cultural nationalism
. . . Nazism
. . . Neutralism
. . . Pacifism
. . . Patriotism
. . . Pluralism
. . . . Cultural pluralism
. . . . Social pluralism
. . . . . Cultural pluralism
. . . Racism
. . . Radicalism
. . . Regionalism
. . . Separatism
. . . Totalitarianism
. . . . Fascism
. . . . Nazism
. . . Traditionalism
. . . Utopia
. Probability theory
. . Expectation
. . . Probable error
. . . Risk
. . . Standard error
. . Game theory
. . Random processes
. . . Markov processes
. . . Queueing theory

Vehicles (cont.)
. Armoured vehicles
. Bathyspheres
. Hovercraft
. Land vehicles
. . Armoured vehicles
. . Road vehicles
. . . Bicycles
. . . Motor vehicles
. Ships
. . Fishing vessels
. . . Seiners
. . . . Seine nets
. . . Trawlers
. . Hovercraft
. . Research ships
. Spacecraft
. . Artificial satellites
. . . Communication satellites
. . . Meteorological satellites
. . Rockets
. . Space vehicles
. Submarines

Vertebrata
. Amphibia
. Birds
. Fish
. . Freshwater fish
. . Marine fish
. . Shellfish
. . . Crustacea
. Mammals
. . Camels
. . Primates
. . . Human species
. Reptiles

Vocabularies
. Index language vocabularies
. . Blank words
. . Concepts (index language)
. . . Isolates
. . Index terms
. . . Abbreviations
. . . . Acronyms
. . . Bound terms
. . . Compound terms
. . . Homographs
. . . Identifiers
. . . . Proprietary names
. . . Subject headings
. . . Synthesised terms
. . Lead-in terms
. . Modifier terms
. . . Qualifiers
. . . Sub-headings
. . Qualifiers

Volcanoes
. Submarine volcanoes

War relief organizations
. Red Cross

Warfare
. Air warfare

Warfare (cont.)
. . Bombing
. Chemical/biological warfare
. Land warfare
. . Urban warfare
. Naval warfare
. Nuclear warfare
. Unconventional warfare
. . Guerilla activities
. . Subversive activities
. . . Sabotage
. . Terrorism

Water currents
. Ocean currents
. . Tidal currents
. . Wind driven currents

Water discharge
. Discharge of rivers

Water sources
. Glaciers
. Groundwater
. . Springs
. . . Thermal springs
. . Underground streams
. . Wells
. Precipitation
. . Rain
. . Snow
. Running water
. . Canals
. . . Irrigation canals
. . Rivers
. . Springs
. . . Thermal springs
. . Streams
. . . Underground streams
. . Underground streams
. . Waterfalls
. Snowmelt
. Standing water
. . Lakes
. . . Lagoons
. . Ponds
. . Reservoirs
. Surface water
. . Canals
. . . Irrigation canals
. . Dams
. . Lakes
. . . Lagoons
. . Oceans
. . . Antarctic Ocean
. . . Arctic Ocean
. . . Atlantic Ocean
. . . . North Atlantic Ocean
. . . . South Atlantic Ocean
. . . Indian Ocean
. . . Pacific Ocean
. . . . North Pacific Ocean
. . . . South Pacific ocean
. . Ponds
. . Reservoirs
. . Rivers
. . Seas
. . . Andaman Sea
. . . Arabian Sea

484

Water sources (cont.)
. . . Baltic Sea
. . . Banda Sea
. . . Barents Sea
. . . Beaufort Sea
. . . Bering Sea
. . . Bismarck Sea
. . . Black Sea
. . . Caribbean Sea
. . . Caspian Sea
. . . Chukchi Sea
. . . Coral Sea
. . . Dead Sea
. . . East China sea
. . . East India Archipelago seas
. . . . Arafura Sea
. . . . Bali Sea
. . . . Banda Sea
. . . . Celebes Sea
. . . . Ceram Sea
. . . . Flores Sea
. . . . Halmahra Sea
. . . . Java Sea
. . . . Molucca Sea
. . . . Savu Sea
. . . . Sulu Sea
. . . . Timor Sea
. . . East Siberian Sea
. . . Greenland Sea
. . . Irish Sea
. . . Kara Sea
. . . Labrador Sea
. . . Laccadive Sea
. . . Laptev Sea
. . . Lincoln Sea
. . . Mediterranean Sea
. . . . Adriatic Sea
. . . . Aegean Sea
. . . . Alboran Sea
. . . . Balearic Sea
. . . . Ionian Sea

Water sources (cont.)
. . . . Ligurian Sea
. . . . Tyrrhenian Sea
. . . North Sea
. . . Norwegian Sea
. . . Philippine Sea
. . . Red Sea
. . . Sea of Azov
. . . Sea of Japan
. . . Sea of Marmara
. . . Sea of Okhotsk
. . . Seto Naikai Inland Sea
. . . Solomon Sea
. . . South China Sea
. . . Tasman Sea
. . . West Scotland Inland Sea
. . . White Sea
. . . Yellow Sea
. . Streams
. . . Underground streams

Wave propagation
. Sound wave propagation

Wavelength
. Ocean wave length

Woodworking
. Carpentry

Writing systems
. Ancient scripts
. . Cuneiform writing
. . Hieroglyphics
. . Ideographic scripts
. . Pictographic scripts
. Cryptography
. Phonetic writing
. Shorthand